# THE TEARS OF SOVEREIGNTY

# THE TEARS OF SOVEREIGNTY

PERSPECTIVES OF POWER IN
RENAISSANCE DRAMA

PHILIP LORENZ

Fordham University Press   New York   2013

Copyright © 2013 Fordham University Press

All rights reserved. No part of this publication may be reproduced, stored in a retrieval system, or transmitted in any form or by any means—electronic, mechanical, photocopy, recording, or any other—except for brief quotations in printed reviews, without the prior permission of the publisher.

Fordham University Press has no responsibility for the persistence or accuracy of URLs for external or third-party Internet websites referred to in this publication and does not guarantee that any content on such websites is, or will remain, accurate or appropriate.

Fordham University Press also publishes its books in a variety of electronic formats. Some content that appears in print may not be available in electronic books.

Library of Congress Cataloging-in-Publication Data
Lorenz, Philip.
 The tears of sovereignty : perspectives of power in Renaissance drama / Philip Lorenz. — First edition.
      pages cm
 Includes bibliographical references and index.
 ISBN 978-0-8232-5130-8 (cloth : alk. paper)
 1. English drama—Early modern and Elizabethan, 1500–1600—History and criticism.  2. Spanish drama—Classical period, 1500–1700—History and criticism.  3. Kings and rulers in literature.  4. Sovereignty in literature.  5. Power (Philosophy) in literature.  I. Title.
 PR649.K55L67 2013
 822'.309358—dc23
                                                                    2012048068

Printed in the United States of America

15 14 13   5 4 3 2 1

First edition

# Contents

*Acknowledgments* vii

Introduction: The Body Is Burning—Sovereignty, Image, Trope 1

1. Breakdown: Analogy and Ontotheology in *Richard II* 33

2. Reanimation: The Logic of Transfer in *Measure for Measure* 59

3. Resistance: Waiting for Power in *Fuenteovejuna* 97

4. Transformation: The Body Moves Out in *Life Is a Dream* 153

5. Return: The "Wrinkles" of Mystery in *The Winter's Tale* 204

After-Image 239

*Notes* 247

*Works Cited* 345

*Index* 371

# Acknowledgments

This book has taken me a long time to finish. During the course of its writing and the many turns that have accompanied it, I have accumulated an enormous amount of debt—but some kinds of debt are good. It is a pleasure to be able to recognize and thank the extraordinary teachers, scholars, colleagues, students, friends, and family, without whom this book would never have been possible.

*The Tears of Sovereignty* began when I was at New York University and worked with Leonard Barkan, Georgina Dopico Black, and Anselm Haverkamp. Leonard has been a sustaining force throughout these years. His intelligence, humor, refinement, and warmth are a continuing inspiration. I thank him for being a wonderful teacher, advisor, and friend. The project was sparked by ideas generated in his graduate seminar on "Word and Image" and began to take shape after a conference on "Political Theologies" in Amsterdam co-sponsored by the Amsterdam School of Cultural Analysis and the Center for the Study of World Religions at the Divinity School of Harvard University, which I was able to attend thanks to the generosity of Anselm Haverkamp. I am especially grateful to Anselm, Michèle Lowrie, and Eva Geulen of the NYU Poetics and Theory Program for supporting the 2002 "Zone 2" Sovereignty conference whose participants, including Georgio Agamben, Gil Anidjar, Judith Butler, Rüdiger Campe, and Richard Falk, articulated the historical and theoretical problems of sovereignty in such compelling and important ways. At NYU, I was privileged to be able to study Golden Age drama with Georgina Dopico Black, who is not only an exemplary scholar and advisor but also a witty, brilliant, and generous friend. At NYU, I was also very fortunate to study with Mikhail Iampolski, whose seminars on sovereignty and symbolic space changed the critical horizon and whose influence is notable in these pages.

I would especially like to thank Anselm Haverkamp for his teaching and his continued and extraordinary generosity, support, and encouragement. Thanks to the trans-Atlantic affiliations he established between NYU, the European University Viadrina, and the Amsterdam School of Cultural Analysis, I benefited from interactions with scholars on both sides of the Atlantic. I am grateful to Anselm and to the members of the Graduiertenkolleg at the Europa Universität Viadrina, including especially Dirk Mende, Mariele Nientied, and Björn Quiring for reading and responding to drafts of this project at various stages and for their invaluable commentary, criticism, and suggestions. I would also like to thank Christoph Menke, Katrin Trüstedt, and the organizers of the "Wrong Again—Tragedy's Comedy" conference for the invitation to present portions of this material at Potsdam University, and, again, to Björn Quiring for the opportunity to test ideas about Suárez, mystery, and theater at the workshop on "The Uses of the *Theatrum Mundi*: Metaphor in Seventeenth-Century England" at the Ludwig-Maximilians-Universität in Munich.

This is a comparative project. I have learned what that can mean from a marvelous group of scholars I am privileged to be a part of who comprise the international research collective on Comparative Renaissance Drama, "Theatre Without Borders." My thanks to Dick Andrews, Michael Armstrong-Roche, Pam Brown, Christian Billing, Pavel Drábek, Rob Henke, Peg Katritzky, Natasha Korda, Paul Kottman, Jacques Lezra, Clare McManus, Bella Mirabella, Eric Nicholson, Shormishtha Panja, David Schalkwyk, Jyotsna Singh, Maria Galli Stampino, Melissa Walter, and Susanne Wofford—whose work reminds us that Renaissance drama travels, transgresses, and is nothing if not international from the start.

My research on Francisco Suárez has carried me across disciplinary boundaries and into territories beyond my professional training, including theology and especially international law. I would like to thank Anne Orford and Martti Koskenniemi for invitations to present portions of this material at a series of conferences and workshops on "International Law and Wars of Religion" at the Faculty of Law at the University of Lund, in Sweden, in 2007; on "Reasons of State: Security, Civility, Immunity, Life" at the Institute for International Law and the Humanities at the Melbourne Law School in 2009; and on "International Law and Empire" at the Erik Castrén Institute for International Law and Human Rights at the University of Helsinki, in 2011.

At Cornell University, I have benefited from the best colleagues and students one could hope to have. Rayna Kalas read and commented brilliantly, incisively, and humorously on numerous drafts. Jenny Mann and Barbara Correll offered helpful feedback and advice. If it weren't for the inspiring work on early modern literature and drama by Walter Cohen, María Antonia Garcés, Mitchell Greenberg, Bill Kennedy, and Tim Murray, I would have never gotten into this in the first place. I would like to offer a special thanks to Bernie Meyler for the invitation to present an early version of my chapter on *Measure for Measure* to the Law and Literature colloquium at the Cornell Law School. Cathy Caruth, Cynthia Chase, Jonathan Culler, Stuart Davis, Debby Fried, Roger Gilbert, Ellis Hanson, Paul Sawyer, Harry Shaw, and Shelley Wong have all supported this book in different ways. Thanks, too, to the members of a Carnegie Mellon seminar on performance at Cornell directed by Amy Villarejo and Andy Galloway. I can't thank Andy enough for his advice, his help with Suárez's Latin, his careful readings of the manuscript, and above all for his generosity as a colleague and friend. Kevin Attell has been a gracious interlocutor and source of wisdom on the work of Giorgio Agamben and Walter Benjamin. Satya Mohanty read two versions of the manuscript and reminded me to continue to think about the book's "core." Neil Saccamano and Molly Hite offered important feedback and encouragement, as has Mary Pat Brady, who I thank for her guidance and advice. I am grateful to Tracy McNulty for our conversations about Lacan and the Bible (as well as for her, slightly twisted, notion of a "work party"). Finally, I would like to thank my dear friend Annetta Alexandridis, who generously discussed bodies, organs, theory, and metaphor during wonderful dinners in Ithaca.

It is a pleasure to acknowledge the amazing graduate students at Cornell who have played an important role in sharpening my focus and who have been a source of inspiration and encouragement. It has been an honor to work with them. I would especially like to thank my brilliant research assistants, Alexis Briley, Jess Keiser, and (unofficially) Shilo McGiff, as well as the students in my graduate seminar, "Theater, Theory, Form: The Question of Sovereignty."

Outside Cornell, many other colleagues have taught me much about early modern law, sovereignty, politics, economy, drama, and philosophy, including especially Peter Goodrich, Gil Anidjar, Mark Netzloff, Paul Kottman, and Margherita Pascucci. I am also grateful to Henry

Turner and to the participants of the seminar on "Shakespeare and Theory: Law, Theology, Sovereignty," sponsored by the Program in Early Modern Studies of Rutgers University for responses to material from Chapter 2.

This book would not exist were it not for Julia Reinhard Lupton and Graham Hammill. To each I owe a debt of professional and personal gratitude that I can hardly begin to express here. I thank both for their helpful comments on the manuscript and for much more. From Julia's early generous invitation to join the seminars she and Graham organized on "Sovereigns, Saints and Citizens" at meetings of the Group for Early Modern Cultural Studies and the Shakespeare Association of America in 2003 and 2005, through many subsequent conversations and collaborations, she has been an unwavering source of intellectual inspiration, good counsel, integrity, and friendship. Graham's elegant work on early modern literature and political theology, too, has been an inspiration. I thank him not only for his scholarship but also for his warmth and generosity.

Jacques Lezra's influence is felt throughout these pages. I am extremely grateful to Jacques for his teaching and scholarship. His singularly brilliant work always reminds me what the aesthetic, political, and philosophical stakes are. Discussing literature and philosophy—or piracy law, Australian rules football, or Spanish politics—over a beer in Melbourne and Madrid has been a pleasure. I am glad for our friendship.

Of the many other kinds of debts upon which this book depends I would like to express my gratitude to a group of people for whom there is no simple category. I would especially like to thank Laura Ahumada, for her generosity, warmth, encouragement, and deep friendship. My thanks, also, to my dear friend Jim Harder, and to Larissa Bonfante, Claire Hills-Nova, Margaret Dieter, and Muhammad Wattoo for their hospitality, kindness, humor, and support.

An earlier version of Chapter 1 was published as "'Christall Mirrors,' Analogy and Onto-Theology in Shakespeare and Francisco Suárez," in *Religion and Literature*. And a much abbreviated form of Chapter 5 appeared in "Notes on the 'Religious Turn': Mystery, Metaphor, Medium," in the special issue of *English Language Notes* on "Literary History and the Religious Turn." A study leave by Cornell University made revisions possible, and I am grateful to the Hull Memorial Publication Fund of Cornell University for its generous support.

I have been extremely privileged to be able to work with Helen Tartar at Fordham University Press. I thank Helen for her guidance, kindness, faith in the project—and *patience*. Tom Lay, Eric Newman, Katie Sweeney, and the staff at the Press have been ideal to work with. Thanks to Nancy Rapoport for her skillful editing and for dealing with my many inconsistencies. I am also grateful to Kate Washington and Karen Mann for their astute editorial suggestions.

Finally, to my family, here and in Spain, for their unwavering love, support, irony (*gracias a Dios* . . . ), and encouragement. To Ena Bronstein Barton, Bob Barton, Nicole and John Furyk—and to Carmen Truyols, without whom none of this would have been possible.

This book is dedicated to my father, Philip Manfred Lorenz, 1935–1992. He would have enjoyed it. In loving memory.

# Introduction: The Body Is Burning— Sovereignty, Image, Trope

> ... as though literature, theater, deceit, infidelity, hypocrisy, infelicity, parasitism, and the simulation of real life were not part of real life!
>
> —Jacques Derrida, *Limited Inc.*, 90

## *Sovereignty Is Burning*

On December 1, 1613, England's King James I ordered that a book, *A Defense of the Catholic Faith against the Errors of the Anglican Sect* (*Defensio fidei*), by the Jesuit theologian and philosopher Francisco Suárez, be burned in front of Saint Paul's Cathedral in London.[1] The Spanish Ambassador to England, Diego Sarmiento de Acuña (Count of Gondomar), described the scene to Spain's King, Philip III, in the following letter:

> [T]oday at noon, by order of the Archbishop of Canterbury, who has jurisdiction over London, a minister preached in the cemetery of St. Paul's Church and in the midst of his sermon produced the book of Father Suarez together with one of Becan [the Jesuit Van de Beeck] and one of Scioppius. After he had informed the people of the contents, he pitched the books down from the height of his pulpit and ordered them to be burned. Immediately on the spot two sacks of books were thrown into the flames.[2]

Prior to this event, a series of diplomatic exchanges between the English and Spanish courts had led up to James's order to burn Suárez's *Defense*. As Suárez's biographer, Joseph Fichter, recounts,

> For almost two years the English ambassador at the court of Philip III in Madrid knew of the impending attack, and like a reliable military scout kept his monarch informed. If the element of surprise was thus eliminated from Suarez' assault, that of anxiety was steadily increased, and when it was finally accomplished it spread like the shrapnel of a high explosive in the camp of the enemy.[3]

Suárez's book landed in England like a bomb, not only challenging Royalist claims that James's power was directly derived from God but also threatening to undermine the king's authority over the bodies and souls of his subjects.[4] James responded with an equal display of violence, publicly condemning the *Defense* to the sacrificial flames of the pulpit.

Perhaps the most philosophically rigorous of numerous Catholic responses to James's 1606 Oath of Allegiance, Suárez's *Defensio fidei* incurred James's wrath by outlining the conditions under which it is licit to violently resist a king.[5] In it, Suárez contends that "even a king who is supreme in temporal matters may be punished with deposition and sentenced to be deprived of his kingdom" and that "it is not sedition to resist a king who is ruling tyrannically." The key passage reads:

> But in the highest pope is this power, possessing in the case of superior [ranks] the jurisdiction for prosecuting even the highest kings, as much as he does in those below him, as is shown above. Wherefore if there are crimes [*crimina*] in spiritual matters, such as the crime of heresy, he can punish those crimes directly [*directe*] in the king's person, even to the point of deposing him from the kingdom, if the king's obstinacy and the providence of the common good of the Church so require it. But if the vices [*vitia*] are in temporal matters, insofar as they are sins [*peccata*], he can also prosecute those things through direct power [*per directam potestatem*]. So as far as such things are temporally noxious to the Christian republic, he will at least be able to punish those indirectly [*indirecte*] inasmuch as the tyrannical kingship of a prince is always destructive to the health of souls.[6]

Suárez's identification of different types of power and jurisdiction takes us straight to the heart of the problem of sovereignty as it was being reconfigured in the early seventeenth century. The explosive nature of the argument, as James clearly recognized, lay in the claim that popes had the power to depose kings, which is, in effect, the theoretical and theo-political precondition for justifying regicide (or "tyrannicide"). Although, as Suárez argues, many conditions for such an act have to first be present, the implications are nevertheless clear: In the extreme case, it may even be necessary to kill the king—*if* this killing is an act of self-defense. Invoking the authority of Thomas Aquinas, Suárez writes that in such a conflict "it is not the king or prince who is slain, but rather an enemy of the state."[7] For Suárez, the 1606 English Oath of Allegiance, along with James's later justification of it (*De triplici nodo, triplex cuneus* [1608]), represent an arrogation of power the King does not possess: "To be sure, Paul said [*Romans*, Chap. xiii, v.1]: 'Let every soul be subject to higher powers'; but nowhere did he add: Let all be subject even to powers that have been excommunicated or deprived [of their authority] by the Pope."[8] Suárez thus subordinates James's sovereignty to the Pope's jurisdiction—a conclusion he knows "will not be pleasing to the King of England."[9]

Suarez's focus on the term "jurisdiction," in particular, introduces a problem that is symptomatic of the difficulties facing any conceptualization of sovereignty in the early seventeenth century. "Jurisdiction" (*jurisdictio*) is not an easy matter to define here. The term identifies a particularly contested site in the wake of Reformation and Counter-Reformation struggles, as Catholic and Protestant princes alike sought to administratively align ecclesiastical jurisdictions with the territories over which they ruled.[10] It does not refer primarily to territorial boundaries, as it would come to do in later understandings of sovereignty, but rather to the nature of the pope's power over Christian souls. The argument is complex, involving not only two forms of time (worldly and otherworldly, or temporal and eternal) but also two types of crime, or transgression. That neither can be subsumed to merely legal or political matters but also involve theological ones is made clear by Suárez's language. When he describes spiritual evils, Suárez speaks of "crimes" (*crimina*)—*but* when he discusses temporal evils he speaks of "sins" (*vitia*) instead—thus subtly blurring the distinction between the different kinds of time and crime and allowing popes to have jurisdiction over both.[11] The *Defense*'s crossing of terms from one domain to the other is central to Suárez's theoretical articulation of the nature of the pope's power. It is also a frontal attack on James's claim that his own sovereignty is directly derived from God and that all English subjects therefore owe their primary allegiance to the king: an act to which every English subject was obliged to acknowledge in writing, in a text that concluded with the phrase: ". . . heartily, willingly, and trewly, vpon the true Faith of a Christian. So helpe me GOD."[12] The crux of the theoretical battle over the changing concept of sovereignty in the early seventeenth century has to do with how we understand these terms and relations.

Suárez's text was hardly the first to justify violent resistance to the temporal sovereign. The *Defensio fidei* extends a trajectory of clerical and, in particular, Jesuit writings supporting what has come to be known as "resistance theory," including the Spanish Juan de Mariana's *On the King and the King's Education* (*De Rege Et Regis Institutione*) (1599), the English Robert Parsons's *A discussion of the answere of M. William Barlow* (1612), and the Italian Jesuit Robert Bellarmine's *De potestate summi pontificis* (1610). Earlier Protestant tracts defending resistance to a ruler viewed as obstructing the path toward the true religion include the *Vindiciae, contra tyrannos* (1579), published under the name of Stephanus Junius Brutus, and the *De jure regni apud Scotos* (1579), by James's former teacher, George Buchanan.[13] Resistance theory thus occupies a central position in the constitutional problematics of the early seventeenth century, as James himself well understood, writing in *The Trew Law of Free Monarchies* (1598) that even a wicked king cannot be resisted "but by sobbes and teares to God."[14]

"Back in Coimbra," Suárez's biographer, continues, imagining Suárez's view of the Oath of Allegiance controversy, "the source of all this agitation and international complication was placidly going about his duties of lecturing and writing."[15] As unperturbed by worldly events as he was devoted to spiritual ones, according to Fichter, Suárez himself was apparently most concerned with the unexpected side effects of the dissemination of his text:

> A young cleric of Oporto had been receiving the pages of the work as it came from the printer, and had been helping Suarez in their correction. Without the author's knowledge this priest read the proofs to a young Englishman deeply interested in the controversy who was staying for a while at Oporto. The truth about the Catholic Church thus gradually unfolded before his eyes so that he came to Coimbra and asked to be received into the Church. Suarez took a childlike delight in telling Aquaviva about the conversion, remarking that good fruit had been produced from the work. "Our Lord has accorded me a very deep consolation, concerning a young Englishman from Oporto, a convert to our holy faith (who declared) that the reading of this book had made him understand where the truth was."[16]

Fichter's biography of Suárez is far from impartial and has been described as "hagiographical."[17] Its ideological concerns are, in fact, part of the problems we will be encountering in the following pages. That is, while Fichter's account of the burning of Suárez's *Defensio fidei* is not in itself particularly illuminating as far as seventeenth-century English and Spanish literary relations go, the trajectory it traces from immolation to conversion, on the other hand, as well as its own perspective of these events, introduce an array of historical and theoretical problems accompanying the formation of the concept of sovereignty at the threshold of European modernity. As a figure of these tensions, Suárez's burning text not only richly captures the state of hostilities between England and Spain, but it also marks the volatility of relations between religion and politics, authority and representation, sacrifice and subjection, underlying the construction of a new body-of-power at the turn of the seventeenth century.[18] The effects of these developments would include one of history's most violent conflagrations, the Thirty Years War, in the early part of the seventeenth century, and begin to move Europe, in the latter part, toward the formation of what would eventually become a new political form: the nation-state.

In some ways, prefiguring these developments, the Oath of Allegiance controversy opens on to two conflicting stories about power, resistance, and theater. Binding them together is the image of Suárez's burning text itself—not only as the object of sovereign power but also as its staging, as the text in flames becomes the site and scene of sovereignty's performance. That is, on the one hand, it reveals sovereignty to be an act and actualization of power. By having Suárez's book publicly burned, James produces his own image of sovereignty, on a stage in which what counts is less the conceptual argument than the effective display of power that destroys it: that which resists sovereignty will be met with a certain violence. At the same time, by forcing James to respond, Suárez's text, on the other hand, also exerts its own form of sovereignty, in effect obliging the king to act. In this view, Suárez's text precedes and even takes a certain form of precedence over James's action. From this perspective, true sovereignty appears in the light of the flames of resistance to that which in the end is not sovereignty; Suárez's text negates through its own negation leaving us with an after-image of what James's sovereignty cannot contain or be. Both images produce the impression that the primary action of power is resistance to power.[19] The destruction of Suárez's text thus brings into view a set of historical, political, and theological problems underlying and in some ways impelling the production of the English and Spanish plays I read in this book.

## Sovereignty

This is a book about Renaissance drama and the concept of sovereignty, a term that refers not simply to power in general, but rather to extraordinary power, that which is above, beyond, or outside all others—the *highest* power.[20] Chiefly understood today as a political concept defining the state's jurisdiction, sovereignty in the seventeenth century was the product of an amalgamation of juridical and theological ideas.[21] The king's, or the pope's, power was understood in terms of the position the sovereign occupied in relation to God—a theorization that (as the term "theory" itself suggests) operates by viewing and looking.[22] How are we to see this "thing," as Hamlet puts it, that is a king?[23] The question is more complex than meets the eye, for a Renaissance king is a hybrid creature, at once a being, a body, and also an image of absolute power. How are we to understand the properties and capacities of this construct? On the one hand, the question is ontological, focusing on the dual—natural and political—status of the king's body, as it was theorized by early modern jurists and clerics.[24] On the other hand, it is also representational, involving the sovereign figure's capacity to signify, and thereby effect, a number of crucial conceptual transpositions: from the particular to the universal, the temporal to the eternal, and the finite to the infinite body-of-power. The representational structure used to express the link between the sovereign's power and God's—a connection historically figured as a "body"—thus becomes increasingly important, as it is asked to bear the conceptual burden of actually performing these transpositions.[25]

The question of sovereignty is, additionally, a terminological and translational one that takes us straight to the heart of one of the increasingly difficult problems of late modernity: the relationship between secularization and political theology. For while the term "sovereignty" is a decidedly modern one, emerging at a crucial moment in the historical process of secularization, it is also the heir of a complex tradition of theo-political terms and tropes. As José Antonio Maravall has shown, in the gradual transition from medieval concepts of imperial rule and papal claims to unlimited jurisdiction, toward the assumption of total power by the governing head of secular states, the Pope's *plenitudo potestatis* gradually began to lose its strictly religious sense. Even as the old Latin terms of the *plenitudo potestatis* and *imperium* continued to be used to refer to the power of secular kings, the new word, "sovereignty" appears, in 1576, with the publication of Jean Bodin's *Six livres de la République*, without clear etymological antecedents in a national idiom, French. Gaspar de Añastro's 1590 Spanish translation of Bodin's text does not use the word "sovereignty" (*soberanía*) once, as Añastro prefers to use the traditional forms instead. On the other hand, with the Spanish translation of Giovanni Botero's *Della ragion di Stato* (1589), the inverse occurs. While the new expression does not appear in the Italian original, the Spanish translator commissioned by Philip II, Antonio de Herrera, replaces the Italian, "*sopranità*," which refers to royal power as "*superiority*" with "*soberanía*."[26] Related to these developments, and at least as important as its terminological transformations, is the central problem of sovereignty's representation. Because of its singular position above all other powers, the concept of sovereignty presents us with a set of philosophical, theological, and representational questions: How are we to understand its being, origin, pathways of derivation, and historical manifestations? What is its proper nature, structure, or form? Like the religious problem of the naming of God, with which it has much in common, the question of sovereignty is always at least a double if not a triple one, of designation, conceptualization, and representation. The following readings suggest that, in the case of sovereignty, these questions in effect converge, on-stage, in different ways, into one.[27]

Recent work on sovereignty has returned to a consideration of the concept's metaphysical structures and ontological relations.[28] For Giorgio Agamben, "sovereignty is not an exclusively political concept, an exclusively juridical category, a power external to law (Schmitt), or the supreme rule of the juridical order . . . it is the originary structure in which law *refers to* life and includes it in itself by suspending it."[29] The fact that this "originary structure" is above all a structure of reference leads Agamben to formulate a series of historical and conceptual difficulties of sovereignty related to language. Agamben explores these by viewing them in the space of his recurring figure of the "zone" (*zona*). Beginning with the problem opened up by the two different Greek terms for "life"—*zoē*, or the simple fact of living, sometimes referred to as "bare life," and *bios*, the way of living proper to an individual or group, the "good" or "political life"—Agamben approaches sovereignty genealogically and conceptually, situating it within a large trajectory of Western thought.[30] Building on the work of Michel Foucault and Hannah Arendt, Agamben's theories of sovereignty identify conceptual borders between an inside and an outside of various orders—legal, logical, and metaphysical—only to then posit their collapse into "*zones of indistinguishability*," in a movement that for Agamben is itself symptomatic of Western political philosophy. What Agamben calls the "paradox of sovereignty" is that the concept lies both inside and outside these orders at once, giving it, in effect, no stable, discernible place.[31] For the philosopher Jean-Luc Nancy, on the other hand, sovereignty presents a different kind of paradox. For Nancy,

> sovereign is the existent who depends upon nothing—no finality, no order of production or subjection, whether it concerns the agent or the patient or the cause or the effect. Dependent upon nothing, it is entirely delivered over to itself, insofar as precisely, the "itself" neither precedes nor founds it but is the *nothing*, the very thing from which it is suspended.[32]

Sovereignty, Nancy argues, necessarily and "essentially eludes the sovereign." This is, in a sense, logical. For if it were otherwise, Nancy continues, "[i]f sovereignty did not elude it, the sovereign would in no way [*en rien*] be sovereign. The same condition that ensures that sovereignty receive its concept also deprives it of its power: that is, the absence of superior or foundational authority." Sovereignty, to be sovereign, cannot depend on or follow a prior authority. Nor can it have a superior. It can only be "under" *itself*, a condition, Nancy argues, that contradicts its "self." For Nancy, this is precisely the paradox of sovereignty: that "the sovereign authority must be essentially occupied with founding itself or with overcoming itself in order to legislate prior to or in excess of any law."[33] Nancy's paradox—the fact that sovereignty "essentially eludes the sovereign"—underscores the peculiar state of sovereignty as that which is at once everything (all power, the power above and beyond all others) and at the same time, nothing—empty. Like Hamlet's ghost, sovereignty in this view is, essentially, no thing; it has no being. What Nancy's description underscores is that in order for the concept to make logical sense, it has to be understood as that which cannot be founded or preceded in any way by another power, or caused to act, other than by its own will. Its conceptual consistency requires us to imagine a sovereignty that draws its basis, authority, and legitimacy only from itself in an act that both presents and negates it.

Sovereignty's conceptualization thus presents us with a set of challenges similar to those raised by the older theological problem of the naming of God. As Ernesto Laclau points out, for a long tradition of Western theological thought, the only proper thing that can be said about God is that He is One. As soon as one starts attributing other qualities to God, one determines and differentiates and therefore limits God in some way.[34] The problem of naming God is akin to the philosophical challenges involved in understanding sovereignty insofar as both hinge on the representational capacities of language to posit a singular being or power superior to all others. Sovereignty always speaks from the "God-place."[35] Sovereignty's twentieth-century theorists, from Laclau and Nancy through Claude Lefort, Louis Marin, Jacques Derrida, Giorgio Agamben, and others, have all variously described this place as an "empty one."[36] One of the purposes of this study is to show how drama provides a particularly powerful vehicle for thinking through the problems of sovereignty. In the chapters that follow, I will consider how Renaissance (or what, for reasons that will become clearer, I will also refer to especially as *baroque*) drama, responds to the paradoxes, provocations, and problems of sovereignty's conceptual emptiness, precisely as problems for theater.

One answer to that question has been put forth, in the twentieth century, by the controversial, arch-Conservative jurist Carl Schmitt. For Schmitt, enemy of liberalism, "godfather of political theology," and "Crown Jurist" of the Third Reich, that answer involves a complex understanding of the relationship between history and representation.[37] Perhaps surprisingly, one place Schmitt sees that relation most illuminatingly revealed is in early modern drama, and, specifically, Shakespeare. While the constitutional law scholar is certainly known more for his sovereignty theory than for his Shakespeare scholarship, it was through an unusual reading of *Hamlet* that Schmitt formulated a compelling account of the relationship between history, sovereignty, and theater.[38]

In his 1956 essay *Hamlet or Hecuba*, Schmitt identifies an "irruption" (*Einbruch*) of historical time into "the time of the play."[39] Reading the drama in relation to historical events surrounding the life of England's King James I, particularly the murder of his father followed by his mother, Mary, Queen of Scots' marriage to the murderer, the Earl of Bothwell, Schmitt focuses on the inside-outside dynamic of literary and political-historical relations as these are marked by the space of the stage. Although "it would be absurd," Schmitt writes, "to be distracted by the historical circumstances," his reading of *Hamlet* nevertheless centers largely on these—or, more specifically, on the way that Shakespeare responds to them. As James waited to succeed Queen Elizabeth during her last years, which are also the years that *Hamlet* was produced and performed (roughly 1599–1603), the question of the play—what Schmitt calls the "taboo of the Queen"—becomes a key index of the permeable border between history and theater in the early seventeenth century. For Schmitt, the double imperative with which the play confronts its audience—to recognize both the Queen's complicity in the murder of her husband (and marriage to his killer), *and, at the same time*, not criticize it—haunts both Hamlet and James. This contradictory double demand is intensified in relation to the historical Elizabeth's claim that she had no role in the death of Mary, Queen of Scots.[40] Although Schmitt argues that the "rift" between literary history and political history, Hamlet and James, is "too deep" to bridge, he nevertheless identifies two moments when history indeed "breaks into" ("irrupts") the play. These occur in what Schmitt calls the "Hamletization" of the hero, and in the play within the play, known as the "Mousetrap." Despite his claims of the deep "rift," Schmitt ultimately sees behind the figure of the revenge hero, the historical King James, whose own family drama, in effect, forms "the substance" of that which is re-played on stage. As Jennifer Rust and Julia Reinhard Lupton have shown, Schmitt reads the play as a "play" (*Spiel*) of immediate historical presence—literally as a "piece" (*Stück*) of time.[41] In the end, although these "intrusions" "disturb the unintentional character of pure play," and, are therefore a "minus," they are also what make it possible for Schmitt to see the figure of Hamlet as a "truth myth," which then (in his eyes) "elevates" the play to a tragedy.[42] Schmitt's reading of *Hamlet* as a "true myth" is connected, as we shall see, to his view of history as rooted in legal substance. The literary myth's function in relation to historical reality, according to Schmitt, is not so much to "interpret" reality, as it is to remind it of what it really consists.[43] I will return to Schmitt's view of reality in relation to theater and law in Chapters 3 and 4.

While his writings have sparked a widespread debate, particularly with regard to his "concept of the political," based on its antithesis of friend and enemy, Schmitt's work has also taken on an enormous importance among twentieth and twenty-first century thinkers on both the right and the left, for its theorization of power. For some theorists, in the wake of the Cold War, neither liberalism's reliance on law nor

Marxism's critique of the production and distribution of wealth could account for a political order in which a new form of violence poses the real possibility of total global destruction.[44] In the face of these inadequacies, Schmitt's work has been seen by some to provide an important critical corrective.

In works such as *Political Theology: Four Chapters on the Concept of Sovereignty* (1922), *Roman Catholicism and Political Form* (1923), and *The Nomos of the Earth* (1950), Schmitt presents a conceptual genealogy of sovereignty within a larger framework of what, at times, appears to be an almost mythological narrative of legal history. Schmitt describes this history in *The Nomos of the Earth* (1950) in quasi-Heideggerian terms of cultivation, containment, and differentiation, in which the law inscribes itself into the earth in three distinct phases. "In mythical language, the *earth* became known as the mother of law. This signifies a threefold root of law and justice":

> First, the fertile earth contains within herself, within the womb of her fecundity, an inner measure, because human toil and trouble, human planting and cultivation of the fruitful earth is rewarded justly by her with growth and harvest . . . Second, soil that is cleared and worked by human hands manifests firm lines, whereby definite divisions become apparent. Through the *demarcation of fields*, pastures, and forests, these *lines are engraved and embedded*. . . .
> Third and last, the solid ground of the earth is delineated by fences, enclosures, boundaries, walls, houses, and other constructs. Then the orders and orientations of human social life become apparent . . . In this way, the earth is bound to law in three ways. She contains law within herself, as a reward of labor; she manifests law upon herself, as fixed boundaries; and she sustains law above herself, as a public sign of order.[45]

While there is much to say about Schmitt's mythology of the earth (including its awkward gendering, in which after "she" is publicly bound and contained, the earth provides "rewards"), for the purposes of introduction I would like to merely note how it presents a concise account of Schmitt's view of history.[46] For Schmitt, the engine of history is law, and historical development is driven by legal processes of division, inscription, and binding to the earth. The earth's relationship with law is itself conceived of in terms of bonds: "the earth is *bound* to law . . ." The importance of the earth's relation to law in Schmitt cannot be overstressed. It is at the heart of his sovereignty theory, and it is also, as we shall see, a crucial starting point for thinkers from Walter Benjamin through Jacques Derrida and Giorgio Agamben, who have all returned to Schmitt's work in order to understand contemporary problems of sovereignty and political theology. Each of Schmitt's stages, from the earth's rewarding of human labor with the gift of law, through the "clearing" of soil and "divisions" of labor, to the "*delineation* by fences, enclosures, boundaries, walls, houses, and other constructs," marks a different aspect of these bonds, as they come together to form the historical ground of geopolitical thought. It is precisely this ground and its legal layering that, for Schmitt, orders the world—prior to any sociological or psychological determination.[47] Schmitt's language reinforces his hierarchical gendering of the earth ("within the womb of her fecundity," "she contains," and so on) by indicating the positions where these borders are inscribed—*within, upon, and above*. What slowly starts to emerge, in *Nomos of the Earth* in particular, is a spatial order created and structured by the originary force of law. It is above all through law, for Schmitt, that the "orientations of human social life" become legible. In order to bear out this view of the relationship between legal history and life forms ("orientations"), Schmitt advances a novel conceptual methodology.

## "Sociology of Concepts"

Although he published his study of political theology in a Festschrift for the sociologist Max Weber, Schmitt goes to great lengths to distinguish his own form of juridical "sociology" from Weber's.[48] For Schmitt, a legal-theoretical understanding of history is different from a psychological one, reliant on the category of "motivation." It is also distinct from a sociology that focuses on "specific types," which is more or less what "brilliant literary criticism" does.[49] Against these, what matters for Schmitt is the "juristic construction." For Schmitt, it is the legal, not the social or psychological, layering that underlies and determines history. In order to demonstrate this, Schmitt turns toward a theory of comparison and what he calls "radical conceptualization" governed by the operation of "correspondences." A sociology of concepts

> aims to discover the basic, radically systematic structure and to compare this conceptual structure with the conceptually represented social structure of a certain epoch. There is no question here of

whether the idealities produced by radical conceptualization are a reflex of social reality, or whether social reality is conceived of as the result of a particular kind of thinking and therefore also of acting. Rather this sociology of concepts is concerned with establishing proof of two spiritual but at the same time substantial identities.[50]

Rather than seeing historical realities "reflected" in concepts, Schmitt's sociology identifies correspondences between, for example, the status of a political form, such as monarchy, and a "general state of consciousness." Between political status and subjective consciousness, form and thought, lie organizational structures that shape historical periods. Schmitt's analyses hinge on the way one conceives of the relationship between legal and political structures and various—social, spiritual, metaphysical, and aesthetic—forms of life. Understanding the nature of the relationship and the logic of the correspondences lies at the heart of Schmitt's methodology.

Schmitt's sociology of concepts raises as many questions as it provides answers for the problem of sovereignty. How, for example, does one recognize "structural correspondences" between juridical, theological, economic, or aesthetic forms? How does one compare a "conceptual" structure with a social one? And how does a "historical-political status" correspond with a "general state of consciousness"—especially in cultures where legal history and even conceptualization itself may take on different forms? What structural or "logical" sense does Schmitt's "correspondence" theory make? In order to answer such questions, Schmitt repeatedly insists on the "systematic" nature of the correspondences—a feature he identifies, perhaps surprisingly, in the form of what he refers to as a "metaphysical image" (*das metaphysische Bild*):

> The metaphysical image that a definite epoch forges of the world has the same structure as what the world immediately understands to be appropriate as a form of its political organization. The determination of such an identity is the sociology of the concept of sovereignty.[51]

Somewhat akin to his contemporary, Martin Heidegger, and his notion of a "world picture" (*Weltbild*), Schmitt's "metaphysical images" have structures that reflect "substantial identities"—above all, in Schmitt's case, ones that can be recognized in political forms. This structuring logic of the image lies at the heart of a "systematic" methodology that attempts to account for the way material and conceptual history meet at the level of representation.[52]

A different kind of "image" emerges in the work of Schmitt's surprising—for some, even shocking—interlocutor on these questions, Walter Benjamin.[53] Benjamin's study of the German baroque "mourning play" (*Trauerspiel*) provides an inverse theoretical perspective to Schmitt's. For Benjamin, too, the question of methodology is inseparable from the practice of criticism (what Schmitt refers to as "scientific" investigation).[54] It is precisely the question of method that Benjamin works out most fully in his study of baroque drama. There, Benjamin—unlike Schmitt, who sees his work as a systematic investigation of radical structural correspondences—describes his own research method not in terms of correspondences, but rather as a process of *detours*. "Method," for Benjamin, "is a digression" (*Methode ist Umweg*).[55] In the "Epistemo-Critical Prologue" to *The Origin of German Tragic Drama* (1928), he links this indirect way of proceeding to the problem of representation (*Darstellung*) in general:

> Representation as digression—such is the methodological nature of the treatise. The absence of an uninterrupted purposeful structure is its primary characteristic. Tirelessly the process of thinking makes new beginnings, returning in a roundabout way to its original object.[56]

Benjamin explains this notion of method as "digression" by comparing it with the mode of presentation used in the scholastic treatise. Here, the "truth-content" of the work is "only to be grasped through immersion in the most minute details of subject-matter."[57] Immersing oneself in the details of the form is central to an immanent criticism in which the interpreted object's availability to knowledge depends on understanding both the internal relation of its elements to each other, and also their relation to the act of interpretation itself.[58] It is interpretation that sets ideas in motion. Interpretation, in effect, stages thought.[59] As Benjamin explains and develops in some detail in *The Origin of German Tragic Drama* (often referred to as the "*Trauerspiel* book"—*Trauer* plus *Spiel* designating "plays of mourning" or of "tragical history"[60]), this double movement of identification and interpretation does not merely "describe" the object it contemplates. Rather, it participates in the actual production of its meaning. It is the object that determines the mode of interpretation, not the other way around.

Like Schmitt, Benjamin's critical method gives central place to what he refers to as "image" (*Bild*). Like Schmitt, too, Benjamin's theory of the "image" lies at the heart of his understanding of historical consciousness. In a famous passage of Benjamin's "Arcades Project" (*Das Passagen-Werk*) Benjamin describes the relationship between what he calls the Then (*das Gewesene*) and the Now (*das Jetzt*) in terms of an instantaneous "flash" (*blitzhaft*):

> It's not that what is past casts its light on what is present, or what is present [casts] its light on what is past; rather, image is that wherein what has been comes together in a flash [*blitzhaft*] with the now to form a constellation. In other words, image is dialectics at a standstill. For while the relation of the present to the past is a purely temporal, continuous one, the relation of what-has-been to the now is dialectical: is not progression but image, suddenly emergent.— Only dialectical images are genuine images (that is, not archaic); and the place where one encounters them is language.
> □Awakening□[61]

Benjamin's "semi-concept" of the dialectical image has sparked an enormous amount of critical commentary in the twentieth century in disciplines ranging from philosophy and political theory, to theology and psychoanalysis.[62] Included among Benjamin's many critical targets here is an understanding of history and historical representation in terms of development and progress. Specifically, Benjamin is countering both a Hegelian conception of world-historical movement and particular aspects of Martin's Heidegger's theory of historicity.[63] Against both of these, Benjamin's "image" posits a materialist conception of history in which what is accessible to thought is a "ruin," the historicity of which is made momentarily visible through the abrupt effects of an interpretive collision. "Not progression but image," Benjamin writes, is what the fleeting encounter between the Then (*das Gewesene*) and the Now (*das Jetzt*) produces. The place where this collision and its illuminating consequences occur, as Benjamin suggests, and as Anselm Haverkamp stresses and develops, is language. "More precisely," Haverkamp writes,

> the paradigmatic instance of the dialectical image's existence in language is citation: language reused and reread. One might be tempted to go so far as to say that the word *image* is the metaphor— and a very suggestive one—for citation, while the word "dialectical" has to be taken as "reading." The expression "dialectical image" has to be translated into and put to use as "reading citation."[64]

The temporality of this "reading" unfolds in a non-linear manner, moving according to a more irregular and iterative, even violent, rhythm. It tears the object away from a history that would situate it within a wider narrative of progress.[65] While Benjamin's theory of the image reaches its mature form in his Arcades project, it is in his earlier study of baroque drama—focusing particularly on Shakespeare, Lope de Vega, and Calderón de la Barca—that he begins to formulate his complex view of the relationship between history, language, and time.[66] It is the Benjamin of the *Trauerspiel* book that I grapple with here.

Benjamin's rich formulation of the connection between baroque culture and twentieth-century modernity guides me throughout these pages, as I draw on his study to understand how baroque drama continues to inform our thinking about the problems of sovereignty and political theology today.[67] One of the theoretical and methodological gains suggested by the dialectical image is that it provides a complex and compelling way of thinking about the relationship between conceptual and material history. While the figures I pursue in the following readings are by no means offered as simple illustrations of dialectical images (nor are they taken from Benjamin's own examples, such as the lightning-like flash [*blitzhaft*], or the frozen image of arrested movement), they nevertheless suggest similar operations of historical and theoretical mediation. It is precisely in their capacity to bridge the early and post-modern problematics that the tropes of sovereignty take center stage. Along with Schmitt's "metaphysical image," then, I take Benjamin's "dialectical image" as a second point of orientation from which to follow the tropological formation of sovereignty on the baroque stage.

Benjamin identifies a strong epistemic link between the seventeenth-century baroque and twentieth-century modernity. This connection has to do in part with the kinds of problems sovereignty poses in both periods. In both the seventeenth and twentieth (and one might now add twenty-first) centuries, some of the conditions that frame these problems include the resurgence of political theology; the development of unprecedented military power, including the technological capacity for world destruction; a constantly present anxiety over the question of security; military, economic, and legal developments related to the administration of global empire; the spatialization of power; a virtualization of politics; and an ongoing theological and political rhetoric of sacrifice.⁶⁸ In addition to these crises of sovereignty, each period also bears witness to a general awareness of, and sophisticated relation to, sovereignty's staging conditions.⁶⁹ Both periods share a complex relationship to the—equally complex—sign-systems of sovereign power. If, in the seventeenth century, the epistemological problems involved in this crisis are explicitly theological ones, they are also, in both periods, what Hent de Vries refers to as "mediatic" ones.⁷⁰ That is, both periods undergo intense philosophical and political-theological crises of the sign. In order to better understand this claim, as well as the complex relationship between sovereignty and its mediation, I rely throughout this book on Schmitt's juridical investigations, as well as Benjamin's still extremely suggestive work on the baroque. For both thinkers, the historical and conceptual problems of the baroque move in tandem with the constitutional and theological staging of sovereignty. For both, too, the crisis of sovereignty is also a crisis of representation.⁷¹

*The Tears of Sovereignty* follows this interplay of historical and conceptual crises as it is registered in the drama of the leading playwrights of the early modern period: William Shakespeare (1564–1616), Lope de Vega (1562–1635), and Calderón de Barca (1600–1681). Specifically, it focuses on representational operations performed on the "body-of-power" in the form of five "events": the staging of sovereignty's collapse in *Richard II* (Chapter 1); a reanimation via an "organ transplant" in *Measure for Measure* (Chapter 2); an autoimmune response to that operation, in Lope de Vega's *Fuenteovejuna* (Chapter 3); a reconstitution of sovereignty in the form of "ciphers and images" (*cifras y estampas*) in Calderón's *Life is a Dream* (Chapter 4); and, finally, a return (with a twist) to a new body-of-power in Shakespeare's *The Winter's Tale* ("wrinkles") (Chapter 5). Collectively, these moments do not form a history of sovereignty's development, so much as they present a set of scenes of its deformation, reformation, and transformation, staged as a series of shifting metaphorical movements.

Each of these movements is a "tear" of sovereignty in a different sense. From the royal *tears* through which we initially view sovereignty's departure in *Richard II*, tears situate us in relation to sovereignty in a second sense, as a figure of the resistance theory against which divine-right kingship defines itself. (As James asserted, a wicked king cannot be resisted "but by sobbes and teares to God."⁷²) The figure of the "tear" also opens onto a third set of problems, regarding the rise of the modern subject, so frequently associated with literature and art of the early modern period, in general, and writers such as Shakespeare, in particular.[73] For Jacques Derrida, for example, providing his own pun and drawing on the work of Andrew Marvell, the "tear" is a figure of that which is "proper to the *eyeII*."[74] At least one part of this pun, however, the "eye," is unable, on its own, to take in the meaning of "tear," in yet a fourth sense—that of the rip, or the cut—in which the term must be heard as well as read, in order to take in its violence. Here, the "tear" functions in the manner of what the Renaissance rhetorician George Puttenham calls an *auricular figure*, a pun, simultaneously conveying the optical and destructive senses of the term. In my chapter on *Richard II*, the secretive and destructive aspects of the tear take center stage, capturing a key element of what I argue to be the epistemological and political conditions in which one always views sovereignty.[75] Finally, but by no means least important, the *tear* is a figure of mourning, an emblem of the *Trauerspiel* or "tragical history" that, for Benjamin, marks our historical entrance into an ongoing, baroque modernity.

*The Tears of Sovereignty* traces the theatrical arrangements and derangements of these figures and forms into some of the displacements, disavowals, and continuing challenges that the concept of sovereignty confronts us with. Against a view of sovereignty's history in terms of chronological development, the readings presented here move more according to the "logic" of the rhetorical trope of *metalepsis* or *transumption*, which, as Leonard Barkan puts it,

> is a figure of rhetoric that also becomes a figure of history. In its rhetorical mode, which one might call *synchronic*, it refers to the movement, or slide among different tropes: say, a kind of domino effect from one metaphor to another instead of the direct reversion from the metaphorical to the literal. In its historical mode, which one might call *diachronic*, it refers to relations among different planes of time that operate not by direct transmission but by the slide from one figure or motif or anecdote to another. These relations do not conform to the rigors of Socratic thinking but operate by pun, by misreading, by free association (which is never free), by condensation and displacement—choose whatever illogical logic you will.[76]

My pursuit of the tropological relations involved in the representation of sovereignty follows its own "slide" from figure to figure. At the same time, the picture of sovereignty presented here is not one that opens on to a history of rhetoric or rhetorical traditions in England and Spain. Neither does it present a general or intellectual history of the concept.[77] Instead, what *The Tears of Sovereignty* attempts to make visible is a series of co-implications between sovereignty's baroque stagings and its contemporary (both seventeenth *and* twenty-first century) theorizations. My readings, therefore, are not restricted to the historical context of the early seventeenth century—even as I argue that the tropes produced on stage during this period are themselves historical events. Taken as a whole, the "illogical logic" of these events suggests less a narrative of historical "development" than an allegory of sovereignty's ongoing migrations and deformations, as the concept moves from early to late modernity. One general trajectory these follow is from sovereignty's representation in the symbolic body of the sacred king, into increasingly fragmented, abstract, and disembodied forms.[78] Accompanying these representational movements are corresponding conceptual shifts in philosophy, in which questions about a being's essence gradually begin to cede to those of its function, and, in theology, in which, understandings of the absolute begin to move away from the notion of "body" and into more diffuse spatialized and decorporealized forms.[79]

The practical and theoretical place of theater is implied in these questions all along. Historically, from ancient tragedy, through the allegorical drama of medieval Mystery plays, to the public theaters of Western Europe in the Renaissance, which have often reinforced the imperial or centralizing policies of what will become the modern state, the institution of theater has played an enormous role in the dissemination of various political theologies. The present study, however, is not a historicist one. Instead, it focuses on a different sense, in which the specific representational capacities of theater as a medium participate in the historical formation of the concept of sovereignty. Here, as I hope to show, theater brings into dynamic view our ongoing entanglement in sovereignty's conceptual logics. Thus, while the following chapters do not offer an intellectual history of sovereignty, they nevertheless aspire to make visible (at least) one aspect of early modern theater's involvement in that history.[80] In the course of attempting to do so, I do not position the plays with or against much of the critical literature concerning British or Spanish theatre history, much less "Renaissance drama" or the *comedia* as a whole.[81] Nor do I address Italian *commedia* tradition or French court and theater.[82] Neither does *The Tears of Sovereignty* situate the plays in relation to archival material, or the playwrights in relation to their minor interlocutors. Finally, even as it draws extensively on the various writings of Francisco Suárez to provide the conceptual and philosophical framework of the early modern problem of sovereignty, I do not, here, explore Suárez's complex relation to his contemporaries, such as Jean Bodin, in France, or other School of Salamanca theorists.[83]

What *Tears* does do, on the other hand, is seek to address an urgent problem that arises at the juncture of political philosophy and literary and cultural studies, in the wake of the return to Schmitt. As Jacques Lezra has shown, the problem concerns two of Schmitt's chief claims: one, that the state inherits its concepts from theology (historical argument), and, two, that sovereignty ultimately legitimates itself in a nonsecularized conception of time. Schmitt's sovereignty theory itself is thus double, and divided, providing, as Lezra argues, both a tenacious historical description of the theologico-political transition to modernity, and at the same time showing that this entire process relies on a structural exception to the historical.[84] *Tears of Sovereignty* focuses on the manner in which theater captures and complicates this dual development. How do Shakespeare's seminal sovereignty and political theology plays, *Richard II* and *Measure for Measure*, stage these divisions? How do the equally paradigmatic Spanish plays by Lope de Vega, the revolutionary *Fuenteovejuna*, and Calderón, the philosophical *Life Is a Dream*, respond? And, finally, how do the political and religious divides separating the two great national theaters not only mark a key moment in the history of sovereignty, as it begins to move into its modern forms in the early seventeenth century, but also expose its conceptual and representational logics?[85]

One of the theoretical premises of this study is that these logics are always metaphor-logics. *Tears* focuses on the production and effects of these logics as they are generated and released on stage. On the way, it explores the close connection between what Benjamin called baroque drama and a modernity that political-theological sovereignty continues to haunt. Thus my readings not only focus on the ways that sovereignty is staged by the leading playwrights of England and Spain in works that have become centerpieces of research on the topic, but it also considers how current theorizations, including those by Derrida, Schmitt, and Agamben, might be considered in a new light when viewed through the logics of tears.

## Methodology

The readings that follow are informed in different ways by the work of Walter Benjamin, Giorgio Agamben, Carl Schmitt, and Jacques Derrida. The book's tropological method, in particular, draws on Hans Blumenberg's theories of metaphorology and non-conceptuality. Blumenberg's wide-ranging studies explore the philosophical and historical challenges to representation posed in particular by phenomena whose truth status cannot be directly verified.[86] In his *Paradigms for a Metaphorology*, Blumenberg provides a theoretical account of different kinds of metaphors. While some metaphors are used to represent entities that are accessible, and whose truth status *can* be verified, others are employed for that which cannot be directly or fully experienced. In the latter case we use what Blumenberg calls "absolute metaphors": metaphors, including images, that function to make "the maximal abstraction of such concepts as 'Being,' 'History,' [and] 'World,'" accessible.[87] "Absolute metaphors" themselves are not conceptual but rather "theoretical" terms. That is, they don't present us with knowledge so much as they provide us with a "point of orientation" in relation to that which cannot be verified. Not unlike Kant's theory of symbols, absolute metaphors are pragmatic tools. They "give structure to a world, representing the nonexperienceable, nonapprehensible totality of the real."[88] Like many theological and metaphysical theories, absolute metaphors are, in this regard, pre-and meta-conceptual.[89] Blumenberg goes on to characterize absolute metaphors as "'translations' that resist being converted back into authenticity and logicality."[90] That is, they cannot be brought back into literal language. "That these metaphors are called 'absolute,'" Blumenberg writes, "means only that they prove resistant to terminological claims and cannot be dissolved into conceptuality, not that one metaphor could not be replaced or represented by another, or corrected through a more precise one. Even absolute metaphors therefore have a *history*."[91] In his later work, Blumenberg moves from a discussion of absolute metaphors in relation to "metaphorology," to a consideration of their place in a theory of what he refers to as "non-conceptuality." Here, the focus shifts from the metaphors themselves to the question of the "life-world" that generates them. In this latter aspect of his project, metaphor is no longer the sole subject but now also includes other tropological forms.[92]

Like Schmitt, then, Blumenberg sees history in terms of its representation. Unlike Schmitt, however, Blumenberg doesn't link his theories of metaphor directly to specific social issues or political forms. He does not see law as the motor of life. Nor does he focus on the "correspondence" between a period's metaphysical images and its political structures. Rather, for Blumenberg, it is a deep linguistic rather than juridical layering that organizes the "life-world." Against Schmitt's mythological legal "soil" (*Boden*), the "metaphorological" strata that Blumenberg focuses on present us with a different view of history's ground. Metaphors, Blumenberg says, are "fossils that indicate an archaic stratum of the trial of theoretical curiosity—a stratum that is not rendered anachronistic just because there is no way back to the fullness of its stimulations and expectations of truth."[93] The pre-conceptual function of absolute metaphors, then, makes them similar, in some respects, to certain aspects of Michel Foucault's notion of "archaeology." Just as the four components that for Foucault constitute "discourse"—concepts, objects, ways of describing, and the position of subjects—relate subjects to concepts in a formal way, Blumenberg's absolute metaphors similarly attempt to grasp the sub-structures of conceptuality.

Nonconceptuality's turn toward the terrain that produces the terms, images, and tropes through which we grasp "maximal abstractions" is a productive starting point for metaphorological study of sovereignty.[94] In early modern Europe, one of the institutions largely responsible for the generation of such terms is theater. At the same time, the readings that follow do not only operate, strictly speaking, in metaphorological terms, in Blumenberg's sense. They could also be viewed, loosely following Foucault, as "archaeological," or archaeo-tropological investigations of some of the key metaphors baroque drama has reconstituted for the concept of sovereignty.[95] How do the tropes produced by Shakespeare, Lope, and Calderón figure and reconfigure sovereignty's conceptual logics? How do exegetical tropes *perform*? In order to answer these questions, literary history itself might hold a special, even privileged, position in relation to other kinds of historical and intellectual discourse. The plays read here not only stage the "body-of-power," but they also generate terms that repeatedly re-trope the concept of sovereignty apart from any particular staging. In this light, the theater's production of sovereignty tropes could itself be viewed as both a conceptual performance and a historical event at once.[96] We think sovereignty, I argue throughout these pages, with and through its tropes.

Perhaps the most recurring of these tropes is the figure of the "body." Historically speaking, sovereignty's reliance on the "body" metaphor appears in theorists from Plato and Aristotle, through Machiavelli, Hobbes, Spinoza, Rousseau, Gilles Deleuze, Antonio Negri, and Michael Hardt. In these and other thinkers, sovereignty is repeatedly understood in relation to the body. This is not accidental. Perhaps *the* conceptual crux of sovereignty is the problem of embodiment—both at the level of the concept viewed as a "body" of power, and also at that concerning the collective or individual bodies subordinated or subjected to it. As religious studies scholars have pointed out, we tend to think of "maximal abstractions" such as sovereignty in terms of a "body" because we ourselves are and have bodies.[97]

Early modern theater has a special, even burning, relation to these "bodies." One of the objectives of this book is to show how the canonical dramatists of the early modern period provide us with an archive of thought-figures for imagining the body-of-power at a crucial moment in sovereignty's conceptual history. In their works, Shakespeare, Lope, and Calderón have produced a reservoir of tropes that continues to inform our understanding of the nature and operations of sovereignty.[98] Following this line, I argue that the paradigmatic plays considered here can be seen to respond to and even—in a paradoxical and anachronistic sense that we will return to—inform the theorization of sovereignty posed by thinkers such as Agamben, Derrida, and Nancy. Consequently, I read early modern theater and late-modern theory together, pursuing their co-implications at the level of metaphor. How, for example, do the metaphysical and juridical relations captured by Agamben's figure of the "zone" appear in the "law voids" differently staged by Shakespeare, in *Measure for Measure*, or Lope de Vega, in *Fuenteovejuna*? What happens when the body-of-power falls into a crisis of indistinguishability on stage? How does the famous monsterscape of Calderón's dream work appear in relation to Nancy's paradox of an always self-eluding sovereignty? How do these canonical baroque plays both mark and expose the conceptual problems of sovereignty that Schmitt, Benjamin, Foucault, and Derrida have singled out as constitutive of modern life?

I explore answers to these questions through readings of plays of the late sixteenth and early seventeenth centuries: Shakespeare's *Richard II* (1597), *Measure for Measure* (1604), and *The Winter's Tale* (1609–11); Lope de Vega's *Fuenteovejuna* (1612); and Calderón de la Barca's *Life Is a Dream* (*La Vida es Sueño*) (1635)—each of which presents its own paradigm of the representation of political-theological sovereignty. I borrow the term "paradigm" here from Agamben to refer to a particular kind of example. What distinguishes a "paradigm" is that it "make[s] intelligible [a] series of phenomena whose kinship had eluded or could elude the historian's gaze."[99] Paradigms, in this view, don't discover origins in time. Rather, they mark "crossings" of diachrony and synchrony.[100] Agamben's definition of a paradigm is indebted to Benjamin's notion of the "dialectical image."[101] Following Benjamin, Agamben argues that "the historical object is never only in the past and never only in the present. It lies in a constellation formed by both: it is there where past and present meet."[102] In this dual (synchronic and diachronic) sense of the meeting place, the plays analyzed here, I argue, are historical objects with respect to sovereignty. Each is paradigmatic, in Agamben's sense, of a particular problem involved in its staging, both "Then *and* Now" (as Benjamin puts it). Each, too, is governed by a controlling figure, one that comes with its own logic, operations, and implications.[103] Taken together, the readings repeatedly underscore different aspects of sovereignty's conceptual dependence on its theoretical—i.e., metaphorical—machinery.

Each of the plays read here either already holds a prominent place in a tradition of sovereignty criticism, or has become a new site in the burgeoning field of theoretical writing on political theology. All of them remain compelling to scholars interested in the historical, philosophical, and political problems posed by sovereignty. Perhaps the most well-known instance of such a turn to theater to theorize sovereignty is Ernst Kantorowicz's reading of *Richard II*, in his foundational study, *The King's Two Bodies: A Study in Mediaeval Political Theology*. Shakespeare's exploration of political theology is pursued in another direction by Debora Shuger, in a major study of the play in relation to sexuality and English religious history. In other arenas, *Measure for Measure* appears, re-troped, in forms as diverse as Wagner's opera *Das Liebesverbot* and even (for some critics) cultural events such as the

Anita Hill–Clarence Thomas trial;[104] Similarly, innumerable critics and producers have turned to Lope's *Fuenteovejuna* to support wildly contradictory positions with respect to sovereignty, from seeing the play as the embodiment of radical democracy, including Lorca's revolutionary re-writing, to totalitarian and fascist appropriations and interpretations. *Life Is a Dream*, too, can be recognized in countless reiterations and adaptations in forms as diverse as Hugo von Hofmannsthal's *Der Turm* and the films *The Matrix* and *Vanilla Sky*. And, finally, *The Winter's Tale* has not only become the object of much intensive recent Shakespeare criticism of a theoretical and political-theological nature, but its experimental form has also been identified as informing works as diverse as Jane Austen's *Persuasion* and Pedro Almodóvar's *Volver*.[105]

At the same time, even as I underscore the substantial place each of these plays already holds in cultural and intellectual history in relation to sovereignty, my intention is not merely to view them as reminders of a tradition that is past. Rather, my contention is that in terms of the tropological machineries they produce and disseminate for sovereignty, we have in a sense never left them. That is, in addition to the rich place each play already holds within Shakespeare or Golden Age studies, each is also paradigmatic precisely for the way it reveals our ongoing relation to the problem of sovereignty. We are still thinking about sovereignty through their logics, viewing it through their baroque tropes, or "tears." This book explores the different "logics" of these tropes at the level of their linguistic and conceptual staging. Each chapter pursues the staging of a different sovereignty "event," from the concept's collapse ("tears"), through its reanimation ("transplant"), resistance, transformation (*cifras y estampas*), and return ("wrinkles"). Collectively, the "tears," or tropes of sovereignty viewed here function in the manner of what the scholastics referred to as "syncategoremata," words that alone do not form subjects or predicates, but that collectively can form an argumentative proposition. The proposition here concerns the different (representational and conceptual) ways of imagining sovereignty as a body-of-power, and the argument is that baroque drama provides constituent metaphors for understanding the workings of that "body." Sovereignty depends on the tropes of its stagings.[106] Without these terms, there is no sovereignty. Sovereignty is troped, or it is not at all.[107]

This is a comparative study, called for not only by the historical nature of the seventeenth-century sovereignty crisis, but also by the role played by the two great national theaters of Spain and England in articulating it. The early modern constitutional problematic of sovereignty is international from the start. Not only does it emerge from the Reformation–Counter-Reformation reconfiguration of Europe along confessional lines, but it is also an epistemic "event" in Foucault's sense, involving the development of new languages for conceiving of what are increasingly becoming global relations of power. As Schmitt shows, both Spain and England play determining roles, especially at the juridical and conceptual levels, in the formation of these modern languages of power. These early modern geopolitical events correspond with the rise of the institution of theater in England and Spain as the dominant popular art form in both countries. Not only does theater play a significant role in the formation of the public spheres of each country—a development that leads in different directions—but the "paradigmatic plays" read here also respond to the early modern sovereignty crisis in ways that have lasting conceptual effects.[108]

## *The Problem of Political Theology*

Political theology is a bridge discourse. It articulates the relation between the political and theological life-worlds, variously imagining them as independent and co-dependent at once. As an explanatory discourse, it focuses in particular on questions of authority, legitimacy, representation, and mediation. One of the most common features of Western political theology is its recurring attempt to construct an "analogy between God and sovereignty, which permits the earthly sovereign to be conceived as the representative of the divine, the lieutenant of God."[109] In this way, it strives to present a coherent conceptual account of the relation of each term to the other. The nature of this relation is, of course, an old problem, differing understandings of which can be found in the Western tradition in a wide range of sources, from Plato's *Laws*, through the Stoic writings, to Hebrew, Christian, and Islamic sacred texts, and beyond. Classical accounts of political theology often begin with Marcus Terentius Varro, whom Saint Augustine discusses in *The City of God*.[110] All of these writings posit and elaborate complex structures of power. In this general sense, then, political theology's objective is to tell the story of the right role of earthly power in relation to its transcendent source(s).

The problem of political theology has reappeared with a burning intensity in the twentieth century in relation to the work of Carl Schmitt. According to Heinrich Meier, Schmitt takes the term "political theology" not from Varro or Augustine, with whom its beginnings are often associated, but rather from the Russian anarchist, Mikhail Bakunin. For Schmitt, Meier argues, political theology is a "weapon in a war in which two irreconcilable armies face one another, one under the banner of Satan, the other under the sign of God."[111] In his well-known formulation, Schmitt defines political theology as the consequence of the transfer of theological concepts to the political sphere:

> All significant concepts of the modern theory of the state are secularized theological concepts not only because of their historical development—in which they were transferred from theology to the theory of the state, whereby, for example, the omnipotent God became the omnipotent lawgiver—but also because of their systematic structure, the recognition of which is necessary for a sociological consideration of these concepts. The exception in jurisprudence is analogous to the miracle in theology. Only by being aware of this analogy can we appreciate the manner in which the philosophical ideas of the state developed in the last centuries.[112]

Schmitt's analysis of the conceptual and juridical processes through which the state inherits theological concepts has become a cornerstone of many debates about secularization and the theologico-political transition to modernity.

Today there is an understandable resistance to the connection between sovereignty and political theology.[113] To many, it appears as a disavowal, if not an outright avoidance of responsibility, to turn from the inheritance of Hobbes, Locke, Hume, Smith, and Kant, back to a "religious" dependence, in which modern, secular life reverts to the irrational fetters, fantasies, and destructive pursuits of its theological origins. For these scholars, it goes against an entire legacy of Enlightenment thought. At the same time, for a wide range of other critics, including but not limited to those indebted to psychoanalytic theory and deconstruction, this legacy itself is unthinkable apart from its ability to question its own relation to its theological origins.[114] Historically and theoretically, then, political theology can be seen as one of sovereignty's necessary, if problematic, siblings, bound to it in different structural and conceptual ways.[115] Both discourses require us to think relationally, demarcating zones above and below, inside and outside the various orders and structures of power. The critical question regarding these spheres is not so much whether one believes in them, but rather how they function implicitly or explicitly to help us understand relations of power.[116]

Political theology poses conceptual challenges to which the literary sphere in particular has responded in significant and influential ways. How, for example, is the difference between political and theological life to be imagined? Are the political and theological worlds autonomous realms? The question is especially one of mediation: how to think the link between the political and the theological? Is the relation to be imagined, as Schmitt argued, as one of "transfer"? Or, on the other hand, is it what Hans Blumenberg describes as a "reoccupation"?[117] Is it an antithesis? A dialectical supersession (Hegel)? An inevitable co-implication (Lefort, Legendre, Jean-François Courtine)? Or the ghostly remainder and reminder of a premature interring (Lefort, Derrida, De Vries, Lezra, Mark Taylor)? In each of these cases, political theology not only explains the relation between the two terms, but it also, more significantly, attempts to account for *our* attachment to that relation. In this regard, political theology operates similarly to ideology, in Louis Althusser's well-known definition: a formation in which that which captures the subject is not the object itself—the real—but always one's imaginary relation to it. Viewed in this light, political theology moves from being understood not only as a strictly conceptual problem but also as what Hent de Vries calls a *mediatic* one.[118] At the same time, it is not—at least not necessarily—a dogmatic one. Rather, as a critical problem, political theology could be viewed to begin with as a question that has as much to do with conceptual positioning as belief.[119] Just as sovereignty historically opens onto the representational problem of the God-place, so, too, does political theology challenge us to imagine both an inside as well as a place outside of the normal orders of being and power. By doing so, it inserts us into its own political-theological imaginary.[120] Historically, the theo-political imaginary has proven to be a rich and productive theater. Political theology provokes the institutional imagination, which has responded by producing an array of fictions and figures, many of which have taken on surprising and unpredictable after-lives. The philosophical, anthropological, epistemological, and representational questions that political theology raises have elicited a wide range of responses. As the seminal work of Ernst Kantorowicz has shown, the desire for political-theological answers to the question of the "beyond" has transformed the most prosaic of texts into rich and mobile "archives" of social and political history.[121]

At the same time, the poetic birth of such creatures gives voice to different kinds of historical anxieties. Related to the fecundity of its imagery, political theology also awakens a corresponding sense of incompleteness, emptiness, and absence. Paradoxically, this sense of emptiness is precisely the condition that sets the representational machinery of political theology in motion in the first place, according to many of its theorists. One way to understand this "machinery" is to see it in relation to what Jacques Lezra has described as the "uneven" and "incomplete" processes of secularization and modernization themselves. For Lezra, political theology raises the question of the historical remains left over by the uncompleted processes of modernization: "What residues of an incomplete secularization, and an incomplete desacralization of the sovereignty's body, haunt European modernity?"[122] Along with theology, two of the institutions that have responded most fully to this question are the theater and the law. Each produces its own form of "answer" to Lezra's "haunting" question. And for each, too, that answer comes in the form of a certain kind of "body."

## *Francisco Suárez (1548–1617)*

To return to Suárez's burning text: Suárez is not just a pivotal figure in the history of sovereignty; in different ways, his diverse writings also bridge early modern England and Spain at the conceptual level, formulating many of the juridical, political, and philosophical problems facing the rising and falling empires at the threshold of modernity. Born in Granada to a wealthy family, Suárez entered the recently founded Society of Jesus in 1564, the year of Shakespeare's birth. Although he was initially rejected for reasons of insufficient intellect (as well as "poor health"), he would eventually be admitted to the order with the status of "indifferent," before proceeding to become the most prominent Jesuit theologian and philosopher of the early modern period.[123] At the University of Salamanca, one of the most important in Europe at the time, and an institution that would play an unparalleled role in the development of many of the legal and economic concepts underpinning the systems of modern empire, Suárez would study theology and later teach philosophy.[124] Today, the *Doctor eximius ac pius* ("Eminent and pious Teacher"), as he is known by the title given to him by Pope Paul V, is recognized as a landmark figure in the history of Western philosophy.[125] Suárez's writings provide us with a unique historical and conceptual archive of early modern thought—particularly with respect to the juridical and ontological terms that are so important to theorists such as Schmitt, Heidegger and Agamben. Consequently, it is to Suárez, rather than to the more familiar figures of Machiavelli, Bodin, or Hobbes, that I continually turn in the following pages, not only for the ways Suárez's work represents the philosophical and epistemological landscape of the early modern sovereignty debate, a terrain itself divided, or even trifurcated into metaphysics, theology, and law, but also for how Suárez's "baroque modernity" continues to illuminate the problem of sovereignty today.[126] Suárez will occupy a central place in the pages that follow, rounding out the "perspectives of power" opened up by Shakespeare, Lope, and Calderón.

"Last of the schoolmen," "father of scientific Mariology," "founder of modernity," Suárez is a "privileged witness" of the problems and processes involved in the formation of sovereignty and political theology and the resistances they produce.[127] Although he is often characterized as a "synthesizer" and "systematizer" of classical and medieval philosophy, Suárez does significantly more than merely summarize. As Suárez's reception history is increasingly showing, he is not only a key transitional figure in the movement from medieval to modern forms of thought but also an important participant in the terminological reconfiguration of that thought. Over the course of a lifetime, during which he would produce a literary *corpus* consisting of over twenty-one million words, Suárez's texts perform subtle but important conceptual translations in the areas of metaphysics, law, and theology, the effects of which carry over from a world fast receding into one that would soon become our own.[128] His influence in the seventeenth century cannot be overstated. His best-known work, the *Metaphysical Disputations* (1597), spread from the Catholic countries of Spain, Portugal, and Italy to Northern European countries. It became a textbook in many Protestant universities, particularly in Germany, where it would greatly influence Wilhelm Leibniz, Christian Wolff, and Arthur Schopenhauer. In the years between its initial publication in Salamanca in 1597, and

1636, it went through seventeen editions, in Venice, Mainz, Paris, Cologne, and Geneva, a publication history that some consider to be "unique in the history of philosophy."[129] For Jean-François Courtine, Suárez's *Metaphysical Disputations* is a "work of passage"; for Heidegger, Suárez is, of all the Scholastics, "the thinker who had the strongest influence on modern philosophy." "Descartes," Heidegger writes, "is directly dependent on him, using his terminology almost everywhere; and it is Suárez who for the first time systematized medieval philosophy and above all ontology."[130]

Largely unknown in Shakespeare studies, apart from his role in the Oath of Allegiance controversy, Suárez himself seems singularly unaware of the fact that drama is Spain's most vibrant genre during his own lifetime. While this can be partially explained by a lifetime spent more in Rome, Salamanca, Valladolid, and Coimbra than in Madrid or Valencia, it is nevertheless striking that the term "theater" (*teatro, theatrum*) is virtually absent from Suárez's immense body of writings.[131] Absence itself, of course, does not mean that it's not *there*, as critics from Freud and Lacan to Blumenberg would all point out. Perhaps paradoxically, then, Suárez is, in some ways, ideally situated to provide the epistemological ground for a study of sovereignty and theater in the age of Shakespeare, Lope de Vega, and Calderón—*as well as* that of Benjamin, Schmitt, and Agamben. Suárez's diverse writings in philosophy, theology, and law are not only themselves seminal events in the history of each discipline, but they also provide us with a conceptual apparatus for traversing those fields, even as they are in the process of being formed. The diversity of Suárez's texts itself indicates the divisions implicit to the early modern period's understanding of "sovereignty" (for which Suárez still uses the older vocabulary of "imperium," "imperio politico," "potestas," "suprema potestas," and "majestas") in relation to its origins, derivations, and representations.[132] Together, Suárez's metaphysical, juridical, theological, and political writings constitute an entire apparatus for understanding relations between law and life in the period, as these are staged and imaginatively played out in various institutional formations.[133] Suárez's work provides a significant view of the "horizon" of philosophical and conceptual thought in the seventeenth century.[134] Thus, I take Suárez as both a pivotal and a paradigmatic figure of the sovereignty situation in the early seventeenth century, his texts not merely "theorizing" but also performing sovereignty's ongoing divides between politics and theology, metaphysics and law, literature and philosophy. Along with Benjamin and Schmitt, then, Suárez provides a third lens through which to view the interplay between the theater and theory of sovereignty in the seventeenth century and today.

CHAPTER I

# Breakdown: Analogy and Ontotheology in *Richard II*

[H]owever one attempts to explain away the impact of the question of analogy on that of being, the simple fact that the notion of analogy *can* and *must* be brought to bear upon the question of being shows that this notion profoundly affects the very concept of being.

—Rodolphe Gasché, *The Tain of the Mirror*, 306[1]

This word *analogy* is not only obscure, like a word whose concept or theorem, whose theoretical tenor, is invisible or inaccessible: it is obscure and dark and black, this word *analogy*, like the reality of a frightening cloud that announces and carries within it the threat of thunder, of lightning, of tempest and hurricane; it is dark because it is heavy with all the (actual and virtual) violences and nameless historical ravages, disasters we won't (already don't) have a name for, when the names of right (national or international), war, civil war or international war, terrorism (national or international) lose their most elementary credit.

—Jacques Derrida, *The Beast and the Sovereign*[3]

ANALOGY, replied my father, is the certain relation and agreement, which different—Here a Devil of a rap at the door snapp'd my father's definition (like his tobacco-pipe) in two,—and, at the same time, crushed the head of as notable and curious a dissertation as ever was engendered in the womb of speculation;—

—Laurence Sterne, *Tristram Shandy* II, 7[2]

"Theory must move among the events," Machiavelli writes in a 1503 letter to Piero Soderini. Ten years later, he writes to Soderini again: ". . . that man is fortunate who harmonizes his procedure with his time, but on the contrary he is not fortunate who in his actions is out of harmony with his time and with the type of its affairs." The question of time, in relation to sovereignty, is one of Machiavelli's central preoccupations, and it stayed with him throughout his work. As the philosopher Antonio Negri has shown, time and theory move together in Machiavelli's thought, particularly in moments of crisis.[4] In this chapter, I view the early modern crisis of sovereignty through the lens of three distinct events. On the historical plane lies the 1606 Oath of Allegiance Controversy, sparked by the passage of legislation in England requiring Catholics to renounce the Pope's ability to excommunicate and depose kings—an event the constitutional historian Charles McIlwain calls a "turning point in the history of modern politics" for the consequences it would have on the future of Church–State relations.[5] At issue here are temporal and jurisdictional questions in relation to the theory of sovereignty. Coinciding with this historical and political event is a literary and philosophical one: the publication in Salamanca in 1597—the same year Shakespeare's *Richard II* was entered in the Stationers' Register—of Francisco Suárez's *Metaphysical Disputations*. On this second, ontological plane, I will be focusing primarily on the problem of analogy and the question of how to view its relationship to sovereignty. Finally, containing and staging both sets of problems (political and philosophical) is the "event" of Shakespeare's play itself, *Richard II*, which—at least since Ernst Kantorowicz's still unsurpassed study on political theology in *The King's Two Bodies*—continues to posit the theoretical and metaphorical crux of political-theological sovereignty: the embodiment and division of power.[6]

On March 21, 1610, James I addressed his parliament:

> So have I now called you here, to recompence you againe with a great and a rare Present, which is a faire and a Christall Mirror; Not such a Mirror wherein you may see your owne faces, or shadowes; but such a Mirror, or Christall, as through the transparantnesse thereof, you may see the heart of your King.[7]

James's metaphor of a "Christall Mirror" that does not reflect the face of the constitutional body assembled before it back to itself but rather purports to open on to a view of the interiority of sovereignty itself—into the "heart of the King"—introduces the central problem of sovereignty's representation. How does sovereignty appear? The question is more than a formal or even sociological one. It is also a philosophical and conceptual one. At the conceptual level, it involves the performance of a transposition of values that constitute and define sovereignty. Thus, while it is a visual and semiotic problem, on the one hand, the question of sovereignty's manifestations could also, on the other hand, be viewed as a theoretical problem: How are we to imagine, as Louis Marin puts it, in the finite body of the King, the infinite body of power?⁸ The problem is juridical and metaphysical at once, and it also involves a certain type of theater, as James's writing begins to make clear:

> The Philosophers wish, That euery mans breast were a Christall, where-through his heart might be seene, is vulgarly knowne, and I touched it in one of my former Speeches vnto you: But though that were impossible in the generall, yet will I now performe this for my part, That as it is a trew Axiome in Diuinitie, That *Cor Regis* is *in manu Domini*, So wil I now set *Cor Regis* in *oculis populi*.⁹

James's "performance" of setting his "heart in the public eye" takes the specific form of a series of analogies. He refers to these as "similitudes":

> There bee three principall similitudes that illustrate the state of MONARCHIE: One taken out of the word of GOD; and the two other out of the grounds of Policie and Philosophie. In the Scriptures Kings are called Gods, and so their power after a certaine relation compared to the Diuine power. Kings are also compared to Fathers of families: for a King is trewly *Parens patriae*, the politique father of his people. And lastly, Kings are compared to the head of this Microcosme of the body of man.¹⁰

The King's power is "after a certain relation" compared with divine power. The name for this relation is "analogy," a term that, from the Greek, "*analogos*" (reason + *legein*, to gather) refers to a "gathering" of the logos, of reason, rationality. Analogy refers both to a way of thinking about relations of being and also to a specific manner of seeing those relations, of setting them into a particular form and visualizing that form. Analogy *works*. It performs what Barbara Stafford calls a "demonstrative or evidentiary practice [of] putting the visible into relation with the invisible and manifest[ing] the effects of that momentary unison."¹¹ Stafford sees this process as "incarnational": "All of analogy's simile-generating figures," she writes, ". . . materialize, display, and disseminate an enigma that escapes words."¹² The concept of sovereignty could be thought of as precisely such an enigma. The crux of analogy's function within religious discourse in general, and Christian theology in particular, lies in its capacity to conceptually embody and "incarnate" that "enigma." Perhaps the paradigmatic example of an enigma of this sort in the early modern period is that of a divine-right king, a theo-political creature, whose divinity requires for its expression both a certain display of itself and at the same time a discursive construction that emphasizes that "self's" ineffability. To understand the theory of a divine-right king not only requires that we attend to the early modern institutional frameworks that govern its articulation, but also that we follow the representational and conceptual forms and devices through which divine-right sovereignty speaks. Perhaps the most centrally important of these is the recurring structure of analogy.

## Analogy

While an exhaustive consideration of the complex history of analogy exceeds the competence of this study, we can, nevertheless, discern within it a general trajectory, as analogy evolves from Aristotle's deployment of it in logic, biology, and mathematics to signify a "structure-providing principle in all things [and] the idea of like functions" to its crucial role in Medieval philosophy as a structure for conceiving of *being* itself.[13] Analogy arises in the Middle Ages as what Paul Ricoeur calls a "compromise figure" in response to a new modification in the challenge that always faces theological discourse. This has to do specifically with the problems of *univocity* and *equivocity*, terms that refer to the unified or equivocal nature of the languages used to understand the meanings of creatures and Creator. As Ricoeur explains:

> to impute a discourse common to God and to his creatures would be to destroy divine transcendence; on the other hand, assuming total incommunicability of meanings from one level to the other would condemn one to utter agnosticism. It therefore seemed reasonable to extend the concept of analogy to theology by means of the invention (after Aristotle) of a third modality of attribution—analogous attribution—equidistant from univocal and equivocal attribution. The doctrine of the analogy of being was born of this desire to encompass in a single doctrine the horizontal relation of the categories of substance and the vertical of created things to the Creator. This project defines onto-theology.[14]

The questions that analogy raises in this regard are both conceptual and representational ones, giving rise to the discourse of what Kant and, later, Heidegger refer to as "onto-theology." Onto-theology asks how we are to conceive of the relations between God and man, knowledge and language, ontology and theology.[15] Historically, one of the most influential responses to these questions is through the structure of analogy. The medieval *analogia entis* (analogy of being) is intended to help us think the link between finite and infinite being. But as Heidegger also noted, this structure itself is not a "solution" but rather a formula,[16] one that he describes as "the most stringent aporia."[17] That is, in the very course of linking the finite and the infinite orders of being, analogy at the same time exposes a gap that separates them. The Middle Ages understood this gap in terms of "proportion." The *locus classicus* for this problem is Thomas Aquinas's description in the *Summa Theologica* Ia.13 of the language we use when we speak of God:

> Whatever is said of God and creatures is said according as there is some relation of the creature to God as to its principle and cause, wherein all the perfections of things pre-exist excellently. Now this mode of community is a means between pure equivocation and simple univocation. For in analogies the idea is not, as it is in univocals, one and the same; yet it is not totally diverse as in equivocals; but the name which is thus used in a multiple sense signifies various proportions to some one thing: *e.g., healthy*, applied to urine, signifies the sign of animal health; but applied to medicine, it signifies the cause of the same health.[18]

For Aquinas, our way of speaking of God is analogical: a way of speaking becomes also a manner of conceiving. Within this conceptualization itself, however, as Heidegger noted, there remains a gap. Language draws us closer to God and provides us with an understanding of Him as well as our relation to Him—but not a total knowledge. God is both more understood and less known at once. For Jean Luc-Marion, this gap lies at the heart of Aquinas's "radical agnosticism."[19] Even though Aquinas proceeds to explain the "five paths" (*viae*) by way of which one can become acquainted with divine transcendence, the very fact that each path terminates in a different name—"first mover," "first efficient cause," "necessary cause," "cause of every perfection," "the end of all things"—leaves God, in the end, unknown, because these names are "relative" and "inadequate." Knowledge of God, in Aquinas, "remains analogical: the gap always remains, even when our knowledge is certain; even if we can know what God is not, we cannot know what He is—He who remains to us 'profoundly unknown, *penitus ignotum*.'"[20]

In the language of creatures, the Creator can never be fully and directly known.

How does this theological discussion of the knowledge and naming of God inform the political discourse of early modern sovereignty? The answer hinges on different understandings of the capacities of language. For the political historian J. P. Sommerville, the prevalence of analogy in early Stuart writings on sovereignty is "overrated"; it is only used for "illustrations, not proofs":

> The use of analogy presupposed relevant similarity. The analogy between God and the king, for example, *presupposed* that both held sovereignty over their subjects. It was all very well to argue that creation was a Great Chain of Being. But the fact that the universe was a hierarchy did not prove anything at all about political society. Was the pope, or were the people superior to the king in the Great Chain? The mere existence of the chain was of little use in answering the question.[21]

While Sommerville is of course correct, in that the "mere existence of the chain" itself did not settle the question, historically, of the sovereign's identity or legitimacy—this is precisely the point of contention between Royalists and Catholics, including Bellarmine, Robert Parsons, and Suárez—he at the same time misses an important part of the point, which is that all theories rely in a fundamental way on the conceptual structures that go into their "illustrations." In this case, apart from "answering the question," the structure of analogy (between Creator and creature, God and Sovereign) is crucial in that it actively configures the political space in which relations of power are imagined to begin with. As Michel Foucault has argued, the "very order of the universe" in the sixteenth century is constituted by the "way in which words are linked together and arranged in space." If this is so, then it is to the specific form of this "reconstitution" through the operation of analogy that we must now turn in order to consider the theoretical problem of sovereignty in more detail.[22]

### Re-Enter Suárez

Largely unknown in Shakespeare scholarship, Francisco Suárez is, nevertheless, a crucial figure for early modern thought. Suárez's work lies at least doubly (historically and conceptually) at the center of the seventeenth-century crisis of sovereignty.[23] Historically, as we have already seen, Suárez (despite his well-known "distaste for controversy") is Pope Paul V's personal choice to respond to King James and his Oath of Allegiance.[24] Suárez's *Defense of the Catholic and Apostolic Faith* (*Defensio fidei*) was published in 1613, but James knew of it beforehand through reports from his secret agent in Madrid, Sir John Digby.[25] Along with that other Jesuit text, Juan de Mariana's *On the King and the King's Education* (*De Rege Et Regis Institutione*) (1599), it would become anathema to Protestants and Royalists alike, for its argument justifying tyrannicide under certain conditions. Conceptually, Suárez's theory of the papal *potestas indirecta* would take the idea of sovereignty into increasingly complex forms of mediation and representation. In the formulations of Jesuit thinkers such as Suárez and Robert Bellarmine, power is divided into its distinct civil and ecclesiastical capacities in the temporal and eternal spheres. James legitimately possesses the first ("civil power"), which operates in the temporal sphere, but only God, whose representative is the Pope, not the King, possesses the second. As we have seen, Suárez argues that in certain cases, like that of heresy, the Pope has an *indirect* coercive power (*potestas indirecta*) that, together with his directive power (*potest directe*), allows him to depose a heretical King.[26] Without this indirect temporal aspect, Suárez argues, citing Aristotle's *Nicomachean Ethics*, the power that Christ granted to the Pope would have been "imperfect and ineffective" ("imperfecta et inefficax") since "directive force is inefficacious without coercive force" ("vis directiva sine coactiva inefficax est").[27] The notion that the Pope's effective power, derived directly from God (unlike James's), could be imperfect is surely absurd, Suárez argues. Consequently, it is perhaps not surprising that, as we have seen, James ordered Suárez's book to be publicly burned.

Suárez's concern for the efficacy of power and his insistence that the Pope's power be effective recall the work of an earlier, but very different, Renaissance thinker, who also understood sovereign power in terms of its effects. In what might be considered Suárez's theoretical counterpart, Niccolò Machiavelli famously declared that his book *The Prince* does not represent things as they are imagined but on the contrary presents "the real"—or rather the "effective"—truth of the thing: "alla *verità effettuale della cosa*."[28] I discuss this notion of effective truth in greater detail in Chapter 5. For now, I would merely like to note that both Suárez and Machiavelli understand sovereignty in terms of its conceptual and representational efficiency. But, as will see, they see this efficiency in different terms.

For Suárez, the question of sovereignty is both a theological and a legal-theoretical one. In texts such as the *Defensio fidei* (Coimbra 1613) or his major treatise on law, *Tractatus de legibus ac Deo legislatore* (Coimbra 1612) (*A Treatise on Laws and God the Lawgiver* [henceforth *De legibus*]) Suárez presents one of early modernity's most fully elaborated conceptualizations of the nature and operations of sovereign power. Like Agamben's structural and philosophical approach to the concept in terms of its distinct "zones," Suárez dissects sovereignty into distinct components and capacities and explains the space of their relation in temporal and juridical terms. As the international law scholar James Brown Scott put its, what Suárez endeavored to do in *De legibus* "was to give us a methodical, connected work tracing the development of law from its divine origin and expounding it as a moral and social instrumentality which should enable man to live in harmony with his fellows."[29]

In Suárez's writings, sovereignty appears as a jurisdictional—or in Agamben's terms, "zoning"—matter of identifying the sovereign's position and capacities in relation to the different spheres of temporality and power. Both Suárez and James view this position as a dual and mobile one, simultaneously straddling a place above and in between the different zones and types of power: If, for James, the royal prerogative allows him to move between ordinary and extraordinary forms, then for Suárez, it is the Pope who (in times of necessity) can draw on his God-given authority to exercise indirect deposing power. The oath of allegiance controversy was instrumental in pushing the conceptualization of sovereignty into more complex institutional forms. While the matter of the division of power would not be settled in Europe (if at all) at least until the Peace of Westphalia, the debate remains significant as a key turning point in the movement toward what most theorists define as the modern resolution of the state-system.[30]

Suárez's importance to the theory of sovereignty, however, far exceeds his response to King James on the occasion of the oath of allegiance controversy. It could even be said to surpass his foundational contribution to the burgeoning field of international law in *De legibus*, which antedates Hugo Grotius's *De iure belli ac pacis* by thirteen years and from which many scholars now agree, Grotius borrowed.[31] In addition to his theorization of the nature of power *within* the jurisdiction of what is on the way to becoming the modern state form, Suárez is perhaps even more important for his conceptualization of sovereign power *among* states. In Suárez, as one scholar puts it, "one first encounters the modern concept of a society or community of sovereign states, tied together by a body of laws applying to their mutual relations."[32] Suárez's massive corpus of texts—divided into theological, philosophical, and juridical writings (filling twenty-six large volumes)—itself reflects the historical and conceptual divisions inherent to the very idea of sovereignty. Suárez's writings not only provide the conceptual and terminological groundwork for the concept in the early modern period, but they also continue to speak to us about some of sovereignty's modern forms and fantasies.

Prima professor of Philosophy at the University of Coimbra, famous for the commentaries published there on Aristotle, Suárez in 1597 published the monumental *Disputationes metaphysicae*, which represents a watershed moment in the historical and philosophical transition to modernity.[33] Jean-Francois Courtine calls the *Disputations* a "work of passage."[34] For Heidegger, Suárez, of all the Scholastics, is "the thinker who had the strongest influence on modern philosophy. Descartes is directly dependent on him, using his terminology almost everywhere; and it is Suárez who for the first time systematized medieval philosophy and above all ontology."[35] The *Disputations* provide us with the seventeenth-century understanding of the metaphysical categories that, for a study like Agamben's, attempts to read sovereignty from its ontological base—*de potentia et actu*—up. Analogy is one of the most important of these grounding structures.

Suárez makes several "corrections" to Aquinas's theory of analogy, beginning with the question of the *proportional* relation it establishes between creatures and Creator:

> *There is no proper analogy of proportionality between God and creatures.* Accordingly, for this [kind of] analogy it is necessary that one member be absolutely such through its own form, while the other be such not absolutely but rather as it is subject to some proportion or comparison with the first. But in the present case this is not so, whether we consider the reality itself or the imposition of the name. For a creature is a being by reason of its own being in an absolute way and considered without any such proportionality, because, without doubt, by that being it is outside nothing and has some actuality. Also the name "being" is applied to a creature not from the

fact that it has some proportion or proportionality with God, but simply because it is something in itself and not absolutely nothing. Indeed, as we will say below, that name can be understood first to be applied to created rather than uncreated being. Finally, every genuine analogy of proportionality includes something metaphorical and improper, just as "to smile" is said of a meadow by a metaphorical transference. But in this analogy of being there is no metaphor or impropriety. For a creature truly, properly, and simply is being. This therefore is not an analogy of proportionality, either alone or in conjunction with an analogy of attribution.[36]

The problem with proportional analogies for Suárez is that they include "something metaphorical and improper," while in the true analogy of being "there is no metaphor or impropriety." For Suárez, this is a preferable way to think about being and therefore a better kind of analogy because a creature is a being "by reason of its own being in an absolute way and considered without any such proportionality." For Suárez, the creature is, and has, being absolutely and "properly," not metaphorically.[37] To this improper analogy of proportionality, Suárez will oppose his own analogy of intrinsic attribution, which for him has the advantage of allowing being to be said "properly" of creatures without reference to the Creator—and, above all, without having to rely on the tricky foundation of metaphor, which always, for Suárez, introduces equivocation.[38] As Ashworth explains, "Aristotle's description of the second mode . . . suggests metaphorical usage [and] encouraged an identification of metaphor with deliberate equivocation and hence with analogy in many logic texts."[39] For Suárez, on the other hand,

> it is evident that a creature is not designated a being in an extrinsic way from the entity or the being that is in God, but rather from its own intrinsic being. And therefore it is called a being not by metaphor but truly and properly.[40]

Today, philosophers disagree over the implications of Suárez's analogy of intrinsic attribution.[41] Perhaps the most far-reaching and important of these recent returns to Suárez is that of the French philosopher of religion and theology, Jean-Luc Marion. Marion sees two major consequences resulting from Suárez's revision of Aquinas's analogy of being. Both of these are central to the problem of understanding sovereignty's relationship to representation. The first is that in Suárez's revisions of analogy, God derives from a univocal concept of being, i.e., a concept that understands all of the modalities of being in the same way. The second, which follows from the first, is that God's knowledge of finite essences therefore derives from a univocal concept. "Creative essences," Marion writes, "do not *derive* from God as their exemplar (as in Bonaventure and Thomas), but are *seen* by God under some representation."[42] The relationship between God's sovereignty and representation thus starts to change. Philosophically, it begins to be viewed from a new theoretical perspective.

This shift in thinking about ontological relations will come to have serious political implications. The crux of these theological and philosophical developments has to do with the way one conceives of God's position in relation to creatures. How are we to view the relationship between infinite and finite being, between "ens infinitum, deus, and ens finitum, creatura"?[43] Suárez approaches the question as a scholastic philosopher would—by making distinctions and divisions. To begin with, the *Metaphysical Disputations* divides being into two categories: the first twenty-seven disputations focus on the category of being in general; disputations twenty-eight through fifty-three focus on "the being of specific beings." This includes, in the final disputation, fifty-four, what are known as "beings of reason." It is here that, for Heidegger, Suárez appears as "the first one who—even if only timidly—tries to show, in opposition to the usual Scholastic opinion, that the *ens rationis* [being of reason] is also an object of metaphysics."[44]

The question of "ideal being" is, in turn, linked to others, including that of the relationship between formal and objective concepts of being (*conceptus formalis entis* and *conceptus objectivus entis*) and, above all for subsequent thinkers such as Heidegger and Marion, that of the relationship between essence and existence. Where for Suárez "the most fundamental" of these distinctions is that between the *ens infinitum* and *ens finitum*, for Heidegger and especially Marion, it is, rather that between essence and existence.[45] For later thinkers who return to Suárez, such as Marion, one of the primary interests of the *Metaphysical Disputations* lies in its analyses of representation in relation to the understanding. This returns Marion to a consideration of Suárez's treatment of the relationship between essences, existences, and statements. God, in Marion's reading of Suárez,

> therefore does not create essences but only their existences. Statements concerning what is logically possible, statements that ground

what we can say about essences, do not depend upon the creative power of God; indeed, they impose themselves upon his understanding.[46]

In order to better understand the nature of the different kinds of statements one can make regarding God's creative power in relation to his understanding, Marion turns to an important passage from Suarez's thirty-first *Metaphysical Disputation*: "'These statements are not true because they are known by God, but rather they are known because they are true, otherwise one couldn't give any reason why God would necessarily know that they are true.'"[47] One of the most significant implications of Suárez's conceptual adjustments to Aquinas, in this view, has to do with knowledge and, above all, representation. "Representation," Marion writes, now

> governs the knowledge God has with respect to possibilities (creatures) as much as it does the knowledge that finite understandings claim with respect to the infinite. To this extent, at least, *God's knowledge is like ours*.[48]

Representation "fills the gap" between finite and infinite orders of being left open by Aquinas's analogy. This conclusion will prepare the way for extremely important changes in the subsequent decades of the seventeenth century, as philosophy crosses over from its medieval to its modern forms. Marion formulates the double blow succinctly: Suárez, on the one hand, "tangentially annihilates analogy through the objective concept of *ens*, almost to the point of rendering it useless, while, on the other hand, he tangentially steers it so far toward univocity as to render it suspicious of being ineffective."[49] The conceptual and representational consequences of this "filling" are important and continue to manifest themselves in different ways in theories of sovereignty today. In Suárez's reconceptualization of the *analogia entis*, the representational structure used to figure the relation between God and creatures is brought to the brink of destruction.

> In the *Disputationes*, Suárez filled the analogical gap between the finite and the infinite by a univocal concept of being (*conceptus univocus entis*), sufficient to represent to the human mind any being whatsoever in a confused and indeterminate way . . . Consequently . . . the ontological gap between the finite and the infinite distinguishes God from his creatures less than the conceptual representation of them as beings joins them.[50]

Viewed through the lens of Suárez's analogy, the seventeenth-century sovereignty problematic—consisting of the what Agamben views as the "zoning" questions of time and power—appears in a new light. Against their author's intentions perhaps, Suárez's theoretical revisions to Aquinas's analogy prepare the way for an ontology of immanence. It is based on just such an ontology that later thinkers, such as the Marxist philosopher Antonio Negri, will elaborate a theory of founding or "constituent power" in relation to an "immanent being." *Contra* a view of sovereignty conceived of in relation to transcendent being, Negri posits a theory of constituent power understood as an

> act of choice, the precise determination that opens a horizon, the radical apparatus of something that does not yet exist, and whose conditions of existence imply that the creative act does not lose its characteristics in the act of creating. When constituent power sets in motion the constituent process, every determination is free and remains free. On the contrary, sovereignty presents itself as a fixing of constituent power, and therefore as its termination.[51]

The philosophical presuppositions of Negri's constituent power reach back to seventeenth-century theorizations of the relationship between finite and infinite being. Work such as Suárez's in the *Defense of the Faith* on the different kinds of power (direct or indirect) or on the nature of being in the *Metaphysical Disputations* constitutes sovereignty's historical and conceptual ground. And it takes us straight to the heart of what remains one of sovereignty's central theoretical problems today: the question of the relationship between ontology and power.[52] Once the vertical relations of being upon which transcendental power and the social contract thinking it gives rise to are broken, a conceptual opportunity presents itself for a reformulation of sovereignty in different terms. What emerges is a concept in which the outside-inside paradoxes of law and time that Agamben identifies appear in another light.[53] That is, once there is no longer an "analogical gap" separating finite and infinite being, then the crucial structural place of the exception that for Agamben lies "outside the law"—"in God's name"—ceases to be the source from which the lethal effects of sovereignty are produced.[54] Power, in this view, is brought down to a horizontal model of relations—not unlike that which Negri and Hardt will later define in terms of "immanence."[55]

This account would go totally against Negri's own characterization of Neo-Scholasticism as that which "wants to be dominated in reformist terms," and "makes the fundamental transcendental a possibility" precisely through its "conception of analogical being."[56] Yet as we have seen in the case of Suárez's understanding of that analogy, the consequences can be understood in precisely the opposite terms. That is, (following Marion's reading), Suárez's analogy of intrinsic attribution could be seen to undermine a transcendental scheme of power dependent upon hierarchical gradations of being. Against Aquinas's analogy of proportion, which posits a relation between Creator and creatures in terms of hierarchical relations of being, Suárez's analogy of *intrinsic* attribution brings being down, so to speak, to the level of creation. Along the way, it returns sovereignty to the problem of representation. The analogy of being underlies and therefore changes the way we imagine the body of power. Among the consequences of this reading of Suárez's analogy, would be a change in the way we understand the hierarchical orders of being implicit in King James's "Christall mirror": "Gods," "fathers," and "heads" are all participants in the same structure, *intrinsically* sharing the same being. What lies "in the heart of a king," in this view is analogy itself. Paradoxically, then, against the grain of Negri's argument, in this light, Neo-Scholasticism appears as a key participant in the transformation of a concept that would eventually arrive at a "positive conception of being," such as Negri's.[57] Suárez's contributions to this development in particular, in his revision of the analogy of being, could be viewed as one of sovereignty's most important theoretical and historical events.

## Richard II

In the light of Suárez's re-conceptualization of analogy and its metaphysical consequences for the representation of sovereignty, I would like to turn to the theater and specifically to the play that provided Ernst Kantorowicz's with his first political-theological model in *The King's Two Bodies*. But first, a preliminary word on Kantorowicz and the legacy of his "two-bodies" theory.

Kantorowicz's work on the constitutional problematics of early modern sovereignty has sparked a vigorous debate among early modern scholars over the question of just how prevalent this way of thinking about sovereignty was. As David Norbrook and Lorna Hutson have shown, the legal fiction of the king's two bodies was only one of several available models invoked in early modern English constitutional debates, and not the most dominant one at that. Norbrook, in particular, has questioned the dominant trend in early modern scholarship of uncritically adopting Kantorowicz's two bodies narrative in order to deploy it against an older, conservative, positivistic historicism. Hutson has similarly shown how an uncritical acceptance of the "two-bodies metaphor in seventeenth-century political thought" has obscured other forms of political consciousness of the period.[58] For Victoria Kahn, on the other hand, the gains of Kantorowicz's study lie elsewhere. For Kahn, among the many achievements of *The King's Two Bodies* is its recognition of the important and complex role that literature, in general, and metaphor, in particular, play in the philosophical history of an idea. As Kahn shows, it is not only legal fictions, such as that of the two bodies metaphor, but also the critical capacity of literature to think that enables Kantorowicz to both theorize and historicize political theology. The literary sphere itself, in this view, is one of the protagonists of Kantorowicz's massive tome.[59] I follow this view, and Kahn's identification of the important place of metaphor in Kantorowicz's study, in particular.[60] My emphasis on the metaphor logics of the "body-of-power" is not meant to discount the richness of early modern political debate that Hutson and Norbrook recover. Rather, my aim is to focus on an ongoing conceptual problem at the heart of political-theological sovereignty. This problem, as Lezra has shown, is empirical and conceptual at once.[61] Rather than focusing on the image-manipulation, or on the charisma of the ruler, I choose to concentrate on the ways the metaphor logics conceptually map the movements of power involved in the sovereign-body relation. How are the transfers, derivations, and delegations of sovereign power imagined as they move from one "body" to another? How does the community envision its own place, specifically in time and space, in such a play of power? Inevitably haunting the debates that Norbrook and Hutson refer to are competing philosophical and theological accounts of sovereignty's embodiment. How is the sovereign's or the representative's (whether of king or parliament) capacity to embody the concept of sovereignty understood? How do we imagine a sovereignty that is *embodied*?

Shakespeare's *Richard II* (published the same year as Suárez's *Metaphysical Disputations*) explores these questions. *Richard II* is a play about a king whose sacred claim to the throne is never in question but whose lawless actions eventually lead to his deposition and murder. The play is one of the most returned to sites in early modern literature for an articulation of the theory of divine right sovereignty. Specifically, what I want to consider is how the play exposes and complicates the jurisdictional or zoning questions of sovereignty in terms of time and being we have seen so far. How does *Richard II* respond to the ontology of sovereignty implied by Suárez's analogy of being?

### "SORROW'S EYES"

In the second act of *Richard II*, Bushy, the King's favorite, tries to console the Queen, who sees in her husband's departure to Ireland the sign of an "unborn sorrow coming towards her." On the contrary, Bushy insists, it is the Queen's sorrow that causes her to misinterpret the meaning of Richard's departure. Bushy proceeds to explain his point in ontological and representational terms:

> Each substance of a grief hath twenty shadows,
> Which shows like grief itself, but is not so;
> For sorrow's eyes, glazed with blinding tears,
> Divides one thing entire to many objects,
> Like perspectives, which rightly gaz'd upon
> Show nothing but confusion; ey'd awry
> Distinguish form.
>
> (2.2.16–22)

"Sorrow's eyes," according to Bushy, cause the Queen to mis-view the event. To gaze upon the world "sorrowfully" is to view it through a perspective glass. Observed rightly, one sees "nothing but confusion." In order to distinguish form, one must look at it *awry*. Yet as Bushy's consolation continues to develop, his simile subjects not only the Queen but also the reader to its own kind of shifting mirror: ". . . so your sweet Majesty, / Looking awry upon your lord's departure, / Finds shapes of grief, more than himself, to wail, / Which, look'd on as it is, is nought but shadows / Of what it is not" (2.2.22–6).

In the second half of the passage, Bushy reverses himself, saying now that it *is* because the Queen looks at Richard's departure awry that she mis-sees it and finds "shapes of grief more than himself to wail." Looking awry this time not only does *not* allow one to discern meaning, but on the contrary leads to error and a kind of excess of meaning. The passage's closing assertion that, were the Queen to look on Richard's departure "as it is," she would see that it is "nought but shadows / of what it is not"—becomes increasingly perplexing. What does it mean to say that the Queen sees only shadows of what does not exist? How, exactly, can the king's exit be a shadow of what is not? Can sovereignty ever really depart?

This is not only a question of English history, but remains an ongoing concern of contemporary theorists of sovereignty. In this regard, it is a variant of that which Giorgio Agamben poses to his philosophical antagonist Antonio Negri in their ongoing debate over the relationship between constituent power and sovereignty. If, for Negri, "the truth of constituent power is not what can be attributed to it, in any way whatsoever, by the concept of sovereignty," then for Agamben, on the contrary, constituent power and sovereignty have a necessary relation.[62] Negri, Agamben insists, "cannot find any criterion, in his wide analysis of the historical phenomenology of constituting power, by which to isolate constituting power from sovereign power."[63] There is, for Agamben, an unavoidable conceptual relation between constituent power and sovereignty. More than for Negri, for whom this is not a question, for Agamben, the philosophical analysis of sovereignty requires a conceptual apparatus through which to view (among others) the relationship between constituting power and sovereignty. Where Agamben's trope of the "zone," and its corresponding topologies, responds, in his view, to this challenge, Shakespeare presents us with another figure, that of the "tear," which allows him to couch the question in terms of gazing "rightly," or "awry." Does focusing on the king have the paradoxical effect of making what I have referred to as the "event" of sovereignty's departure unreadable?

> "AS IF THE WORLD WERE ALL DISSOLVED TO TEARS . . ."
> RICHARD II (3.2.108)

Viewed within the overall context of the play's events, the Queen, of course, does not mis-see at all, but quite correctly perceives that Richard's departure to Ireland signals a coming sorrow: the rise of Bolingbroke. At the same time, another tilt of the perspective glass shows that Bushy is also correct in a way to call what the Queen pictures "nought but shadows," in that by the time Richard leaves for Ireland, he will have *de facto* already lost his authority and power—arguably the substance of sovereignty. The crossing of paths marked by Richard's exit to Ireland and Bolingbroke's return entrance to

England effectively punctuates the end of one rule and the beginning of another. Once Richard finally returns to kiss English soil, one could very well argue that, in terms of a theory of the sacred *essence* of sovereignty, Richard has simply become a "shadow" of his former self.

Read alone, either half of Bushy's consolation seems to make sense. Combined into a whole, the passage's shifting of perspective eludes our attempts to see its meaning rightly. The two specific questions raised here—first, how to distinguish between the essence and reflection of a thing, and second, how to interpret the event of a King's departure—both point to the larger historical problems we have been tracing regarding the nature, representation, and temporality of sovereignty at the end of the sixteenth century.

The perspective glass passage is not only a parable of the rise and fall of kings; it also presents us with a unique allegory of the problem of sovereignty itself. What Shakespeare shows us is that to make sense of the event of sovereignty, we have to *see* its movement and operations correctly. Critics have often remarked on the distorting process of *anamorphosis* to which the perspective glass passage alludes, most often illustrated by Hans Holbein's painting *The Ambassadors*.[64] What I would like to focus on instead is the metaphor of the Queen's tears.[65] If, as Christopher Pye has persuasively argued, the Queen can be seen as an exemplum of the modern political subject, then how does that subject view the absence of sovereignty created by the king's exit?[66] The question leads in different directions, dividing (like the concept of sovereignty) and multiplying itself according to the views opened up by multiple perspectives: How are we to view the king's exit? How do others, including the Queen, see it? How does Richard, himself, understand it? Why does Shakespeare figure Richard's vision as "ill"? (2.1.99). The figure of "tears" ties these questions together in different ways. For in addition to signifying *sorrow*, tears are also a figure for that which distorts fragments, and multiplies vision. Recalling the challenges to representation that give rise to Blumenberg's "absolute metaphors," as well as the paradoxes presented by Giorgio Agamben and Jean-Luc Nancy, then, in an epistemological sense, fragmentation and distortion might be the condition through which one always views a "maximal abstraction" such as sovereignty.

In the famous deposition scene, the centrality of the *tear* becomes even greater, as Richard is forced to hand over his crown[67]:

> Here, cousin, seize the crown.
> On this side my hand, and on that side thine.
> Now is this golden crown like a deep well
> That owes two buckets,[68] filling one another,
> The emptier ever dancing in the air,
> The other down, unseen, and full of water.
> That bucket down and full of tears am I,
> Drinking my griefs whilst thou mount up on high.
> (4.182–9)

The transfer of sovereignty is figured as a rising and falling movement motored by the sheer weight of the sovereign's tears. In order to convey this movement, Shakespeare returns to—but also transforms—an old metaphor. The image of rising and falling buckets contains more than meets the eye. Originally a medieval metaphor for fate (*fortuna*), the rising and falling buckets are now re-troped in rich and complicated ways.[69] In Richard's conceit, his fall is brought on by the weight and substance ("water") of his own tears. He—not Bolingbroke, his figure suggests—is responsible for it. Bolingbroke, on the other hand, is light, insubstantial—and empty, dancing high in the air. Central to the image is the dynamic movement of history itself.[70]

To return, for a moment, to Benjamin's study of baroque drama, recall that there, time and the image enter into a complex relationship in which historical legibility is imagined in a dependent and sorrowful, if not tragic, relation to the concept of sovereignty. For Benjamin, in the baroque drama not only of the German playwrights but also of Shakespeare, Lope, and Calderón, "chronological movement is grasped and analyzed in a spatial image. The image of the setting or, more precisely of the court, becomes the key to historical understanding."[71] While Shakespeare's figure of the buckets of tears for the transfer of sovereignty is certainly not an "illustration" of Benjamin's "dialectical image," the new function Shakespeare gives it, to move from a medieval metaphor of fortune to a figure for the transfer of sovereignty, nevertheless performs what Benjamin calls a certain "coming into legibility of a particular kind of historical image." The crucial point, for Benjamin, is that this "dialectical image" appears only at a particular time:

> For the historical index of the images doesn't simply say that they belong to a specific time, it says above all that they only enter into

legibility at a specific time. And indeed, this "entering into legibility" constitutes a specific critical point of the movement inside them . . ."[72]

As with the perspective glass passage, the figure of the rising and falling buckets allows us to glimpse an aspect of historical time that becomes accessible only through the partially legible traces left in its wake. More precisely, the "sorrow" that propels history forward, in Richard's conceit, is itself generative. It invokes a field of metaphors, including those generated by the divine right king's association with Christ's *Passion*. As Kantorowicz's analysis of *Richard II* has shown, Richard is a *christomimetes*: "Not all the water in the rough rude sea / Can wash the balm off from an anointed King" (3.2.54–5). Richard's bucket full of "tears" figures the relentless weight and wasting power of time, *as well as* the sacred permanence that presumably resists time's eroding force. As if both pained but also amused by the implications of his own image, Richard calls for a mirror to be brought to him. In this famous mirror scene, Richard's sovereignty paradoxically reaches a certain apex. As a multitude of critics of the play, at least from Kantorowicz on, have observed, it is precisely at this moment in the play, when Richard's *political* sovereignty is vanishing, that his theatrical and in a sense conceptual power begins to move into its own complex forms of supremacy. This is not a power that can be confined to a chronological narrative of a monarchical succession. Rather, what Shakespeare, in effect, invents through Richard is modern sovereignty's image as an image of fragmented mediation.

Once Richard receives the mirror, instead of gazing into it, he smashes it into the ground. In addition to its fragmenting and distorting power, here we see a third, crucial sense of the tear as an agent of reflection and a figure of the mirror. The scene concludes with what Walter Pater calls an "inverted rite . . . of degradation," as Richard proceeds to perform a mock *undoing* of what, according to its own idea, historically, can never be undone: the anointing of a sacred king.[73] While it is customary at this point to underscore the fragmentation of the image produced by the shattered mirror—which makes it impossible to re-assemble the king's body into anything resembling a proportional whole—it is equally important to note that what Richard destroys is the representational medium itself through which James had attempted to present to Parliament the "heart of the king." For

## Analogy and Ontotheology in Richard II 53

James, recall, the architecture of this device consisted of a series of analogies. For Richard II, on the other hand, the very structure of that mirror, capable of representing sovereignty's inside and outside at once, is now no longer operative. Shakespeare, in effect, deposes James's "Christall mirror," along with Richard II. The dual destruction of king and thing, sovereign and glass, corresponds with an "emptying out" of sovereignty at the representational and conceptual levels, as the play begins to move sovereignty toward a new "body."

Just as the Queen's tears, produced by sovereignty's departure, had earlier figured more than just a personal sorrow, here, too, the destruction of the mirror marks the end of an entire world order built on the structure of analogical correspondences.[74] Against the by now familiar argument that Shakespeare invents the modern subject, the Queen's tears instead present us with a vision of subjectivity completely emptied out of interiority.[75]

### "TIME IS THE SUBSTANCE OF POWER"—ANTONIO NEGRI

In his closing soliloquy, Richard, deposed, imprisoned, and shortly to be assassinated, hears music playing outside his cell:

> Music do I hear?
> Ha, ha! keep time—how sour sweet music is
> When time is broke and no proportion kept!
> So is it in the music of men's lives.
> And here have I the daintiness of ear
> To check time broke in a disordered string;
> But for the concord of my state and time,
> Had not an ear to hear my true time broke:
> I wasted time, and now doth time waste me;
> For now hath time made me his numb'ring clock;
> My thoughts are minutes, and with sighs they jar
> Their watches on unto mine eyes, the outward watch,
> Whereto my finger, like a dial's point,
> Is pointing still, in cleansing them from tears.
> (5.5.41–54)

In perhaps the play's most complex conceit, Richard's fall is marked by the inversion of his relationship to time. His language moves from positioning him as a king in control of time—the "representative of history," in Benjamin's words—thematized at the opening of the play by the power of his mere breath to change the period of banishment, to a king now subjected to time's power. Richard has become a mere "thing," as Hamlet puts it.[76] But not a thing, as we shall see, quite of "nothing."

The temporality upon which the old king-Christ analogy relied is broken: The king is no longer *like* God, but is reduced instead to a mere measuring device for the passing of time. The time of divine right sovereignty—and with it the viability of Aquinas's proportional analogy—has come to its end: "No proportion kept." Yet as we have seen, this clock is also a mirror ("dial"). It is thus not at all clear whether the vision that marks the King's fallen state removes or creates more metaphors for sovereignty. For political theory, the question will become whether the metaphysics of transcendental power have also been disrupted, as the king's body gradually ceases to be the site of sovereignty's sign-system. Historically, we know this power will reconstitute itself in the course of the seventeenth century around the figure of the Leviathan and the social contract theory introduced by Hobbes—a theory that, according to Negri, ultimately requires transcendence.[77] In the interval, a conceptual space has opened up—an "empty place"—soon to be represented by the "untimely bier" carrying Richard's body in the play's last line, in which, once again, and finally, tears play a role. Here, the new king, Bolingbroke, declares a time of national mourning:

> Come mourn with me for what I do lament,
> And put on sullen black incontinent.
> I'll make a voyage to the Holy Land,
> To wash this blood off from my guilty hand.
> March sadly after; grace my mourning here
> In weeping after this untimely bier.
>
> (5.5.47–52)

Unlike with Richard, who had a different conception of the relationship between the inside and outside of sovereignty, Bolingbroke's tears expose an *arcanum* of political-theological sovereignty with a slightly different secret.[78] Bolingbroke's tears perform in a different way and tell another story. The mystery of sovereignty here is something that gets belatedly exposed as having been at its theatrical heart all along.

Thus, as opposed to the humanist subject Harold Bloom and others find "invented" in Shakespeare, *Richard II* moves us toward a less comforting picture of modern subjectivity, closer to the conflicted and alienated subject of psychoanalysis and Marxism than the autonomous agent of humanism. Once again, Benjamin provides perhaps the best account. That is, if the baroque sovereign is a prototype of modern subjectivity, as Benjamin scholars (Nägele and Weber) have suggested, then this is a subjectivity doubly in peril. Shakespeare drives the point home to its unnerving consequences. The extremely compressed language of Richard's final speech transforms the king from a sacred being to a hybrid mechanism of consciousness and mechanical measurement, the metaphor turning his body into a machine that both attacks and protects the eye/I. Thinking itself becomes quantifiable here, and the result is painful and contradictory. Richard's thoughts "jar / their watches" into the same eyes ("the outward watch") that protect him. Shakespeare's compression of the operations of thought, measurement, vision, and protection, all in the single term "watch," is disorienting. Consciousness, in Richard's conceit, becomes both scientific (quantifiable) and lethal, attacking the very system of self-protection it relies on.

The immediate consequence of this movement is a functional shift in the body-of-power. By play's end, Shakespeare has begun to prepare the way for a new understanding of the relationship between sovereignty and its sign system. That is, sovereignty begins to acquire a different kind of legibility, as the sovereign—"representative of history"—becomes a different text for reading—or perhaps always mis-reading—what Negri calls the historical "mutation."[79]

To return to where we have been: the fall of analogy, theorized in one way by Suárez, and staged another by Shakespeare, sparks a variation, if not a totally new model of sovereignty. If the sovereign is the "representative of history" in the Baroque period, then when the representational principle of this representative changes, then so, too, does our understanding of history. Sovereignty and historical time move together. Time, in Richard's view, subjects the king to its "wasting power." The consequences are complex, and will be long lasting, involving questions not only of political philosophy and philosophies of subjectivity, but also of aesthetic theory and the autonomy of art. The process begins when Richard's thoughts start to transform his body into a clock, the movement of which, as we have seen, "jars into his eyes" producing tears. This time, however, the tears produced, unlike those of the Queen, which had (in Bushy's view) distorted historical vision, enable a certain historical perspective to come into view.

Richard's tears "cleanse" his vision, allowing him to correctly perceive not the end or effacement of sovereignty, but rather its transformation and transfer to a new time as well as place: "my time / Runs posting on in Bolingbroke's proud joy . . ." (5.5.58–9).

Against Richard's "true time," time now runs with Bolingbroke. As Richard's extended simile suggests, this time is clock time, what Benjamin calls the "mechanical time" of modernity. The "messianic time," which once had the possibility of being "fulfilled," is broken. Replacing it is the mere "spatial measure of the passing of chronological events." In the writings leading up to the *Trauerspiel* book, Benjamin referred to this time as "musical time." This mode of representation, he argued, resists similarity and recognizes only relationship instead. Most provocatively, Benjamin saw this form of representation as "related to pure feeling," precisely that which, in Benjamin's view, resists analogy.[80]

*Richard II* closes with *tears*. Through their lens we view a de-positioning and a de-composition of analogy that paves the way for a new perspective of power.[81] What this lens opens onto is an emptiness, which waits to be filled with—according to Louis Marin—representation itself. No more tears—until, that is, they reappear, in the future in another play that will look back to Richard's body. In *Henry V*, Bolingbroke's son, Hal, or Henry V, will re-bury Richard with his own tears:

> I Richard's body have interrèd new,
> And on it have bestowed more contrite tears
> Than from it issued forcèd blood.
> Five hundred poor have I in yearly pay
> Who twice a day their withered hands hold up
> Toward heaven to pardon blood. And I have built
> Two chantries, where the sad and solemn priests
> Sing still for Richard's soul.
>                     (*Henry V*, 4.1.277–9)[82]

The movement of *Richard II* carries us—and with us the concept of sovereignty—across the threshold from one state to another. The play's dialectic of "forcèd blood" and "contrite tears," violence and repentance, crime and pardon, leads us into a new relationship to sovereignty.

Returning to James's "Christall Mirror," we are now, perhaps, in a better position to view what lies "in the heart of the King." What lies there, Shakespeare suggests, is in fact nothing—emptiness. More than four centuries before Jean-Luc Nancy can formulate his paradox of sovereignty, Shakespeare has already presented us with the point: Sovereignty *is* nothing. Yet this is not quite right either. Sovereignty takes its bearing from what bears it. As we have begun to see through the perspective of the *tear* opened by Shakespeare and staged by Suarez's deposition of analogy, what is borne in Richard's "untimely bier" is a subtle but crucial conceptual shift. In its emptying out of the old structures and forms, the play leaves us with a new possibility for conceiving of the relation between sovereignty and its sign-system. What this emptying out provides us with is an opportunity to re-envision the body-of-power as it begins to move away from the king's body and into another form. The container structure that bears the dead king announces the advent of a new body-of-power: one that comes in the guise of a "well-graced actor" entering the theater (5.2.23). Through the opening of the "tear," history peers into sovereignty's changing condition, as well as its future precondition. Through this exceptional and emptied-out space, the force of sovereignty—i.e. its potentiality—speaks. Through the lens of this distorting and fragmenting—but also, as we have seen, in some ways, necessary—trope of the tear, the contours of modern sovereignty begin to come into view. It is no longer the presence of the body inside the coffin, but rather the entourage and its movement that signify and effect the force of sovereignty. Louis Marin links this "mediatic" condition directly to analogy and to the necessary relation of sovereignty to its signs:

> It could well be that analogies of mimesis and proportions of resemblance, far from being manifestations of the *law* of the world and of being, are only flukes, erratic "coincidences." But the necessity of the effects clings to this "fluke" and, retroactively, makes it destiny.[83]

Sovereignty, at the end of *Richard II*, is no longer located in one place or one body. Rather, it is dispersed—in mediation itself. Before his death, Richard is the first to recognize this. That is why, having discovered sovereignty's secret, before he dies he tries to destroy the representational medium, the mirror that looks into the heart of a king. The "secret of the political" is, precisely, as Louis Marin puts it, that power is secretive—that it, like tears, *secretes*. But from where? From where does sovereignty originate? If we follow Suárez's *almost* univocal theory of being, the answer would appear to be: from an immanent source within creatures themselves. On the other hand, as long as the political space remains conceived of in terms of the descending grades of being required by proportional analogies, sovereignty will continue to operate according to the logic of the "empty place."[84] It is only once analogy no longer conceptually functions to represent the concept of being—once it breaks under the strain of what Benjamin calls the "over-extended transcendental impulse" of the baroque[85]—that the theory of power must reconstruct itself around a new representational logic and figure. *Richard II* prepares the way. What we will begin to see in the plays that follow are the contours of a gradual theatrical and theoretical reconfiguration of sovereignty, in which the now deposed vertical relations of the *analogia entis* are replaced by a new set of horizontal lines provided by that great leveler that is the stage.[86]

CHAPTER 2

# Reanimation: The Logic of Transfer in *Measure for Measure*

> What is re-presenting, if not presenting anew (in the modality of time) or in the place of (in the modality of space)? The prefix *re-* introduces into the term the value of substitution. Something that was present and is no longer is now represented.
>
> —Louis Marin, *The Portrait of the King*, 5

> The sovereign is not an angel, but, one might say, he who plays the sovereign plays the beast.
>
> —Jacques Derrida, *The Beast and the Sovereign*, 60[1]

> "O, that it were as like as it is true"
>
> —*Measure for Measure* (5.1.108)

In the second installment of his "brain-dead trilogy," *Todo Sobre Mi Madre* (*All About My Mother*), Pedro Almodóvar tells the story of Manuela (Cecelia Roth), a mother and Transplant Coordinator at the Ramón y Cajal hospital in Madrid. Manuela's job is to train doctors for the delicate task of informing a relative that a loved one has died and then requesting permission to take his/her organs.[2] Rehearsal quickly gives way to reality when, in a sad and ironic turn, Manuela's son is killed in a car accident after watching a performance of *A Streetcar Named Desire*. Suddenly, the very doctors Manuela has been training now approach her, using the techniques she has taught them, to inform her of her son's death—and ask for his organs.

The film moves briskly. After consenting to donate her son's heart, Manuela follows the disembodied organ to its new recipient in La Coruña, where she abandons it and leaves for Barcelona to search out the boy's father, Lola, a transsexual, to inform him/her of their son's death. In Barcelona, Manuela re-encounters an old friend, Agrado, another transsexual, as well as the theater troupe that had performed *Streetcar* the night her son was killed. Manuela and Agrado become involved in the production of *Streetcar*, and, in the film's centerpiece scene, Agrado walks on stage to announce the cancellation of that night's performance (due to the overdose of one of the principals). In place of the performance, Agrado offers to tell the audience the story of her life:

> AGRADO: [Ladies and Gentleman] the show has been cancelled. Those who wish can have their money back. But for those who have nothing better to do, for one of the few times you come to the theater, it would be a shame to leave. If you stay, I promise to entertain you by recounting the story of my life . . . [People begin walking out.]
>
> Good-bye, good-night, so sorry . . . [Continues to those remaining] Ok, then, if I bore you, you can snore like this [snore, snore]. I'll get it immediately, and you certainly won't hurt my feelings. *Really*.
>
> They call me "La Agrado" [from the Spanish *agradar*, "to please"] because I've always tried to make people's lives agreeable.
>
> As well as being agreeable, I'm very authentic: Look at this body! Everything made to measure. Almond-shaped eyes, 80,000. Nose, 200,000. (Waste of money because the next year another beating left it like this. I know it gives me a lot of character, but if I'd have known, I wouldn't have touched it.) Let me continue . . . Tits. Two. (Because I'm no *monster*.) 70,000 each—but I've more than earned that back. Silicone . . .
>
> AUDIENCE MEMBER: Where?!!
>
> AGRADO (POINTING IN ORDER): Lips, forehead, cheeks, hips and ass. A pint costs about 100,000, so you work it out, I've lost count. Jaw reduction, 75,000. Complete laser depilation—because women too, just as much, or even more than men, come from apes—60,000 a session. It depends on how hairy you are. Usually, two to four sessions. If you're a flamenco diva, you'll need more.
>
> So as I was saying, it costs a lot to be authentic, ladies and gentleman. And with these things one can't be stingy. Because the more you resemble what you've always dreamed you were, the more authentic you are.[3]

In place of the canceled play, Agrado recounts the story of her life: a history of surgical operations, violence, and desire. While Agrado stresses the price of each piece of this history, what is most important to her is the fabrication of her "authenticity" through her self-narration. In telling her story on stage, Agrado does much more than narrate. She actually performs her subjectivity through a complex combination of discursive and material operations. Her "authenticity" is not only socially constructed; it is produced, live, on stage. At the same time, this type of performance (to be distinguished from the early modern self-fashioning identified by the new historicism) is not only discursive. It is also literalized through the technological aid of surgery and silicone. In certain ways, Agrado exemplifies what some theorists describe in terms of a "labor" of self-making; she could be viewed as a type of postmodern "assemblage." Hers is an alternative, affective hybrid subjectivity.[4] While Agrado stresses the costs of this assemblage, what is most important to her is the actualization of her "authentic" body-of-power according to her desires. In this regard, the figure of Agrado not only sets many things right, as far as a post-modern understanding of the relationship between power, gender, representation, and the body goes, but she could also be viewed as an heir (or heiress) of a theater tradition in which the concerns of this relationship are played out with a particularly complex historical and conceptual force. While the story of Agrado's life would seem to have little in common with the concerns of seventeenth-century English Puritanism, and *All About My Mother* may strike readers as an unusual reference for a study of Renaissance drama and sovereignty, in its treatment of selfhood, authenticity, and what I have been referring to as the body-of-power, *All About My Mother*, nevertheless, invokes the very operations of power explored in Shakespeare's "problem play," *Measure for Measure*. For at the risk of being excessively tropological, what both Almodóvar's film and Shakespeare's play stage is a paradigm of sovereignty, in which authenticity, the political body, power, and law are all not only restored, but also produced through the effective operation of a theatrical "organ transplant." In this sense, Almodóvar could be seen as Shakespeare's heir.

Like *All About My Mother*, *Measure for Measure* opens with a transfer. In this case, however, the transferred thing is not a heart, not even the heart of the king, as we saw in the last chapter, but something more abstract: power. What is an authentic body-of-power? And what about the bodies subject to that power? What does it mean to have a body, authentically? How does the law "have" a body? What (legal) sense does the question even make, especially when the body in question, the Counter-Reformation believer's body, is itself already divided between competing allegiances to the here-below and the beyond?[5]

Shakespeare takes up these questions in *Measure for Measure*—his only play with a biblical title—specifically as questions of government. Vienna's ruler, Duke Vincentio, will be leaving town, he tells the Lord Escalus, and has chosen ("elected") a substitute, Angelo, to rule while he is away:

> Of government the properties to unfold
> Would seem in me t'affect speech and discourse,
> Since I am put to know that your own science
> Exceeds, in that, the lists of all advice
> My strength can give you. Then no more remains
> But that, to your sufficiency, as your worth is able,
> And let them work. The nature of our people,
> Our city's institutions, and the terms
> For common justice, y'are as pregnant in
> As art and practice hath enriched any
> That we remember. There is our commission,
> From which we would not have you warp.

(At this point, if I were an actor, I would gesture or pause to mark the enigmatic status of this "commission," its non-place and non-being: *Where* is it? *What* is it?)

> Call hither,
> I say, bid come before us Angelo.
> What figure of us, think you, he will bear?
> For you must know, we have with special soul
> Elected him our absence to supply;
> Lent him our terror, drest him with our love,
> And given his deputation all the organs
> Of our own power. What think you of it?
> 
> (1.1.1–21)[6]

The Duke's commission—wherever it lies—will "dress" Angelo with "love" and bequeath to him "all the organs" of his power, leaving Angelo's body doubly endowed with the "*marks* of sovereignty," terror and love.[7] Like *All About My Mother*, *Measure for Measure* is—metaphorically speaking, of course—a play about an organ transplant, or at least about the possibility of performing this operation on the body politic that is the play's "Vienna." That possibility, however, raises multiple questions for our thinking about sovereignty: How are we to understand the nexus of "pregnant," "bearing," and "organs" in the Duke's speech? Why—if Escalus is the one "pregnant" with the knowledge of human nature, civic institutions, and the "terms" of justice—does the Duke turn to Angelo instead? How does one revivify as well as restore order to a body politic that is rotting in the absence of law? More abstractly, how can power ever be effectively transferred? But perhaps *the* central question the play's opening lines raise, and which the play insists on re-raising throughout, is that of the figure that the substitute sovereign will "bear."

Included among the play's answers to this last question—all related to the substitute's name, "Angelo"—are the figures of legal currency, messengering, and of divine beings.[8] But the response *Measure for Measure* most consistently provides to the question of sovereignty's figure is one that is tied to the operation of representation itself—and, even more specifically, to its substitutional logics. One body part is as good as another, the "organ" transplant metaphor seems to suggest, to satisfy the desire of the "re-awakened" law.

While the term "organ transplant" may strike some critics as an anachronistic one to apply to a seventeenth-century text, the trope of bodily exchange already occupied an important place in the early modern cultural imaginary, as Leonard Barkan has shown.[9] Recounting the story of the Christian saints Cosmas and Damian—the twin brothers and great physicians who are tortured and decapitated by the Roman proconsul in Syria for refusing to sacrifice to the gods—Barkan reconstructs an allegory of historical attitudes toward the body, as they are produced around one of the miracles the saints are said to have performed. Jacobus de Voragine's thirteenth-century *Golden Legend* recounts that Pope Felix

> erected a noble church in Rome in honour of Saints Cosmas and Damian. In this church a man whose leg was consumed by a cancer devoted himself to the service of the holy martyrs. And one night as he slept, the saints appeared to him, bringing salves and instruments, and one said to the other: "Where shall we find new flesh, to replace the rotted flesh which we are to cut away?" The other replied: "This day an Ethiop was buried in the cemetery of Saint Peter in Chains; do thou fetch his leg, and we shall put it in place of the sick one!" Thereupon he hastened to the cemetery and brought back the Moor's leg, and they cut off the leg of the sick man and put the other in its stead. Then they anointed the leg which they had cut off, and attached it to the body of the dead Moor. When the man awoke and

felt no pain, he put his hand to the leg, and discovered that the wound was no longer there. Wondering whether he was himself or another, he held a candle to the leg, and still found no ill in it. Then, overjoyed, he leapt from his bed, and narrated to all what he had seen in his dream and the manner of his curing. Speedily therefore they sent to the Moor's tomb, and found his leg cut off, and the sick man's leg laid in the tomb beside the Moor.[10]

Following the myth's development in Renaissance paintings "from third-century Constantinople, through early Christian Rome, to medieval Spain and Germany, and finally to the High Renaissance in Florence, when Cosmas and Damian become the patrons of the Medici" (the name itself means "doctors," as Barkan points out [224]), Barkan traces various "fault-lines" in the narrative that lie around the problem of verification: "Just as (in certain respects) the transplant miracle symbolically prefigures modern medical practice, so the representation of the scene of verification prefigures an education system for anatomy and medicine where, once again, the body becomes the locus of real demonstrations and verification."[11] Perhaps the most puzzling aspect of the myth lies in the double direction the organ transplant operation takes: "Here, we touch upon the most powerful mystery in this legendary operation, more significant even than the race of the donor but, I think, closely related to it: that is, the fact that the gangrenous white leg gets attached to the corpse with the same logic as the healthy black leg gets attached to the living man."[12] The attachment logic in question here is also a representational logic—or rather an "il-logic"—that marks a departure from the normal physical and temporal orders of being, and that is itself a constituent feature of the discourse of sainthood. While the myth of the replacement of a dying Christian's live but rotting leg with the dead leg of a Moor inverts the trajectory of substitutions on which *Measure*'s resolution is effected (in which the pirate Ragozine's dead head preserves the live head of Claudio the lover), the "organ transplant" figure nevertheless presents a logic of representation that is central to *Measure for Measure*'s representation of sovereignty.

## *Institutional Desire*

In order to understand the centrality of the figurative problem in *Measure for Measure*, it is necessary to recall the play's setup. Forming a triangular relationship with the courthouse and the prison, the brothel is the institution that most powerfully characterizes the play's social space. Preceding the action proper, Vienna is established as a place of exchange. As we will quickly learn, one of the defining features of this public sphere is an economy of money for sex (the play's first substitution). The first act then opens with the Duke's selection of Angelo—(the coin/angel)—his "absence to supply" (the second substitution). Angelo restores a defunct statute and orders Claudio's execution to serve as an example that law has been restored (Claudio's head for Juliet's stolen maidenhead is the third substitution). Isabella pleads for her brother's life, which Angelo says he will spare if she sleeps with him (Isabella's maidenhead for Claudio's head is the fourth substitution). Meanwhile, other substitutions are taking place: The brothels in the suburbs are "plucked down," while those in the city are allowed to "stand for seed" (a fifth substitution). The Duke, who of course isn't absent at all but is observing these events in disguise, "like a true friar" (1.3.48), arranges to send Mariana in place of Isabella (Mariana for Isabella is the sixth substitution); Angelo sleeps with Mariana, reneges on his promise, and demands Claudio's head. (Back to head-for-head.) The Duke then plans to have another head—Barnadine's—sent in place of Claudio's. Barnadine refuses. Finally, yet another head, Ragozine the pirate's ("more like to Claudio" [4.3.68]), goes in place of Barnadine's, in place of Claudio's, in exchange for the stolen child's head.

I have reviewed *Measure for Measure*'s plot in order to remind us to just what degree the comedy plays with the question of the easy commensurability of these heads. From its opening transfer of power to its concluding pardonings and marriage arrangements, *Measure*'s plot is propelled along by a series of bodily exchanges, deferrals, and substitutions that, together, ultimately work to satisfy the law. Will any head do, the play asks, to restore law and satisfy the sovereign (himself the head of a body politic figured as a whore/horse "whereon the governor doth ride" [1.2.149])? Is there a *uniqueness* to this or any head, or to the head of any body? Or—as the play seems to suggest—does substitution itself (*likeness*) satisfy the law's desire?

Numerous critics have underscored the centrality of substitution in the play. For Nancy Leonard, a substitutional logic underlies the comedies' treatment of identity in general; Alexander Leggatt finds in it Shakespeare's theory of theater; and in a famous essay, William Empson analyzes the play's treatment of the substitution of one meaning of "sense" for another.[13] In this chapter, I focus on the play's treatment of substitution in the construction of political-theological sovereignty. Viewed in terms of the play's representation of sovereignty, *Measure for Measure*'s restoration of law through—and as—a series of substitutions, I will argue, presents a representational paradigm of a theologico-political sovereignty, in which the "absence" created by the departed sign creates an institutional desire that can only be satisfied by the substitution of another sign. The legal historian Peter Goodrich describes this dynamic as an operation of "political love":

> The structure of political desire replicates that of faith in God and demands a comparable and unthinking love. Political love is directed towards the images of a power that is never present in a body but only ever represented emblematically and vicariously by the delegates of its absolute yet invisible source. The sovereign may embody the law, and classically both the sovereign and the judiciary were thought somehow to incorporate the law, either by carrying its spirit in their breast or by giving it birth in their speech, but they nevertheless were only ever representatives of a source of law in whose name they spoke. The authority of law was an abstract one which could only ever be mediated by its secular representatives, so much so that the medievals adopted the maxim that only where the body was absent could authority be present (*absens corpore, praesens auctoritate*).[14]

Taking the representational ratio of the absent-present body of law as its point of departure, *Measure for Measure* explores various ways in which the absence of an authoritative body functions not only as sovereignty's provocation but also its conceptual precondition. Returning to Carl Schmitt's definition of political theology as a systematic *transfer* of theological concepts to the modern theory of the state, I will re-read *Measure for Measure* through the lens of Schmitt's theory in order to see how Shakespeare might modify that theory. How does *Measure for Measure* respond to Schmitt's thesis about a systematic transfer of concepts from one "body" of knowledge (theology) to another (law)? For *Measure* is precisely Shakespeare's most sustained interrogation of the functions, fault lines, and (lack of) effectiveness of this transfer. How is the relationship between theological and political sovereignty marked in Shakespeare's only play with a biblical title—a "comedy" about legal punishment, disease, death, and judgment?[15] In order to answer these questions, I would like to return to the "transfer" with which the play begins.

To "re-awaken" the sleeping law, the Duke explains to Friar Thomas that he intends to transfer "all the organs" of his power from his own to Angelo's body, knowing that Angelo, who has a reputation for severity, will be able to restore order without incurring the people's wrath:

> Sith 'twas my fault to give the people scope,
> 'Twould be my tyranny to strike and gall them
> For what I bid them do . . . Therefore indeed, my father,
> I have on Angelo impos'd the office;
> Who may in th'ambush of my name strike home,
> And yet my nature never in the fight
> To do in slander.
>
> (1.3.35ff)

The Duke gives to Angelo "all the organs of his power" so that the substitute will be able to "strike" *in the name of* the absent sovereign, without doing his "nature" any harm. Meanwhile, disguised "as 'twere a brother" of Friar Thomas's order, the Duke will remain in Vienna in order to observe the effects of the transfer:

> And to behold his sway,
> I will, as 'twere a brother of your order,
> Visit both prince and people. Therefore, I prithee,
> Supply me with the habit, and instruct me
> How I may formally in person bear
> Like a true friar.
>
> (1.3.35ff)

"How I may formally in person bear . . .": The Duke does not say *what* he is to "formally" bear. He does not supply the word "myself," as a reader of these lines might unconsciously do in order to complete the thought: "bear *myself* like a true friar." Rather, what he is supposed to bear is left blank. It has no figure—yet. At the same time, read another way, the line explicitly states what the Duke is to "bear": "instruct me how I may formally in person *bear like* a true friar." He is to bear "*like*." The Duke's language (like that of some American teenagers) is to bear the simile ("like") itself, the (non) weight of similarity. Like the perspective glass passage in *Richard II*, in order to arrive at whatever meaning it may have, one has to read it awry. What I would like to consider here is the possibility that "how I may formally in person *bear like* a true friar" is not just a bad sentence or the indication of a lapse but rather that, in its omission of *what* is to be borne, it felicitously hits on the problem this "problem play" is principally about. For in addition to being Shakespeare's most sustained exploration of political theology, *Measure for Measure* is also, perhaps, Shakespeare's most penetrating analysis of the function of what King James had referred to as the "similitudes" in the conceptualization and performance of sovereignty. The reasons for which it will come to focus on the space between the "like" and the "true," between representation and reality, in relation to sovereignty, with such intensity, are already indicated in the play's opening lines. These have to do with the fear that—as Jean-Luc Nancy's paradox put it—sovereignty is, in fact, *nothing*. The anxiety that this possibility raises is at least as much of a theological problem as it is a political one. It is above all, in Shakespeare's view, a representational one.

In addition to the question of the figure the substitute sovereign will make, the success of the Duke's plan will also depend on the degree to which he will be able to "bear" the figure not of secular but of spiritual authority: "like a true friar." The play produces the space between the secular and the spiritual through a substitution that will eventually elide the distinction, as the Duke, disguised as Friar Lodowick, takes confessions and offers absolutions. Before a distinction can be erased, however, it must first be marked—and read. The borderline between the reality and the representation of power in *Measure*'s Vienna increasingly becomes a matter of reading, or a reading of matter, and specifically body-matter. Thus, *Measure*'s opening dramatic problem is a legal problem related to the reading of a body. Out of wedlock, Juliet's and Claudio's "mutual entertainment" "with character too gross is writ on Juliet" (1.2.143–4). This is *Measure for Measure*'s unique way of saying that Juliet is pregnant. The body that is repeatedly bound and read in *Measure for Measure* is not only the object of moral censure; it is also the target and text of law. The relationship between law, reading, and the body is perhaps the play's central concern—as it is also in the competing sovereignty theories being formulated by King James and his oath of allegiance opponent, Francisco Suárez. Where James, for example, will write to his son in the *Basilicon Doron*, "let your owne life be a law-booke and a mirror to your people; that therein they may read the practice of their owne Lawes," emphasizing the sovereign's legible public performance, Suárez pursues the connection between law and reading into the term's theo-political etymology.[16]

Suárez opens his important legal text, *De legibus ac Deo legislatore* (1612) (*On Laws and God the Lawgiver*), with a definition of law ("lex") that underscores the historical relationship between reading and binding that lies at law's conceptual heart. In some ways, anticipating Michel Foucault's well-known argument that the force of law always requires a readable body, Suárez points out the etymological link between Thomas Aquinas's derivation of law from the Latin term "ligandum" (binding) and Saint Isidore's reading of "lex" as "legendum," that which is to be read:

> From these considerations, St. Thomas . . . held that the term ["law"] was derived from *ligandum* (binding), since the true effect of law is to bind, or place under a binding obligation. This view was adopted by Gabriel (on the *Sentences of Peter Lombard*, Bk. III). Clichtove . . . quoted the same explanation of the etymology of law, from Cassiodorus, and approved it. Moreover, the opinion in question is in agreement with Scripture, which speaks of laws as bands, in a passage from *Jeremias* (Chap. ii [v. 20]): "Thou hast broken my yoke, thou hast burst my bands . . ."
>
> But Isidore (*Etymologies*, Bk. II, chap. X and Bk. V, chap. iii) believes that law (*lex*) is so called from *legendum* (that which is to be read), a conclusion which he deduces from the fact that law ought to be written, and therefore is something to be read. However, since we are now dealing with law in a rather broad sense, the word *legendum* should be extended to include internal reading or reflection, as Alexander of Hales has noted ([*Summa Universae Theologiae*] Pt. III, qu. xxvi, memb. I), in order that this etymology may be suited to every law. For, just as the natural law is said by Paul (*Romans*, Chap. ii. [v.15]) to be written in the heart, so it can and should also be read there by the mind . . . Moreover, in harmony with this same etymology is the Hebrew name for law (*Tora*), which signifies "instruction."[17]

Following Isidore's interpretation, the text of "law" (*lex*) for Suárez is distinctly "something to be read." Yet in order to enable this "reading," external or internal, there must first be a readable "body"—or at least a body part (the "leg" of "legendum"). *Measure for Measure* develops this notion of the readable and "speaking" body in various ways. When Escalus attempts to mitigate Angelo's severity by suggesting that he himself may have once been in a similar position to Claudio (which we later learn to, in fact, be true), Angelo responds:

> 'Tis one thing to be tempted, Escalus,
> Another thing to fall. I not deny
> The jury passing on the prisoner's life
> May in the sworn twelve have a thief, or two,
> Guiltier than him they try. What's open made to justice,
> That justice seizes. What knows the laws
> That thieves do pass on thieves? 'Tis very pregnant,
> The jewel that we find, we stoop and take't,
> Because we see it; but what we do not see,
> We tread upon, and never think of it.
>
> (2.1.17ff)

For Angelo, justice "seizes" what it sees.[18] Without this visibility, the object of law's desire ("jewel") would pass by unperceived. The lesson is "very pregnant." Echoing the Duke's opening metaphor of Escalus as "pregnant" with legal knowledge, Angelo reiterates what will become one of the play's central themes: The law in *Measure for Measure* speaks through the body—starting with that of the substitute himself. Angelo is not only "the *voice* of the recorded law" (2.4.61), but also, in Claudio's words, the "damnedst body to invest and cover / In precise guards!" (3.1.94–6).[19] Lucio, the "fantastic," has another view. For him, Angelo was

> not made by man and woman, after this downright way of creation . . . Some report, a sea-maid spawned him. Some, that he was begot between two stockfishes. But it is certain that when he makes water, his urine is congealed ice; that I know to be true. And he is a motion ungenerative; that's infallible. (3.2.99–108)

As critics have pointed out, Lucio's view of Angelo as a monstrous figure, an impotent fish that urinates ice, reflects anti-puritan sentiment of the early seventeenth century—particularly that of English royalists.[20] In this regard, Angelo represents a hypocritical relation to and representation of law—which of course, as an "actor," he is![21] But the law also speaks through other bodies in the play—or, rather, body parts. That is, if Angelo is the over-zealous representative of the law, then the constable, "Elbow," is simply incompetent: "I do lean upon / justice," Elbow says to Angelo and Escalus, "and do bring in here before your good / honour two notorious benefactors" (2.1.46–9):

> ANGELO: Benefactors? Well, what benefactors are they? Are they not malefactors?

ELBOW: If it please your honour, I know not well what they are. But precise villains they are, that I am sure of, and void of all profanation in the world, that good Christians ought to have.

(2.1.51–6)

As Escalus later puts it, Elbow "misplaces" (2.1.87). His inversions—"benefactors" for "malefactors"; "void of all profanation in the world that good Christians ought to have"; (and later) "detesting" for "attesting"; "cardinally" for "carnally" given; "suspected" instead of "respected"—mirror the corrupt state of the play's body politic, in which law has been asleep for some fourteen, or perhaps nineteen,[22] zodiacs. But they also mark a problem that obliges me to qualify my earlier claim that the law "speaks through the body" in the play. For what Shakespeare seems to equally insist on, whether it's through the "pregnant" bodies of Escalus and Juliet, the "damnedest" body of Angelo, the "leaning" body of Elbow, or the disguised body of the Duke, is that the law *misspeaks* through the body. That is, our understanding of the legal body depends on how we view it, which, in turn, depends on how it's figured.

Much of *Measure* criticism focuses on one of two sets of problems: those having to do with power, surveillance, and the law, on the one hand, and those regarding family, sexuality, and incest, on the other.[23] Linking both—i.e., both the force that writes itself on the body, and the threat posed by unpoliced sexuality—is the operation of metaphor.

While metaphor theory in general far exceeds the purview of this study, one well established way of understanding metaphor's conceptual function is to see it as a comparison that operates in terms of substitution: One term stands in for another in order to present a similarity between the two. In Aristotle's well-known formulation, "metaphor consists in giving the thing a name that belongs to something else; the transference being either from genus to species, or from species to genus, or from species to species, or on grounds of analogy."[24] The key term in Aristotle's definition is "transference." Metaphor initiates a certain movement, from the proper to "something else." Early modern metaphor theorists stressed not only its ornamental function, but also especially its capacity to move between various levels of sense. For Puttenham, for example, metaphor

> is of two sorts: one to satisfy and delight only by a goodly outward show set upon the matter with words and speeches smoothly and

tunably running; another by certain intendments or sense of such words and speeches inwardly working a stir to the mind. That first quality the Greeks called *enargeia*, of this word *argos*, because it giveth a glorious lustre and light. This latter they called *energia* of *ergon*, because it wrought with a strong and virtuous operation. And figure breedeth them both . . .[25]

Criss-crossing from sight to sound, Puttenham classifies metaphors, first, into those which "delight the *ear* by a goodly *outward show*," and, second, those capable of "*inwardly working a stir to the mind*"—an outcome he describes as a "strong and virtuous *operation*." At the center of this crossover operation lies metaphor's capacity to initiate a conceptual movement from one term, and one sense, to another. For this reason, metaphor becomes, for Puttenham, precisely a "figure of transport." While *Measure for Measure* is not a play specifically about the problem of metaphor, its representation of sovereignty highlights the power effect produced by this "figure of transport." It does so by invoking a metaphor—that of the "organ transplant"—that will come to play a pivotal role in political theory. In what Otto von Gierke termed "association theory," the sovereign's will is seen precisely, as Carl Schmitt puts it, as "the organ of the people convoked to express legal consciousness as it emerges from the life of the people." Commenting on von Gierke's theory, Schmitt writes, "the personal will of the ruler is spliced into the state as if into an organic whole"[26]—as if, in other words, it were an "organ transplant."

This is, of course, a connection that can only be made on the basis of a highly metaphorical reading. And one could argue that in associating the "organ transplant" metaphor of association theory, and the "operations" involved in Puttenham's *figure of transport*, I am playing fast and loose with the very different terminologies of rhetorical and political theory, moving irresponsibly from the vocabulary of one discipline and discourse to another. The stakes of the debate are high, for it is important to be careful about confusing a metaphor ("organ") deployed in one kind of theater from the very same term in the world of another. This tension is, in fact, very much a part of a seventeenth-century debate, in which conceptual definitions and the metaphors on which they ride are on the move.

As Jacques Lezra has shown, ". . . the lexical effort to define power during this period is in flux between force and power."[27] In the important seventeenth-century dictionary, *El Tesoro de la lengua Castellana*, for example, Sebastián de Covarrubias Orozco defines "power" in terms of the capacities and processes of delegation, substitution and transfer: "POWER. From the Latin verb, *possum, potes.* Power, noun, the faculty one gives to another so that, in place of that person, he may do something."[28] The question of when, and how, to take a metaphor is inextricably bound up with the ways that we understand such fluctuating processes and capacities.

Recall the scene with which this book opened. In the Oath of Allegiance polemic between King James and Suárez, Suárez identifies the King's theological errors as problems of reading in general and conceptual and terminological distinctions in particular. In a section of his *Defensio Fidei* dedicated to the "Errors Regarding the Catholic Faith Professed by King James of England," Suárez argues that James is unable to distinguish between the terms "representation" and "metaphor." The test case, as usual in Counter-Reformation debates, is the Eucharist ceremony, which itself fast became a kind of primal scene for the baroque problem of sovereignty. The crux is the meaning of "representation." For Suárez, "[t]o represent is the same as to make the thing present" (*Representare idem est quod rem præsentem facere*). In the Eucharist ceremony, the function of representation is to make *the very being* of God present:

> TO REPRESENT IS THE SAME AS MAKING THE THING PRESENT. Let St. Jerome be the third witness who, interpreting Christ's words in Chapter 26 of St. Matthew, says: *after having observed (celebrated) the typical Easter and eaten the flesh of the lamb with the apostles, he takes the bread, which comforts men's heart, and goes on to the true Sacrament of Easter, so that—in a similar way as Melchisedec, priest of the great God, had done by offering bread and wine—He also would represent the reality of his body and blood.*
>
> Perhaps with reference to this some heretic will interpret the word "represent" in a fictitious or metaphorical sense. But the sense and intention of San Jerome are clear: to represent is the same as making a thing present, especially when it deals with something that had been previously promised, or that had been foretold or desired.[29]

To understand the Eucharist ceremony, according to Suárez, one has to know when a metaphor is just a metaphor and when it's something else. Citing one of *Measure*'s key source texts, the Gospel of St. Matthew,

Suárez argues that while a "heretic" might interpret St. Jerome's use of the word "metaphorically," the correct meaning of "to represent" is *to make something present*, and above all something that had been "promised, predicted, *or desired*" ("quod rem præsentem, facere, præsertim quæ antea promissa erat, vel futura prædicta, aut desiderata"). Like Covarrubias's definition of "power," representation, in the performance of the Eucharist ceremony, has the capacity of actualization.

Shifting from sacred ritual to secular theater, the representational "operation" staged in *Measure for Measure* veers off in an important sense from this actualization.[30] For *Measure*'s chief representational operation consists *not* of presenting the body that is called for, but rather of repeatedly producing *another* body, similar but not identical to the one the law demands. For the purposes of "justice," nevertheless, this "other body" would seem to be perfectly satisfying—that is, effective. What links the two bodies in question is that both respond to a particular representational expectation, or, as Suárez puts it, "desire." *Measure*'s reliance on the figure of simile to fulfill the law's desire to "have the body" echoes but also diverges from a theological understanding of representation. Simile, in *Measure for Measure*, does actually make something present. It's just not the same thing that was promised, predicted, or desired. Nevertheless, as far as law is concerned, it works.

Between a representation with the force of actualization and an authority with the power to stage it lies a zone crucial to the play's conceptualization—as well as its production of power. That is, just as with Agrado's authenticity, the performance of power in *Measure for Measure* is not only produced (in this case, without silicone), but it is also represented. The play's primary question, then, might be: How does theater theorize this representation? And how might this theory differ or coincide with theories of representation in political science, such as Gierke's, or theology? What is the relationship between the type of representation Suárez sees at work in the Eucharist ceremony, and the substitutions set in motion by Duke Vincentio to restore law and order in Vienna? If substitution is indeed the controlling metaphor of the play, as is so frequently argued, then how does Shakespeare's use of this operation mark and re-mark upon the theory of sovereignty being developed in the early seventeenth century? Jonathan Goldberg begins to provide an answer to some of these questions. For Goldberg, too, it begins with a certain recurring notion of law:

> Substitution is the law of the play and inherent in justice, the law of society as well. The "mystery" in these multiple replacements and substitutions centers on the Duke, sovereign in both realms . . . Sovereign power, real and stamped, sustains the exchange system of society, the endless refiguration of the king in representative acts of substitution.[31]

If substitution is "the law" not only of Shakespeare's play, but also "of society as well," then what governs its operations? How is its effectiveness monitored, its economy generated? Is it a political act? Legal? Theological? Economic? Acts of substitution, of course, underlie all of these. In the broadest of senses, too, the operation of substitution—one head going in place of another—could be said to govern the play's conception of selfhood, theater, law, commerce, and sex, as so many have noted. But this is still too general a definition to provide an efficient accounting of sovereignty's force in *Measure for Measure*. Goldberg's conclusion takes the problem to its radical point, locating sovereign power in language itself:

> It is . . . in language that the king represents himself; it is in language that power is displayed. And the language of power, the sovereign's speech/writing, is, like the sovereign himself, *sui generis*. It, like himself, points beyond itself, but does not establish a final referent. The sovereign depends upon sustaining contradictions, and the stage is his place of re-presentation where he is doubled. Its doubleness is an essential quality of language and of power, of language insofar as what language does is represent itself.[32]

In focusing on the duality of both, Goldberg identifies a commonality between language and power that is crucial to *Measure for Measure*'s construction of sovereignty. One might take Goldberg's point further, even into the contrary direction. That is, one of the implications of this "doubleness" might be not that the "language of power . . . is . . . *sui generis*," but rather that it is like *all* language, already metaphorical, double, and on the move. This is what *Measure* actually shows.[33] Giorgio Agamben develops Goldberg's point by carrying the relationship between sovereignty and representation into a consideration of fundamental ontological categories. Focusing specifically on the problem of *potentiality* as formulated by Aristotle, Agamben writes that

> Sovereignty is always double because *Being* as potentiality, suspends itself, maintaining itself in a relation of ban with itself in order to realize itself as absolute actuality.[34]

The crux of sovereignty, for Agamben, lies in the space that defines this duality. That is, sovereignty, as it has developed historically and conceptually, has moved into an increasingly gray zone, what Agamben repeatedly calls a "zone of indistinguishability." Specifically, the *being* of sovereignty, for Agamben, is a mode, revealed as much by its capacity *not* to act. Sovereignty suspends but also retains its power of actualization. This leads Agamben to one of his key terms, not only for sovereignty, but also for the forms of life: potentiality. It's a difficult mode. How can this "potentiality" be figured? Agamben's example is Avicenna's figure of the scribe, precisely "in the moment in which he does not write."[35] The question of how to figure sovereign potential leads us back once to the problem of metaphor and its related figure of simile, the figure which performs the bulk of sovereignty's representation in *Measure for Measure*.[36] How does one figure sovereignty in action? And what about when it doesn't act, but withholds its potential to do so?

Where simile relies on relations of resemblance, and metaphor those of identity, *Measure* shows the two to be indistinguishable from each other with respect to their effects: Likeness of identity is indistinguishable from sameness as far as law's representational needs go. Returning to Puttenham's definition, we see that relations of power ("force") become increasingly important to Puttenham's understanding of metaphor.

> There is a kinde of wresting of a single word from his owne right signification, to another not so naturall, but yet of some affinitie or conveniencie with it, as to say, *I cannot digest your unkinde words*, for I cannot take them, in good part: or as the man of law said, *I feele you not*, for I understand not your case, because he had not his fee in his hand . . . . Or to call the top of a tree, or of a hill, the crowne of a tree or of a hill: for in deede *crowne* is the highest ornament of a Princes head, made like a close garland, or els the top of a mans head, where the haire windes about, and because such terme is not applied naturally to a tree, or to a hill, but is transported from a mans head to a hill or tree, therefore it is called by *metaphore*, or the figure of *transport*.[37]

One of the reasons we use this "figure of transport," according to Puttenham, is to "enforce a sense and make the word more significative."[38] Prior to this "enforcement" of one particular sense, the word remains more open to the multiple senses that may be available to it. We might say that sense lies in waiting, in between one or the other of its possible meanings, until force arrives in the form of metaphor to fix one superior sense in place. Until then, metaphor might not be able to deliver its goods. To return from this sense of metaphorical force underscored by Puttenham's *figure of transport*, to Agamben's analysis of sovereignty, we see a similar situation with regard to the space (or what Agamben calls the "zone") that lies between various possibilities and potentialities. That is, like metaphor, sovereignty, for Agamben, also lies waiting in a state in-between potentiality and actuality, the inside and the outside of law, bare life and the good life. Sovereignty exists in between the power of law to inscribe itself on the body, and the actual inscription. Uniting the two "laws"—of metaphor and sovereignty—is Empson's "keyword" for the play, "sense."

As Empson saw, *Measure for Measure* takes the space and movement between one sense of a term—and in this case, the term "sense" itself—and another, as its primary problem and provocation. As Empson points out, the term "sense" bears a productive ambiguity between common sense, on the one hand, and sensuality, on the other.[39] Empson's path-breaking essay called attention to *Measure for Measure*'s investment in the problem of the displacement between the two senses itself—and the ensuing anxiety this displacement releases. Anticipating Derrida's, Agamben's, and other post-structuralist readings, Empson argued that the play's *order* depends on both stabilizing this semantic and logical movement and revealing its instability. Keeping Empson's observation in mind, I would like to return to two of the main claims made by Agamben and Schmitt with regard to life and law.

Recall that, for Schmitt, the sovereign's principal operation is to decide on the exception ("sovereign is he who decides on the exception"). The sovereign does not *derive* this decision from a norm, but simply decides, separating the inside of law and exception, in a stroke. In terms of the language of bodily inscription I have been following in my reading of *Measure* so far, Schmitt's argument that the decision "represents the inscription within the body of the *nomos* of the exteriority that animates it and gives it meaning"—is itself "animated" by a play that seems to take Schmitt at his word. For Schmitt, the mark of sovereignty is the decision that "represents the inscription within the body of the *nomos* of the exteriority that animates it." The "body," in this case the body of the law, for Schmitt, exists inside a law-zone but is "animated" from outside that zone. The "inscription within" comes from a position without—from an "exteriority." In this sense, law is not itself, and neither does the "body" give itself its own life. The law speaks, and more specifically, as Schmitt puts it, *writes* ("inscription") its force on the body from a position outside the law. In terms of the legal institutions responsible for producing, administering, and enforcing the law, Schmitt's argument has unsettling implications, starting with the question of the legitimacy of these institutions themselves. For one way of understanding Schmitt's claim that the law does not coincide with itself is to conclude that the law is fundamentally ungrounded in law, i.e. in legal norms, parliamentary procedures, democratically arrived at decisions, rational deliberations or collective arguments. The legal institution does not produce the law but rather receives it—from without. Law does not arrive, deduced, from logic or norms, human rationality or democratic process. Rather, the sovereign, and only the sovereign, in an act modeled on biblical creation, simply decides.

To return to the question of embodiment with which we began, then, and which Jacob Taubes showed was central to the question of sovereignty in relation to political theology, what we see here is a striking case of estrangement with regard to law. The "body" that orders the social and that gives legal sense-making its sense—is also a body outside itself. The inside and the outside don't coincide in a "zone of indistinguishability," as Agamben would have it, but rather remain separate, dependent on each other, but apart. Instead, there's a space in between them, conceptual to be sure—but also legal. And that space itself is not only therefore "real," but it is also determining for the forms of life that traverse it. It provides what Schmitt calls "the normal structuring of life relations."[40]

For Empson, the error that both the Duke and Isabella make is to think that they can avoid the pitfalls of sense and somehow "get outside the world and above justice,"[41] because there is no "outside." For Schmitt, on the other hand, law arrives precisely from such an outside space. The body-of-power in *Measure for Measure*, insofar as it is a legal body, is "animated" from outside. Consequently the inhabitants of Vienna, whose individual bodies are subject to its now reanimated law, also receive their "inscription" from without. The law writes its force on their bodies, and "animates" those bodies, just as it is itself animated not by itself or by legal institutions, or even Angelo, but from somewhere else. But from where?

Agamben returns to Schmitt: "The sovereign decides not the licit and the illicit but the originary inclusion of the living in the sphere of law or, in the words of Schmitt, the 'normal structuring of life relations,' which the law needs."[42] For Agamben, this "structuring" turns out to be largely a linguistic structuring. The relationship of the inside to the outside, law to the body, and sovereignty to life, is marked by language. Thus, following Aristotle, Agamben begins his analysis of sovereignty by asking two questions about the relationship between sovereignty and language: First, "in what way does the living being have language?" And second, "in what way does bare life dwell in the polis?"[43] Both questions are, of course, extremely complex and could elicit responses from a variety of disciplines, including linguistics, anthropology, biology, sociology, political science, and philosophy, from which Agamben himself is drawing them. To situate these questions within the framework of *Measure for Measure*, Shakespeare's initial response to the first would seem to be that living beings have language, insofar as that "having" allows them to move—to negotiate the channels and "structurings" of life, which, the play shows, are not only legal, but also economic, moral, political, and political-theological. Language, in this light, might be viewed as the *tool* that for both Schmitt and, in a different way, Hans Blumenberg provides us with our orientation in relation to this structuring. (Recall here Schmitt's claim, discussed in the Introduction, that the legal ordering of the earth *orients* human social life—as well as Blumenberg's argument that absolute metaphors provide a "point of orientation [and] give structure to a world representing the nonexperiencable, nonapprehensible totality of the real."[44])

Agamben's second question—"In what way does bare life dwell in the polis?"—takes us straight to the structural and theo-political crux of the play. If the course of Western politics has been to gradually move the two Greek senses of life, "*bios*" (the good, political life) and "*zoē*" (bare life) into a "zone of indistinguishability," as Agamben argues, then the motor that produces this movement is language, in general, and metaphor, in particular. This argument raises the dual questions of how one has language and how one dwells in the polis. *Measure for Measure* seems to respond to the first by suggesting that the living being "has" language insofar as he/she is able to deploy it in operations of exchange, or substitution, that allow him or her to negotiate the channels of authority and desire the play explores. The mechanisms of linguistic substitution (which is one, but only one, way of understanding metaphor) operate by first positing and then relying on relations of similarity. The epistemology of metaphor, as Paul De Man describes it, does not so much present a simple substitution of one term for another in order to create meaning, as it poses a new logic, in which the substitution, in the end, is merely a simulation of the creation logic—or, rather, a dissimulation. Describing the dependence of our concepts of being on language, De Man writes that "the attribute of being is dependent on the assertion of a similarity which is illusory, since it operates at a stage that precedes the constitution of entities."[45] For De Man, metaphysical concept formation operates by asserting a similarity *prior to* the "constitution of the entity." Before a thing is made, a similarity is imagined—and posited. Imagination precedes *being*; similarity is prior to existence. With regard to sovereignty, then, one might say that prior to sovereignty's *being* lies an imagination and simulation of what does not yet exist. The road to sovereignty runs through language, in general, and as *Measure for Measure* emphasizes, simile in particular. Thus, theo-political sovereignty thinks itself through existing similes available to theorize the sovereign's exceptional power. The king's, or the pope's, power is *like* God's: located outside the normal (temporal and spatial) orders of being. To imagine it we must go through a transfer that cannot be logically questioned, only re-described.

At the heart of this transfer is the operation of metaphor. The problem of metaphor keeps returning in *Measure for Measure* because as far as the play's representation of sovereignty goes, metaphor, one might say, is the very matter and material of law. Metaphor, according to the literary and legal scholar Stanley Fish, is the law's "roadway":

> [T]he law is continually creating and recreating itself out of the very materials and forces it is obliged, by the very desire to *be* law, to push away. The result is a spectacle that could be described (as the members of the critical legal studies movement tend to do)—as farce, but I would describe it differently, as a signal example of the way in which human beings are able to construct the roadway on which they are traveling, even to the extent of "demonstrating" in the

course of building it that it was there all the while. The failure of both legal positivists and natural law theorists to find the set of neutral procedures or basic moral principles underlying the law should not be taken to mean that the law is a failure, but rather that it is an amazing kind of success. The history of legal doctrine and its applications is a history neither of rationalistic purity nor of incoherence and bad faith, but an almost Ovidian history of transformation under the pressure of enormously complicated social, political, and economic urgencies, a history in which victory—in the shape of *keeping going*—is always being wrested from what looks like certain defeat, and wrested by means of stratagems that are all the more remarkable because, rather than being hidden, they are almost always fully on display.[46]

Although Fish uses the term "rhetoric" instead of "metaphor," the "almost Ovidian history of transformation" within legal doctrine that he describes is perpetuated by semantic and conceptual movements performed by metaphorical transfers within the language of law. Rhetoric, in general, and metaphor, in particular, both work by "effacing [their] own rhetoricity."[47] For Fish, rhetoric is the "trick by which the law subsists," and thus both the law's malleability and its ability to "*keep going*" depend on the linguistic and pragmatic capacities of language to construct the meanings we come to rely on.[48] Perhaps the biggest "trick" effected by metaphor is the production of legal authority itself. Law, for Fish, is "in the business of producing the very authority it retroactively invokes":

> Why should law take *that* self-occluding and perhaps self-deceiving form? The short answer is that that's the law's job, to stand between us and the contingency out of which its own structures are fashioned. In a world without foundational essences—the world of human existence; there may be another, more essential one, but we know nothing of it—there are always institutions (the family, the university local and national governments) that are assigned the task of providing the spaces (or are they theaters) in which we negotiate the differences that would, if they were given full sway, prevent us from living together in what we are pleased to call civilization. And what, after all, are the alternatives? Either the impossible alternative of grounding the law in perspicuous and immutable abstractions, or the unworkable alternative of intruding that impossibility into every phase of the law's operations, unworkable because the effect of such

intrusions would be so to attenuate those operations that they would finally disappear. That leaves us with the law as it is, something we believe in because it answers to, even as it is the creation of, our desires.[49]

Fish doesn't cite *Measure for Measure*. But his argument that the law "answers to, even as it is the creation of, our desires" could not more aptly describe the play's view of law as a complex force and form of life. "We believe in law because it answers to our desires," he writes.[50] What does it mean to say that law "answers to our desires," or that "the law [itself] desires a formal existence"? It means, for Fish, that it doesn't want to be absorbed by another structure, doesn't want "to need completing by some other, supplementary discourse." The law's autonomy is "threatened," in Fish's words, by morality, and by interpretation.[51] Its autonomy is threatened by morality because the identification of law with morality would leave every individual his or her own judge, and in place of a single standard, we'd have many. Consequently, "in order to check the imperial ambitions of particular moralities, some point of resistance to interpretation must be found, and that's why the doctrine of formalism has proved so attractive." Yet at the same time, Fish argues that the law *cannot* have a "formal existence." It cannot because our specification of what the law is will already be "infected" by interpretation and will therefore be challengeable. Finally, for Fish, this challenge-ability is a good thing in the end. And the law does *not* fail to have a formal existence after all. The law "succeeds," and the nature of this "success" is a "political/rhetorical achievement."[52] The law's desire to have a "formal existence" is, indeed, sufficiently satisfied by rhetoric and by the rhetorical performance of metaphor.[53]

Like metaphor, in this view, sovereignty's performance in *Measure for Measure* operates by similarly substituting one category for another and treating it *like* another. As we will see, however, this performance does not consist solely of acts of substitution, but we can start with substitution. For Agamben, the meaning of "life" in modern political entities has come to acquire its legal sense not from itself but, just as in Schmitt's theory, from something outside of itself.

In Agamben, the inside-outside relation is even more complex with regard to the status of the life that these spaces capture, in that for Agamben the inside of law captures life by excluding it. Excluding, however, does not mean not governing. It also doesn't mean simply substituting one meaning or sense for another. There's nothing simple about this legal capture, which is exactly what *Measure for Measure* shows. As with the Schmittian decision, *Measure for Measure* starts out as an experiment with the possibility that this "animation" can be provided by an internal substitute, while the "real" representative of sovereignty and the law is "away." What is required is a certain fusion, or confusion between the inside and outside of life, law, and the body.

Walter Benjamin finds a technical name for the conceptual performance of this type of confusion in drama. For Benjamin, baroque drama provides us with a capacity to understand the space of fusion or con-fusion between what Agamben might see as two senses of life. Indeed, I would suggest that Benjamin might even see Agamben's argument as a theatrical discovery. In his explanation that temporal movement in baroque drama is represented not chronologically but "choreographically," he begins, somewhat surprisingly, with a consideration of the significance of the term "confusion" itself. For Benjamin,

> "Confusion" [*Verwirrung*] is already a technical term in the dramaturgical theories of the Nuremberg school. The title of Lope de Vega's drama *Der verwirrte Hof* [The court in confusion; Spanish: *El palacio confuse*] is typical.... The term "confusion" is to be understood in a pragmatic as well as in a moral sense. In contrast to the spasmodic chronological progression of tragedy, the *Trauerspiel* takes place in a spatial continuum, which one might describe as choreographic. The organizer of its plot, the precursor of the choreographer, is the intriguer. He stands as a third type alongside the despot and the martyr.[54]

Confusion is a "technical" term, Benjamin insists. We might understand the technique in question to be that of the political scientist, or the anthropologist—or both. But Benjamin gets it from drama, and baroque dramaturgy. It is precisely from these areas that he derives his understanding of political anthropology and its theories of what we would call the subject:

> The uniformity of human nature, the power of the animal instinct and the emotions, especially the emotions of love and fear, and their limitlessness—these are the insights on which every consistent political thought or action, indeed the very science of politics must be based . . . Human emotions as the predictable driving mechanism of the creature—that is the final item in the inventory of knowledge

which had to transform the dynamism of world-history into political action. It is at the same time the source of a set of metaphors which was designed to keep this knowledge as alive in the langue of poetry as Sarpi or Guicciardini were doing in historiography.⁵⁵

Benjamin moves swiftly from the political anthropology of Machiavelli and Dilthey to the operation of metaphor. The metaphor that is "designed to keep this knowledge alive" is that of the clock. As we saw at the conclusion of the last chapter, the sacred body of the king, Richard, transforms itself precisely into this object. There, the stage prop of the king as clock becomes the new sovereign body-of-power.

What the play also underscores is that in order for this exchange system to operate, not only for the law but also for and within the very concept of sovereignty itself, it first needs to *have* this body. The body is always sovereignty's pre-condition. As we have already seen, in all of its historical formulations, from Aristotle through Hobbes to Deleuze, Derrida, and Agamben, the concept of sovereignty relies on the metaphor of the body for its figuration. Following Foucault, the new historicism has seen this body as an "anchoring point for the manifestation of power," the site where the force of sovereignty becomes visible.⁵⁶ For the new historicism, the body is especially well suited to satisfy sovereignty's visual requirements, for as Goldberg puts it, "sovereignty is a matter of sight."⁵⁷ Accordingly, *Measure for Measure* stages these requirements in terms of the body—with the exception that, as we have seen, rather than providing a whole body to be read by the law, Shakespeare's comedy presents instead mere body parts, above all the heads. Heads fill the "absence" produced by the Duke's feigned departure from Vienna; they are the "supply" created by his transfer of "the organs of his power" to the substitute, Angelo. Like the coin to which his name (as well as the term "sovereign") refers, Angelo bears power in *Measure for Measure* as a currency, which, as the play proceeds to make clear, is economic in the political and sexual senses as well. Angelo's sovereignty rapidly reveals itself to be a currency of desire. "Voice of the recorded law," his sovereignty speaks first of the law's general desire to have the body (that is, Claudio's), in order to signify its restitution, and, second, of the sovereign's personal desire to have Isabella's body in another capacity. To say that to speak this way is "only metaphorical" is to miss *Measure*'s repeated rhetorical point, which is largely about the power of metaphor itself, in sovereignty, including the power over life and death. This power is productive and *pragmatic*, as Blumenberg notes, in his analysis of "absolute metaphors." More than in Shakespeare's representation of sovereignty in the history plays or the late great tragedies, *Measure for Measure* takes the crossing of sovereignty and metaphor as one of its principal concerns, for as the play repeatedly shows, as far as the restoration of law in the play's Vienna goes, they are, in a sense, codependent. Like metaphor itself, which consists of a linguistic transfer of meaning (from $x$ to $y$), Angelo's sovereignty begins when the Duke transfers to him the "organs" of his power, in an operation that does not merely state but, in effect, *creates* power. In this regard, the play's opening question of the "figure" this newly made sovereign will "bear" is not a question of just any figure, but precisely of metaphor as the sovereign figure. For as Paul Ricoeur puts it, metaphor is not "just one figure of speech among others." Rather, metaphor itself could be seen as the sovereign figure of figurative speech. Ricoeur describes the operation of the transfer—the "epiphora"—of metaphor, particularly in terms of movement:

> The second characteristic is that metaphor is defined in terms of movement. The *epiphora* of a word is described as a sort of displacement, a movement "from . . . to . . ." This notion of *epiphora* enlightens at the same time as it puzzles us. It tells us that, far from designating just one figure of speech among others such as synecdoche and metonymy (this is how we find metaphor taxonomized in the later rhetoric), for Aristotle the word *metaphor* applies to every transposition of terms.[58]

It could be said that this is exactly what a "sovereign body" *is*, a sign capable of effecting this transposition. As *Measure* proceeds to figure this re-containment, however, it begins to point to a relationship between force and theater—and the manner in which one arises from the other—that is, now *not* figuratively speaking, built into the very notion of sovereignty.

Sovereignty's representational history is one of movement across pathways of exchange and substitution. From the image used in Roman imperial funerals to "substitute for the missing corpse," to attempts of entire discourses (theology, magic, science, law) to displace competitors from their positions of authority,[59] the history of sovereignty could be viewed as a history of substitutions and displacements. At stake in all of these exchanges and transformations is the formation of a body-of-power and the question it subsequently gives rise to: how to "read" it? *Measure for Measure*'s answer to this question shows us that at least part of what is involved is a competition for control over signification itself. How, the play asks, can we not only signify force, but also enforce signification? The usual answer is through the body. Power writes its force on the body. This is, of course, Foucault's well-known argument in *Discipline and Punish*, in which Foucault reads seventeenth-century penal practice and torture in relation to their capacity to produce the readable signs of sovereignty on the body:

> If torture was so strongly embedded in legal practice, it was because it revealed truth and showed the operation of power. It assured the articulation of the written on the oral, the secret on the public, the procedure of investigation on the operation of the confession; it made it possible to reproduce the crime on the visible body of the criminal; in the same horror, the crime had to be manifested and annulled. It also made the body of the condemned man the place where the vengeance of the sovereign was applied, the anchoring point for a manifestation of power, an opportunity of affirming the dis-symmetry of forces.[60]

The body, in Foucault's formulation, is an "anchoring point for a manifestation of power," a readable text demarcating a "dis-symmetry of forces." Foucault will later develop his analysis of sovereign power by distinguishing between "government," whose objective is "to govern things," and "sovereignty," which has as its aim "the common welfare and salvation of all":

> "the common good" means essentially obedience to the law, either that of their earthly sovereign or that of God, the absolute sovereign. In every case, what characterizes the end of sovereignty, this common and general good, is in sum nothing other than submission to sovereignty. This means that the end of sovereignty is the exercise of sovereignty. The good is obedience to the law, hence the good for sovereignty is that people should obey it. This is an essential circularity; whatever its theoretical structure, moral justification, or practical effects, it comes very close to what Machiavelli said when he stated that the primary aim of the prince was to retain his principality. We always come back to this self-referring circularity of sovereignty or principality.[61]

The "essential circularity" of sovereignty, which has as its "end" its own "exercise," consists of a potentially endless capacity to refer to itself. The "body" operates as a target zone needed to make the power of sovereignty visible. *Measure* makes this general representational requirement—that sovereignty be visible—more specific by explicitly figuring the condemned body as a legible one. The precondition of controlling the body is reading the body. Reading the body, in turn, requires some form of writing on the body. Thus, the "essential circularity" staged in *Measure* becomes a circularity of texts and inscriptions, and the play's construction of power takes the form not only of writing in general, but also of a specific kind of writing in particular—a *legal* writing, known technically (as Claudius himself puts it) as a "writ." As Claudius tells us, his crime, or "entertainment" (deciding *which* one and how sex should be viewed is one of the play's questions) "[w]ith character too gross is writ on Juliet" (1.2.143–4). Claudius's complex syntax here nicely reinforces the fact that language and sexuality, text and sex—and above all the legislation of their relation—are precisely what are at stake. Rather than saying that his crime is grossly "written" on Juliet's body in the "legible" form of her pregnancy, his copulative verb ("is") is made to wait until the middle of the sentence before it can make its binding function known. That the sentence itself begins with the word "character," i.e. handwriting, nicely underscores the dramatic situation in which the legal determination of Claudio's character will have to wait until the end of the play. The sentence performs the play's structuring logic of delay and deferral with regard to judgment and understanding. The production and reading of *lex* in *Measure* requires just such a combination of language and law, body-writing and legal-binding. The term that Shakespeare has Claudio use here to refer to Juliet's body, "writ," invokes a specific legal history having to do precisely with the law's relation to the body—the history of *habeas corpus*. In an elaboration of, as a well as a shift away from, Foucault's argument, Anselm Haverkamp and Cornelia Vismann point out a subtle but important displacement of the relationship between the body and writing built into the history of *habeas corpus*. Haverkamp and Vismann identify an important historical and conceptual shift from the habeas corpus *writ* to the habeas corpus *act*. In the course of this shift, not only the status of the body but also that of sovereignty in relation to the body is altered. As they point out,

The *Habeas Corpus Act* is celebrated as a major success against the king's rule, although the *Habeas corpus writ* had previously been a prerogative of the king. The transition and translation from the king's order to "produce" the body to the liberty of "having the body" are significant, the false understanding of the original Latin notwithstanding. Shifting from "having" in the one sense to "having" in a second sense, the Latin idiom of *Habeas* provides a suggestive bridge and documents a displacement easily overlooked, the literal displacement of the *corpus* in question—it may go as far as "freedom of movement." To whom belongs this body? The king's, the law's, the subject's? And whose subject? To whom is this body subject?[62]

In a sense, the body's "freedom of movement" is also metaphor's movement—the movement to (as Puttenham put it) "enforce a sense." Here, however, this movement escapes the law's desire to contain or enforce any particular sense. Yet a question remains. "Whose is this body?" The sovereign's? The political-theological subject's? God's? However one answers the question, the body remains a necessary target of signification. For as Haverkamp and Vismann insist:

> Without the body there is no act, although the desire for the body is *not* to have the act executed and the power exemplified through violence. Rather the body is to focus the decision, while the decision itself remains undecided between grace and execution, discretion and representation. It is, however, to be taken. The casuistry of substitutions, of cash and delay, rather than the incessant and monotonous shame of executions, keeps the force of law forceful.[63]

*Without the body there is no act*—no activity, action, or play. The theater of sovereignty requires the body for its play. *Measure for Measure* shows that it is precisely this "casuistry of substitutions" that keeps the force of law forceful. The "body" of the subject must remain exchangeable for the successful operation of sovereignty's transfer to occur.

Marc Shell and Deborah Shuger have underscored different ways that *Measure* marks competing historical, legal, religious, and especially sexual claims to this body.[64] More recently, Julia Reinhard Lupton has explored the play's treatment of substitution in relation to the dialectic of the particular and the universal built into the discourse of citizenship. For Lupton, Isabella's choice for her own chastity over her brother's life—"a decision in Carl Schmitt's sense of being made without reference to precedents or norms"—marks the border of "the one immoveable quantity in a world defined by fluid circulation."[65] The public political conception of a *citizen*-body, as opposed to the private theological construction of the secret interiority of the *believer*'s body, form the two poles of contention in which the subject is simultaneously connected to and disconnected from the world.[66]

All of these bodies depend on a certain theologico-political *desire*. In *Measure*'s "unfolding" of the "properties of government," this desire is displaced in a series of substitutions, all organized around sovereignty's need for a "body": the Duke's, the legal subject's, and, finally, as Louis Marin puts it, the body of representation itself:

> Representation in and through its signs represents force: as delegates of force, signs are not the representatives of concepts but rather the representatives of force, which can be grasped only in their representation effects: the power-effect of representation is representation itself.[67]

Representation, for Marin, puts force into signs. Unlike Haverkamp and Vismann's observation that the body, in law, and in the *habeas corpus* act, in particular, is to "focus the decision" and not to "exemplify power through violence," Marin sees in all representation not a "focusing" device, but rather a force that arises out of the destruction of another, inferior power. Representation, for Marin,

> carries out the substitution for the exterior act, where a force is manifested in order to annihilate another force in a struggle to the death, of signs of force, which need only be *seen* as a force to be *believed*...
>
> A force is force only through annihilation, and in this sense all force is, in its very essence, absolute, since it is such only to annihilate all *other* forces, to be without exterior and incomparable.[68]

But what is a force that is "without exterior" and "incomparable"? How is it to be made representable if it cannot be compared to anything? What "figure" can bear it? For Marin, this kind of force becomes visible only through its effects. These are precisely what allow one to retrospectively fill out the conceptual body-of-power. Marin explains this by putting power and representation into the dynamic relation of a rhetorical chiasmus:

> Power is the tendency toward the absolute of the infinite representation of force, the desire for the absolute of power. From then on,

representation (whose effect is power) is at once the imaginary satisfaction of this desire and its real deferred satisfaction. In representation that is power, in power that is representation, the real—if one understands by "real" the always deferred satisfaction of this desire—is none other than the fantastic image in which power will contemplate itself as absolute.[69]

Power is produced through a reciprocal capture of the mirror. The paradox of Marin's theory, as well as of political-theological representation on the whole, is that the "real" (in Spanish, the "royal," *real*) is the image itself. It is the image that satisfies the subject's "desire for the absolute of power." Power, here, is the Real. And the Real is always deferred. The Real is an image. Marin takes this desire for an almost universal condition, in which the subject, as a desiring machine, is always constituted by a representation that comes in the form of a "fantastic" image:

> How, then, is representation the satisfaction of the desire for the absolute that animates the essence of all power, if it is not by being the imaginary substitute for this satisfaction, that is by being an image? The portrait of the king that the king contemplates offers him the icon of the absolute monarch he desires to be . . . The king is only truly king in images.[70]

Representation and desire move in a circular way here, caught up in the "essential circularity of sovereignty" Foucault describes. Representation for Marin is something both more and less than satisfying at once. By being an "imaginary substitute" for that which satisfies the desire for the absolute, representation keeps the signifying chain moving. For Marin, the king himself is never, in fact, his—sovereign—self. Rather, that self is *produced* in the movement between the king's gaze and the image of himself that he contemplates in his portrait. Between gaze and portrait is created a circuitry of desire that keeps the circularity of sovereignty turning. Sovereignty is thus a desire machine, or, rather, a *desiring* machine. It desires to have the body that it is not, since this desire is never fully satisfied other than by "imaginary substitutes." "Representation" is Marin's name for that which provides "the satisfaction of the subject's desire for the absolute," a desire that is never fully satisfied, except through a ceaseless production of more substitutional figures. This condition, he argues, "animates the essence of all power."[71]

Yet if the "power-effect of representation is representation itself," then this "effect" meets its limit with at least one figure in *Measure for Measure*. Barnadine simply refuses to participate in the economy of exchanges needed to keep the desiring machine desiring. His veto of his own execution (extremely strange, given his seemingly powerless position) obstructs the processes of transfer the play has been running on, and thereby renders the "casuistry of substitutions" ineffective:

> DUKE: Sir, induced by my charity, and hearing how hastily you are
> to depart, I am come to advise you, comfort you, and pray with
> you.
> BARNADINE: Friar, not I. I have been drinking hard all
> night, and I will have more time to prepare me, or
> they shall beat out my brains with billets. I will not
> consent to die this day, that's certain.
> DUKE: O sir, you must; and therefore I beseech you
> Look forward to the journey you shall go.
> BARNADINE: I swear I will not die today for any man's persuasion.
> DUKE: But hear you—
> BARNADINE: Not a word. If you have anything to say to me, come to
> my ward: for thence will not I today. *Exit*
>
> (4.3.49–62)

Barnadine's response halts the disguised Duke. His refusal to listen to the "Friar's" advice silences the sovereign. Immediately after this, the Provost asks him how he finds the prisoner, and the Duke replies: "A creature unprepar'd unmeet for death; / And to transport him in the mind he is / Were damnable" (4.3.66–8). The play's "law of substitution" would seem to meet its limit with Barnadine, who stops *Measure*'s "organ transplant" operation dead in its tracks: "Not a word." No more discussion. The exchanges of law's desire for death seem to have ended here. And, as Jacques Lezra notes, Barnadine "threatens to interrupt the path of any criticism based upon the trope of substitution."[72] To "transport him in the mind he is / Were damnable." To "transport" is also, as we have seen, Puttenham's description of what metaphor does. In Puttenham's view (following Aristotle's), it is the very function of metaphor. Thus, as Lezra points out, to stop the "transport" would be to break down the "tropological system," would be, that is, to break down the system necessary for the perpetuation of sovereignty.[73] Where Barnadine arguably breaks down the sovereignty system, he does not quite undo its reliance on metaphor. What *Measure* shows, rather, is sovereignty's continuing need for metaphorical substitution. Substitution ends up becoming to sovereignty what metaphor is to language: the representational transfer that doesn't "supply" but rather defers or displaces judgment, while restoring order at the same time.[74] Substitution underlies the hermeneutical transfer that enables the movement from what Agamben calls a law-void, to the actualization of power. As long as it is able to speak through an institution (Church, prison) that effectively figures its authority to "have" the body, sovereignty works. *Measure* shows that what sovereignty requires above all is that the chain of deferrals and deferments needed to keep the law forceful be kept intact. Hence, the "organ transplant" that opens the play and that, ultimately, re-vivifies the body politic not only names a one-time operation, but rather becomes a figure for the ongoing making, unmaking, and remaking of the conceptual "body" of sovereignty itself. Surpassing mere transport, the organ transplant figure reveals a logic of representation in which success depends on the body's capacity to receive the new part, to keep what Foucault calls its "self-referential circularity" alive. In this sense the power of sovereignty is the power of representation to have the body it desires. Just as the history of *habeas corpus* bears a distinction between the "habeas" of the law's desire "to have" and that of its desire to *produce* the juridical body in question, *Measure*'s organ transplant figure also reveals a certain displacement in relation to the body-of-power. In the play, sovereignty perpetuates itself through an ongoing presentation of representational bodies, all which collectively reanimate the body-of-power and the force of law. It successfully presents and re-presents itself only as long as it is able to effectively employ the signs of absolute power, which as Schmitt argues, it draws from a theological body of concepts and transfers to the political-juridical corpus. It does this not concretely, but through a logic of representation that mirrors the political-theological operation in Schmitt's secularization thesis—if only to undo it. For as Kantorowicz has shown, the very being of a "king," who doubles the image of God, depends on the success of this operation: "the king, otherwise an individual man, is *in officio* the type and image of the anointed in heaven and therewith of God."[75] The actualization of this image requires that properties formerly reserved for the church be transferred to the law.[76] The representational logic of the organ transplant is theological and theatrical at once, allowing for what Derrida calls the "[p]roduction and reproduction of the unproducible absent in place."[77]

In both cases, the bodies made present—of power and of law, but also of the subject, and of the community—are produced through the representational effects of a transfer.[78]

### THE "PROBLEM" WITH THE PLAY

If, however, the "body" in *Measure for Measure* satisfies what Haverkamp and Vismann call the law's institutional desire to *cite* it, the play at the same time questions the legitimacy upon which this satisfaction rests. Barnadine's refusal to be executed, through a double negation of self and language: "Friar, not I" (4.3.52) and "Not a word" (4.3.61)[79]; Lucio's constant interruptions; Angelo's preference for death to marriage with Mariana; and Isabella's silence in the fifth act[80] all represent forms of resistance to a completely satisfied desire. And all also problematize the play as comedy, even before its famously unsatisfying quadruple marriage and conclusion.[81] For contrary to what occurs in Shakespeare's romantic comedies—in which the "casuistry of substitutions" Haverkamp and Vismann allude to affirms what Nancy Leonard describes as "a versatility of the self"—selfhood and sovereignty here are both subsumed in a legal structure that relies on the exchange of the un-exchangeable.[82] Quite apart from the similarity that satisfies law, *Measure*'s figures of sovereignty continually frustrate an operation of comparison that relies on substitution.

The "body of the condemned" resists sovereignty's desire to write its mark on it. "Not a word," Barnadine insists, making clear that sovereignty's desire for a "body" is not only always satisfied but also terminated by the operation of similarity: "like doth quite like . . ." (5.1.408). And in this sense, too, *Measure*'s closing substitutions of body parts for life not only doubles but also, finally, cancels the operation that has been effective throughout the play:

> . . . sweet Isabel, take my part;
> Lend me your knees, and all my life to come
> I'll lend you all my life to do you service.
> (5.1.428–30)

This final proposed exchange of body parts (Isabella's "knees") for Mariana's "life to come"—is met with one of Shakespeare's famous silences. Here, the closing exchange re-introduces the operation of substitution underlying *Measure for Measure*'s rhetoric from the start—but with a difference:

> Most bounteous sir:
> Look, if it please you, on this man condemn'd
> As if my brother liv'd. I partly think
> A due sincerity govern'd his deeds
> Till he did look on me. Since it is so,
> Let him not die. My brother had but justice,
> In that he did the thing for which he died:
> For Angelo,
> His act did not o'ertake his bad intent,
> And must be buried but as an intent
> That perish'd by the way. Thoughts are no subjects;
> Intents, but merely thoughts.
>
> (5.1.442–52)

As Debora Shuger argues, Isabella's pleas for Angelo's life by distinguishing his thoughts from his actions invoke the jurisdictional boundaries traditionally understood to prevail between state and church, civil and ecclesiastical law: "The claim advanced by the papal theologians of the eleventh and twelfth centuries that civil law dealt with crime, canon law with sin was precisely an attempt to untangle them, to differentiate the state from the church. The line they drew followed the seam between body and soul. . . ."[83] Isabella's thought seems to follow the contours of this seam throughout the entire play, and it is not at all clear, at the play's end, whether she will be able to make the transition from one sphere to the other, or, rather, whether she will continue to inhabit the borderline position that she seems to maintain from the beginning of the play. (Recall that we meet Isabella in the nunnery in the first act, "wishing a more strict restraint" [1.4.4] but "as yet unsworn" [1.4.9].) *Measure* closes with the presentation—as well as the return—of the body whose status has been in question since the opening scenes of the play. The Provost brings on to the stage the muffled (covered) Claudio:

> PROVOST: This is another prisoner that I sav'd,
>     Who should have died when Claudio lost his head;
>     As like almost to Claudio as himself.
> DUKE: [to Isabella] If he be like your brother, for his sake
>     Is he pardon'd; and for your lovely sake
>     Give me your hand and say you will be mine.
>     He is my brother too—
>
> (5.1.485ff)

Or he presumably will be. If she were to marry the Duke, then Claudio would become the Duke's brother-in-law. *Measure*'s restoration of sovereignty both works and leaves us uncertain. Its construction of power, in which force is actualized through a representational transfer, operates according to the logic of metaphor, a logic with effects and demands. Like sovereignty, metaphor needs a body in order to produce its power-effects. And like both sovereignty and metaphor, the operation of substitution is both what keeps the law forceful in *Measure for Measure*—or rather restores force to a law that had been "asleep"—and at the same time endows the "law" in Vienna with a somewhat dubious being. As we have seen, the law's desire for the body in *Measure for Measure* is constantly deferred rather than finally satisfied. But the deferral itself is effective—and along with sovereignty's need for a body, any body, could be seen as a representational paradigm for the representation of theo-political sovereignty. Shakespeare's staging of sovereignty-*as*-substitution presents a glimpse of the imminent replacement of one representational mode, centered on the symbolic body of the ruler, by another, in which power is already beginning to break off from the king's physical body and assume another form.[84] From its opening question of the "figure" power will bear in the sovereign's absence, to its closing re-containment of the bodies at its disposal, *Measure for Measure* thus answers its own opening question of the figure sovereignty will bear not so much with a single trope as with a process (of representational substitution), as well as a logic of transplant, that we can take as a paradigm in Agamben's sense, i.e., as a kind of example. This figure of sovereignty not only writes its force on the body, but also attempts to make sense of this writing in terms of the organ transplant logic. Between the function of a metaphor to (as Puttenham puts it) "enforce a sense" and a Catholic conception of non-metaphorical representation as that which supplies a body lies a void and empty space. Although the law in *Measure for Measure* works hard to fill this space by providing the requisite imaginary substitutes for that which it desires (the body), that desire remains, in the end, only temporarily satisfied. Yet, for now, it is satisfied by what is provided for it on stage and in the "empty space" (as Peter Brook calls it) of theater itself. What is at stake in this space is not only the making present of the absent authority of sovereign power, but also the conferring of that power's sense itself.[85] Like Almodóvar's Agrado, *Measure for Measure* presents a new sense of sovereignty as a juridical and theatrical production of the body. Before this operation will become complete, however, the historical body-of-power will resist the organ transplant logic and present in its place another figure of sovereignty, the construction of which forms the subject of my next chapter. For now, I close with *Measure for Measure*'s presentation of a first paradigm, and a first representational logic of the construction of political-theological sovereignty, in which the law's desire for a body is satisfied through the figure of the organ transplant.

CHAPTER 3

# Resistance: Waiting for Power in *Fuenteovejuna*

The sovereign is the representative of history. He holds the course of history in his hand like a sceptre. This view is by no means peculiar to the dramatists. It is based on certain constitutional notions. A new concept of sovereignty emerged in the seventeenth century from a final discussion of the juridical doctrines of the middle ages. The old exemplary problem of tyrannicide became the focal point in this debate.

—Walter Benjamin, *The Origin of Tragic Drama*, 65

Great is the confusion of a Christian judge
when, in an atrocious case, Fuente Ovejuna
with a daring and vengeful hand
without God, without King, without law, unifies
itself *de facto* around a barbarous and inhumane act
in which no clarity is to be found.
Who might be guilty, who innocent in a
community of so many people?

—Sebastián de Covarrubias Orozco, *Emblemas morales*,
Madrid, 1610, f. 297

Can a patrimony of organs revolt against a normalizing order? . . .

—Julia Kristeva, *The Sense and Non-Sense of Revolt*[1]

How to make politics sweet? Natural? Nourishing? Not only for the "good life," but for *all* life? "How is it possible to 'politicize' [what Aristotle refers to as] the 'natural sweetness' of *zoë*?"[2] These are among the questions Giorgio Agamben asks in his philosophical critique of sovereignty, *Homo Sacer: Sovereign Power and Bare Life*. The following chapter explores one, baroque, response to Agamben's questions, as well as to the question of sovereignty itself, as it has been posed for us so far by the analogy and metaphor logics of *Richard II* and *Measure for Measure*. Turning from the *tears* and "organ-transplant" perspectives of power staged by Shakespeare to the Spanish stage of Shakespeare's contemporary Lope de Vega (1562–1635), we see a different paradigm and problem for sovereignty.

## The Case of Fuenteovejuna

On April 23, 1476, in a small village near Córdoba in the south of Spain, the commander of the military-religious Order of Calatrava was dragged from his house, murdered, and mutilated by a furious mob of peasant men, women, and children. According to the chronicles, his body parts were carried off in different directions and publicly paraded—especially, of course, the head.[3]

Read as an "answer" to the questions of sovereignty posed by *Measure for Measure*, *Fuenteovejuna* responds by staging a number of productive and disturbing contradictions. The most immediate of these has to do with the concept of sovereignty itself. If, as the last chapter showed, *Measure for Measure* stages a successful restoration of power to a diseased body politic through a representational logic of the "organ transplant," then Lope's *comedia* responds to the crisis of sovereignty in a different way. While the sovereignty question *Fuenteovejuna* asks is similar to that posed by *Measure for Measure* ("how to 'supply' its 'absence'?"), the response Shakespeare's play offers (through representational substitutions) no longer works in Lope's. Reading the two plays together for the representational and conceptual questions and answers they raise about sovereignty, then, requires that we re-imagine the problem and its demands. More specifically, each asks how to restore order to a "body" that has either been rotting in the absence of law, or, as we will see here, on the verge of internally destroying itself, through civil war. While in both cases, the body politic is threatened by a law that is either divided or perverted in some way, Lope's play will figure the people's response to that threat in a different way from that which we have seen in *Measure for Measure*.

One way to understand this difference is to consider the immediate concerns of each play. Where *Measure for Measure* explores tensions between political and theological modes of rule in relation to English Puritanism (the play was written in 1604, the year James signed a peace treaty with Spain, one year before the Gunpowder plot, and two years before the Oath of Allegiance controversy and its subsequent reprisals against English Catholics), the immediate political concerns surrounding Lope's play are different.[4] Written roughly ten years after *Measure for Measure*, *Fuenteovejuna* explores the transition from feudal to absolute structures of power in the face of the problem of tyranny.[5] Additionally, each is based on a different kind of source material. Where

Shakespeare's dark comedy reworks material from the morality play stories of the "corrupt magistrate" and "disguised ruler" (as well as the "substituted bedmate") from Giraldi Cinthio's *Hecatommithi* (1565) and *Epitia* (1583), and George Whetstone's *The Right Excellent and Famous Historye of Promos and Cassandra* (1578), Lope's play is based on chronicle accounts of relatively recent events in Spanish history.⁶ At the same time, despite these differences between the "fabular" and the historical in source material, both plays witness a deep cultural and conceptual anxiety about the problem of sovereignty. These include worries over its foundation, preservation, and representation.

As we have seen in *Measure for Measure*, if the "organ-transplant" logic of representation staged there suggests anything about the demands of theo-political sovereignty, it is that the law desires to "have" the body—whether in person, or through a substitute representative. Where Shakespeare ultimately figures this desire as satisfied through the operation of representational transfers and a sufficient "supply" of heads, Lope's play poses a complication to the "organ-transplant" logic. Here the attempt to perform such an operation and restore sovereignty will meet with a case of resistance that gives pause to the body-of-power. Sovereignty in *Fuenteovejuna* becomes a matter of time.

Lope de Vega was fifty years old in 1612 when he wrote *Fuenteovejuna* at the height of his creative powers.⁷ Several years earlier, he had given a speech to the literary Academy of Madrid that would become a famous manifesto regarding the "new art of writings plays," *El arte Nuevo de Hacer Comedias* (1609).⁸ In his speech, Lope was very specific about how the playwright should deal with time:

> El sujeto elegido escriba en prosa
> y en tres actos de tiempo le reparta,
> procurando, si puede, en cada uno
> no interrumpir el término del día.
>
> Write out the plot in prose, dividing it
> into three acts, three sequences of time
> contriving, if you can, within each one,
> not to disrupt the time-frame of a day.
>                                   (211–14)⁹

Each one of the *comedia*'s acts was to contain its own temporal sequence. Each act was a performance of its own time. The trick for the playwright, then, according to the treatise, was to not to allow an interruption (what

Schmitt might call an "irruption" [*Einbruch*]) of time in between: "No interrumpir." "Do not disrupt the time-frame of a day." Despite the three separate sequences within each act, the day and the play were also to appear to move continuously through time. Maintaining this combination of autonomous sequence *and* non-interruption was crucial to holding the audience in suspense:

> ponga la conexión desde el principio
> hasta que vaya declinando el paso,
> pero la solución no la permita
> hasta que lleque a la postrera escena;
> porque en sabiendo el vulgo el fin que tiene,
> vuelve el rostro a la puerta y las espaldas
> al que esperó tres horas cara a cara;
> que no hay más que saber que en lo que para.[10]

> . . . show how the plot develops from the start
> up to the point when things begin to change,
> but don't allow the outcome to be obvious
> until you reach the very final scene,
> for once the audience guess the end they turn
> their faces to the exit, and their backs
> on actors who've been three hours on the go;
> how all concludes is all they want to know.
> (232–9)[11]

It is not only, then, that the new form has to be a hybrid one, something in-between the comic and tragic modes; it also has to hold its audience's attention and keep them waiting—*until* the very end: "*Until you reach the very final scene*" ("hasta que vaya declinando el paso, / pero la solución no la permita / hasta que lleque a la postrera escena"). "[H]asta que vaya *declinando* el paso," which Dixon's renders as—"up to the point when things begin to change"[12]—is one way to describe how a play moves through time. It declines. The Spanish "declinando" comes from "declinar," which means "to diminish (in health, wealth, or intelligence)"; "to come to the end"; "to change the nature of a thing into its opposite, including from virtue to vice, or strength into weakness."[13] In his seventeenth-century dictionary, Covarrubias defines the term in relation to grammar, astrology, and law:

> DECLINAR. Cerca de los gramáticos es variar las terminaciones de los nombres, por sus casos, con que se distinguen los unos de los otros.

Y así *declinare* es dicernir y apartar una cosa de otra. Declinar jurisdición, término forense, cuando uno se vale de otro tribunal como propio suyo, apartándose del que no le es competente. Declinar el sol, es irse acercando al poniente. Los astrólogos tienen este término de declinación Declinación de la calentura, cuando se va acabando. Cerca de los gramáticos hay nombres declinables, que se varían, y nombres indeclinables, que en todos los casos tienen una mesma terminación.[14]

With the grammarians, "declinar" is to vary the endings according to the [grammatical] case in order to distinguish some from others. Such that *declinare* is to discern and distinguish one thing from another. To *decline jurisdiction* is a forensic term used when one recurs to another tribunal as belonging to your own in order to separate yourself from one that is not competent. For the sun to *decline* means that it is moving toward the west. Astrologers have this term. A decrease of warmth as it is ending. In grammar there are declinable nouns that differ from the non-declinable ones, which in all cases end with the same termination. (my trans.)

In grammar, the word "declinar" has to do specifically with making distinctions of case—and with word endings. With a declinable noun, the ending changes depending on the grammatical case. Dixon's translation of "hasta que vaya declinando el paso," as "up to the point when things begin to change" does not, of course, bear this cumbersome etymological history along with it. Still, as we shall see, it is not unimportant to the subject matter of *Fuenteveojuna* that a definition of theatrical movement should articulate itself in relation not only to grammar and astrology, but also especially to law. The linguistic and the legal move together in time. Time doesn't just *pass* in *Fuenteovejuna*; it "declines," in both the grammatical and juridical senses of the term.[15]

Lope makes time's movement a significant player in the comedia, opening his first act with a Commander, who is made to wait: "¿Sabe el Maestre que estoy en la villa? ¿Y sabe también que soy Fernán Gómez de Gúzman?" (1, 4–5). ("Does the young Master know that I'm here? Does he know who I am?") The Commander of the Religious-Military Order of Calatrava, Fernán Gómez de Gúzman, walks on stage, demanding to know whether his host, the young Master of Calatrava, Rodrigo Téllez Girón, knows that he has arrived—which he couples with the question of his identity: Does the Master know that *he's there*?

The question of whether the Commander has been recognized recurs throughout the play, like a leitmotif. From his initial appearance here, through the opening of Act Two when a soldier similarly doesn't recognize him and asks, "Is the Commander here?" and another answers, "Don't you see him before you?" (1105–6), to the third act, when he is about to be killed and desperately addresses the people of Fuenteovejuna: "It is I who address you, I your lord" (1887)—the question repeats itself, insistently and anxiously. By the time we arrive at this point, however, the villagers will no longer recognize Fernán Gómez as their lord. Instead, while they kill him and mutilate his body, they invoke the names of their new lords, the "Catholic Kings" Isabel and Fernando, of whom the young Master will come to say by the end, "They are the sovereigns, as such I recognize them" ("Son señores soberanos, / y tal reconozco yo" [2150–1]).

As its thematics of recognition and mastery are so central to the play, *Fuenteovejuna* has lent itself to readings of subject-formation in terms of Hegel's theory of Master and Slave. For Anthony Cascardi, for example, "the central social drama of the play asks to be read in the light of Hegel's account of the struggle for recognition." For Cascardi, in particular, the nature of that social drama has to do with subjection: The play "illuminates a mode of subjection that offers resistance to the transformative work of history by the most peremptory means, namely by the cultivation of what Foucault described as the 'fascism within,' the desire of individual subjects to seek their own domination."[16]

A different understanding of resistance emerges in psychoanalytic criticism of the play. For Peter Evans, *Fuenteovejuna* resists the reductive ideology of sexual identity staged in many plays of the period: "In this play, for all its many ambivalences, and for all its own contradictions, Lope allows women an opportunity to speak for themselves, to rise up against intolerable trivialization and victimization by men who treat them only as the gratifiers of their libido."[17] Evans compares the village of Fuente Ovejuna to Freud's Rome, "a psychic entity as well as a physical structure, representing various layers and stages of human development, drives and instincts."[18] Mitchell Greenberg shifts the focus slightly, from the question of whether the play supports a conservative ideology, to its treatment of the "ideology of subjectivity."[19] Focusing on the play's representation of sexuality, Greenberg points out that "the two faces of community, the external ('politics') and the internal (the sexual) are combined in the person of Fernán Gómez. He is the only character who joins the exterior to the interior, the outside world of Castilian history to the inside world of the village, bringing the one into the other."[20] For Greenberg, the Commander occupies a position of "a perversion in which it is impossible to separate political treason and sexual aggression."[21] Greenberg's reading moves us closer to an understanding of the ways *Fuenteovejuna* has participated, historically, in the ongoing production of a political and cultural imaginary. Returning to Louis Althusser's "famous (and hotly debated) definition of ideology," Greenberg points out that the word "imaginary" itself is

> the bivalent hinge uniting the individual spectator to the represented universe and, at the same time, to those other spectators, that is, his or her reality, around him or her. The exploration of the ideology of the play, therefore, would be an exploration of its "textual unconscious": forces in the text that are not reducible to an extratextual reality, and yet maintain with that exteriority very real and tendentious ties. Only in this way, in this crisscrossing of the textual universe and its historical context, might we be able to resolve one of the major dilemmas facing any commentator of a text that arrives (through what circuitous paths) in our present as a transhistorical fragment, a symptom of a vanished world.[22]

Greenberg's assertion that *Fuenteovejuna*'s "textual unconscious" is "not reducible to an extratextual reality" focuses specifically on the play's representational logic. The representational question, in turn, takes us straight to the heart of the play's conceptualization of sovereignty— and of life. Recall that for Giorgio Agamben, the archaic Roman law figure of the *homo sacer*, the "(sacred man), *who may be killed and yet not sacrificed*," exposes a complex in which "life" is always conceptualized by virtue of its exclusion.[23] Sovereignty approaches life and, in a sense, captures it, by including one of its conceptual forms—of *bios*, the "good" or "political life"—even as it excludes another, *zoē*, the prepolitical form of "bare life." Embodying the paradoxes of this exclusionary inclusion, the *homo sacer* occupies a structural position similar to that of the sovereign, with respect to his "zone" qualities.[24] Like the sovereign, the *homo sacer* is not subject to law, but stands inside and outside, within and above the juridical orders at once. Agamben thus describes the space of sovereignty as a "zone of irreducible indistinction" between the juridical norm and the exception—and proceeds to "discover" within this zoning, nothing less than the "hidden foundation" of Western politics itself:

> [W]hat characterizes modern politics is not so much the inclusion of *zoē* in the *polis*—which is, in itself absolutely ancient—nor simply the fact that life as such becomes a principal object of the projections and calculations of State power. Instead the decisive fact is that, together with the process by which the exception everywhere becomes the rule, *the realm of bare life*—which is originally situated at the margins of the political order—*gradually begins to coincide with the political realm*, and exclusion and inclusion, outside and inside, *bios* and *zoē*, right and fact, enter into a zone of irreducible indistinction.
>
> At once excluding bare life from and capturing it within the political order, the state of exception actually constituted, in its very separateness, the hidden foundation on which the entire political system rested.[25]

As we have already seen with Carl Schmitt, for Agamben, too, "the political" rests not on legal norms, but rather on the exception. Unlike Schmitt's *decisionism*, however, Agamben's sovereignty works through the continual production of "states of exception"—which, paradoxically, become the norm, as well as modern politics' hidden foundation. From outside the norm, the juridical exception founds the norm, secretly.[26]

Lope's *comedia* stages a conceptual resistance to such secret foundations. In Lope's play, the logic of representational transfer (or "transplant") that was successfully staged in *Measure for Measure* meets with a certain resistance. *Fuenteovejuna* presents sovereignty's desire to "have the body" with a limit, as the two principal political "bodies" of the play, those of the individual community members, but also that of the body politic itself; both resist sovereignty's desire to contain and inscribe them. This double resistance will not only suspend the "organ transplant" logic of sovereignty we saw in the last chapter, but it will also present us with a new paradigm of political-theological sovereignty. In order to understand this operation we have to attend to the play's construction of both the metaphysical and also the metaphorical machinery of sovereignty.[27] If the representation of sovereignty is the very *being* of sovereignty, as I have argued throughout these pages, then *Fuenteovejuna* treats this being in a complex and unique way. Here, the question becomes not so much how to restore health to a body politic rotting in the absence of law, as in *Measure for Measure*, but rather how to and—whether to—form a new body-of-power, when one of the organs (in this case, also the "head") attacks the body? How can an attack of the political body against itself be resisted? In the course of answering these questions, Lope's play will significantly complicate the paradigm of successful sovereignty we saw staged in *Measure for Measure*.

From the opening scene between the Commander and the Master, the play next shifts to the perspective of the peasants, who despite not being able to read (II.372), proceed to debate the meaning of "love" by drawing on arguments from Plato (*Symposium*) and Aristotle (*Politics* and *Nichomachean Ethics*). Thus, for example, for the play's comic figure (*gracioso*), Mengo, love's "value" is *natural*:

MENGO:
Del natural, os advierto
que yo no niego el valor.
Amor hay, y el que entre sí
gobierna todas las cosas,
correspondencias forzosas
de cuanto se mira aquí;
y yo jamás he negado
que cada cual tiene amor
correspondiente a su humor,
que le conserva en su estado.
Mi mano al golpe que viene
mi cara defenderá;
mi pie, huyendo, estorbará
el daño que el cuerpo tiene.
Cerraránse mis pestañas
si al ojo le viene mal,
porque es amor natural.
        (383–99)

MENGO:
As far as the natural world goes,
I don't deny that it has value.
There is love which rules
all things through a
forceful correspondence
of what one sees here.
I have never denied that each

person has love
proportionate to his humor,
which preserves him in his state.
My hand will defend my face
against the coming blow,
my foot, fleeing, impedes
harm to the body.
My eyelashes will shut,
if something harmful comes to the eyes,
because this is natural love.

                        (my trans.)

"Natural love," for Mengo, operates according to a rule of powerful correspondences ("correspondencias forzosas") that govern all things and whose end is self-preservation. Thus the separate parts of the body function together to protect the whole, in a world figured as threatening and harmful ("my hand will defend . . . my foot impedes . . . my eyelashes will shut"). Consequently, this view leads Mengo to understand love in terms of self-defense, in which "natural love" plays a conservative role, maintaining power relations in their place, state, or status ("que le conserva en su estado" [392]).[28] Barrildo responds that for him, on the other hand, love is a sign of universal harmony and accord: "Armonía es puro amor / porque el amor es concierto." ("Harmony is pure love, because love is concord" [381–2].) To this, Mengo retorts that he doesn't reject the "value" ("valor") of natural love ("Del natural, os advierto / que yo no niego el valor"), simply its harmonious purpose, a point emphasized by the association produced by the concluding rhyme of "mal" / "natural" (398–9). Finally, Laurencia "synthesizes Barrildo's idealistic and Mengo's naturalistic philosophy" by taking the position of Plato's *Symposium*, and defining love as a "desire for beauty" ("un deseo de hermosura") [409]).[29] When Mengo asks Laurencia whether she herself loves ("¿amas tú?"), she answers by introducing one of the central problem terms of Golden Age drama: *honor*. I love "my own honor" ("mi propio honor," I.434–5).

In his seminal study of the concept of honor in Spanish Golden Age drama, Américo Castro reminds us of the medieval distinction between two notions of honor: honor as social reputation (*honra*), and honor as an objective ideal (*honor*). "The language," Castro writes, "distinguishes between the ideal and objective notion of 'honor' and the functioning of that notion as it is realized in the process of life."[30]

Castro's specific phrase "*process* of life" ("en un proceso de vida") reminds us that what is at stake is an understanding of life in formation, life in movement. His decision to examine how these processes are understood on the Spanish *corrales* reflects his view that life processes are not only in flux and in the states of transformation, but that they are also always in some ways constructed and performed. Theater stages and remarks upon the "life process" as it is actualized on-stage. Within this theatrical life laboratory, language, in general, and metaphor, in particular, operate as key processing agents. It is not only that a term such as "honor" plays a determining conceptual and ideological role in Spanish culture; it is also that those roles have to be staged and processed through tropes. This is another way of thinking about what sovereignty's tropes do, and show: In addition to elaborating its "logics," sovereignty's tropes, in effect, also perform its processes. They show, for example, the way that the conceptualization of "life," such as in Agamben's theory, is "worked up," if not "worked out," as Anselm Haverkamp puts it, through metaphors.[31] Concepts are presented and elaborated, if not "solved," by their tropes. Sovereignty works through tro-political processes. "Honor *is*," Castro writes, but "'honra' belongs to someone, acts, and is moving in life."[32] *Honra* is additionally distinguished from *honor* by its association with notions of wholeness and rupture: "The word *honra* appears more connected to the soul of the one who feels that what once existed openly and securely has been destroyed or diminished . . . The *comedia* thrived on presenting cases of fracture [*casos de fractura*] and the reconstitution of violated honors" (my trans.).[33] As Castro points out, honor is less a "concept" than a *contradiction*.[34] Spatially and conceptually, *honra* is distinguished from *honor* by its relationship to wholeness and to the threat of rupture. Castro thus situates "honra" in relation to loss, mourning, and, specifically, to "cases of fracture" that are activated by the problem of the readable body.

Perhaps more acutely than other institutions of the period, early modern Spanish theater understood and capitalized on the anxieties involved in this contradiction. On the one hand, these anxieties can be related to the theater itself and to the kinds of criticism theater generated in both England and Spain. On the other hand, the "cases of fracture" that the honor plays stage are also anxiety laden for the ways that they recognize a constitutional division within the various "bodies" of early modern communities.[35] The topic of honor remains at the heart of the problem of sovereignty in Spain throughout the seventeenth century. In his influential work, *Idea de un príncipe politico christiano representada en cien empresas* (1640) (*The Idea of a Christian Political Prince*), dedicated to the prince, Baltasar Carlos, political philosopher Diego Saavedra Fajardo begins his fifty-eighth *Empresa* (emblem) by reminding the prince that

> Es el honor uno de los principales instrumentos de reinar. Si no fuera hijo de lo honesto y glorioso, le tuviera por invención política. Firmeza es de los imperios.
>
> Honor is one of the principal instruments of rule. If it weren't already a child of honesty and glory it would have to be a political invention. Steadfastness of Empires. No one can sustain him/herself without it.

The emblem treats the theme of *majesty as light*. The engraving depicts two hands entering symmetrically from each side of the frame (emerging from either clouds—or what appear to be ostrich plumes) extending to light a candle, above which reads the inscription, "Sin Perdida de Su Luz" ("Without Loss of Its Light"). The accompanying explanatory text (*epigramma*) cites Aristotle: "Querer exceder en las riquezas, es de tiranos; en los honores, de reyes." ("To want to exceed in wealth is for tyrants, in honors, for kings.") The epigram proceeds to discuss the value of honor in monetary terms: "esta moneda pública del honor . . . ." (this public coin or currency of honor), and is the "cheapest price to pay for great feats and heroic actions" ("el precio más barato que pudieron hallar los príncipes").[36]

Castro's distinction between honor's *being* (el honor *es*) and its movement ("la honra . . . actúa y *se está moviendo* en una vida") endows the latter term with a performativity that the more static and unwavering virtue of the former presumably lacks. While critics have pointed out that by the seventeenth century, this originally medieval distinction was starting to disappear, much of Golden Age drama, nevertheless, revolves around the problem and latent force of the movement of one term within the other.[37] As Lope was one of the first to recognize, theater's effectiveness to capture its audience lies largely in its capacity to harness the power of this movement and transform the conflict of interiority and exteriority into drama. For while the integrity of *honor* could be taken as a universally admired quality, *la honra*, on the other hand, as Lope's audiences knew, always requires a staging.

In his *New Art of Writing Plays* (*Arte Nuevo de Hacer Comedias*), Lope links the movement of *honra* to the power of the new *comedia* form to affect its audience:

> Los casos de la honra son mejores,
> porque mueven con fuerza a toda gente,
> con ellos las acciones virtuosas,
> que la virtud es dondequiera amada;
> (lines 327–30)[38]

> The cases of honor are the best,
> because they move everyone with
> force, [toward] virtuous actions,
> since virtue is everywhere loved;
> (my trans.)

Honor cases provide the best material for the *comedia* because they supply the force (*fuerza*) that moves people toward virtue. Through this force, Lope's "New Art" implies, the honor play collapses the border between spectator and spectacle and thus, on a popular level, assumes the power not only to reflect but also to actually produce its community—or at least to capture the *vulgo*'s attention (and secure their money). For Walter Benjamin, the *comedia*'s reconfiguration of the honor dialectic not only reflects the period's complex understanding of a subjectivity that operates in terms of "recognition" and "violability," but it also participates in the institutional production of what he calls "creaturely exposure" in the sixteenth and early seventeenth centuries: The "unparalleled dialectic of the concept of honour in the Spanish drama permitted a uniquely superior, indeed a conciliatory representation of the creaturely exposure of the person."[39] At the practical and political levels, the "creaturely exposure" Benjamin refers to underlies a social and semiotic system in which the human subject is conceived of not only in terms of "inviolability," but also, as the honor code insists, legibility. At this point, it is worth recalling the centrality of the blood purity statutes that were drafted in early modern Spain as a part of the Inquisition's attempt to ensure a pure Christian State, to begin with by attempting to exclude one of Spain's "internal enemies"—the Jewish other, in 1492. As Georgina Dopico Black points out, this process of exclusion turned out to have paradoxical and proliferating consequences:

If the expulsion and forced conversion program instituted by the Catholic Monarchs was intended to either banish or incorporate (through baptism) the semitic Other under the banner of a monolithic, Christian Spain, then once that program was successfully negotiated and the Jewish Other had been at least symbolically eradicated from the cultural landscape, the need arose for a *new* Other against which the Self could articulate itself. While this vacancy was partly filled by the body of the Morisco and, from across the ocean, by the body of an indigenous, American Other that conveniently appeared on the scene at this precise juncture, its pull was so forceful as to elicit the institutionalization of a secondary division within the category (Christian) that previously conferred sameness. The demarcation that emerged—between cristianos viejos and cristianos nuevos—formed the basis for what would become perhaps *the* central cultural obsession in Spain through the sixteenth and seventeenth centuries; the preoccupation over limpieza de sangre.[40]

As Dopico Black has noted, among the many cultural anxieties that are created by such an attempt to produce a homogenous society, one has to do with the status of the body. The "pure blood" statutes become, in part, an epistemological problem as well as a hermeneutic question regarding the knowledge and readability of the body. The threat of illegitimacy coincides with the anxieties of "legibility" that lead to ever more stringent attempts to reign in somatic and semantic excess. The notion of a legible human body is central to a problematic Spanish political history in which, for example, as the medieval legal codex of Alfonso el Sabio, *Las siete partidas*, puts it, "Jews must be marked so that they be recognized: cómo los judíos deben andar *señalados* porque sean conoscidos."[41] In his important Spanish (Castilian) dictionary (the first of its kind) *El Tesoro de la Lengua Castellana*, the seventeenth century writer Sebastián de Covarrubais Horozco distinguishes between *signal* (*seña*) and *sign* (*signo, indicio*) in the following manner:

> SEÑAL: Unas veces sinifica lo mesmo que seña, y otras el indicio de la cosa ausente, la huella del jabalí impresa en la tierra es señal de que anda en aquel lugar, y por ella suelen los monteros discurrir sobre si es la res grande o pequeña y otras cosas de que ellos están muy diestros. La cicatriz que queda de la herida llamamos señal, y el que la tiene en la cara, señalado, en mala parte y en Buena. Señalado, es

el hombre valeroso, o por armas o por letras, o por gran virtud y santidad, etc. Señalarse uno entre los demás, aventajarse a todos.⁴²

SEÑAL: Sometimes it means the same as *seña*, (seña could have many meanings, but I understand *signal* here) and other times the indication of the absent thing, the footprint of a wild boar on the ground is a sign that it is roaming around that place, and from it (the footprint) the hunters usually infer if the animal is large or small or other things at which they are good experts. The scar that is left from a wound we call *señal*, and he who has it we call *señalado*, both for the good and for the bad. Señalado is the worthy man, whether by arms, letters, great virtue or sanctity, etc. *Señalarse* (*signaling oneself*) among the rest, to surpass all others.

Covarrubias defines the term "señal" (sign, trace, mark) in relation to hunting, scars, and (male) honor in attempting to distinguish between a "signal" (*seña*) and a "sign" (*signo, indicio*). Covarrubias's definition not only notes that *señal* "signals" an "absent thing," but it also proceeds to offer examples—including that of the wild boar that hunters pursue—that reinforce the division between *what* is designated and *where* it is or is not ("the absent thing"). The definition ascends, hierarchically, from the animal trace to the human scar (which can be interpreted as good or bad), before arriving, finally, at the sign that distinguishes the "worthy man," who surpasses all others: the man, in other words, who is sovereign. That Covarrubias's definition of "señal" would itself arrive at sovereignty is by no means surprising. As we have seen throughout this book, between sovereignty and *signs* there is a special relation of codependence—and performance. As Louis Marin puts it, with regard to French absolutism, signs mark the "quite empty place of true justice or science . . . and by doing that . . . [justify] their imaginary justice or truth by striking the imagination."⁴³ *Fuenteovejuna* underscores the lethal effects that this relation can produce, when one institution takes control over the interpretation of its meaning.⁴⁴

The play invokes the social system that both threatens and protects subjectivity. Translating into the language of honor what is fundamentally a politics of blood, the honor code simultaneously structures and de-structures the world of the play.⁴⁵ The commander exploits the code, arguing that raping a peasant elevates her socially by mixing his blood with hers so that she is "honored by it" (998). At the same time, as a hermeneutic system that orders the social and political world, the honor code breaks down strikingly in *Fuenteovejuna*, along with other forms of writing and reading in the play. Act Two opens with the astrologers' inability to read the present (869ff); Mengo cannot read (yet knows the arguments of Plato, Aristotle, and the Scholastics—and even, anticipatorily on self-defense) [372]), and the fashion of the day is to speak (like *Measure for Measure*'s "Elbow") in disjointed language that mis-names and refers to what is not (320ff). The play's reflections on language, and the "logic" of breakdown it makes visible, include the theological, political, and aesthetic systems involved in performing the village's "normative function." All come together at the level of the body. As Dopico Black points out, the honor code is itself a problem that focuses on three different "bodies"—that of the wife, the linguistic sign, and the Other. Linking all three are theoretical questions involved in the much-discussed Catholic "sacraments of transformation." As Dopico Black notes, these are

> all heatedly (and at times bloodily) debated in early modern Europe and America and, given their importance to Counter Reformation theology, politics, and even aesthetics, the subject of long sessions at Trent: the one flesh doctrine of matrimony (which putatively renders the wife of the same flesh as her husband), the transubstantial conversion of the *hoc est corpus meum* (that converts the bread of Communion to the body of Christ), and the baptismal conversion of the Jewish or Islamic or Amerindian Other into a Christian, specifically, a Catholic "self."[46]

Lope's theory of the new *comedia* describes its own art of subjective "capture" in terms that have similarities to the "normative function" and subjective formation that Pierre Legendre sees effected by law. Specifically, Lope's theater theory coincides with Legendre's theory of subject-formation at the level of image. For both, subjectivity is traversed by a collective desire that crystallizes in the form of an image. And for both, this subjective "capture" is structured by institutionally generated discourses of "love." In this understanding of "image," as Legendre stresses, affective movement is itself at least as important, if not more so, than any particular visible object.

For both Lope and Legendre, then, what is at stake in the transfer between subjective desire and image is the effect and internalization of power. What Lope describes as the *comedia*'s capacity to "move with force" (particularly when it stages an honor case) anticipates Legendre's psychoanalytic account of the subject's internalization of law. As Peter Goodrich puts it, for Legendre,

> The institution and more specifically the law enters the subject not through rules but through language and through images. The image of power—of the law-giver or sovereign, of God, emperor, legislature or even something as unconscious as the "rule of recognition" or "basic norm"—is a *point of transition* between the public and private space of subjectivity. The structure of that entry of law into the subject is a structure of *love*, or in Augustine's terms it is a *structura caritatis*.[47]

Love marks the subject's entry into the structure of law. What is significant here is that the social images of power that the subject comes to love are those produced in an in-between space: the zone that links but also divides the public and private spheres and their various "orders." Subjectivity arises out of the interplay of attraction and threat that originates and is then reduplicated in the familial, juridical, and religious orders that govern life. For Legendre, it is above all in the familial order that "blood and love [as well as] law and pleasure are most directly mixed and contained, [and] it is for this reason that an analysis of law cannot escape addressing either the role of the father in the institution or the role of the institution in the father."[48]

Read in relation to *Fuenteovejuna*, Legendre's ideas would seem at first to do nothing but confirm Cascardi's argument that Lope's play dramatizes the internalization of authority and bears witness to a "cultivation of the fascism within." Subjectivity, in this view, is fabricated historically by an authoritative tradition whose function it is to produce an internalization of the paternal image. The Law-of-the-Father inscribes itself in the subject, in a "writing" that takes the form of "love." For Legendre, the "internal principle or inscription of authority also helps explain the coincidence of power and love, of normativity and desire. The institutional structure of submission is infantile, the subject loves the law like a child loves its parents."[49] The legal structure thus mimics a psychic structure that, in Freud's view, is always already constituted by resistance.[50] As Peter Goodrich explains,

> What law institutes, in other words, is not simply an exterior limit or subjection, but equally an interior emotional structure which will bind the subject through fear and through love, through fascination and through fealty, to the theater of justice and truth.[51]

*Fuenteovejuna* consistently figures this *binding* of the subject to the legal and political orders (feudal, familial, and royal) that constitute the play's world as a relation of "love." At the same time, perhaps one of the most interesting aspects of the play is that it simultaneously stages resistance to this binding, in the name of love or law, by presenting an alternative "theater of justice and truth" in which the institution of binding (what Legendre calls power's performance of the "normative function") is delayed or (as we shall see) at least deferred. For while the villagers fear the Law (the "prototype," God, the Father), their response to its institutionalizing desire, at the same time, inverts the power relations that legal force depends on for its capture of subjectivity. If sovereignty "speaks" through the institutional orders (feudal, familial, and royal) that govern "life" and inscribes its force on the body, then in the play's two pivotal events—a violation and a revolution—the "body" resists sovereign power and frustrates the law's desire to "have" it.

### Revolution: Laurencia's Curse

In the climactic scene of Lope's play, Laurencia, having escaped from the Commander's attempted rape, staggers into the Town Hall meeting, where the village elders are debating how to respond to the Commander's abuses.[52] Laurencia does not so much ask, as *demand*, to know from the stunned men whether they recognize her: "*¿Conocéisme?*"(1718). "Do you *know* me?" The question echoes back to the opening scene and the frustrated Commander's complaint that he has not been recognized. It is a return, however, with a difference. Here, it is Laurencia who is in the position of the questioning Commander. What has happened to her in the meantime will turn out to affect everyone: "I come in such a changed state that my difference throws you into doubt over who I am." ("Vengo tal / Que mi diferencia os pone / En contingencia quién soy" [1720–2]).[53] Laurencia's question emphasizes the complex interactive nature of the honor code and its precarious treatment of life. *Her* difference, Laurencia insists, not only makes the men uncertain of who *she* is, but it also throws them into doubt over who *they* are, or (as we shall see) who they will have become. The code's manner of linking male honor to the public perception of female integrity places both in radical doubt. Not only is one's identity made to depend on the other, but both are constantly in question, made to rely on an always changing "reading" of signs and, above all, bodies.

Laurencia's violation thus throws the men into a state of "contingencia": "Mi diferencia os pone/en contingencia quién soy" (not *de* quién soy—of whom, or over whom, I am). The Spanish term "contingencia" is not identical to the English "contingency," with its connotations of uncertainty, randomness, or chance. As Donald McGrady notes, "contingencia" was "unknown in dictionaries" of the time (Covarrubias has no entry), but it has subsequently come to be known primarily as "una cosa que puede suceder" (a *thing that could occur*).[54] Over time, the word becomes increasingly associated with questions of value and quantity. Among the meanings a recent (2007) *Diccionario de la Lengua Española* lists are: 1) *cosa que puede suceder* (thing that can occur); 2) *parte que cada uno paga o pone cuando son muchos los que contribuyen para un mismo fin* (the part each one pays in a group contribution to the same end); 5) *numero de soldados que cada pueblo da para las quintas: leva* (number of soldiers each village contributes for a military contingent); and *riesgo* (risk). In juridical terms, "contingencia" means "eventuality" as well as "possibility."[55] Not only will each one of these meanings—of temporality, value, military unit, and risk—begin to emerge as Laurencia's speech continues, but collectively, as we shall see, they will come together to throw the men as well as the order on which identity itself is configured in the play into a state of doubt:

> Llevóme de vuestros ojos
> a su casa Fernán Gómez:
> la oveja al lobo dejáis,
> como cobardes pastores.
>         (1742–5)

> Before your very eyes, Fernán Gómez
> took me off to his house:
> the sheep to the wolf you abandoned
> Like cowardly pastors.
>         (my trans.)

The question returns us to the opening scene of the play. Here, however, it is Laurencia, not the Commander, who demands to know whether she has been recognized. Once again, selfhood and power are understood in terms of recognition. Just as Mengo's flesh, after having been whipped, is "darker than ink," and just as another peasant is given an "enema of dye" (1494), here it is Laurencia's body that has been written on and which she demands not only her father but all the village fathers read. Laurencia insists that they attend to her speaking body—that they perceive her changed value. Can they bear to see the visible "signs" (*las señales*) of violation? Before giving them a chance to respond, Laurencia continues, re-creating the scene herself:

> ¡Qué dagas no vi en mi pecho!
> ¡Qué desatinos enormes,
> qué palabras, qué amenazas,
> y qué delitos atroces,
> por rendir mi castidad
> a sus apetitos torpes!
> Mis cabellos, ¿no lo dicen?
> ¿No se ven aquí los golpes,
> de la sangre y las señales?
> (1746–53)

> What daggers I saw at my breast!
> What tremendous ravings!
> What words, what threats,
> and what atrocious crimes
> to [force me to] surrender my chastity
> to his vile desires.
> My hair doesn't say it?
> Don't you see here the blows
> of the blood and the signs?
> (my trans.)

Situated at the dramatic heart of the play, Laurencia's speech not only accuses the men of having failed in their responsibility to protect her and the women, but it also initiates a series of inversions that attack the logic of the honor code. The code, and along with it the responsibility to perform what Legendre would refer to as the village's "normative function," has broken down. The symptoms of breakdown include a rearrangement of the relationship between power, the body, and writing, as Laurencia tears from the honor code its power to subject the woman's body to a "reading," in which not only her own value but also that of the "man" is publicly "written" and read. Laurencia appropriates sovereignty's inscribing function, determining for herself what the meaning of her body is to be—and then (like Almodóvar's Agrado), performs it: "Don't the signs [*las señales*] of violation speak?" "Don't my bruised and bleeding face and my disheveled hair *say* it?" she demands to know.⁵⁶

What Laurencia emphasizes above all is that not only her value, but that value itself has changed: Its determination now lies in her own "account," no longer "running through" that of her father ("por tu cuenta corre") or of the order of fathers at all, which, along with the religious-military order of Calatrava, have all failed to protect her. She will no longer accept their account, or for her own value to be that which is accountable to them. Instead, she insists that they picture what has happened to her, a demand for imagination that comes with its own exigencies for sympathy and recognition: "Doesn't my hair *say* it?"

> Mis cabellos, ¿no lo dicen?
> ¿No se ven aquí los golpes
> de la sangre y las señales?
> (1750–2)⁵⁷

While Victor Dixon translates the passage as "Does this my hair not tell the tale? / Can you not see these scars / These signs of savage blows, this blood?" a more literal rendering might be, "Don't you see here the blows of the blood *and of the signs*?" That is, Laurencia's speech is not only an attack on the men's failure to have protected her, but it is also an attack on the very system of protection itself—including, above all, the sign system of the honor code. Her curse is a curse on the code's practice of reading the body as sign (of purity, chastity, fidelity, and so on). Here, not only are these signs the legible traces of violation, but they have also, in a sense, produced the violation itself and therefore become part of the attack: "No se ven aquí los golpes / de la sangre, y las señales?" ("Aren't the blows of the blood *and the signs* visible?") While the syntactical ambiguity of the preposition "de," which can mean both *in* (as in "los golpes se leen en la sangre") or *caused by* (as in "los golpes que causan las señales") is not a case of a literal reading revealing what a figurative one obscures,⁵⁸ it can, nevertheless, be taken to suggest that the village's signifying order itself comes with a violence that expresses itself on the body—whether that of the individual subject, the collectivity, the institutional structure, or the linguistic form through which all of these are thought. The violence of the honor code "speaks." It is its very sign-system (*las señales*) that becomes legible on Laurencia's body, bearing the (bad) blood of its blood politics in unavoidable fashion. Where formerly the responsibility for the interpretation of these signs had lain with the men, now, Laurencia insists, women will do their own "reading" and provide their own "account." In terms of the honor code and the crossing of language and bodies that it plays on, as Dopico Black has shown, Laurencia's body not only bears the signs of violence as a kind of stage, but it also re-directs them toward the sign-system of the honor code itself. At this moment, the play's various treatments of "signs" begin to converge. Laurencia's question marks *Fuenteovejuna*'s pivotal turning point into revolution. For the first time in the play, a woman refuses to be interpellated into the signifying systems of the village's normative structures. Instead, like Almodóvar's Agrado, she assumes control over her own self narration, twisting the dynamics of the honor code on their head. ("¿No se ven aquí los golpes, de la sangre y las señales?" [1746–53]). Don't the men perceive her changed state, if not *value*? "Doesn't it *tear* their insides apart" to picture *her* experience? Isn't it painful? ("¿Vosotros, que no se os rompen / las entrañas de dolor, de verme en tantos dolores?" [1756–7]). Her questions are "rhetorical" ones, in the sense Paul de Man made famous in his discussion of Archie Bunker's bowling shoes.[59] That is, she is not waiting for an answer. In contrast with other moments in the play, where waiting is precisely the marker of power—or of having the power to make others wait—here, Laurencia is no longer waiting for the men's "answer." The time for their knowledge or action is over. It is now her turn to give meaning to the event.

The various ways in which institutional violence "writes" its force on the body have been explored in the influential work of Michel Foucault.[60] In their analyses of power, thinkers such as Gilles Deleuze, Antonio Negri, and Michael Hardt have focused in particular on Foucault's argument that "resistance is prior to power." For Negri and Hardt, for example, the power of empire is inseparable from the forms of resistance that it brings into being.[61] Lope de Vega could be seen to anticipate Foucault's argument here, showing, in *Fuenteovejuna*, how the exercise of sovereignty leads to not one but at least three levels of material, conceptual, and linguistic resistance. The simultaneity and excess of this triple response is linked to something "ungovernable" about Laurencia's curse. Her curse targets the honor code and its blood politics, which has been largely responsible for the villagers'—and especially the women's—understanding of their subjective "value."

Encompassed in the code are presuppositions of gender, class, race, nationality—and religion.

> ¿Vosotros sois hombres nobles?
> ¿padres y deudos?
> ¿Vosotros, que no se os rompen
> las entrañas de dolor,
> de verme en tantos dolores?
> (1755–8)

> Are you noble men?
> Fathers and relatives?
> Doesn't it tear your insides
> with pain
> to see me in such sorrow?
> (my trans.)

Returning to the question posed to the Queen in Shakespeare's *Richard II*, Laurencia now asks the men what they *see*? As in *Richard II*, the question is linked to that of the departure of a certain form of sovereignty. Her curse is a declaration of the end of an old order of sovereignty, aimed directly at the village's symbolic structure of power and protection. In terms of its figuration of a theo-politics, the curse attacks what Foucault described as "pastoral power," a form perfected by Christian political theology, in which what is at stake is also the governance of something as ineffable as honor: the care of subjects' souls:[62]

> Ovejas sois, bien lo dice
> de Fuente Ovejuna el nombre.
> Dadme unas armas a mí,
> pues sois piedras, pues sois bronces,
> pues sois jaspes, pues sois tigres . . .
> —Tigres no, porque feroces
> siguen quien roba sus hijos,
> matando los cazadores
> antes que entren por el mar
> y por sus ondas se arrojen.
> Liebres cobardes nacistes;
> (1760–70)

> Oh, sheep you are; how well the
> name of Fuente Ovejuna says it.

>      Give me weapons and let me fight,
>      since you are stones, since you are
>      bronze, since you are jasper, since
>      you are tigers—no, not tigers, for
>      tigers fiercely attack those who steal
>      their offspring, killing the hunters
>      before they run to the sea
>      and throw themselves into the waves.
>      You were born timid hares;
>                         (my trans.)

As she continues, Laurencia not only inverts the gender order, she also places the men outside the national and religious orders:

>      bárbaros sois, no españoles.
>      Gallinas ¡vuestras mujeres
>      sufrís que otros hombres gocen!
>      Poneos ruecas en la cinta.
>      ¿Para qué os ceñís estoques?
>      ¡Vive Dios, que he de trazar
>      que solas mujeres cobren
>      la honra de estos tiranos,
>      la sangre de estos traidores,
>      y que os han de tirar piedras,
>      hilanderas, maricones,
>      amujerados, cobardes,
>      y que mañana os adornen
>      nuestras tocas y basquiñas
>      solimanes y colores!
>      A Frondoso quiere ya,
>      sin sentencia, sin pregones,
>      colgar el Comendador
>      del almena de una torre;
>      de todos hará lo mismo;
>      y yo me huelgo, medio-hombres,
>      por que quede sin mujeres
>      esta villa honrada, y torne[63]
>      aquel siglo de amazonas,
>      eterno espanto del orbe.
>                         (1771–95)

>      you are barbarians, not Spaniards,
>      Hens! allowing other men

to enjoy your women!
Put distaffs in your scabbards.
Why do you wear swords?
By god, I swear that only women
will avenge [get paid back for]
the honor [stolen by] these tyrants,
and the blood of these traitors,
and they should stone you,
you spinning girls, sissies,
effeminates, cowards.
Tomorrow you should deck
yourselves out in our bonnets and
skirts and wear our makeup.
The Commander wants to hang
Frondoso from a merlon of the
tower, without let or trial, and
to all of you he will do the same.
And I'll be glad—you half-men—
that this honorable town will be
rid of women. And may the age of
the Amazons return, to the
eternal horror of the world.
           (my trans.)

To curse is to draw a line ("trazar")—a speech act that, like Agamben's sovereignty, excludes what it includes.[64] In part, what is re-drawn here are the lines of a psychosexual economy in which human value emerges not only as a function of speech, but also as part of the wider process in which a society's orders (political, sexual, economic, theological, social, and so on) come together to perform what Legendre calls its "normative function"—a *binding* of the subject to the structures that govern life. Laurencia first exposes the binary divisions of the village's normative order—men/women (effeminates), Spaniards/barbarians, humans/animals—only to then reject them for the possibility of another order: that of the Amazon epoch ("y torne aquel siglo de amazonas, eterno espanto del orbe"). By doing so, she at least momentarily brings sovereignty's fault-lines into view. Lope figures her vengeance in terms of different kinds of economy. Laurencia and the women, she swears, will be "paid back" for the honor that has been stolen from them ("que solas mujeres cobren la honra des estos tiranos..."). Her curse draws the line between the ending of an old set of orders and the potential contours of a new one.

To curse is, thus, at the same time to inscribe one's wish in some material form. "Trazar" invokes the notion of inscription.[65] Laurencia's oath, "By God, I swear that only women will avenge / be paid back for the honor stolen by these tyrants" ("¡Vive Dios, que he de trazar . . .") continues to develop the play's understanding of life in terms of an economy of blood debts. Linking the value of life to payments that can only be made in blood, Laurencia reiterates the honor code's implicit rule: Violation must be repaid in violence.[66] The two are simply inseparable. In addition to her provocative reminder that the honor code plays on and perverts God's injunction in *Romans* 12:19, "Vengeance is mine; I will repay" (*Romans* 12:19), Laurencia's language also specifically introduces what Walter Benjamin saw as the key term of the code's implicit theory of subjectivity. For Benjamin (following Hegel), that term is "violability": "Honour is, as Hegel defined it, 'the extreme embodiment of violability [*das schlechthin verletzliche*]' . . . '[I]t contends simply for the recognition and formal inviolability of the individual subject.' This abstract inviolability is, however, no more than the strictest inviolability of the physical self, the purity of flesh and blood in which even the most secondary demands of the code of honour are grounded."[67] While Hegel's reading may seem antiquated, its implicit understanding of the relationship between *value, violence*, and *violability*, nevertheless, articulates a central problem in *Fuenteovejuna* and also moves us toward a way of thinking that starts to approximate that staged in Agamben's complex topographies. What we see in the "zones of indistinction" between bare life and the good life is a coincidence of forms, which depends, in the end, on time.

In *Fuenteovejuna*, value, violence, and violability are intertwined in a complex system that the village's institutions are responsible to uphold—a "system" Legendre would understand in relation to its ability to perform a "normative function," the binding of "the biological, the social and the subjective (inclusive of its unconscious dimensions) orders which constitute the human."[68] Laurencia's curse makes clear to the men not only that the system has broken down but also that the signs of this breakdown have inscribed themselves on her body. The village orders have failed to protect her, failed in their responsibility to protect.[69]

The play understands this failure in relation to time as well as in relation to a certain notion of accounting. Revenge consists of being "paid back," in blood, for what the tyrants have stolen. As Laurencia points out, *until* the wedding night, the responsibility for the daughter's protection remains with the father; it "runs through" his "account" ("por tu cuenta corre"):

> Aun no era yo de Frondoso,
> para que digas que tome,
> como marido, venganza;
> que aquí por tu cuenta corre;
> que en tanto que de las bodas
> no haya llegado la noche,
> del padre, y no del marido,
> la obligacion presupone;
> (1730–7)

> I was not yet Frondoso's wife,
> so you cannot ask that
> he take revenge as my husband,
> since in this case *it lies in your account*,
> for, as long as the wedding night has not
> arrived, the obligation rests with the
> father, not the husband.
> (my trans.)

According to *Fuenteovejuna*'s symbolic economy of honor, protection, and love, the bride remains a virgin until nightfall. Until then, the obligation for protection resides with the father. Yet even as Laurencia understands accountability in the language of "debts" taken from the old order, her speech also begins to move the play into a new direction. Marking this double movement is a "call" that has become one of the most hotly debated moments of the play. Laurencia: "¡Ah, mujeres de la villa! / ¡Acudid, por que se cobre / vuestro honor, acudid todas!" (1818–20) ("Ah, women of the town! / Come, gather around me, so that / your honor is avenged!").

In order to both render these accounts visible, and also to overturn them, Laurencia calls for *both* a return (*torne*) *and* also a revolution of the village "orders." Her curse is aimed directly at the heart of the system that had previously performed *Fuenteovejuna*'s normative function: its combination of local council and military-religious protection. Laurencia depicts a world turned upside down as a result of the multiple and simultaneous failures of the men—to be themselves, to have protected the women, to be Spanish, and even to be human: all aspects of *honorable* life, according to the previous value system. The consequence is that they have become animals, impotent creatures, and freaks: "hens," "half-men," and "spinning girls," who should be stoned and banished.

This point marks one of the most disturbing aspects of Laurencia's speech. What is, on the one hand, a powerful moment of resistance to political and sexual oppression, Laurencia's curse seems, on the other hand, not only to leave the overtly sexist, racist, and violent presuppositions of the honor code intact, but also to actually reinforce and perpetuate them. It's a complex and crucial moment in the play's figuration of resistance. After rhetorically transforming the village elders into "women," ("spinning girls," "sodomites"), Laurencia also banishes them for having failed to protect their loved ones ("que quede sin mujeres esta villa"). What remains? At this point, Laurencia invokes a new order in which what *would* remain *would* be a state without women: ". . . que quede sin mujeres esta villa honrada, y torne / aquel siglo de amazonas, / eterno espanto del orbe" (1792–5). ("So that this honorable village may be without women / may the age of the Amazons return.") She and the others (former women of the village, primarily Jacinta and Pascuala) are included in the call to replace the defunct patriarchs with the new order of "Amazons."

Lope, more than his contemporaries, held a "recurring fascination" for the figure of the Amazon, about which he wrote at least three plays. But in each, including here, the figure is almost always re-subsumed within the dominant order.[70] Here, the performative effect of Laurencia's curse is to call something—in this case a political order and a time—into being by excluding what it also includes. What the double curse, expressed in the complex temporality of the subjunctive mode (". . . que quede sin mujeres esta villa honrada, y torne / aquel siglo . . .") imagines is a purging that has little to do with Aristotelian catharsis.[71] Here, the subjunctive wish for a new time and being of power—that it remain *and that it also* return—in a sense echoes the performance of the priest's performative words in the Eucharist ceremony: "hoc est corpus meum." Cleansed of its "women" ("effeminates"), Laurencia appeals to a future anterior time—the time of the "will have been"—for a model of revolution in which what returns is the "age of the Amazons, eternal terror of the world." This would seem to almost perfectly correspond to Cascardi's argument that the play presents an "imaginary means through which Spanish society was able to simultaneously confront and resist the transition to modernity, by presenting the processes of recognition as having been achieved by a return to the hierarchies of the past."[72] At the same time, what occurs here is also different in at least one crucial, if subtle, respect. Both of Cascardi's claims—that the play stages a "return to the hierarchies of the past" and that it dramatizes the cultivation of the fascism within"—are contingent upon a certain view, even ontology, of sovereignty that Lope's play seems determined to question. At the center of this ontology is the problem of time.

The version of power in which the subject seeks his/her own subjection presumes an order of sovereignty that is stable over time—an order that Derrida might describe as "self-same." [73] For Cascardi, it is precisely such an order of sovereignty into which the peasants seek to reinscribe themselves: "tuyos ser queremos," "we want to *be* yours" (2434). In this view, their call for a return to the authoritarian and patriarchal structures is premised on the unchanging existence of such orders over time. But the play is *not* merely seeing the future in terms of the past, and Laurencia's call is not a call for a "return" in that sense. In fact, as we will see, this aspect of her vision drops out altogether, and the Amazon order is not mentioned again. Yet it is nevertheless this moment, perhaps more than any other that has produced the most lasting and compelling image of the play. Laurencia's invocation of an Amazon order raises questions of political, sexual, and temporal order. Above all, in the midst of a curse that rejects the existing male orders that govern life within and without the village, it raises (if only momentarily) the possibility of a different power arrangement. One name for such an arrangement, historically, as it has been conceptualized in Western political theory, is "friendship." Laurencia's encounter with the Commander not only puts her into a new state, but it also gives her a new *status* with regard to sovereign power. Such a state would have implications for all of the surrounding orders, from that of the village itself, through the military-religious order of the Knights of Calatrava, all the way up to the sovereign order of Catholic Kings. Laurencia's curse presents us with a glimpse of an order that opens on to a new time. She invokes a world that looks in two directions at once—both backward, toward a "return" of the amazons ("y torne aquel siglo de las amazonas"), and forward, in a projection of the future in which what *will have remained* is a community without "women"—a term that now signifies *all* members of the village in their current dishonored state. Laurencia invokes a double time, a temporality of survival as well as a new form of association of women that has not yet arrived. It is precisely this combination that underlies Derrida's analyses of politics in terms of "time of friendship." In the *Politics of Friendship*, Derrida identifies a "double exclusion" at the heart of the Western tradition of political philosophy: "the exclusion of friendship between women [and] the exclusion of friendship between a man and a woman."[74] If "brotherhood" is the figure of the political, and especially of democracy, then sisterhood, for Derrida, represents democracy's untried horizon. At the same time, the figure of the sister always presents a certain threat to what has functioned, up to now, as a dominant logic within the tradition of political democracy. For "the sister will never provide a docile example for the concept of fraternity. This is why the concept must be rendered docile, and there we have the whole of political education." This reflection, in turn, leads Derrida to a question: "What happens when, in taking up the case of the sister, the woman is made a sister?"[75] *Fuenteovejuna* dramatizes one answer to this question.

Derrida's analyses of Aristotelian friendship hinge on many of the themes that are central to *Fuenteovejuna*: honor, theatre, love, enmity, counting-accounting, and especially the question of democracy. Underlying these all is the problem of time. In his reading of Aristotle's *Nicomachean Ethics and Eudemian Ethics*, Derrida links the question of friendship to time in general and, specifically, to the complicated temporality of the experience of mourning and survival: friendship, "... *philía* begins with the possibility of survival. Surviving—that is the other name of a mourning whose possibility is never to be awaited."[76] For Derrida, the temporality of *survival* relates to the concept of friendship in the form of a mutual giving: the "time of surviving thus gives the time of friendship."[77] "*But*," Derrida continues—and this is perhaps the central point to be made here—"such a time gives itself in its withdrawal. *It occurs only through self-effacement.*"

Viewing Lope's play through the lens of Derrida's readings, what Laurencia makes apparent is that, in order for this mutual exchange to occur, she must first present herself as a survivor of a time that she is, in fact, in the process of rhetorically creating. Derrida reads Aristotle's example of "what the women do in Antiphon's *Andromache*" in relation to mourning. Laurencia, on the other hand, figures her survival *both* in connection to lost honor but also, above all, most markedly in relation to revolution—"y torne aquel siglo de las amazonas" (1794) "may the time of the amazons return." At this moment, Laurencia raises the possibility of a new time and order of sovereignty.

Neither historical nor merely mythological, Laurencia's call for a return invokes what can at best be considered a *possible* political model. Its vision of the political calls up not that of the historical events of 1476 on which the play is based. Neither does it refer directly to the play's 1612–14 historical context, as critics often suggest (a moment in which, according to these same critics, Lope is taking advantage of the known aftermath of the events of the play to curry favor with the ruling power).[78] Instead, the image of Amazon time that temporarily emerges is one whose sense could only really be completed in what is essentially an impossible time. Here, I am invoking Derrida's critique of the metaphysics of presence, in which any understanding of the political must understand its precondition as that which could always only occur *in time*. One of the implications of this for Derrida is that no political "order," least of all that of democracy, can ever be fully present. On the contrary, it is the very definition of democracy that it changes—and more specifically, rotates—in and over time.[79]

What is the temporality of democracy? Is there a link to be found between this and the way that *Fuenteovejuna* imagines the temporal and ontological states of its political crises? What is (to roughly quote Julia Kristeva and Antonio Negri) "the *time* of revolution and reconstitution?"[80] The crux of *Fuenteovejuna*'s treatment of sovereignty, I propose, lies in the play's understanding of the relationship between power and time. At the crossing of the two is the recurring motif of *being made to wait*. That is, *Fuenteovejuna* doesn't figure sovereignty as a problem of time in general; it figures it as a problem of *waiting*. Furthermore, it does so in a way that is not "religious"—if that term is taken to mean "messianic" or eschatological. Rather, the play's understanding of the logic of sovereignty is "political" in precisely the sense that Derrida elaborates in *The Politics of Friendship*. It understands the political specifically in relation to the horizon of time. *Fuenteovejuna* is structured according to a chiastic logic of representation in which power is figured in temporal terms, and time is linked to powerful events. And neither one is understood, primarily, in relation to providence.

From the play's opening scene, in which the Commander is made to wait for the Master, through its closing moment (about which more is still to come) the act of waiting turns out to be the play's governing figure, if not mood. Examples range from the Master's waiting to come of age, which, in the meantime is "supplied" (i.e., vouched for) by the Commander ("hasta suplir vuestra edad") (58); waiting "until the time is riper for revenge" ("hasta que llegue occasion . . . ") (1058); the Commander's reference to the pleasure of waiting: "the spice of waiting" ("Rendirse presto desdice / de la esperanza del bien") (1090); waiting to decide (1465); waiting for the council to begin (1653); Laurencia's abduction that takes place during the waiting period between the marriage ceremony and its consummation (1730ff); and, as we shall see, the return of waiting at the play's ending.[81]

The Amazon myth has a complicated relation to the political legacy Derrida discusses, falling outside of it for the most part. At the same time, it introduces what Derrida sees as the excluded figure of Western political thought: the figure of the sister. For Derrida, the sister provides the most un-tame of examples for this tradition. What I would like to consider here is the way that the order of sisterhood invoked by Laurencia's curse introduces the possibility of a different political and temporal order than the one normally operative—an order that would move according to a different time.

In his reading of various texts on friendship, in *The Politics of Friendship*, Derrida arrives at an interesting connection between friendship and time. As with his analyses of sovereignty, the possibility of democracy, the gift, the pardon and forgiveness—all also central problems of *Fuenteovejuna*—the horizons of Derrida's readings move through and with time. Friendship is no exception. For Derrida, there is a "*time* of friendship." Just as "friendship [itself] is never a given in the present [but] belongs to *the experience of waiting*, of promise, or of commitment," Laurencia's speech thus appeals to a possible future model in which what is at stake is precisely the possibility that the new power lies in waiting.[82] However, unlike the form through which power is exercised at the beginning of the play, when the Master keeps the Commander waiting, and has been understood in the play up to this point, here, "waiting" begins to take on a new connotation. As both prayer and curse, as well as demand to be read, Laurencia's performance opens on to the mode of a temporality that lies at the heart of what Aristotle calls "primary friendship (e protè philía)." On the other side, the antithesis of this temporality shows itself precisely in tyrannical power.

> In primary friendship, such a faith must be stable, established, certain, assured (*bébaios*); it must endure the test of time . . . Plato . . . associated *philía* with the same value of constancy and steadfastness. *The Symposium* recalls a few famous examples. A friendship that has become steadfast, constant or faithful (*bébaios*) can even defy or destroy tyrannical power.[83]

Tyranny, for Lope, is a recurring problem. He often thinks of it in relation to processes of repetition and of the reproduction of order, whether those terms are understood in the historical (Cascardi's "hierarchies of the past"), familial (Oedipal), representational (as we saw in *Measure for Measure*'s substitution logic), or theatrical (*mimesis*) sense. Here, Laurencia's "reading" sparks a revolution in which another body, that of the tyrannical Commander, is dismembered and paraded around the village as a sign of a new order. Later, yet another act of violence on the body occurs when the king's judge is sent to torture the villagers into revealing the name of the Commander's killer. Laurencia's curse, thus invokes the political arrangement that Derrida argues runs counter to the dominant model of sovereignty at work "in all the great ethico-politico-philosophical discourses on friendship," the model of *fraternity*. What the complicated double performance of Laurencia's curse invokes instead is the counter-order of sorority.[84] To return to Derrida's question, "What happens when, in taking up the case of the sister, the woman is made a sister?"[85]

## *The Case of the Sister*

Fuenteovejuna could be seen to respond to Derrida's question, as well as his observations that there is a "double exclusion" in politics, each side of which focuses on one aspect of the particular nature of the crime the "sisters" commit: namely, tyrannicide. In what sense, if any, is this violence a political violence, this crime a political crime—"that crime," as Derrida puts it "in which for Carl Schmitt . . . the concept of politics in its most powerful tradition is constituted: the 'real possibility of the enemy being killed'"?[86] This "possibility" and the politics that, for Schmitt, it implies, are also at play in Lope's work. In order to confront the politics of *Fuenteovejuna*, therefore, we have to ask what kind of enemy Fernán Gómez is.

### The Enemy—A "Love" Story?

The *enemy* is the hidden figure of sovereignty, the inexorable pivot that locks its future into a relationship with its past.[87] Sovereignty, in this sense, needs an "enemy."[88] At least that's Carl Schmitt's view. As is well known, for Schmitt, "the specific political distinction to which political actions and motives can be reduced is that between friend and enemy."[89] Yet the question of the enemy is not so simple, combining, as it does in Schmitt's writings, a mixture of philosophical, juridical, and theological or quasi-theological ideas that ultimately come together to form Schmitt's complex and problematic notion of the enemy:

> [T]he political enemy need not be morally evil or aesthetically ugly; he need not appear as an economic competitor, and it may even be advantageous to engage with him in business transactions. But he is, nevertheless, the other, the stranger; and it is sufficient for his nature that he is, *in a specially intense way, existentially something different* and alien, so that in the extreme case conflicts with him are possible.[90]

Schmitt's definition begins simply enough, first demarcating the political from, for example, the aesthetic or economic spheres, as that which is based on its own autonomous criteria, the friend-enemy distinction, as if these were autonomous zones, before efficiently arriving at what is for Schmitt ultimately important. Schmitt links the question of the enemy to the problem of the relationship between public and private space:

> An enemy exists only when, at least potentially, one fighting collectivity of people confronts a similar collectivity. The enemy is solely the public enemy, because everything that has a relationship to such a collectivity of men, particularly to a whole nation, becomes public by virtue of such a relationship. The enemy is *hostis*, not *inimicus* in the broader sense; *polémios*, not *ekhthrós* . . . The often quoted "Love your enemies" (Matt. 5:44; Luke 6:27) reads "diligite inimicos vestros," . . . and not *diligite hostes vestros*. No mention is made of the political enemy. Never in the thousand-year struggle between

Christians and Moslems did it occur to a Christian to surrender rather than defend Europe out of love toward the Saracens or Turks. The enemy in the political sense need not be hated personally, and in the private sphere only does it make sense to love one's enemy, i.e., one's adversary.[91]

It is not only that the enemy is the *public* enemy (*hostis*), not the private (*inimicus*), says Schmitt, engaging in a philological analysis for the time being. What Schmitt's reading of Jesus's *Sermon on the Mount* ultimately attempts is to demonstrate a conceptual compatibility between Christianity and the politics of war. The *hostis-inimicus* distinction undergirds a political-theological relation based on what Reinhard Koselleck refers to as "counter-concepts."[92] The political enemy is the *public* not the private enemy—*hostis*, not *inimicus*. One's relations with him are, therefore, not those of "hatred" but of *enmity*. What is at stake here is one's "way of life." In the end, what is important to Schmitt is the "special intensity" of the distinction.

"Paranoia haunts the Schmittian state," as Anselm Haverkamp puts it.[93] At the center of this paranoia, in Schmitt's own work, is the problem of representation, in general, and the vexed relationship between metaphor and what Schmitt calls the "concept" of the political, in particular. As we have seen, Schmitt's "sociology of the *concept*" of sovereignty works by identifying "correspondences" between political forms and *"general state of consciousness."*[94] What that "identification" relies on is both the possibility of a structural relation between the two and also a sufficient amount of available forms, whether present or in the future—that is, of a certain amount of *possibility* itself. Of this possibility, Haverkamp writes:

> Schmitt's concept of "the political" is conceptual to the extent that it comes to firm grips with, defines and decides, what is real, the result and idea of which is the political in its totality, as totality. The rhetorical emphasis on the reality of the possible highlights a condition of possibility in which politics is reality because of the "concrete" possibility of the enemy as the always existing horizon of life and death in general. Everything underlies, is subjected to, the condition of possibility that is the political. Its evidence, in short, is no evidence, and its possibility no possibility as such but the latent condition of the enemy as real, a condition which conditions—as a "priority of consequence"—the political and organizes its paranoia as a conceiving of reality in the totality of what is effective.[95]

Insofar as he threatens the villagers', and in particular, the women's, *private* lives, Fernán Gómez would not be considered an "enemy" in Schmitt's terms, for he could hardly be viewed as "existentially something different and alien" from the villagers themselves. Yet at the same time, Fernán Gomez is, of course, *also* a threat to the village's political structure of pastoral power, precisely because he represents a different order, constituted by the notion of blood superiority, in both the class and also ontological (or at least political-theological) senses. The chief critical gain of reading Schmitt's concept of the political together with *Fuenteovejuna* is not that Lope exposes the instability of Schmitt's friend-enemy distinction. Rather, what Lope's revolutionary (precisely in the sense of tropological) play makes visible is that Schmitt's "concept of the political" proves to be no "*concept*" at all. Staging cases of honor that themselves turn on turning—whether it's the turning of the (torture) wheel, or that of the "weak concept" of democracy and the tropes on which it survives and moves—itself proves to be unstable, as the second term further divides into its public and private forms.[96] For Schmitt, it is "only the actual participants [who] can correctly recognize, understand and judge the concrete situation and settle the extreme case of conflict."[97] In *Fuenteovejuna*, too, we see that it is up to the villagers themselves to determine whether the Commander is their public "enemy" or not, and whether he threatens their "own form of existence." Once it is recognized that he does, i.e., that his rapes[98] are indeed political crimes, then it is clear that Fernán Gómez would indeed constitute a "political enemy," in Schmitt's terms, as his acts of violation and humiliation, not to mention the appropriation of goods, threaten the villagers' "way of life." Perhaps surprisingly, the question of the public-private distinction returns us to the problem of reading.

To return to the problem of the Spanish honor code, Schmitt's distinction between the public and private enemy corresponds to the divisions of the honor code posited by Castro (social reputation [*honra*] versus objective ideal [*honor*]), insofar as the meaning of both depends on its *public* legibility. Thus, Dopico Black sees the honor problematic of *Siglo de Oro* drama in terms of a "linguistic containment" that corresponds to

> a social construction that depends, almost exclusively, on public opinion; deshonras, accordingly, must be kept secret. But the

cleansing of a stained honor requires that the perceived offenses be washed with blood. For the "cure" to be effective, it must be publicly inscribed and acknowledged, if not by society in general, then by a worthy representative of the patriarchy (king or other father figure).[99]

The *Symposium*'s examples of friendship capable of destroying tyrannical power return us to the central *crime* of *Fuenteovejuna*: the killing of Fernán Gómez:

> LAURENCIA:
> Parad en este puesto de esperanzas
> Soldados atrevidos, no mujeres.
> (1890–1)

> LAURENCIA:
> Stop here at this vantage point
> Daring soldiers, not women.
> (my trans.)

To Laurencia's assertion that the women are now "daring soldiers, not women," Pascuala counters that they *are* women in at least one respect: They exact revenge for crimes committed against their honor. That type of blood "payment," according to Pascuala, can only be made to women: "¡Lo que mujeres son en las venganzas! / ¡En él beban su sangre!" (1892–3). Where Angel Flores translates these lines as "Only women know how to take revenge! / We shall drink the enemy's blood" (Flores 70), emphasizing the Commander's role as "enemy," Victor Dixon shifts the focus to the women and to the vampiric nature of their desire for vengeance: "What furies women are when they seek vengeance! / We'd best stay here, so they can drink his blood."[100]

In line with the play's inversion of the "orders" of sovereignty, Jacinta, in particular, who has been most violently abused, now craves the opportunity to pierce the Commander's body in return: "Su cuerpo recojamos en las lanzas" (1890–4). Jacinta's rage seems to be more personal than political, a case of hatred for the private, not political enemy. Yet "sisterhood" in *Fuenteovejuna* refuses to be understood in Schmitt's terms, which are under the rubric of a "*concept* of the political" that requires a political enemy. Perhaps, the plays shows, this is one of the reasons that this model remains the excluded possibility of the Western political tradition. For, in contrast to Schmitt, Laurencia's "order" destabilizes a model of sovereignty that requires the figure of the enemy and initiates instead what Peter Evans calls a shift of symbolic spaces "from the private to the public domain," from the house (domesticity) and the river (sex, laundry) to the battleground and the law court."[101] Here in this very un-Schmittian construction of public space, *Fuenteovejuna* proposes its own model of "political love," which is also contra to Legendre's account of the subject's attachment to the law.[102] If, in one view of the history of Western political philosophy, love is precisely that which can *not* take on public political form, because of its "inherent worldlessness," as Hannah Arendt has argued, then Lope's *comedia* can be viewed as a challenge and, perhaps, even countermodel to that tradition. While for Arendt, "love, in distinction from friendship, is killed, or rather extinguished, the moment it is displayed in public," Lope's play begins to suggest a model of "political love" in which the private and public are—at least temporarily—fused.[103] This new "love" is the force at the heart of the rebellion and it is what moves the villagers, just as cases of honor move the spectators, in Lope's view. As Frondoso tells the Commander: "love has moved them" ("que amor les ha movido" [1864–6]). Like the force of honor, in Lope's theory of the new *comedia*, "love" generates a new political energy that leads to revolution and the annihilation of the old political order.

In contrast to the play's nascent order of "sisters," the male "body" that forms during the uprising continues to operate according to the logic of the old order. Invoking the state of exception established by the Commander himself, they vow to kill the Commander and his men—who are themselves "*inormes*" (1805), who stand outside the normal order—"sin orden" ("without order"):

JUAN ROJO:
¿Qué orden pensáis tener?
MENGO:
Ir a matarle sin orden.
Juntad el pueblo a una voz;
Que todos están conformes
En que los tiranos mueran.
               (1803–10)

JUAN ROJO:
What order are you planning to have?

MENGO:
To kill the Commander
without order. Unify the village
around one voice. Everyone
agrees that tyrants should die.
                (my trans.)

In deciding "without order" to kill the tyrant, the village men, in effect, declare a state of emergency, arguing, characteristically, that the only way to restore "order" is actually to step outside of it. This, however, is exactly what the women refuse to do. They present a different case and another kind of "order" altogether:

JACINTA:
Di, pues, ¿qué es lo que pretendes?
LAURENCIA:
Que puestas todas en orden,
Acometamos a un hecho
Que dé espanto a todo el orbe.
Jacinta, tu grande agravio,
que sea cabo; responde
de una escuadra de mujeres.
JACINTA:
No son los tuyos menores
LAURENCIA:
Pascuala, alférez serás.
PASCUALA:
Pues déjame que enarbole
en un asta la bandera:
verás si merezco el nombre.
LAURENCIA:
No hay espacio para eso,
pues la dicha nos socorre:
bien nos basta que llevemos
nuestras tocas por pendones.
PASCUALA:
Nombremos un capitán.
LAURENCIA:
Eso no.
PASCUALA:
¿Por qué?

LAURENCIA:
Que adonde
asiste mi gran valor,
no hay Cides ni Rodamontes.
                    (1830–49)

JACINTA:
Tell, then, what you plan to do?
LAURENCIA:
Let all of us, placed in order,
Commit an act that will horrify
the entire world.
Jacinta, your great injury will be
our corporal; you're in charge of a
squadron of women.
JACINTA:
Your injuries are no less.
LAURENCIA:
Pascuala, you'll be the standard-bearer.
PASCUALA:
Then let me raise the flag on a pole;
you'll see that I deserve the post.
LAURENCIA:
There's no room for that,
since our fortune will help us:
it will be enough for us
to wear our bonnets as banners.
PASCUALA:
Let's name a captain.
LAURENCIA:
That no!
PASCUALA:
Why not?
LAURENCIA:
Because where my great courage is
present, there are no Cids or Rodamontes.
                    (my trans.)

Although Laurencia initiates the address to her "squadron" by adopting the terms and rankings familiar from the military order, appointing Jacinta a "cabo" (corporal) and naming Pascuala an "alférez" (ensign), she suddenly changes course, rejecting the hierarchical classification of the military and replacing the model of epic heroes with one built on what she calls her own valor ("mi gran valor"). She begins to describe an alternative order of power that corresponds with the play's overall plot movement from home to court, a movement marked by a pronounced shift in language, beginning with the term "cabo" itself, which slowly grows, from signifying military ranking (corporal) at the beginning of Laurencia's speech, to its additional senses of "extremity" by the end, at which point it refers both to Jacinta's violation and also to the ending knowledge it will lead to ("cabo"—"to put an end to," "to know what's what," "to carry out," "to know all about the matter"). Here, "cabo" provides us with the added turn, or return, to the play's thematic of reading and power—a relation in which what is precisely at stake is the attempt to get to the end of the matter, the knowledge of truth and power. (Idiomatically, in Spanish, one way to describe reading an entire book is to read it "de cabo a cabo"—"from cover to cover.")

Jacinta's violation ("su grande agravio") leads to the founding of a new order, a "squadron of women" ("escuadra de mujeres") that will re-write the village's power structure *de cabo a cabo*, "from cover to cover." In this new language of power, the women point to the possibility of a political space that would reject the hierarchy ("Cides" or "Rodamontes")—and the language of the military-religious order into new forms. Before any of this is realized, however, a series of debts must be paid.

### *Legendre: Psychoanalytical Jurisprudence*

Like Agamben, French jurist and psychoanalyst Pierre Legendre returns to Roman law to understand the problem of sovereignty. Drawing on one of Jacques Lacan's central arguments—that subjectivity is always produced in relation to an institutionally shaped imaginary—Legendre's psychoanalytic jurisprudence returns to founding juridical and theological texts of the Medieval and early modern period in order to analyze the production of the modern subject. Subjectivity, Legendre argues, arises historically, as an effect of the legal and religious orderings that collectively "institute life." Specifically, Legendre focuses on the historical production of what Aristotle refers to as "speaking being," which it is the task of legal and religious institutions to produce. He describes the task of his "psychoanalytic jurisprudence" as "that of opening an abandoned domain to interrogation":

> It is that of the domain which the Roman jurists evoked by means of the formula *vitam instituere*—to institute life. In terms of a structural logic, which is to say in terms of the order which presides over the fabrication or structuration of speaking beings, to institute life means the following: to bind or to combine three distinct but indissociable registers, to know the biological, the social and the subjective (inclusive of its unconscious dimensions) orders which constitute the human. The ability to combine these three registers is definitive of the normative function.[104]

Like the discourse of political theology, the crux of the "normative function" is its capacity to form bonds. A successful normativization, according to this account, consists of the production of a "speaking being" who integrates the biological, social, and subjective orders that govern life. Thus, a normative functioning (or at least a normative functioning effect) is produced by the institutions (political, legal, theological, economic, scientific, and so on) that shape, or "institute," life at the discursive level. Institutions are binding, in the sense that they provide the subject with the languages he/she uses to participate in collective life. The first of these is the "intimate relation which ties the phenomenon of the institution to the problematic of speech [itself]."[105] Following Lacan's work on the pathways and procedures of this binding, Legendre locates the production of subjectivity in the paradoxical space of the subject's relations to his/her own inside-outside, the space of what Lacan refers to as "extimacy."[106] Here, the bonds of subjectivity are so "intimate" that they can paradoxically only ever appear in the exterior.[107] That which one experiences as the most *intimate* aspect of subjectivity, interiority itself, is always produced in relation to a social and institutional exteriority. Subjectivity, properly speaking, is never properly one's own.[108] What constitutes the human according to Legendre, then, is a complex synthesis of the orders that govern life.

One way to begin to understand this synthesizing is to turn to language, and to the particular terms and logics through which these operations are figured and understood. How do the social, political, and theological orders come together to form what Legendre refers to as a political-theological "dance"? How are a society's ideals transformed into a "second body" (of law) that governs the individual bodies that participate in the construction of these ideals in the first place? Legendre explains this circularity—in which source and effect ultimately converge—through a metaphor ("dance") that he sees as a governing trope of many of the texts of especially the Second Scholasticism. Describing this as a "metaphysical idea which was prevalent in the scholasticism of the Counter-Reformation," Legendre argues that "dance is not a physical question, but rather a question of a beyond of the physical," which it is the job of institutions to convey.[109] As embodiments of an authority that is derived from the beyond—the space of absolute power—institutions articulate a law (including that over reproduction) which the subject internalizes and perpetuates. The challenge of understanding and critically engaging this beyond rests not only with how one imagines it, but also, more importantly, with how this conceptualization leads to an internalization of the rules that ultimately come to govern the movements of one's own body. Legendre argues that "that which this Law signifies" is itself a "body," in particular, the human body.[110] The law, as a body, is always also a mystified body, one that perpetuates itself by governing the laws of sexual reproduction. Legendre's term for this reproduction, in a theory that starts to approximate something like a psycho-political anthropology, is breeding:

> It is on the strength of this complex mystification of the body and equally by reference to the amnesiac discourse which supports it, that the various species of dance inscribe their pervasive formulae. The strongest evidence of this is to be found in the classical forms of breeding, which were later taken up by Christianity and by industrial cultures, which all practiced a particular form of domestication which became intrinsic to our historical forms of organization. They dictated to all the bodies present, standing respectfully and greedy to be loved, a mother tongue (which in contemporary Europe is inseparable from the national language), conformity of manners and of gestures, and a doctrine of rectitude. Everyone comes to dance with the Law.[111]

*Everyone comes to dance with the Law.* Legendre's psychoanalytical jurisprudence provides an interesting theoretical lens through which to view subject formation in relation to sovereignty and political theology. Agamben's *Homo Sacer*, another. In Lope's play, the production of "life," which Agamben sees as an outcome of juridical *zoning*, and which Legendre understands as an effect of an institutional *ordering*, is introduced as a conflict set in motion by the dynamics of recognition.

What we will see here is that what is at stake in the play, specifically, is the notion of a certain resistance itself—not only in its political forms and psychoanalytic forms, which invite us to re-think the problematics of revolution and insurgency, but also above all with regard to the conceptual and representational questions resistance raises for sovereignty.[112] As we have seen in the last chapter, all of these questions tend to converge, historically, on sovereignty's relation to the body. In *Fuenteovejuna*, however, this "convergence" runs into trouble. Unlike Shakespeare's play, in which sovereignty's desire to "have" the body is satisfied through a representational logic of substitution, or what I have referred to as "organ transplant," *Fuenteovejuna* troubles the transplant solution, presenting in its place a complex staging of resistance, at both the representational and conceptual levels. Thematically, the play presents one of the most famous examples in the Western canon of a collective, popular resistance to tyrannical rule. For this reason, it has been appropriated by a wide range of often contradictory political movements, particularly in the nineteenth and twentieth centuries.[113] But additionally, there are the representational and conceptual resistances built into Lope's treatment of resistance. These become particularly visible when Lope's play is placed alongside Shakespeare's.

In his treatment of recognition here, Lope is, of course, drawing on an older, medieval political terminology of love. Recognition, in this sense, is always an act of "love." Thus, the Commander complains to the Master:

COMENDADOR:
Tenía
muy justa queja de vos;
que el amor y la crianza
me daban más confianza,
por ser, cual somos los dos,
vos Maestre en Calatrava,
yo vuestro Comendador
y muy vuestro servidor . . .
Debéisme honrar,
que he puesto por vos la vida
entre diferencias tantas,
hasta suplir vuestra edad
el Pontífice.
(44–58)

COMMANDER:
I have a
just complaint against you;
as love and upbringing
had given me more confidence
that in being who we are
you, the Master of Calatrava,
and I your Commander
and very faithful servant . . .
you must honor me
as I've put my life out for you
in the midst of many contentions
[down to] convincing the Pope to
supply your age.
(my trans.)

The Commander alludes to the debt Rodrigo Téllez Girón owes him for having convinced the Pope to "supply his [legal] age" ("suplir vuestra edad") and thereby enable Téllez Girón to become "Master" of the Order. As in *Measure for Measure*, sovereignty's conceptual and representational demands begin by expressing themselves in terms of the need for a serviceable—that is "legible"—body. In this case, the juridical prerequisites for the young Master to assume his post are met with the aid of the Commander, who intervenes to persuade the Pope to "supply his age," that is, to produce a *legal* body that can step in to fill a political void. In order to do this, the Pope makes an exception, the consequences of which include creating an inversion of power relations, in which the child-as-*Master* acquires authority over the father figure who facilitated his ascendance in the first place.[114] This is what the Commander wants the Master to acknowledge at the beginning of the play. Thus, Fernán Gómez can only indirectly assert his claim to recognition, which he does by invoking the feudal notion of love ("el amor"), which expresses itself through the language of service ("muy vuestro servidor"). The medieval rhetoric of love-as-service undergirds the feudal structure of the Order of Calatrava, whose Commander not only "serves" his young superior by ruling him, but also provides protection to the villagers in exchange for their obedience—as well as their taxes ("love").[115] Repentant, the Master replies to the Commander in terms of the filial relations the play will proceed to develop, and then question:

MASTER:
Es verdad.
Y por las señales santas
que a los dos cruzan el pecho,
que os lo pago en estimaros,
y como a mi padre honraros.
                    (55–9)

MASTER:
It is true,
and by the holy signs
that cross both of our breasts
I will pay you in love
and honor you as my father.
                    (my trans.)

The young Master declares that henceforth he will "*honor*" the Commander as his father and "pay" him with love. The "holy signs" ("señales santas") of the Order that he swears by represent a system in which filial debts, first of all to his own ancestors, require "payments" of love (recognition):

COMENDADOR:
Sacad esa blanca espada,
que habéis de hacer, peleando,
tan roja como la cruz;
porque no podré llamaros
Maestre de la cruz roja
que tenéis al pecho, en tanto
que tenéis la blanca espada;
que una al pecho y otra al lado.
entramabas han de ser rojas;
y vos, Girón soberano,
capa del templo inmortal
de vuestros claros pasados.
                    (129–40)

COMMANDER:
Unsheathe your white sword,
dye it red in battle till it matches
the cross upon your breast.

> For I cannot call you the
> Master of the Red Cross
> as long as your sword is white:
> both the sword you bear and the
> cross you wear
> must be red.
> And you, mighty Girón,
> must add the crowning glory
> to the immortal fame of you ancestors.
> (Flores trans., 37)[116]

In order to legitimize his name, as well as his role as the Master of the Order, Téllez Girón must "dye" his virgin white sword as red as the bloody cross he wears ("tan roja como la cruz") by killing those living in Ciudad Real. Without this symbolic "baptism" into the Order, he cannot, in the Commander's view, justify his "sovereignty" ("Girón soberano") or honor his ancestors ("capa del templo inmortal de vuestros claros pasados"). Thus, as we have already seen in *Measure for Measure*, sovereignty's desire expresses itself as a desire to inscribe its force on the body. Lope's treatment of this desire proceeds by linking sovereign inscription to the wider institutional performance of what Legendre calls the "normative function." *Fuenteovejuna* is thus structured in relation to a series of "orders," from the religious-military Order of the Knights of Calatrava, whose members include the Commander and the Master, through the order of the villagers, represented politically by town council, and finally to the burgeoning new, future order of absolute monarchy represented by the Catholic Kings. Each one of these orders is constituted, in part, by its own "rules for the reproduction of human beings." And each, also, defines these rules precisely in the language of "love."

## Debts and Accounts

As I have been arguing throughout these pages, sovereignty speaks through its stagings. It requires these for its very being. Within sovereignty's own history, one of "the fairest marks" of this "being," identified by Bodin and later developed by Hegel, is the right to pardon.[117] The pardon is a kind of legal forgetting, a swearing not to *"recall misfortunes* wrongs," as Nicole Loraux puts it.[118] For Derrida, who in the latter part of his life devoted many seminars to the problems of forgiveness, pardon, and amnesty, forgiveness is "transcendent to punishment." Forgiveness—"if there were such a thing," as Derrida puts it, in his analyses of justice, the gift, and democracy—would be a private experience.[119] For forgiveness to be "sincere," Derrida argued, it must be private. Is *Fuenteovejuna*, then, a forgiveness play? Is it a "pardon" play?[120]

Lope's play would seem to have little to do with "sincere" forgiveness. It does not present us with a case of a staged forgetting, but on the contrary, a re-staged resistance to the law's desire to have the "body"—whether of its individual members, or of the village itself. The play is not even a celebration of revolutionary violence. It is a memorialization of a revolt and then—almost immediately afterward—a restitution of order. I say "almost immediately" because, of course, in the meantime, horrific events occur: a violent (and particularly vicious, according to the chronicles) murder of the tyrannical overlord, including a tearing apart of his body while he was still alive and public display of celebration over his dismembered corpse, followed by a systematic torturing of the villagers, including women and children. This is what happens "in the meantime," before the restitution of order. It is not nothing. It is also not *forgetting*. In place of a staged forgetting, *Fuenteovejuna* presents a repeat performance of a violent dismembering and remembering. And only then, the pardon. It's not a case of forgiveness at all, in Derrida's sense. It is, rather, one of *resistance.* Contra Dixon's claim that the village is defending Laurencia's (still preserved) honor, not committing revenge, the villagers explicitly understand their violence in terms of revenge. And they do not ask for forgiveness. Instead, they ask to be *given* over to the new order of sovereignty—that of the Catholic Kings: "Tuyos ser queremos." ("We want to be yours.") The crux of the play's treatment of sovereignty, however, lies in what happens next.

After having killed the Commander, the entire village is subjected to torture. The Catholic Kings send an inquisitor to discover the criminal and punish the guilty party—as an *example* to the people (2023) ("para ejemplo de las gentes"). Yet no one will confess, and the frustrated Judge must return to report to the Catholic kings that "not a page has been written that could confirm [the crime]" ("una hoja no se ha escrito que sea en comprobación" [2367–8])—to which the king responds: "Pues no puede averiguarse el suceso por escrito, por fuerza ha de perdonarse." ("Then, since the event cannot be determined in writing, by necessity it must be pardoned" [2445–8].)

JUEZ:
Trecientos he atormentado
con no pequeño rigor . . .
Hasta niños de diez años
al potro arrimé, y no ha sido
posible haberlo inquirido
ni por halagos ni engaños.
Y pues tan mal se acomoda el poderlo averiguar,
o los has de perdonar,
o matar la villa toda.
(2373–84)

JUDGE:
Three hundred persons were tortured
quite ruthlessly,
down to ten-year-old children
I stretched on the rack and still it wasn't
possible to find out, neither through
flatteries nor tricks.
And since it was so difficult to
be able to discover what happened,
you're either going to have to pardon
them or kill the entire village.
(my trans.)

The Catholic Kings' dilemma: They must either pardon the villagers or kill them all. It's no choice, really. And yet it is precisely here, in relation to the seemingly forced choice the sovereigns are confronted with, that the play becomes most compelling with regard to the play's conceptualization of sovereignty. To the judge's frustrated complaint that he, finally, was unable to determine what occurred, the King replies in the play's penultimate lines:

Pues no puede averiguarse
el suceso por escrito,
aunque fue grave el delito,
por fuerza ha de perdonarse.

> Y la villa es bien se quede
> en mí, pues de mí se vale,[121]
> hasta ver si acaso sale
> Comendador que la herede.
> (2445–52)

> Then since the event cannot
> be determined in writing,
> even though the crime was serious,
> there must, by necessity, be a pardon.
> And the village shall remain
> in me, as its worth is mine,
> until we see if another Commander
> appears to inherit it.
> (my trans.)

The truth of the event cannot be "subjected" to legal reason ("averiguarse, sujetarlo [la verdad] a la razón"). The Commander's killing eludes the law's desire to name it, to tie it down, to subject it to legal reason ("averiguarse," related to L. *verificare*—"to verify")—and thus to "have" it. No verification means no possession—and therefore, in this case, no execution. While "por fuerza" is usually translated as "by necessity" or "without remedy," it can also be read, literally, to mean, "by force." One kind of force—the force of law—has now been outmatched by another—the force of the collective body that resists the law. The law's desire for the body is frustrated. Its power has, in Louis Marin's terms, been "annihilated."[122] This leads to the conferring of a pardon, the mark of sovereignty itself, for Hegel:

> Pardon is the remission of punishment, but it does not annul the law (*Recht*). On the contrary, the law stands and the pardoned man remains a criminal as before. Pardon does not mean that he has not committed a crime. This annulment of punishment may take place through religion, since something done may by spirit (*Geist*) be made undone in spirit. But *the power to accomplish this on earth resides in the king's majesty alone and must belong solely to his self-determined decision.*[123]

If we were to follow Hegel, then Cascardi would certainly be right. The play leaves us with an image of sovereign majesty restored, and even internalized. Yet, what *Fuenteovejuna* actually shows is that the power to pardon, the mark of sovereignty itself, in Hegel's formulation, is here inverted, and turned, instead, into an obligation forced upon the monarchs by the villagers ("por fuerza ha de perdonarse"). Because the entire village, collectively, defies sovereignty's attempt to subject the event to a legal decision, the Catholic Kings are *forced* to pardon them. Sovereignty's desire to make of the village an *example* is forced to settle for an *exception* instead.

Still, it is difficult to know whether Lope's play figures an *example* or an *exception*.[124] Perhaps, as the reception history of *Fuenteovejuna* makes clear, what the play offers us instead is a theatrical paradigm of a paradigm of sovereignty itself: a "showing beside" each other the problems and co-implications of the example and the exception. Lope's play thus presents us with an *exemplary* case of sovereignty's desire to speak through—(to "have")—the "body," as we have seen in *Measure for Measure*, as well as a paradigmatic instance of that "body's" collective and individual resistance to that desire. While this conclusion might seem to be belied by the villager's own call to belong to the Catholic Kings ("tuyos ser queremos") at the end, it would be misleading to restrict the interpretation of this call to a desire to cultivate the "fascism within."[125] While that reading is, of course, available, and Cascardi's analysis is not "wrong," it is also insufficient. For as the reception history of the play itself makes abundantly clear, *Fuenteovejuna* moves with time.

In its staging of the body's resistance to inscription, *Fuenteovejuna* leaves this particular case history impossible to fully resolve. What this leaves us with is a "without path"—that is, a genuine *aporia:* an undecidable occurrence that, at the same time, requires a (in this case legal) decision, in order to reinstate order.[126] The effect of this indeterminability is to momentarily clear the political space, as the power of the sovereigns meets its limit. Into this vacuum, the villagers insert their own, founding, act of resistance, presenting sovereignty with a case of resistance that it can only respond to by granting *immunity*, or, rather, what Derrida might call *"auto-immunity."*

In one of Derrida's favorite tropes, he links the language of economy to that of law and biology. Through Derrida, we can link Laurencia's economic lexicon of "debts" and "accounts" to a political and philosophical epidemiology of sovereignty, in which

> [t]he "immune" (*immunis*) is freed or exempted from the charges, the service, the taxes, the obligations (*munus*, root of the common of community). This freedom or this exemption was subsequently transported into the domains of constitutional or international law (parliamentary or diplomatic immunity), but it also belongs to the history of the Christian Church and to canon law . . . It is especially in the domain of biology that the lexical resources of immunity have developed their authority. The immunitary reaction protects the "indemnity" of the body proper in producing antibodies against foreign antigens.

They destroy the system of protection itself, leaving themselves, if only temporarily, suspended in a state, and status without sovereignty—in Schmitt's terms, or any others. The name, or rather the figure for such an event, in Derrida's terms, is "autoimmunity." At the same time, the autoimmunine logic of sovereignty staged in *Fuenteovejuna* also differs from Derrida's account in (at least) one crucial regard. While immunodepressants may be administered to humans to "facilitate the tolerance of certain organ transplants," it is precisely the attempt to transplant a new organ into the old "body" that *Fuenteovejuna* rejects. The only immunity they receive is a legal immunity for the killing of Fernán Gómez. He is killed, not with impunity (as if he were Agamben's *homo sacer*) but rather with immunity, because the act of collective resistance (led by an order of sisterhood destined to disappear) explodes all of the old orders that had previously performed (in Legendre's terms) the village's "normative function."[127] *Fuenteovejuna*'s villagers receive legal immunity. They are exempted from the charges of homicide. Lope's play stages the failure of feudal relations, based on reciprocal duties of protection for obedience ("love"). Instead, the villagers' destruction of the Commander could be seen to produce its own type of "autoimmune" response.

It would be nice at this point to argue that the play itself replaces a politically repressive form ("political love") with what I have been edging toward describing as a better, more democratic model. But that's not exactly what we see either. Rather, the Amazonian order of sisterhood, which Laurencia invokes, is activated but not actualized in the play. We glimpse its possibility, but not—as we will see—its realization. Lope does not go that far. The "Amazonian siglo" isn't mentioned again, and it is nowhere to be seen at the end of the play. It will take *Fuenteovejuna*'s reception history to show us that. As for Derrida, if the trope of "autoimmunity" figures a process in which the "body's" own system of protection is depressed in order to "facilitate the tolerance of certain organ transplants," then *Fuenteovejuna* itself resists this operation. Lope's *comedia* interrupts the representational transfer of bodies, leaving us in a state of suspension. For where does sovereignty lie at the end of the play, if not somewhere in between the jurisdiction of the Catholic Kings and the autonomy of the villagers? Technically speaking, it lies no place. One might argue, along with the early modern theorists who supported popular sovereignty, that power has been *delegated* from the dead Commander to the Catholic kings, but this is clearly not the case. Their sovereignty is assumed. The question, however, is in what state specifically does the village remain at the end? And what is its relation to the sovereignty of the kings? The villagers are clearly to be ruled, from afar, as belonging to the kings, incorporated in the larger unit of what would be come the centralized monarchy. As the king puts it, "the village shall remain / *in me*, as its worth is mine" ("Y la villa es bien se quede / en mí, pues de mí se vale . . .").[128]

What I would prefer to say—and what I believe *Fuenteovejuna* actually shows, however, is that it lies waiting for its time, some time in the future—"hasta ver si acaso sale / Comendador que la herede" (2451–2) ("until we see if *perhaps* emerges [another] Commander to inherit it [the village]")—and that's not entirely promising either. There is no sovereign decision here—other than the decision to postpone decision. Instead, the play tells us, we must wait to see what the "inheritance" of the revolution will be. *Fuenteovejuna* thus stages a rejection of the law of the Father followed by the Order of the Knights of Calatrava. *Autoimmunity* interrupts the transfer, as well as the political subject's "alienation" of civil power, in theories such as Suárez's.[129] If sovereignty's desire for a body is satisfied in *Measure for Measure* by the substitution of one body part (the head or the "leg" of "lex") for another that keeps the force of law forceful, then *Fuenteovejuna* resists the "organ transplant" paradigm.

Thus, to put Cascardi's reading in a counterlight, *Fuenteovejuna* does *not* present us with a case of the subject's desire to be reinscribed into the operations of absolutism or "cultivate the fascism within." Nor does the play participate in a collective national project of resistance to modernization. Or not exactly. Rather, what *Fuenteovejuna* stages is a suspension of power, not foreseen in Suárez's or other Catholic treatises on what will come to be known as sovereignty, which can be figured only in terms of waiting: "hasta ver" ("until we see"). Until then, the Commander's place—but also that of the Catholic Kings' in relation to the village—remains vacant, empty, at best deferred to a mode of waiting. In this very empty space—the space of the theater itself—Lope's *comedia* presents a case of resistance that is neither a return to a pre-modern form of sovereignty nor the pre-figuration of sovereignty's modern forms (fascism, totalitarianism).[130] Against both of these desires to claim it, *Fuenteovejuna* opens, if only momentarily, a space of incalculability. What the play poses for—perhaps "weak"—thought, then, is the conceptual possibility (not the actualization) of something like what Derrida calls a democracy *á-venir*.[131] For Derrida, the phrase, "Democracy to come" does not mean a future democracy that will one day be "present":

> Democracy will never exist in the present; it is not presentable, and it is not a regulative idea in the Kantian sense. But *there is the impossible*, whose promise democracy inscribes—a promise that risks and must always risk being perverted into a threat. There is the impossible, and the impossible remains impossible because of the aporia of the demos: the demos is *at once* the incalculable singularity of anyone, before any "subject," the possible undoing of the social bond by a secret to be respected, beyond all citizenship, beyond every "state," indeed every "people," indeed even beyond the current state of the definition of a living being as living "human" being, *and* the universal of rational calculation, of the equality of citizens before the law, the social bond of being together, with or without contract, and so on.[132]

Derrida returns us here, by way of "immunity," to the "empty space" of sovereignty. Sovereignty appears in different conceptual guises in the work of Derrida, Agamben, and Lope de Vega, to be sure. At the same time, when the three "theorists" are read together, something recurring about the concept, or fantasy, or desire for sovereignty comes into view. To Derrida's opening up of sovereignty to the philosophical space between the "incalculable singularity of the demos" and the "universal, rational calculation" of the citizen, and to Agamben's reframing of it in a "zone of indistinction" between bare life and political life itself, Lope adds a third, compelling and complex twist. In its movement from keeping power *waiting* at the beginning of the play to the suspension of law at the end, *Fuenteovejuna* returns, in its closing moments, to the questions of recognition in relation to sovereignty and subjection, with which it opened. The state of suspension in which the village is left—*"waiting to see"* whether another Commander shall inherit it—is also a suspension of the transfers between power and desire, law and love, body and sign that sovereignty has come to depend on. The play puts this operation on hold, asking us, like the Commander at the beginning of the play, to wait.

Why, one might ask, does Lope stage *Fuenteovejuna* in 1612? Why does he write a play projected back in time? Is it really, as Cascardi has argued, to resist the processes of modernization confronting Spain? Alternatively, can the seemingly most conservative of thinkers be *at the same time* the most revolutionary.[133] As we have seen from the beginning, the play's investment in the problem of temporality is a complex one. It is also one that is inseparable from its treatment of sovereignty.[134] If, as some scholars have argued, the "future" of *Fuenteovejuna* is the Spanish Second Republic, then as the play's reception history, especially in Russia and Spain, including Federico García Lorca's adaptation, shows, this future will be a markedly divided one.[135] While both (Republican and Nationalist) sides turned to Golden Age texts in general, and to *Fuenteovejuna*, in particular, to support their positions, differences in their relation to the play emerged[136] One of the most important of these had to do specifically with time. As Duncan Wheeler notes, "Whilst Republican forces looked to adapt Golden-Age works to fit the needs of the present, Nationalist forces saw the needs for the present to be rooted in the past."[137] Regarding the interpretability of *Fuenteovejuna* in terms of either conservative (Spanish *Nationalist*) or revolutionary (Republican) politics, as many critics have pointed out, the play does not settle debates so much as defer and perpetuate the question. It was really only in the nineteenth and especially twentieth centuries that the play became canonical in the first place, championed by advocates on the left and right. What is clear is that, as the term "revolution" itself suggests, the wheel will keep turning. In the meantime, that is the time of the play (as Schmitt might put it), while we wait for a decision, *Fuenteovejuna* leaves us with two enduring and troubling images of sovereignty: the turning wheel of revolution, and the twisting rack of legally sanctioned torture.

Recalling Aristotle's distinction between *bios* and *zoē*, we may now again ask Agamben's question: "How is it possible to 'politicize' the 'natural sweetness' of *zoē* [bare life]?"[138] In its multiple resistances to sovereignty, *Fuenteovejuna*—or, in its perhaps more historically correct etymology, *Fuente Abejuna*[139]—"bees' source"—provides the glimpse of an answer, in which a political model built on the deferral of sovereignty momentarily comes into view.[140]

CHAPTER 4

# Transformation: The Body Moves Out in *Life Is a Dream*

> For hardly has an argument begun, than it is immediately transformed by one or other of the speakers into a metaphor which keeps on being extended... Thus it is that ideas evaporate into images...
>
> —Walter Benjamin, *Origin of German Tragic Drama*, 199

> A cipher has two meanings. When we come upon an important letter, whose meaning is clear but where we are told that the meaning is veiled and obscure, that it is hidden so that seeing we shall not see and hearing we shall not hear, what else are we to think but that this is a cipher with a double meaning?
>
> —Pascal, *Pensées*, 260

Calderón de la Barca's *Life Is a Dream* (*La vida es Sueño*) (1635) has been described as the "ultimate work of theatrical theology."[1] Considered one of the most philosophically complex works of the early modern period, *Life Is a Dream* not only raises theological and political questions of power, but it also poses epistemological and ontological challenges to thought, particularly in relation to the increasingly sophisticated representational capacities of baroque theater. Like Suárez, in Jean-François Courtine's account, and against a long-standing tradition that views the Jesuit playwright as a bastion of Spanish conservatism, Calderón, too, could be viewed as a "figure of passage" from the early to the late modern periods.[2] As William Egginton puts it, "[w]hen Calderón dreamt, in the middle of the century of novelty, his dream marked the new space of modernity's relation to the possibilities of its own knowledge."[3]

*Life Is a Dream* explores this space in ways we haven't seen in *Richard II*, *Measure for Measure*, and *Fuenteovejuna*. In relation to his Spanish colleague in particular, Calderón's play marks a departure from Lope's *Fuenteovejuna* and its "new comedy" views in at least three crucial ways. A member of the second generation of Golden Age dramatists, Calderón (1600–81) returns to many of the aesthetic precepts Lope had rejected in his *Arte nuevo*. First, Calderón employs a difficult style of "Latinate or Gongorine language" and complex rhetoric, learned at the Colegio Imperial of the Jesuits (1608–13) and, later, at the universities of Alcalá and Salamanca.[4] Second, his work takes advantage of the new playing spaces that opened in the second half of the seventeenth century, especially the Buen Retiro palace and the Coliseo.[5] One consequence of this shift away from the *corrales*, as Jonathan Thacker notes, is that a successful playwright such as Calderón would more likely "aim to write for the pleasure of the court [than] for the entertainment and education of the masses."[6] Finally, Calderón's theater, unlike Lope's, could use the sophisticated technical innovations, including the perspective scenery that was increasingly being imported from the Italian theater. As a result of these changes, Calderón's theater reflects a greater investment in the visual capacities of the stage than Lope's had.[7]

This shift toward rhetorical compression and visual complexity coincides with developments related to the representation of sovereignty in seventeenth-century Spain. These involve a greater emphasis on visual depictions of the king, in painting or through the medium of architecture, including the construction of "that paradigm of royal propaganda, the '*Salón de los Reinos*' (The Hall of the Realms) in the Palace of the Buen Retiro, built in Madrid by Philip IV in the 1620s."[8] At the same time, despite this emphasis on the capacity of visual depictions to convey sovereign power, political theorists also increasingly advised the King to become more "untouchable, inaccessible, and 'invisible.'"[9] As Antonio Feros observes, this "sacralization of the king's body and the steps taken to reduce the accessibility of the monarchy in practice deeply affected public perceptions of royal majesty in the seventeenth century."[10] This simultaneous movement toward the visual displays of painting and architecture and away from the king's body created opportunities for "theorists of poetics [who] began to assert that poetry, and more particularly, drama, should serve to promote the sacred image of the monarch." As Feros notes, it "was Lope de Vega who most aptly addressed the role of the poet in relation to royal power," writing, "Who may doubt that the birth of Princes / Should be celebrated with verse? / [For] Kings are gods on earth." (Quien duda que naciendo humanos Príncipes / Será justo alabarlos con los versos? / [Pues] los reyes son Dioses de la tierra.)[11]

The tension between the increasing sacralization of the king's body in the seventeenth century and the king's simultaneous withdrawal from display creates a new moment for the drama of sovereignty. In my last chapter, I argued that the political ontology of sovereignty in *Fuenteovejuna* is above all a temporal one: The power of sovereignty is the power to keep one waiting. In *Life Is a Dream*, written roughly two decades later, for the new playing spaces of the Buen Retiro palace and the Coliseo, Calderón turns from an understanding of sovereignty primarily in terms of its temporality, to that of its visual and spatial representation.

*Life Is a Dream* could be read as an "answer" to the questions raised by the dual deposition of sovereignty and analogy jointly staged by Shakespeare and Suárez in *Richard II* and the *Metaphysical Disputations*. By "answer," I do not mean that Calderón writes his play as an explicit response to *Richard II*. Rather, my contention is that in its evocation of the earlier play's metaphorical and metaphysical landscapes, *Life Is a Dream* returns us to the conceptual problems raised by the earlier play, on the way to providing its own its own tropological solution. What literal and figurative bodies arise out of the ashes of the multiple theoretical and theatrical destructions that mark the end of sovereignty's old metaphysical orders?[12] What appears, in Calderón's theater, to fill the conceptual space opened up by the collapse of divine right theory and the analogical structure on which it rests? For a response to these questions, I turn from the emptiness of Richard II's "untimely bier," to the space and tropes of sovereignty created, in perhaps the best-known play of Spanish Golden Age drama, *La vida es sueño*.

*Life Is a Dream* "responds" to *Richard II* in at least three ways. To begin with, Calderón presents us with an alternative view to the deposing of divine-right theory in the earlier play. Here, Calderón's play draws on what the historian J. P. Sommerville refers to as a "Catholic theory of civil society," based on a separation of powers, formulated by thinkers such as Augustine and Thomas Aquinas, and modified by Suárez and other theorists of the "Salamanca School."[13] Second, in contrast to both the empty "mechanical time" in which we're left at the end of *Richard II*, in which the sovereign body itself is figured as a mere measure of time, or to the time of waiting at the end of *Fuenteovejuna*, *Life Is a Dream* continually invokes an Augustinian conception of time, premised on the fullness and possibility of divine presence.[14] Finally, in the wake of Shakespeare and Suárez's dual collapse of sovereignty and analogy, *Life Is a Dream* reconstructs a transcendental model of sovereignty through the representational mode of allegory, the nature of which the following chapter explores in detail. Once again, I take Walter Benjamin as my guide, as we move into Calderón's *laberinto* of political-theological sovereignty.

Calderón holds a privileged place in Benjamin's thought. Along with Shakespeare, Calderón provides Benjamin with a comparative critical lens through which to view the "inferior" forms of German drama. *Life Is a Dream*, in particular, represents for Benjamin the "perfect form" of the *Trauerspiel*, whose object, unlike that of tragedy, is "historical life *as it was conceived at that time*."[15] "Nowhere," he writes, "but in Calderón could the perfect form of the baroque *Trauerspiel* be studied. The very precision with which the 'mourning' [*Trauer*] and the 'play' [*Spiel*] can harmonize with one another gives it its exemplary validity—the validity of the word and of the thing alike."[16] Yet despite Calderón's centrality to Benjamin's analysis of the baroque, his relation to Calderón is complex, not least for reasons of language and translation. As Jane Newman has shown, Benjamin read both Shakespeare and Calderón "in German-language translations heavy with politically inflected commentary of a particular sort."[17]

In a December 28, 1925 letter to Hugo von Hofmannsthal, whose adaptation of *Life Is a Dream* Benjamin much admired, Benjamin writes that "Calderón's use of metaphor is dazzling and seems to me quite different from Shakespeare's: if this were the case, they would certainly be revealed as two distinct and significant poles of the figurative language of the baroque (Shakespeare's metaphor being the 'image and trope' of the action and the individual, Calderón's the romantic intensification of speech itself)."[18] Benjamin does not pursue the project of contrasting Shakespeare's and Calderón's treatment of metaphor further (leaving us with the intriguing characterization of Shakespearean metaphor as "image" and the Calderonian as "intensification"), but when he publishes *The Origin of German Tragic Drama* three years later, his thinking has changed. It is now not only Shakespeare's metaphor that presents what he calls in the same letter the "image and trope" of action and individuality, but also Calderón's dream play that provides Benjamin with the particular trope that he will go on to develop so distinctively: allegory. For Benjamin, Calderón's *comedias*, in general, and *Life Is a Dream*, in particular, present the "perfect form" of the baroque mourning play—that is, a play that responds in telling ways to the theological, political, and philosophical losses produced by the Lutheran critique of good works. For Benjamin, understanding these losses (something Benjamin refers to as the "contemplative necessities" of the period) is a precondition of criticism:

> One of these, and it is consequent upon the total disappearance of eschatology, is the attempt to find, in a reversion to a bare state of creation, consolation for the renunciation of a state of grace. Here, as in other spheres of baroque life, what is vital is the transposition of the originally temporal data into a figurative spatial simultaneity. This leads deep into the structure of the dramatic form . . . [19]

What is "vital" to understanding the problematic of the baroque, as Benjamin sees it, is the conceptualization of space. The "transposition" of temporality into "spatial simultaneity" presents a new development with regard to the representational problems of sovereignty. In contrast to the logics of transfer, transplant, and resistance we have seen so far, *Life Is A Dream* moves into a different configuration of temporal and spatial coordinates on the way to providing its own metaphors for the representation of political-theological sovereignty.

## First Movement: The Reading of Time

Like *Richard II* and *Fuenteovejuna*, *Life Is a Dream* begins its approach to sovereignty by focusing on sovereignty's relation to time. At the beginning of the play, the king of Poland, Basilio, a student of mathematics and astrology, decides to reveal to the people the hitherto concealed history of his son, Segismundo, their rightful Prince.[20] The boy's birth not only cost his mother her life, but was also accompanied by a series of celestial signs, which Basilio interpreted as signaling the coming of tyranny and violence. Consequently, Basilio has imprisoned Segismundo in an "enchanted tower" ("encantada torre") in the mountains to ward off the coming disaster. Later, in order to test the heavenly signs' accuracy, he drugs the now fully grown Segismundo with a dream potion and returns him to the palace to see how he will respond: If he behaves well, the people will have their rightful heir. If he proves to be the monster that was prophesied, Basilio will return Segismundo to the tower and tell him the whole experience was a dream. Complicating the main story of the king and his son is a corresponding plot regarding the history of the king's advisor, Clotaldo, and his daughter, Rosaura, whose fall onto the stage initiates the drama.

The play opens with a bang. Disguised as a man[21] and bearing (unknown to herself) her father's sword, a young woman, Rosaura, is thrown from her horse into the hostile land of "Poland": "Poorly, Poland, do you receive / a foreigner, writing with blood / his entrance in your sand." ("Mal, Polonia, recibes / a un extranjero, pues con sangre escribes / su entrada en tus arenas . . ." [17–19]) The world Rosaura falls into is remarkably similar to that prophesied for England by Shakespeare's Bishop of Carlisle in *Richard II*—a desolate landscape of deception, disproportion, and above all violence:[22]

> Hipogrifo violento
> que corriste parejas con el viento,
> ¿dónde, rayo sin llama,
> pájaro sin matiz, pez sin escama,
> y bruto sin instinto natural, al
> confuso laberinto
> desas desnudas peñas
> te desbocas, te arrastras y despeñas?
> Quédate en este monte,
> donde tengan los brutos su Faetonte;
> (*LVS* 1–10)

> Violent Hippogryph,
> who ran hand in hand, together
> with the wind, where, ray without
> flame, bird without plume, fish
> without scale and brute without
> natural instinct are you hurling
> yourself from those naked cliffs into
> this confused labyrinth?
> Stay in this mountain, where the
> beasts will have their Phaeton;
> (my trans.)

Rosaura's fall from the "violent Hippogryph" into the "confused labyrinth" of Segismundo's cave not only sets the play in motion, but it also initiates a chain of transformational events, understood from the beginning in relation to the power (or violence) of signs.[23] A series of divisions mark her crash, with elements that normally correspond in nature here violently separated: flash without spark, bird without color, fish without scales, animal without instincts, and above all, person without honor. The latter represents, as we saw in *Fuenteovejuna*, the "fracture" that Américo Castro sees at the heart of Golden Age plots. As Ciriaco Morón explains, Calderón employs the term "*violento*" here in the technical, Scholastic sense of contradiction.²⁴

In the early seventeenth century, the neo-Scholastic work of Francisco Suárez expands on and explores that sense in great detail.²⁵ For Suárez and other important theorists from the Salamanca School, the relationship between power or violence and nature is a matter of law. It is through law that Suárez theorizes the "right relation" among the natural, social, and political orders. Like Carl Schmitt, Suárez "sees social relations essentially as legal relations."²⁶ Suárez's seminal *De legibus* (Coimbra 1612) outlines the hierarchical relations governing the juridical, metaphysical, and above all theological discourses that bind "baroque bodies" to power.²⁷ For Suárez, the study of laws is "a large division of theology; and when the sacred science treats of law, that science surely regards no other object than God Himself as Lawgiver."²⁸ The objective of the Catholic theologian, jurist, and philosopher, then, is to articulate the "harmonious division of the sciences."²⁹ This division, including particularly the question of the right relation between power and law, is one of the central philosophical concerns of *Life Is a Dream*. It is also precisely the question of the relation between power, or violence, and justice that emerges when the baroque becomes a problem of, and for, sovereignty.³⁰

For Giorgio Agamben, this division takes us directly to the theoretical heart of the problem of sovereignty. In the "Nomos Basileus" chapter of *Homo Sacer*, Agamben explores this relation by returning to a passage from Hesiod's *Works and Days*. Here, Hesiod discusses the same triad of bird, fish, and beasts that Calderón inherits from antiquity. "What is proper to the fish," Hesiod writes, "the wild beasts, and the winged birds / is to devour each other, since there is no *Dike* [justice] between them. / But to men Zeus gave *Dike*, which is much better."³¹ The relationship hinges on the question of what is *proper*. According to Hesiod, what is proper to man, unlike animals, is justice (*Dike*)—the justice given them by the gods. "Wild" creatures, on the other hand, possess neither justice nor metaphor, only violence. For Hesiod, this division is *natural*. Agamben contrasts Hesiod's view of the relationship between violence and justice with Pindar's:

> While in Hesiod the *nomos* is still the power that divides violence from law and, with it, the world of beasts from the world of men, and while in Solon the "connection" of *Bia* and *Dike* contains neither ambiguity nor irony, in Pindar—and this is the knot that he bequeaths to Western political thought and that makes him, in a certain sense, the first great thinker of sovereignty—*the sovereign nomos is the principle that, joining law and violence, threatens them with indistinction.*[32]

Thus begins Agamben's genealogy of modernity, with its corresponding genealogy of sovereignty, inaugurated by what he repeatedly refers to as a movement into conceptual "indistinction." The crux lies with the question of division. More specifically, the problem Agamben identifies is one that emerges in the movement from the clear divisions of violence and law, beast and man, force and justice, into an ambiguity in which law and violence become tied up in a "knot." As one of the earliest writers to articulate this relation, Pindar becomes, for Agamben, the "first great thinker of sovereignty." Agamben next turns to Carl Schmitt's reading of Pindar's fragment in *The* Nomos *of the Earth*. There, Agamben notes:

> [I]n the chapter "First Global Lines," Schmitt shows how the link between localization and ordering constitutive of the *nomos* of the earth always implies a zone that is excluded from law and that takes the shape of a "free and juridically empty space" in which the sovereign power no longer knows the limits fixed by the *nomos* as the territorial order. In the classical epoch of the *ius publicum Europaeum*, this zone corresponded to the New World, which was identified with the state of nature in which everything is possible (Locke: "In the beginning, all the world was America"). Schmitt himself assimilates this zone "beyond the line" to the state of exception, which "bases itself in an obviously analogous fashion on the idea of delimited, free and empty space" understood as a "temporary and spatial sphere in which every law is suspended."[33]

Agamben is less interested in the historical specificity of Schmitt's claim—the production of a "juridically empty space" in relation to New World conquest—than he is in identifying a recurring conceptual principle: sovereignty's dependence on the production of extralegal zones. Schmitt's idea that this zone is "void" of law contributes to a conceptualization of sovereignty as an "event" that literally emerges out of nothing, and therefore forms part of Schmitt's essentially theological view of the sovereign decision. For Agamben, on the other hand, the state of exception is not a "suspension" of, or in, time or space, so much as it is a principle internal to the concept of sovereignty itself. It is, above all, what Agamben will refer to as a "complex topological figure." The state of exception is, in other words, a trope.

At the same time, it's a complicated trope. Agamben's analysis of the state of exception, for example, which works through a "complex topological figure," underscores the movement of "passing through" from one state into another—a movement that itself becomes a figure of historical process:

> The state of exception is thus not so much a spatiotemporal suspension as a complex topological figure in which not only the exception and the rule but also the state of nature and law, outside and inside, pass through one another.[34]

This, according to Agamben, is how modern thought about life has worked from the beginning, first distinguishing, and then twisting and turning the distinctions so that they inevitably converge as to always exclude what they include: *life*. It is the turning movement of exclusive-inclusion that for Agamben characterizes the historical process in "which we are still living." For this, Agamben himself returns to Schmitt:

> The process (which Schmitt carefully described and which we are still living) that began to become apparent in the First World War, through which the constitutive link between the localization and ordering of the old *nomos* was broken and the entire system of the reciprocal limitations and rules of the *ius publicum Europaeum* brought to ruin, has its hidden ground in the sovereign exception. What happened and is still happening before our eyes is that the "juridically empty" space of the state of exception (in which law is in force in the figure ... of its own dissolution, and in which everything that the sovereign deemed de facto necessary could happen) has transgressed its spatiotemporal boundaries and now, overflowing [*riversandosi*] outside them, is starting to coincide with the normal order, in which everything again becomes possible.[35]

Agamben's illustrations are never random. His figure of the exception that, in the form of a force "overflowing" (*riversandosi*) its boundaries, recalls a famous earlier example of a similar process of "overflowing" force. In Chapter 25 of *The Prince* (c.1513), Niccolò Machiavelli theorizes sovereignty's relation to history through the figure of a river, similarly "overflowing" the normally operative natural limits:

> I compare fortune to one of those violent rivers [*uno di questi fiumi rovinosi*] which, when they are enraged, flood the plains, tear down trees and buildings, wash soil from one place to deposit it in another . . . there is no possibility of resistance. Yet although such is their nature, it does not follow that when they are flowing quietly one cannot take precautions, constructing dykes and . . . . So it is with fortune. She shows her potency where there is no well regulated power to resist her, and her impetus is felt where she knows there are no embankments and dykes to restrain her . . . . Italy . . . is a country without embankments and without dykes: for if Italy had been adequately reinforced, like Germany, Spain, and France, either this flood would not have caused the great changes it has, or it would not have swept in at all.[36]

Yet there are differences between the two Italian sovereignty theorists, starting with their relation to time. Where Machiavelli's "river" becomes an opportunity for the Prince to read and act on what Antonio Negri refers to as the "historical mutation," as we saw in Chapter 1, Agamben's exception operates on a different political and philosophical plane. Unlike Machiavelli's "theater" of mutations that the sovereign can take advantage of, Agamben's "zones" depict a process internal to the *nomos* itself in which sovereign agency is de-activated and certainly de-personalized. For Agamben, the overflowing river seems to be part of an inexorable historical trajectory. History is not a text for the sovereign to read but rather an effect of an always life-excluding form. For Machiavelli, on the other hand, the historical process is indeed legible by and for the sovereign. It is precisely this possibility that should inspire the modern prince to anticipate contingency and take precautions in order to avert a catastrophe. The difference between Machiavelli and Agamben thus inversely mirrors that between Benjamin and Schmitt with regard to the sovereign exception. Ironically, in this reading it is Agamben who uncomfortably occupies the position of Schmitt's sovereign, who doesn't avert an exception but rather declares one.[37] For Machiavelli, the "overflowing river" is a consequence of an insufficient relation to contingency.

At the same time, for both thinkers—and, indeed as with *all* of the thinkers we have encountered up to now—the theory of sovereignty continues to work itself out through its tropes. In Agamben's case, his thought moves repeatedly and restlessly from concept, or pseudo-concept, to metaphor, and back. Like Benjamin's thought, Agamben's philosophy is perhaps its most original and powerful when it works itself out through literary interpretation. Whether he is attempting to define the temporal and spatial coordinates of the state of exception, the structural positions of sovereignty, or the ontological status of forms of life, Agamben continually recurs to texts and tropes. Above all, Agamben repeatedly recurs to his own master trope of the "zone" to trace the conceptual-historical movements that interest him. That these movements consistently arrive at points of suspension or "indistinction" has frustrated his critics. But as Jacques Lezra points out, "Agamben is not being gratuitously confusing but is in this shadowy way applying to the definition itself the topology that the definition describes."[38] Agamben's theory is, in this view, a conceptually and linguistically performative one, relying on the labor of metaphor to figure complex (historical and conceptual) processes of convergence that distinguish modernity. A crucial aspect of this process, as Lezra has shown, is Agamben's understanding not only of conceptual space, but also of spatiality itself. Lezra calls attention to an important distinction within Agamben's thought: It is not only a "suspension" of space and time that distinguishes sovereignty. It is "a particular use or aspect of spatiality, a process expressed as, or mapped onto a space or *a figure.*"[39] Figures come to play an enormously important role in Agamben's thinking, serving not as "illustrations" but rather as conceptual stages on which thought plays itself out.

Calderón takes on this problem as a question of the complex mirror relation between the baroque stage and the multiple theo-political crises enveloping Europe at the time of the play's development. The violent opening of *Life Is a Dream* reflects the wider political-theological moment of the seventeenth century. As Marcel Gauchet has described it, this is precisely a moment of violent rupture. For Gauchet, the Christian believer and specifically the Counter-Reformation subject, whether Protestant or Catholic, is confronted by conflicting political and theological demands, between inward isolation and outward subjection. For Gauchet, the

> true originality of the relation to the world established by Christianity lay in this axiomized ambiguity, which was a direct refraction of the union of the two natures in Christ. It made the Christian into a being torn between a duty of belonging and one of distancing,

between forming an alliance with the world and being estranged from it. But also a being in whom this shuttling between worlds is to come to an end—a being who will one day reconcile choice for the beyond and systematic commitment to the here-below.[40]

Once again, we view the problem of sovereignty through a "tear"—this time that of the Christian subject, torn apart by a divided duty, "to double business bound," as Hamlet might put it. The tear here at once unites and divides the subject's relation to sovereignty, even as it divides sovereignty itself into its political and theological poles. The question Calderón faces in dramatizing this dilemma is one of what Gauchet calls the "constituting aporia" of Christianity: How can the Christian believer tear himself away from a world he cannot leave?[41] As Benjamin puts it, it is a religious problem without a religious solution: "For all that the increasing worldliness of the Counter-Reformation prevailed in both confessions, religious aspirations did not lose their importance: it was just that this century denied them a religious fulfillment, demanding of them, or imposing upon them, a secular solution instead."[42] Central to the question, as Calderón's play has made clear from the beginning, is the problem of time. The problem lies in the Christian construction of world history. As Gauchet has shown, the problem of the future, now becomes the crux of a theo-political construction that speaks in a prospective mode, as the Counter-Reformation subject is not only asked but forced to look in two directions at once, an epistemic condition that tears him/her apart.[43] Calderón responds to these divisions and demands by refiguring the relationship between history and vision in a new form.

## Enter Image

The problem of the representational image in the early seventeenth century is an extremely complex one, different aspects of which are taken up by thinkers in a huge variety of philosophical, theological, political, juridical, and scientific texts.[44] Within the specific context of theo-political sovereignty polemics in the Counter-Reformation, the stakes could be high, given that debates over depicting and venerating the Deity linked the question of what one could imagine and represent to what one could believe. In the most general of terms, one could start by saying that Catholicism and Protestantism pursue different paths regarding the question of the subject's relation to images in the early modern period.

In the English context, for example, the problem of the image is often approached as a question of law. In his analysis of what is often taken to be a work of Elizabethan propaganda, the Tudor group portrait, *Edward IV and the Pope; or, An Allegory of the Reformation* (ca. 1548–49) legal historian and theorist Peter Goodrich has argued that the blank spaces in Reformation portraiture in general function as "direct expressions of the new, image-less or literal form of law." Goodrich shows how the portrait's depiction of empty spaces, along with its "blank frames," are "to be understood as crucial if paradoxical visual representations of the Reformers' iconoclastic doctrine." Citing John Fortescue's *De natura legis naturae*, Goodrich argues "that what is at stake in the image and in writing is the archive or memory of the origin of law. The Holy Spirit (*ymaginem*) engenders a law of nature from which justice and the law derive." Historically, Goodrich argues, the "writing of law has archetypically taken place through the destruction of idols or false images, [and] the representation of power has required an icon of legitimacy, an inaugural image or first law which cannot take either a figurative or literal form."[45] If the archetypal writing of law inaugurates itself through an image that is neither figural nor literal, then what form can it take? Goodrich's answer to this question is again the form of emptiness itself:

> The power of the image is thus given its strongest expression in an empty space or blank frame. The power of law exceeds representation; its image is an absence, an iconography of nothing, an empty space that is both not yet and immanent, both a becoming and an always already there, but in its nature unseen.[46]

For the Reformers, the power of the image lies in an emptiness that at the same time serves as a representational vehicle to figure the unrepresentable source of law. In this Counter-Reformation context, the image that "exceeds representation" becomes a provocation to representation. The image is paradoxical because it arises from an emptiness that is at the same time its source, the source of a legal fullness and presence. It is the origin of law. Law arises from absence. The legal foundation is empty.

On the Catholic side, Suárez writes one of the first philosophical treatments of the image in the early seventeenth century, his commentary to Aristotle's *De anima: Commentaria una cum quaestionibus in libros Aristotelis De anima*. The "work has a rather complicated textual history," as James South explains; it was not published in Suárez's lifetime, but the thinker revised the material for publication before his death in 1617.[47] In it, Suárez's understanding of the role of the image in human cognition differs from that of Aquinas. For Suárez, unlike in the English example we have seen, the question of the image has to do with the internal sense operations of the mind. Suárez identifies distinct mental operations related to the mind's capacity to produce images, starting with the creative imagination itself. The creative imagination is a mental power to "construct[s] fictional objects," including "impossible beings,"[48] which are mental creations, similar to phantasms. Phantasms are images in the "internal sense," whose function it is to mediate between the external sensations of accidents, and the internal, intellectual knowledge of essences.[49] Related but not identical to the image or phantasm is the "phantasy" (*phantasia*), the operation that conserves the images of things in their absence so that we can know all sensible objects, including external sensible objects, even when they are not present.[50] Finally, there is "imagination" (*imaginatio*). Imagination, too, is an operation—indeed the same operation as phantasy, with the additional ability to compose and divide mental objects, as well as to create impossible beings.[51] Imagination, therefore, is an operation the mind engages in when it thinks and even creates "impossible beings." It is the precondition for thinking impossibility. Where, for Aquinas, "the proper object of the intellect" is the "common *essence* present in material singular objects," Suárez argues that the "proper object of the intellect" is the "*material* singular object."[52] As South points out, the startling implication of this shift is that Suárez's view of the "internal sense" in humans is "little different than the internal sense in animals."[53] Here Suárez closes a certain gap between human and animal life with regard to their shared powers of imagination and cognition, much as he does with Aquinas's theory of analogy, with regard to the relation between immanent and transcendent being.

### Enter Monster

"There is probably no word that is more characteristic of Calderón de la Barca's art," Roberto González Echevarría writes, "than *monstruo*, 'monster.'"[54] From the *comedia*'s opening invocation of the mythological hippogryph—Ariosto's fabulous hybrid creature in the *Orlando Furioso*, part eagle, part horse—monsters take on an "obsessive presence" in *Life Is a Dream*.[55] The monster, which combines in one being elements that do not correspond in nature, is a figure of a "violent" ontology, according to the technical sense of the term in Scholasticism, as Ciriaco Morón explains.[56] The figure of the monster plays a key role in Calderón's theater of sovereignty, which attempts to articulate the right relation among theo-political, metaphysical, and aesthetic orders.

*Comedia* critics often note the parallel between the play's two principal "monsters," Segismundo, the man-beast, and Rosaura, the man-woman.[57] Both present unnatural qualities that must eventually be re-naturalized, either through marriage or education, before order in the state can be restored. Dramatizing the movement toward the restoration of such an order is certainly one of the aims of *Life Is a Dream*. The predominance of the figure of the monster in *Life Is a Dream* also marks a corresponding obsession with the question of sovereignty. Like monstrosity, sovereignty is not only a historical and political problem, but in Calderón's theater, it is also a conceptual and representational one. As Georgina Dopico observes, the monster's "dwelling place" is one that exists in relation to

> that radically unstable line—or lines—between one species and another, between human and animal, between fascination and repulsion, ultimately between identity and difference. The monster has consistently been bound up with the very problem of defining, of creating categories, of ordering taxonomies.[58]

A moving border, the "radically unstable line" of the monster's dwelling recalls the movement into "indistinguishability" of Agamben's zones. Like monstrosity, sovereignty, too, in Agamben's view, dwells in the in-between and ambivalent space created by shifting juridical and metaphysical borders.[59] In Agamben's political ontology, the body-of-power is always, in a (conceptual) sense, a monstrous one. For Agamben's version of sovereignty not only combines elements and positions (between norm and exception, the inside and outside of law, potentiality or actuality) that are normally kept separate to maintain conceptual clarity, but it also emerges out of an unstable and "unnatural" space of indetermination. The difficulty of figuring this in-betweenness leads to some of Agamben's most interesting and complex examples, including the figure of the Möbius strip.[60]

As we have seen, Agamben stages sovereignty's conceptual drama in the complex space of the "zone," the distinguishing feature of which is precisely the indistinguishability of its elements. Bare life and political life, the inside and the outside of law, norm and exception, potentiality and actuality—all converge, according to Agamben, into a space of "indistinction." Sovereignty, in Agamben's theory, itself is never entirely stable, never fully in one state or the other. Rather, its very existence is linked to its in-betweenness. Sovereignty emerges, in this view, from what Carl Schmitt calls a "juridically empty place," or what Agamben refers to as a "law void."[61]

In the many theories we have encountered so far, sovereignty is repeatedly characterized in terms of its juridical, metaphysical, and political absence. Schmitt's "law void," Ernesto Laclau's "empty signifier," Jean-Luc Nancy's "nothingness," and Louis Marin's invocation of Pascal's view of the "empty place" of the king all point to the recurring paradox of the concept of sovereignty: that it is both everything and nothing, supreme power and absolute cipher at once.[62] How are we to understand this concept that, logically, or ontologically, emerges out of a "law void," but that is also so determining a structuring fiction that it completely organizes political and theological life? Taken together, all of these assertions present challenges to thought, as sovereignty comes to resemble, in the end, both a logical and conceptual, if not empirical, impossibility, and a real and ongoing problem. How to imagine such an impossible being?

In the Scholastic tradition, "impossible beings" or "thought beings" are also known, perhaps paradoxically, as "beings of reason." Beings of reason are not entities but creatures of the intellect. The example Plato introduces, Aristotle elaborates, and Scholasticism inherits is that of the mythological "goat-stag." The goat-stag is something the mind can think but that doesn't exist. It "has meaning but no truth," as Aristotle puts it.[63] Suárez's preferred term for such a creature is the *chimera* ("ut chymaera"). In his 54th *Metaphysical Disputation*, Suárez explains thought-beings such as the chimera as follows:

> For many things are thought by our intellect which do not have real being in themselves, although they may be thought in the manner of beings, as is clear from the examples brought up of blindness, a relation of reason, etc. Likewise, many things are thought which are impossible, and are fashioned in the manner of possible beings, for example, a chimera, which does not have any other being besides being thought.[64]

According to Suárez, the human intellect imagines such impossible beings as abstractions and negations for three reasons:

> First, there is the knowledge which our intellect tries to pursue concerning those negations and privations which are nothing . . . [S]econd, from the imperfection of our intellect. For since it sometimes cannot know things as they are in themselves, the intellect conceives them by comparison with one another, and in this way forms relations of reason where there are no true relations . . . [T]hird . . . from a certain fecundity of the intellect, which can construct figments from true beings by uniting parts which cannot be combined in reality. In this way, it fashions a chimera or something similar, and thus it forms those beings of reason which are called "impossibles" and are said by some to be "prohibited" beings.[65]

The chimera is the product of a series of contradictory intellectual operations, resulting from the mind's attempt to imagine absence. It emerges from the intellect's capacity to imagine and conceptualize abstract relations and negations, and thereby construe knowledge of "impossibles"—beings that cannot otherwise be known. Later, Suárez will also refer to these impossible beings as "prohibited beings." The chimera is an effect of the mind's ability to form "prohibited beings" by "uniting parts which cannot be combined in reality."[66] It is what the mind performs as a consequence of a deficiency—an "imperfection of the intellect," confronted by that which cannot be known directly. Here, the problem is both that the intellect is imperfect, lacking certain abilities, and also that the thing it is trying to imagine does not exist. The intellect thus compensates for this double lack by recurring to what it can know and imagine. The chimera is the result: the intellectual product of a figure to fill in for an original absence of being. Paradoxically, however, the chimera is also the effect of a certain excess within the intellect—a "fecundity" that "constructs figments from true beings by uniting parts that cannot be combined in reality." Like the monster, it combines contradictory elements. The chimera, in other words, is a productive fiction. Suárez relates the intellect's capacity to form images of impossible beings to its own constitution. That is, in the intellect, the potentiality for excessive production lies side by side with that of insufficient production. For the English philosopher Francis Bacon, the imagination operates in a different way. Bacon argues explicitly against the philosophy of the "schoolmen," contending that it breed[s] for the most part one question as fast it solveth another; even as in the former resemblance, when you carry the light into one corner, you darken the rest. So that the fable and fiction of Scylla seemeth to be a lively image of this kind of philosophy or knowledge, which was transformed into a comely virgin for the upper parts, but then "Candida succinctam latrantibus inguina monstris." So the generalities of the schoolmen are for a while good and proportionable; but then when you descend into their distinctions and decisions, instead of a fruitful womb for the use and benefit of man's life, they end in monstrous altercations and barking questions.[67]

Like the misogynistic ravings of King Lear, Bacon's image of Scholasticism "descending" from the "comely upper parts of the virgin" and "fruitful womb for the use and benefit of man's life," to the monstrous nether regions of "barking questions" marks not only an anxiety over the relationship between signs and bodies that will not cease to haunt both the English and Spanish political imaginaries, but also returns us to the problems of sovereignty, imagination, and monstrosity. Against the Scholastic view of a thinker such as Suárez, who tries to understand cognition and the production of mental images in moral and ontological terms ("prohibited beings"), Bacon's view of the imagination takes on a more explicitly political hue. For Bacon, the

> imagination is not simply and only a messenger; but is invested with or at leastwise usurpeth no small authority in itself, besides the duty of the message. For it was well said by Aristotle, That the mind hath over the body that commandment, which the lord hath over a bondman; but that reason hath over the imagination that commandment which a magistrate hath over a free citizen; who may come also to rule in his turn.[68]

Reason rules over the imagination not only like the mind over the body, but also as a magistrate over a free citizen. In a quick turnaround, however, the very "free citizen" that is ruled over by the magistrate may "come also to rule in his turn." Bacon suggests that it is just a matter of time before the imagination in turn (and, I would add, through turns, i.e. tropes,) comes to "rule" over reason—and, by implication, body over mind, "free citizen" over magistrate. This potentiality spells trouble. No mere "messenger," the imagination for Bacon quickly oversteps its "duty" in order to "usurp" "no small authority in itself."

Bacon links this somewhat alarmist (if familiar, at least since Plato) view of the imagination's subversive potential directly to its political implications. Bacon's imagination is a sovereign force—but one that operates at the same time, in a republic of citizens—*as* a citizen, and not a subject of monarchy. The implications for royal absolutism and theater are important. Bacon underscores the power of the imagination in political terms, seeing its crucial role in the organization and functioning of political sign-systems.

Sovereignty is *always* an effect of its sign-system. But sign-systems don't occur in historical vacuums. Rather, they depend on the operations of the imagination. What we see in these early seventeenth-century descriptions of how the imagination functions is, on the one hand, a familiar rehearsal of classical debates, from Plato and Aristotle through Sir Philip Sidney and Lope de Vega, on the potential political danger of harnessing its public force, to, on the other, novel figurations of precisely that force's increasingly administrative structure.

At the turn of the seventeenth century, both English and Spanish theories of kingship demonstrate an increasingly sophisticated awareness of the interactive nature of sovereignty and representation. Whether it's through the public display of the sovereign's body, portraits, insignias, coins, processions, or other forms, sovereignty is increasingly understood as an effect of its sign systems. At the same time, this understanding leads in different directions in England and Spain as we move from the sixteenth to the seventeenth centuries. While sixteenth-century Tudor texts stress the importance of the sovereign's public visibility, Spanish tracts of the early seventeenth century begin to emphasize the monarch's need to remain invisible instead. The sovereign should avoid being too accessible.[69] As Antonio Feros points out, the dramatic change in thinking about the representation of sovereignty in Spain from the sixteenth to the seventeenth centuries has to do in part with the Spanish conquest of Mexico. Partially in response to Hernán Cortés's descriptions of the emperor Montezuma, Spanish attitudes about the display of the king's body began to shift. Whereas in the early sixteenth century "the monarch needed to be public [and] accessible to his subjects, and to the community of which he was an integral part," by the end of the century, "the Spanish monarch was described with language similar to that used by Cortés to describe Montezuma: a detached, inaccessible, untouchable, and almost invisible monarch, God's representative on earth whose sacred gaze was terrifying." Spanish theorists at the beginning of the seventeenth century thus increasingly stressed the advantages of withdrawing the king's physical body from the public eye.[70]

## The Fade Out

The body-of-power once again takes central stage in Calderón's *comedia*—although this time that "body" begins to assume a significantly different look from what we have seen so far. Unlike the collapse of sovereignty's theoretical structures in *Richard II*, or the body politic's reanimation via "organ" transplants in *Measure for Measure* (and the resistances these produce in *Fuenteovejuna*), *Life Is a Dream* presents us with a vision of sovereignty that begins to move away from the body—or at least any single, human, body—altogether. On Calderón's stage, sovereignty appears fragmented from the start. As if in response to the constitutive dualities staged in *Richard* and theorized by Agamben, *Life Is a Dream* divides and multiplies the body-of-power even further, locating different aspects of sovereignty in four representative figures, each with his or her own potentiality: the king, Basilio; his son (and potential king), Segismundo; Rosaura; and, finally, the play's clown, Clarín. We begin, as is fitting, with the king.

> Ya sabéis que yo en el mundo
> por mi ciencia he merecido
> el sobrenombre de docto;
> pues, contra el tiempo y olvido,
> los pinceles de Timantes,
> los mármoles de Lisipo,
> en el ámbito del orbe
> me aclaman el gran Basilio.
> Ya sabéis que son las ciencias
> que más curso y más estimo,
> matemáticas sutiles,
> por quien al tiempo le quito,
> por quien a la fama rompo
> la jurisdicción y oficio
> de enseñar más cada día;
> pues cuando en mis tablas miro
> presentes las novedades
> de los venideros siglos,

le gano al tiempo las gracias
de contar lo que yo he dicho.
                    (*LVS* 604–23)

You already all know that
for my science I have merited in the world
the title of "doctor," since
against time and forgetfulness
the brushes of Timanthes and
the marbles of Lysippus, have acclaimed me
throughout the world
Basilio the Great.
You all already know that it is the sciences
which I most study and esteem,
subtle mathematics,
through which I steal from time
and fame their jurisdiction
and function [office] of
teaching more every day;
since when I see as present in my tables
the events of coming centuries
I win from Time
the gratitude for recounting
what I have said.
                        (my trans.)

Although, as I have suggested, *Life Is a Dream* may be said to open in the violent landscape of disproportion prophesied by the Bishop of Carlyle in *Richard II*, the *comedia* also quickly moves away from the conceptual terrain of the earlier play, particularly in its figuration of sovereignty. Unlike Shakespeare's treatment in *Richard II*, which concentrates on the status and readability of the king's body, Calderón's *comedia* begins to shift the perspective, complicating the question of sovereign power by turning it into a problem of reading time. To be sure, in *Richard II*, too, the representational question of the king's body is linked to the temporal problem, particularly in the closing scenes of the play, where the king figures his body as having been reduced to a "numb'ring clock" of the painful and self-destructing passage of time.[71] Nevertheless, in contrast to a poetics of power that speaks primarily through the single (if complex) figure of Richard's wasted and decomposing body, Calderón's sign-system of sovereignty moves with an almost complete disregard for the king's body. By doing so, Calderón shifts the question of sovereignty from that of a political ontology of the sacred body to a more abstract political-theological epistemology. For Calderón, the question is less what the king *is* than what Basilio does and *knows* about sovereignty. How does the king function in relation to sovereign power? Calderón's answer to this question works itself out through the performance of reading.

Thanks to his "science," Basilio believes that he will be able to steal from time that which is proper to it: its "jurisdiction and office" (*la jurisdicción y oficio*). He assumes time's function to teach (*enseñar*) and to recount (*de contar*) the future, appropriating these for himself, moving them into his own "jurisdiction." The power of sovereignty is shifted here, from the sacred body that is read, to the reader who is able to decipher the signs of the times. Basilio lauds his own power to recount (*contar*) the movement of time in the stars. In his own terms, he sees this divining ability as both a victory and a usurpation (like Bacon's imagination) of a theo-political office, the function of which is to foresee future events. In a recent edition of the play, Gregory J. Racz translates the lines "le gano al tiempo las gracias/de contar lo que yo he dicho," as "The dupe is dull chronology/As we glimpse first what's yet to come."[72] "Dull chronology" alone, however, is only part of the problem. More significantly, what is at stake is the relation between language, time, and knowledge. Basilio aspires to the knowledge of what, in Calderón's eyes, only God can know: the course of time itself. His error, which constitutes the play's pre-history as well as its initial dramatic and political-theological provocation, is to arrogate to himself the power to read the divine will. Describing the portents accompanying Segismundo's birth, Basilio explains the manner in which nature itself seemed to speak to him:

> Los cielos se escurecieron,
> temblaron los edificios,
> llovieron piedras las nubes,
> corrieron sangre los ríos.
> En este mísero, en este
> mortal planeta o signo
> nació Segismundo, dando
> de su condición indicios,

pues dio la muerte a su madre,
con cuya fiereza dijo:
hombre soy, pues que ya empiezo
a pagar mal beneficios.
                (LVS 696–708)

The skies darkened,
the buildings shook,
the clouds rained stones,
the rivers ran blood.
In this misery, in this
planet or sign of death
was born Segismundo,
giving indications of his
condition, by killing his mother,
with whose fury he said:
"I am man," since I already
begin to pay back good with evil.
                (my trans.)

Seeing in Segismundo's birth "indications" (*indicios*) of what the future will be, Basilio proceeds to justify his decision to have his son imprisoned by explaining that Segismundo was born under a "sign" (*signo*) of coming evils that only he, Basilio, could read. As he gives a more detailed account of his reading of time, the signs themselves begin to move, and Basilio arrives at what I take to be one of the play's central figures of sovereignty:[73]

Esos círculos de nieve,
esos doseles de vidrio
que el sol ilumina a rayos,
que parte la luna a giros
esos orbes de diamantes,
esos globos cristalinos
que las estrellas adornan
y que campean los signos,
son el estudio mayor
de mis años, son los libros
donde en papel de diamante,
en cuadernos de zafiros,
escribe con líneas de oro

en caracteres distintos
el cielo nuestros sucesos
ya adversos o ya benignos.
Estos leo tan veloz,
que con mi espíritu sigo
sus rápidos movimientos
por rumbos y por caminos.
                    (*LVS* 624–64)

Those circles of snow,
those canopies of glass
that the sun illuminates with rays
and the moon breaks into turns,
those diamond orbs,
those crystalline globes
that the stars adorn,
and which give the field to the signs
are the main study
of my years, are the books
where, on diamond paper
in sapphire notebooks
heaven writes in golden lines
and distinct characters
our events, whether
adverse or benign.
These I read so quickly,
that with my spirit
I follow the rapid movements
of their paths and directions.
                    (my trans.)

The "distinct characters" that Basilio reads—"circles of snow," "canopies of glass illuminated by the sun's rays," "diamond orbs," and "crystalline globes"—in heaven's books (*los libros . . . donde escribe . . . el cielo nuestros sucesos*) are also images. More specifically, they are images set in motion by the changing light. The matter of their visibility becomes complicated by their movement, which has the effect of producing even more images. Enfolded in the "sapphire notebooks" ("cuadernos de zafiros") of the heavens, the images quickly proliferate into the form of what becomes figured as a "writing" that represents history and historical movement. Basilio's desire to follow this rapid movement into its own pathways ("sus rápidos movimientos / por rumbos y por caminos"), as well as his misplaced faith that he can interpret what he finds there and translate it into political knowledge, turn out to be his error. As the play shows, Basilio's reading is a misreading. Only God can know the course of time.

Basilio's (mis)reading of these images constitutes the central problem of the play. His presumed victory over time proves short lived, as the spatial bodies and signs (*signos*) that he interprets as confirmation of the future turn out not only to be "illuminated" by the stars, but also to surrender to them and their companions. The stars "give the field" to the signs: "que las estrellas adornan y *que campean los signos*." Stanley Appelbaum's translation captures the military sense in which the constellations of signs have the power to "occupy" space: ". . . those spheres of crystal, / which the stars adorn / and the constellations occupy / are the principal study / of my years."[74] The celestial bodies here do not accede to the king's desire to read them (as the human bodies do in *Measure for Measure*), but on the contrary recede into themselves, resisting Basilio's attempt to know and decipher them as signs and indications (*indicios*) of God's will. The body-of-power withdraws into the semiotics of the image.

Basilio's failure illustrates the predicament of the baroque sovereign, according to Benjamin: his desire to make a decision that effectively wards off a coming historical catastrophe but his constitutional (in the political but perhaps also psychoanalytic sense of the word) incapacity to do so.[75] For Benjamin, the baroque sovereign's impotence is itself a symptom of modernity's malaise.

Time appears "enfolded" in images in space. For the French philosopher Gilles Deleuze, the metaphor of the "fold" is the master trope for the Baroque period's overall project of formulating a new understanding of the relationship between matter and soul. For Deleuze, the fold responds to the desire to understand that relation no longer in terms of essences, but rather, following Bacon's inductive method, in terms of function. The fold marks the Baroque period's representational operation *par excellence*: the conceptual performance that allows a range of seventeenth-century thinkers to imagine the matter-soul relation in a new way.[76] Above all, "le pli" is a productive metaphor. As the first sentence of Deleuze's study reads, "The Baroque refers not to an essence but rather to an operative function, to a trait. It endlessly produces folds."[77] According to Deleuze, the philosopher Leibniz develops this figure, along with that of the "labyrinth," most effectively, as a way of understanding the correspondence between matter below and the soul in heaven.

It is not clear whether Deleuze read *Life Is a Dream*, but he could certainly have drawn on the landscape Calderón constructs, a "confused labyrinth of bare cliffs" ("laberinto confuso / desas desnuda peñas") into which Rosaura falls at the beginning of the play.[78] If one were to pursue the connection, one might say that Rosaura's fall places her in the position of the baroque philosopher, who, in order to negotiate his or her situation in a world of confusion, functions as a "cryptographer." According to Deleuze, the cryptographer "must be able at once to account for nature and decipher the soul, to peer into the crannies of matter and read into the folds of the soul—to read both the outside and the inside of a 'body.'"[79] Rosaura, who is of course not a philosopher, on the other hand, will engage in her own form of body reading.

Rosaura is not confronted with the abstract "body" of matter or soul that the philosopher or theologian faces. Rather, she must ward off the violent approach of the all too real and frightening figure of Segismundo, who encounters her in a precarious state of endangerment in the cave. In order to maneuver through this labyrinth, Rosaura must first decipher Segismundo's mystery in the form that it appears to her through the layers of "doubtful light" enclosing his crypt:[80]

>¿No es breve luz aquella
>caduca exhalación, pálida estrella,
>que en trémulos desmayos,
>pulsando ardores y latiendo rayos,
>hace más tenebrosa
>la obscura habitación con luz dudosa?
>Sí, pues a sus reflejos
>puedo determinar, aunque de lejos,
>una prisión obscura,
>que es de un vivo cadáver sepultura.
>Y porque más me asombre,
>en el traje de fiera yace un hombre
>de prisiones cargado
>y sólo de la luz acompañado.
>Pues huir no podemos,

> desde aquí sus desdichas escuchemos,
> sepamos lo que dice.
> (LVS 85–8)

> Is it not faint, this light
> expired exhalation, pale star
> that, in trembling faints
> by pulsing burns and beating rays
> makes the obscure habitation
> even more tenebrous with doubtful light?
> Yes, since from its reflections
> I can make out, although from afar,
> a dark prison,
> a tomb of a living cadaver.
> And to my further astonishment [to see that]
> in the clothes of a beast lies a man
> weighed down by chains
> and only accompanied by light.
> Since we cannot escape from here,
> let us listen to his misfortunes
> let's know what he says.
> (my trans.)

Although Segismundo is only accompanied by doubtful, brief, and violent light (*latiendo rayos*), what distinguishes Rosaura's intellectual approach to him (if we understand that term in the Scholastic sense of sense capacities) is that it begins not with light and vision, but rather with sound and speech. In order to decipher the mystery of the "living cadaver" that is Segismundo, Rosaura must first hear the tale emerging from the darkness and reflections of his mountain prison—a setting itself linked to the malformed condition of Segismundo's being. The physio-poetic crossings of "doubtful light" (*luz dudosa*) and sound, vision and hearing ("let us listen," *escuchemos*) produce a confusion that "accompanies" Segismundo not only in his prison, but also throughout much of the play. When Segismundo first sees Rosaura, on the other hand, as she stumbles into the prohibited site of his "obscure prison" in the form of a man, he is not only captivated by "his" beauty, but Segismundo's eyes themselves begin to undergo a kind of transformation:

> Con cada vez que te veo
> nueva admiración me das,

> y cuando te miro más,
> aún mas mirarte deseo.
> Ojos hidrópicos creo
> que mis ojos deben ser,
> pues cuando es muerte el beber
> beben más, y desta suerte,
> viendo que el ver me da muerte
> estoy muriendo por ver.
> <div align="center">(<i>LVS</i> 223–33)</div>

> Each time I see you
> I admire you anew
> and the more I look at you
> the more I desire to look.
> Dropsy eyes I think
> my eyes must be,
> since when it's death to drink,
> they drink [even] more, in such a way that
> [even though] I see that seeing is killing me,
> I'm dying to see.
> (my trans.)

Unlike the queen's tear-filled eyes ("sorrow's eyes") in *Richard II*, which distort but also enable her to correctly perceive the meaning of her husband's (and with him, sovereignty's) departure, Segismundo's vision is figured as diseased through and through. His "dropsical" or, in Appelbaum's translation, "morbidly thirsty" eyes (*ojos hidrópicos*) become the site of a problematic view of reality in this early moment of the play.[81] When viewed through the lens of his diseased vision, Rosaura appears to him in a captivating but ultimately erroneous form. Unlike in Protestant allegories, such as Edmund Spenser's *Faerie Queene*, where the enticing vision of the bower of bliss has the power to corrupt healthy souls, Segismundo is compromised from the start. The sight of Rosaura only accentuates and actualizes his deprived and depraved soul. Viewed in relation to Spenser's Guyon—whose eyes, similarly transfixed by the lavish spectacle of the bower, turn from "sober," then to "greedy," and then to "wandering," before they are finally met with the Palmer's rebuke—Calderón's beast-man will eventually have to learn that all material appearance is a dream.[82] More specifically, Calderón's Catholic allegory differs from Spenser's Protestant one in that Segismundo must learn, by play's end, not to destroy the object of attraction, which is merely a sign, but rather to understand that all earthly vision consists of illusion, hence the play's title. Segismundo's "ojos hidrópicos" figure a vision of the world rooted in insatiable desire, the cure for which will require turning away from the visible into a new mode and movement. That is, Segismundo will have to be taught not only a new way of seeing but also a new way of "reading" earthly signs. He will have to learn a semiotics of sovereignty that distinguishes material from spiritual realities, signs from things, in order to, in Augustine's formulation, "raise the eye of the mind above things that are corporal and created to drink in eternal light."[83] At this early moment in the play, however, Segismundo's "dropsy eyes" still prevent him from seeing the path he must eventually take to regain his rightful position on the throne.

Critics have approached Segismundo's vision from various angles. For Leo Spitzer, part of what is at stake in the *comedia* is a neo-Platonic understanding of visual forms.[84] Ciriaco Morón points out that, additionally, Segismundo must learn the "civilizing power of beauty" that Rosaura represents.[85] In addition to these moral, philosophical, and aesthetic arguments, *Life Is a Dream* initiates a departure from the representation and conceptualization of sovereignty we have encountered thus far. In the plays we have considered, the chiasmus of seeing-dying/dying-seeing marks both the beginning of the *comedia*'s treatment as well as a certain end and conceptual death of seeing sovereignty. Moving away from the various logics of representation and specific figures for viewing the body of power—tears, transplants, and resistance—*Life Is a Dream* presents a new critical lens through which to contemplate the "body" of absolute power: precisely as that embodied in the king. From its first to its concluding act, in *Life Is a Dream* the body-of-power speaks from a different position and through a different figure than what we have seen in *Richard II*, *Measure for Measure*, and *Fuenteovejuna*. No longer is the king's (or the Duke's, or the Commander's) body the principal site of power. Rather, as we will see, as the play develops, sovereignty moves into increasingly abstract forms.

### Rosaura the Monster

Focusing on a key moment near the end of the play, Echevarría views Rosaura as one of the play's monsters, along with Segismundo. In Act III, after having passed the middle section of the drama playing Astrea, servant of Estrella (or Star, now engaged to the man who jilted Rosaura in Moscow), Rosaura returns to her opening costume. Dressed once again as a man, bearing a sword and dagger, Rosaura appeals to the newly liberated Segismundo to defend her honor and kill Astolfo. She begins her appeal by reminding Segismundo that this is their third encounter:

> Tres veces son las que ya
> me admiras, tres las que ignoras
> quién soy, pues las tres me has visto
> en diverso traje y forma.
> La primera me creíste
> varón en la rigurosa
> prisión, donde fue tu vida
> de mis desdichas lisonja.
> La segunda me admiraste
> mujer, cuando fue la pompa
> de tu majestad un sueño,
> una fantasma, una sombra.
> La tercera es hoy, *que siendo*
> *monstruo de una especie y otra,*
> entre galas de mujer
> armas de varón me adornan.
> 		(*LVS* 2713–25, my emphasis)

> Three times, now,
> you admire me, three you ignore who
> I am, since three times you've seen
> me in different costume and form.
> The first time you thought
> I was a man, when, in your harsh
> prison, your life was a
> comfort to my misfortunes.
> The second time you admired me
> as a woman, when the pomp
> of your majesty was a dream,
> a ghost, a shadow.
> The third time is today, when *being a*
> *monster of one species and another*
> between woman's robes,
> a man's arms adorn me.
> 		(my trans.)

Once again, Rosaura is figured as an in-between creature, divided but also doubled according to the play's social and political orders. The *comedia*'s three-act structure has developed this combination from the beginning, and it plays an important role in organizing this moment. Reviewing the three forms she has assumed throughout the play—man, woman ("Astrea"), and, now, man-woman—Rosaura here presents herself to Segismundo in a synthesized form, as a "monster of one species and another" ("monstruo de una especie y otra"). As Echevarría notes, the term "species"—from the Latin *spicere*, to look or to see—takes on the specific meaning in Scholastic epistemology of "the image the mind conjures of an object." For Echevarría, then, the phrase, "Monstruo de una especie y otra" refers to

> two things: on the one hand, a logical and discursive impossibility, as it is a matter of contradictory attributes; on the other hand, an impossible, ambiguous vision, which is difficult to interpret because it consists of warring appearances. We are confronted here with an epistemological and expressive impasse, a kind of aporia, analogous to those Cervantes is known for. The essence of the "monstruo de una especie y otra" is its changing nature, something which cannot be adequately conveyed by language.[86]

Echevarría identifies some of the difficulties involved in conceptualizing the monster. These have to do, in particular, with the dualities, contradictory natures, and other forms of conceptual ambiguity the figure requires us to imagine and think through.

Echevarría's account raises important questions. It is certainly true, for example, that Calderón emphasizes the "changing nature" of the "monstruo de una especie y otra" in his figuration of both Rosaura and Segismundo. At the same time, one might ask whether this "nature" is in fact an "essence" that "cannot be conveyed by language"? How does drama respond to a Counter-Reformation philosophy of essences? And how does the stage figure its own relation to these through language? For doesn't *Life Is a Dream* bear witness, on the contrary, to the stubborn fact that the changing nature of the monster can *only* be conveyed and staged in and through language, and that the very concept of monstrosity (like any other), relies on its representation for its actualization? Echevarría's observation questions the degree to which images rely on linguistic mediation.[87] How heavily does the image depend on the word, in Calderón's play? And what is the representational mode through which concepts like monstrosity and sovereignty—with which it is certainly kin, if not kind—speak during the baroque period? Before we can see what form this reconfiguration will take, however, we must first consider the play's final figure of monstrosity, Clarín.

## Clarín

The fourth sovereign monster in *Life Is a Dream* is the play's clown, Clarín, the *gracioso*, whose function, as his name indicates, is to call out, or trumpet. As the comic figure, Clarín presents an alternative perspective to the visions of power we've seen in the play so far. We first meet Clarín at the beginning of the play, complaining to Rosaura that he wants to be included in all of the story, and not merely the suffering part: "¿No es razón que yo sienta/ meterme en el pesar y no en la cuenta [in the tale]?" (32–3). Clarín's fear that he may not be taken into account foreshadows his eventual exclusion from the plot, precisely for the threat that his continually trumpeting presence poses to the structure of sovereignty. Clarín's parodic repetitions point to slippages within the play's figuration of sovereignty's representatives. Clarín thus plays a largely subversive role, continually calling attention to the more disturbing aspects of the concept, in which sovereignty comes to appear virtually indistinguishable from its opposite. That is, Clarín exposes the ambivalence at the heart of sovereignty. Playing on the comic potential opened up by the conceptual divisions and positions identified by theorists from Suárez and Bodin up to Agamben (including that between the inside and outside of law, temporality and eternity, potentiality and actuality), Clarín's voice is a constant and troubling reminder of sovereignty's constitutive ambivalence. By referring to sovereignty in a rhetoric that doubles the already doubled and divided thing that is a king, Clarín constantly reintroduces into sovereignty's representation precisely what Suárez tries to avoid: a tropological excess with the potential to divide sovereignty into its impotent double. We see this almost from the beginning of the play. After Rosaura and Clarín are captured by Clotaldo and told that they will be killed for having violated the king's decree prohibiting anyone from visiting Segismundo's hidden cave, Rosaura begs for mercy, invoking the sovereign's traditional dual prerogative of mercy and force (*piedad y rigor*): "Muévate en mí la piedad/ que será rigor notable/ que no hallen favor en ti/ ni soberbias ni humildades" (*LVS* 343–6). ("Let pity move you sir;/ it would be bad for me / if you happened to dislike / Humility as much as Pride" [Honig 14].)[88] To which Clarín then adds:

> Y si humildad y soberbia
> no te obligan, personajes
> que han movido y removido
> mil autos sacramentales,
> yo, ni humilde ni soberbio,
> sino entre las dos mitades
> entreverado, te pido
> que nos remedies y ampares.
> (*LVS* 347–54)

> And if neither humility nor pride
> can move you (being the two stock characters we see
> traipsing on and off stage
> in the same old moralities),
> I, who can't say I stand for Pride or Humility,
> but for something in between
> beg only, from where I'm standing,
> for your help and your protection.
> (Honig 14)

Clarín's view of himself as being somewhere (or some *thing*) "in-between" the stock characters of the morality plays, Humility and Pride, not only echoes the play's ongoing treatment of identity as a theatrical construct—a kind of chimera—but, more important, it also, interestingly, doubles the position of Agamben's *homo sacer*, situated within "zones of indistinction" between the inside and the outside of law, the potentiality and the actuality of power. After Clotaldo informs Rosaura and Clarín that he will spare them, despite the fact that they have violated the king's prohibition, Rosaura responds gratefully to Clotaldo, "I kiss your feet a thousand times" ("Tus pies beso mil veces"), to which Clarín adds, "y yo los viso": "and I authorize them; for what's a letter more or less among friends?" ("que una letra más o menos / no reparan dos amigos" [896–8]). Clarín's addition of a "letter," as well as his continual word play (in this case between "*beso*"—"I kiss," and "*viso*"—"I authorize"), take advantage of language's ongoing potential to deform sovereign authority by subverting its meaning, as well as its rituals and ceremonies. In this vein, Clarín's assertion that "they call all deformed princes 'Segismundos'" ("Segismundo llaman todos / los príncipes contrahechos" [2264–5]) not only underscores the co-implication of sovereignty and monstrosity established throughout the play (as well as his own role as a deformer of language and power), but it also names the very condition of sovereignty as that which has become "*contrahecho*": literally, "made against itself."[89] Subjected to Clarín's voice, sovereignty's claims for its own coherence, unity, and self-containment are de-formed.

From the play's point of view, then, in order to maintain or re-contain sovereignty's ideological integrity, Clarín's subversive presence must be eliminated. This is so, not only because his words continually undermine the hierarchy of power in the play, but also especially because his insistence that the world is governed by an order of fate ("la inclemencia del hado") rather than providence threatens to undermine the Augustinian time frame on which *Life Is a Dream* relies. Consequently, apart from the servant who Segismundo throws from the balcony, Clarín is the only principal character in *Life Is a Dream* who dies—which he does, ironically, reaffirming the inevitability of the "force of destiny":

> pues no hay seguro camino
> a la fuerza del destino
> y a la inclemencia del hado;
> y así, aunque a libraros vais
> de la muerte con huir,
> mirad que vais a morir
> si está de Dios que muráis.
> (*LVS* 3089–95)

> And there's no safe highway
> leading past the force of destiny
> or fate's inclemency.
> So if by fleeing you now attempt
> to free yourselves from death,
> remember, you die when it's
> God's will you die.
> (Honig 108)

Sovereignty will no longer be represented through the dominant figure of the King and the successful English fiction of the two bodies, as in Kantorowicz's well-known narrative. Rather, it will begin to move into the kaleidoscopic figures of movement itself that Basilio attempts to read in the heavens. The representational mode that best responds to the conceptual and historical demands of this movement, as Calderón shows us, is allegory.

But this form of allegory is different from the theological allegory of much medieval and early modern thought, which functions ideologically, to explain a series of relations. While this is the style of allegory that much Calderón scholarship (such as that of Rupp) has focused on, it is not the type critics such as Echevarría or Cascardi discuss; they focus instead on Benjaminian allegory. No longer does analogy, or even metaphor, respond to sovereignty's "contemplative necessities," as Benjamin calls them. Instead, *Life Is a Dream* opens sovereignty up to new theoretical demands; at the same time, it empties the concept of sovereignty out, leaving us pathless with regard to its symbolic space.

Against Echevarría's claim that "the essence of the monster cannot be adequately conveyed in language," what the plays shows, on the contrary, is that this changing nature is one that can only be conveyed by language. The monster becomes one (principal to be sure, but not exclusive) element, in a wider construction of metaphors Calderón deploys to imagine historical movement. It is not so much a question, then, of whether monstrosity—and its shadow sovereignty—can be conveyed by language, as it is one of the particular arrangement and performance of the language in question. The more specific question the play asks, with regard to sovereignty in particular, is whether that language is one that speaks through images.

As we have seen, Basilio's mistake at the opening of the play is to believe that he can read "the course of history" in the divine writing in the sky—a "writing" that comes in the form of images: "the books / where, on paper of diamonds / and sapphire folds / heaven writes in distinct characters / in golden lines our events." His error is double, involving both a presumption of jurisdiction and interpretation, as a historicist reading of the play reminds us, pointing out that his view of himself as a "scientific" king would have been "absurd," for Calderón as well as his public.[90] As Suárez's Jesuit predecessor, Juan de Mariana, succinctly puts it, in his treatise on kingship,

> Oh, sweet prince . . . avoid all superstition. Take all art [*toda arte*] that aspires to the knowledge of heaven in order to investigate the future [*indagar lo futuro*] as futile and vain. Never devote that which

is owed to your duties [*debido a los negocios*] to leisure or to the contemplation of time.[91]

Read in ideological terms, one of the play's messages is clear enough: God's "writing" can never be *directly* read, not even by a king. Rather, the duty of a king instead is to exercise his office with prudence, a key term in early modern Spanish political theory. A prudent king is to "work well" in the service of God and his kingdom, to "*obrar bien*," "do good," an expression that corresponds to the Catholic formula *caritas forma fides* (against the Lutheran, *sola fides*).[92] As Segismundo will later put it, in one of the play's best-known passages:

> . . . sea verdad o sueño,
> obrar bien es lo que importa;
> si fuere verdad, por serlo;
> si no, por ganar amigos
> para cuando despertemos.
>       (*LVS* 2423–7)

> whether it be truth or dream,
> to do good is what matters;
> if it were true, for being true,
> if not, in order make friends
> for when we wake up.
>       (my trans.)

That the sovereign must act with prudence is one of the lessons repeatedly stressed in early modern Catholic treatises on kingship, most of which follow Aquinas's *De regimine principum* and *Summa theologica*. As we have already seen, Diego de Saavedra Fajardo's emblem book, *The Idea of a Christian-Political Prince* (*Idea de un príncipe político-cristiano*), presents 100 lessons to the sovereign in the form of pictures. In the twenty-eighth *empresa* (emblem), an hourglass supporting a scepter, around which is wrapped a crowned serpent, reads, "Prudence is the measure and the rule of the virtues" ("Es la prudencia regla y medida de las virtudes"):

> Por estos aspectos de los tiempos ha de hacer juicio y pronosticar la prudencia de V.A., no por aquellos de los planetas, que, siendo pocos y de movimiento regulado, no pueden (cuando tuvieran virtud) señalar la inmensa variedad de accidentes que producen los casos y

dispone el libre albedrío, ni la especulación y experiencia son bastantes a constituir una sciencia segura y cierta de causa tan remotas.⁹³

Because of these aspects of time, your majesty must judge and predict with prudence, not following the planets, which are few and whose regulated movements are incapable (if they had virtue) of signaling the immense variety of accidents that produce events [*los casos*] and dispose the free will, nor are speculation and experience sufficient to constitute a sure science of understanding such remote causes.
(my trans.)

Where prudence is central to sovereignty, representation is central to prudence. Prudence requires knowledge of the proper relationship between time and representation. Saavedra Fajardo's sovereign serpent sees future and past at once, collapsing dual temporalities into one, in the two mirrors placed by his sides. What kind of "vision" is this? The twenty-ninth *empresa* reiterates the warning against divination:

La presunción de saber lo futuro es una especie de rebeldía contra Dios y una loca competencia con su eterna sabiduría, la cual permitió que la prudencia humana pudiese conjeturar, pero no adivinar, para tenella más sujeta con la incertidumbre de los casos.⁹⁴

The presumption to know the future is a kind of rebellion against God and a mad competition with His eternal wisdom, which permitted human prudence to conjecture but not to divine, so that it would be more subjected to the uncertainty of events.
(my trans.)

The sovereign may "conjecture" but not "divine" ("pudiese conjeturar, pero no adivinar"). Both *empresas* stress the importance of "reading" time (especially future time) with prudence.⁹⁵ Calderón similarly emphasizes that before order in the state can be restored, Basilio must learn that heaven's will is not directly legible, even to a king. Paralleling the play's overall thematic and conceptual movement, from disproportion to restoration, is the path Basilio's understanding must also travel, as the king moves from being a "rapid" (*veloz*) reader (661) to a "prudent" servant of God. At the center of this drama lies the question of the "signs" (*las señales*) the king reads. For Calderón, these signs come in the form of "ciphers and images."

Related to the mathematical concept of zero, as well as to the modern notion of the "code," the "cipher" (which in modern Spanish can refer to "secret writing," or to "figure") is a preeminently enigmatic figure. For this reason, I suggest that it is also particularly well suited for a conversation about the meaning of sovereignty. As the 1611 dictionary of lexicographer Sebastián de Covarrubias makes clear, "cifra" was understood precisely as an "enigmatic writing":

> CIFRA. Escritura enigmática, con carácteres peregrinos, o los nuestros trocados unos por otros, en valor o en lugar. Y el mesmo nombre está corrompido, porque San Isidoro, lib. 1, cap. 21, *De notis*, la llama *criphia*, y con esta nota de una ce inversa y un punto en medio ↄ, dice así: "*cryphia, circuli pars interior cum puncto ponitur in his locis, ubi quaestio dura et obscura aperiri, vel solvi non potest.*" Es término griego, y díjose del nombre κρύφιος, *occultus*. Tengo escrito un tratado de cifras, al cual remito lo que dellas se podia aquí decir, porque hará volumen entero, y para lo que yo pretendo en el trabajo de las etimologías, pienso se ha cumplido con lo dicho. Sánchez Brocense, *cifras adag, scytala laconica,* tiene este nombre cifra por arábigo. Cuando queremos encarecer lo que dejamos de decir, pareciéndoles a los oyentes que se ha dicho mucho informando en algún negocio, solemos añadir: "Esto es cifra para lo que pudiera decir"; y así sea esto cifra de la cifra. Cifrar, recopilar una cosa y reducirla a pocas razones. Descifrar, declarar algunas palabras obscuras.[96]

> CIFRA. Enigmatic writing, with characters [letters, words] that peregrinate or that become confused with others in worth or place. And this same name is corrupted, because Saint Isidro, in book 1, chapter 21 of *De notis*, calls it *criphia*, and with this note of an inverted letter C and a point in the middle ↄ, he says, "*cryphia, circuli pars interior cum puncto, ponitur in his locis, ubi quaestio dura et obscura aperiri, vel solvi non potest.*" It is a Greek term, and one sense of the name κρύφιος, *Occultus*. I have written a treatise on ciphers, to which I base what can be said about them here, because it would form an entire volume. For what I want to convey regarding etymology I think I have achieved it with what I've said. Sánchez Brocense, *cifras adag, scytala laconica*, considers this name "cipher" to be Arabic. When we want to make what we have more valuable, so that it seems to the listeners that one has said a lot, we usually add, "This is a cipher of what could be said [about it]"—and like that, may this [definition] itself be a cipher of a cipher. To cipher is to recompile something and reduce it to a few reasons. To "decipher" [is to] declare some words obscure.

(my trans.)

Part of the reason that the "cipher" (*cifra*) is an "enigmatic writing" is that it is a writing that is constantly in motion, "with characters that peregrinate" ("con carácteres peregrinos"). Its movement contributes, to no small degree, to the difficulty of its reading. In order to interpret the cipher, one must literally arrest its motion—an activity that, in a sense, also negates it. Hence the term "de-cipher" (*descifrar*), which can be read both as an undoing of the cipher, and also as its decoding. After citing his Greek and Latin sources, as usual, Covarrubias seems to doubt whether he should offer more of a discussion, given that the term is so complex that elsewhere it has led him to write a separate "treatise" on ciphers that "would form an entire volume." Nonetheless, he proceeds to add that "cifra" is also the name for the rhetorical gesture we engage in when we want to make something appear like it has more value than it does. Covarrubias then cleverly (and not without a little cheek) has his own definition perform this very gesture, by closing with the flourish: "When we want to make what we have more valuable, so that it seems to the listeners that one has said a lot, we usually add, 'This is a cipher of what could be said'—and like that, let this [definition] itself be a cipher of a cipher" (!). Thus ends Covarrubias's definition of the *cifra*, in a humorous and marvelous performance of the baroque gesture *par excellence*—the *mise-en-abîme*.

In addition to the cipher (difficult enough to interpret, as we have just seen), the second figure of sovereignty—the images (*las estampas*)—present their own challenges to reading. "Estampas" can be translated as "images," "scenes," "pictures," or more generally, "examples," "representations," "portraits," "personifications," or even "presences."[97] Calderón further complicates the question by linking their legibility to the morality of the reader. The correct reading/viewing of these signs, the play argues, depends on the moral conditioning of the reader/viewer. Against the Machiavellian maxim that the new prince must know how to read the "historical mutation," for Calderón, as well as Catholic theorists of sovereignty, such as Mariana or Suárez, history never appears in a directly legible form. On the contrary, it is precisely through the motif of non-legibility that *Life Is a Dream* begins to re-establish the Thomistic vertical relations of being that we saw deposed in *Richard II*. For Calderón, it is not only the king but *all* Christian subjects, who must be reminded that all temporal power is merely "loaned power" (*poder prestado*) (2370). This is the power that, for Suárez and others, the political community transfers to the king, who, in turn, employs it for their well-being. Ernst Cassirer summarizes the notion of political power that is being deployed here.[98] Even though a "Catholic" theory of sovereignty, such as Suárez's, generally accords to the temporal ruler a more indirect access to ultimate power than King James's theory does, nevertheless, for Calderón, Basilio must still be able to "read" time's movement to some degree. But he must do so prudently. The subtlety of this necessity poses problems. These begin with the text that is to be read. Calderón figures this text as one that comes with specific indicators (*indicios*) of God's will, a "text" that *Life Is a Dream* transforms into one in which the signs of history appear, as Benjamin puts it, "in the setting":

> If history is secularized in the setting, this is an expression of the same metaphysical tendency which simultaneously led, in the exact sciences, to the infinitesimal method. In both cases chronological movement is grasped and analysed in a spatial image. The image of the setting or, more precisely, of the court, becomes the key to historical understanding.[99]

## *Allegory's Schema*

The figure of the court becomes Benjamin's key image for understanding the processes of both sovereignty and historical movement.[100] The court completes Benjamin's baroque tableau, in which the sovereign is history's representative and the court its stage, history's "setting." Benjamin takes his *schema* of the "court" from Lope de Vega's *El Palacio Confuso* (*The Confused Palace/Court*), which not only provides the title but also the emblem for what Benjamin sees as the distinctly baroque mode of representing history. The court, that is, lies at what he calls the baroque's "allegorical way of seeing."[101] "Allegory," Benjamin writes,

> in its most developed form brings with it a court (*einen Hof*); around the figural center, which is never missing from genuine allegories, in opposition to conceptual circumlocutions, a host of emblems is grouped. They seem arbitrarily arranged: *The Confused "Court"*—the title of a Spanish mourning play—could be cited as the schema of allegory. "Dispersion" (*Zerstreuung*) and "Collection" (*Sammlung*) name the law of this court. Things are brought together according to their meaning; indifference to their being-there (*Dasein*) disperses them once again.[102]

Where allegory is the figure of history, Lope de Vega's play is a figure of allegory. Its rhythms of collection and dispersion, like the contracting and expanding of the human heart, structure the movement of life in the seventeenth century.[103] The setting of the court that lies at the figural center of Benjamin's schema of history here is itself is a "confused" thing. It is also a spatial image, that of a complex historical process of gathering and dispersion.[104]

Benjamin's allegory is as notoriously difficult as it is important to twentieth-century criticism in theory. It is not my intention here to give a full account of its complexities, of which much has been written, but rather to concentrate on three specific aspects of the figure that are notable in Benjamin's discussion and that have directly to do with the representation of sovereignty: first, its emergence in response to a theo-political crisis; second, the centrality of the image to allegory; and third, its relation to historical and poetic movement.

Benjamin's allegory emerges in response to what he describes as the "contemplative necessities . . . implicit in the contemporary theological situation."[105] It is linked to the religious problematic of the seventeenth century, by which Benjamin means the perceived loss of a relation to transcendence as a result (as we have seen) of the "emptying out" of an eschatological perspective:

> The hereafter is emptied of everything which contains the slightest breath of this world, and from it the baroque extracts a profusion of things which customarily escaped the grasp of artistic formulation and, at its high point, brings them violently into the light of the day in order to clear an ultimate heaven, enabling it, as a vacuum, one day to destroy the world with catastrophic violence.[106]

The mechanism designed to gather and exalt meaning has itself become empty, merely mechanical. This emptying out has multiple consequences. Not only does it bear catastrophic violence, but it also implies the destruction of the conceptual structure formerly dominant in the philosophical schema linking God to his creatures—the *analogia entis*. As we have seen in Chapter 1, this structure was brought to its breaking point in the early seventeenth century, as the result of many factors, including Suárez's reconceptualization in his twenty-eighth *Metaphysical Disputation*. The eventual deposition of the mode in philosophy and theology prepares the way for the entrance of a new design.

Allegory does not arise from a simple interplay or competition between a philosophy of transcendence and one of immanence, or the replacement of one by the other. Rather, it bears witness, in Benjamin's view, to a paradoxical return or enfolding of one into the other, as the entire face of Nature undergoes a radical reconfiguration. As one of Benjamin's most authoritative readers, Samuel Weber, explains, "What the baroque rejects," in Benjamin's reading,

> is any admission of the limitation of immanence, and it does so by emptying transcendence of all possible representable content. Far from doing away with transcendence, however, such emptying out only endows it with a force that is all the more powerful: that of the vacuum, of the absolute and unbounded other, which, since it is no longer representable, is also no longer localizable "out there" or as a "beyond." The otherness that is no longer allowed to remain transcendent therefore reappears this side of the horizon, represented as a "cataract," abyss, or fall. Or, even more radically, such transcendence will be represented by, and as, *allegory*.[107]

The conceptual deposition of eschatology's authority corresponds with the simultaneous tearing apart of the sovereign into the three figures of tyrant, martyr, and intriguer. Sovereignty fragments and falls down. It is no longer representable in relation to an elevated "outside." Because this representational option has been cut off, in Benjamin's reading, the concept of sovereignty itself collapses, and transcendence along with it, only to suddenly reappear, in an ironic turnaround, within the realm of fallen materiality. Given this "historical" and theological predicament, the options for representing sovereignty change. Once again, our understanding of it will come to depend on its representational possibilities.

As if he were aware of the representational opportunities presented by the political and theological situation that Benjamin is describing, Calderón makes the "throne room" the centerpiece of a key political-theological movement:

> El dosel de la jura, reducido
> a segunda intención, a horror segundo,
> teatro funesto es donde importuna
> representa tragedias la fortuna . . .
> (2440–3)

> . . . the throne room,
> split by duplicity and horror,
> becomes again the grisly stage where
> urgent fate enacts its tragedies.
> (Honig 87)

The passage is crucial for the complexities that allegory introduces to the scene of sovereignty. The "dosel de la jura" (literally, the canopy under which is created royal jurisdiction) is, here, "reducido"—that is, "reduced" or "degraded" to another stage that lies behind the scenes—a shadow stage. Although this has been translated by Honig in terms of a "splitting," the meaning of "reducido a" suggests an activity that is quite a bit more complex than a mere splitting or division. No longer understood in terms of the dualities of the king's two bodies, the formal and juridical space of sovereignty created by Calderón's "dosel de la jura" cannot simply be "split." Rather, it is subject to a complex process of transformation. "Reducir a" can mean many different things, including to return a thing (*volver algo*); to diminish something; to change currency (*cambiar moneda*), and to summarize a narration (*resumir en pocas razones un discurso, narración*). With regard to "bodies," specifically, it can refer to their division, *but also* (as in chemistry and physics) to their liquefaction or decomposition (*dividir un cuerpo en partes menudas; hacer que un cuerpo pase del estado sólido al líquido descomponer un cuerpo en sus principios o elementos*). Additionally, it can mean to subject one to obedience (*sujetar a la obediencia a quienes se habían separado de ella*).[108] Many of these senses of transformation and subjection are at play here. But above all, what is at stake in Calderón's scene of sovereignty's "reduction" is a transposition within sovereignty itself, from one scene into another. In its reference to "a second horror," the line suggests that there is more than mere oath-taking at stake here. There is, behind or apart from the manifest scene, another grisly, horrible, and vile "theater of sorrows—where meddling fortune represents tragedies" ("teatro funesto es donde importuna / representa tragedias la fortuna" [2442–3]). The event of sovereignty's collapse is thus more complicated than that of a simple division or splitting.[109] In order to understand this we have to continue to read.

As the play proceeds, sovereignty's transformation undergoes a double movement. First, as we have seen, *Life Is a Dream* breaks sovereignty off from the body, dispersing its attributes among the four "monstrous" figures of Basilio, Segismundo, Rosaura, and Clarín. At the same time, along with this process of disembodying facets of sovereignty, a second movement occurs in which the concept is re-embodied in the abstract form of allegorical writing in space. It is to this spatial text of moving images that Calderón turns to work out his vision of sovereignty. Sovereignty's force is figured as occurring within the movement of the images. This is also what makes the concept rather inscrutable, not only to Basilio but also to all involved. The play's conclusion returns us to this reconfigured sign system, as it also reiterates its opening point that—precisely because of this new "body-of-power"—sovereignty will ultimately remain illegible. As Segismundo says at the end of the play:

> Lo que está determinado
> del cielo, y en azul tabla
> Dios con el dedo escribió,
> de quien son cifras y estampas
> tantos papeles azules
> que adornan letras doradas,
> nunca engañan, nunca mienten;
> porque quien miente y engaña
> es quien, para usar mal dellas,
> las penetra y las alcanza.
> (*LVS* 3162–71)

> What is determined by heaven
> and written on blue tablets
> with God's finger, are
> *ciphers and images* of Him,
> so many blue papers
> adorned by golden letters
> never deceive, never lie;
> since the one who lies and
> deceives is he who, to use them
> badly [would] penetrate and grasp them.
> (my trans.)

The divine will appears in writing. What God determines, comes in the form of "ciphers and images" (*cifras y estampas*) "adorned by golden letters" (*que adornan letras doradas*)—which, on the one hand, must be read by the king, but, on the other, can never be fully deciphered.

"Cifras y estampas" are thus both the form through which God's will appears and also the mark of its inscrutability. They warn the reader intent on interpreting the divine writing to avoid false adulation, as the encryption of the word "adorar" in the juxtaposition "adornar-doradas" might even be taken to suggest. Returning to the play's opening figure for problematic viewing, Segismundo's "ojos hidrópicos" (dying to see / seeing to die) present us with a rhetorical crossing of vision and death that could be extended to the meaning of the play as a whole, with respect to the conceptualization of sovereignty as a "body-of-power." The changing relations of vision, death, and desire, contained and crossing in complex ways in the poetics of "dying to see / seeing to die," lie at the heart of sovereignty's transformation and, ultimately, end. That is, the play prefigures the imminent death of one mode of viewing the conceptualization of sovereignty—as embodied. As an indication of this demise, Calderón's language not only figures Segismundo's vision, it also dis-figures it, and along with it, the very mode through which we view sovereignty in the play. Here, the chiasmic structure of Segismundo's vision—the form through which Calderón allows us to see him—also marks the vacated place of sovereignty, the place where sovereignty is not. Thus, by play's end, it is impossible to fully see Segismundo's body because it is in constant motion, changing through the forms of the living skeleton, animated corpse, human monster ("esqueleto vivo / animado muerto—hombre de las fieras / fiera de los hombres") and, finally into invisibility itself. If we follow Calderón's figuration of Segismundo closely, from beginning to end, we see that Calderón begins to imagine sovereign power as a force that manifests itself through the effects of its representation on others. Sovereignty's "speech," that is, is viewed in the bodies of those who admire Segismundo: "Tu ingenio a todos admira" (3302). Sound into sight, cause into effect, concept into space, sovereignty exists in the transference. The concept "is" nowhere: its existence depends on the motion of the signs. Sovereignty in *Life Is a Dream* is this motion itself and the power to set it off. This is a power that lies not with the reader of the signs, as Basilio mistakenly assumes at the beginning of the play, but rather with the sign system itself and the logic that governs it. By the time we arrive at the play's conclusion, the body-of-power is no longer embodied in the king at all—in fact, in either of them (Basilio *or* Segismundo). Rather, it has become fragmented, dispersed, and only then recollected—in the structure of allegory. Allegory is that which, in Benjamin's words, presents the "non-existence of what it presents."[110] The convoluted nature of the description is a reflection of the relation between absence and a turning movement it attempts to capture. It shows that what is presented to us is no thing. Like Suárez's goat-stag, what the trope represents has no real being. Precisely for this reason, allegory is perhaps modern sovereignty's most adequate scheme, a trope that presents its reader neither with what the trope enframes, nor with any being outside its framework. A quintessential baroque constellation, allegory, like Calderón's *perpetuum mobile* of the cipher and the image, presents that which isn't there but which, nevertheless, through its very presentation, continues to bind us to its images.[111]

Benjamin's illustration at this point is a significant one. He concludes his study by turning to the philosophical question of the problem of evil. Citing the German baroque playwright Sigmund von Birken, Benjamin's conclusion opens with the figure of *tears*—"Mit Weinen streuten wir den Samen in die Brachen / und giegen traurig aus." ("Weeping we scattered the seed on the fallow ground and sadly we went away.") Like von Birken's sad characters, "Allegory goes away empty-handed," Benjamin writes. And then,

> Evil as such, which it cherished as enduring profundity, exists only in allegory, is nothing other than allegory, and means something different from what it is. It means precisely the non-existence of what it presents. The absolute vices, as exemplified by tyrants and intriguers, are allegories. They are not real, and that which they represent, they possess only in the subjective view of melancholy; they are this view, which is destroyed by its own offspring because they only signify its blindness. They point to the absolutely subjective pensiveness, to which alone they owe their existence. By its allegorical form evil as such reveals itself to be a subjective phenomenon. The enormous, anti-artistic subjectivity of the baroque converges here with the theological essence of the subjective. The Bible introduces evil in the concept of knowledge. The serpent's promise to the first men was to make them "knowing both good and evil." But it is said of God after the creation: 'And God saw everything that he had made, and behold it was very good.' Knowledge of evil therefore has no object. There is no evil in the world. It arises in man himself, with the desire for knowledge, or rather for judgment.[112]

Benjamin's move to the Bible seems striking here. One of his objectives throughout the *Origin of German Tragic Drama* has been to consider the relation between language, materiality, and knowledge in the seventeenth century. One way he does this, as we have seen, is to situate the question within the problematic of what he calls the "contemplative necessities" of the baroque.[113] These are largely theological "contemplative necessities," starting with the question of language, after the Fall, thrown into renewed crisis with the Reformation's critique of mediation. Additionally, they include the theo-political construction of baroque sovereignty, in which the sovereign must avert a state of exception but is, at the same time, constitutionally incapable of doing so. Finally, they include changes in both Protestant and Catholic cultures to the authoritative place held by eschatological narratives, which have now been "emptied out" under the period's "over-strained transcendental impulse."[114] Thus, Benjamin's claim that "a critical understanding of the *Trauerspiel*, in its extreme, allegorical form, is possible only from the higher domain of theology," refers at the same time to the historical and representational implications that theology's changing face in the seventeenth century brings into view [115]

At the same time, Benjamin's understanding of theology is difficult.[116] That Benjamin situates the question of language within the theological and especially political-theological problematic of the seventeenth century, in which subjectivity can only emerge in relation to these "contemplative necessities," does not mean that his analysis of baroque drama is equivalent to a historical study of religion.[117] To recall his epistemo-critical prologue, his concerns throughout are at least as much about the question of representation and the availability of knowledge in the face of cataclysmic political and theological events as they are properly "theological" or "sociological," in Carl Schmitt's sense. Consequently, one of the book's consistent questions is that of how historical change manifests itself at the level of dramatic form. How do ideas appear in relation to their real historical conditions? And what kind of relationship does the critic have to both these ideas and their materiality on stage? It is partly in response to these questions that Benjamin begins to formulate his singular notion of the dialectical image. As critics note, this is as good a place as any to have an example of Benjamin's dialectical image.[118]

In addition to the catalyst it becomes for Benjamin to think through the epistemological problems and questions of dialectical representation, baroque drama, and particularly that of Calderón, also provides Benjamin with material for his re-theorization of allegory. In the final sections of the *Trauerspiel* book, Benjamin links what he describes as the "anti-artistic" and "theological" subjectivity of the baroque to the problem of theodicy. Taking as a point of departure an Augustinian understanding of evil as that which neither is nor contains any being, Benjamin turns to the representational capacities of allegory to represent such a non-being: "Evil as such . . . exists only in allegory, is nothing other than allegory, and means something different from what it is.[119] It means precisely the non-existence of what it presents."[120] Allegory is the mode through which the non-being of evil speaks. Like evil, what allegory presents, in the end, is nothing. Or, rather, it shows that what is presented to us—for example, sovereignty—is nothing. It has no *being*.[121] It neither refers to, nor does it contain, any substance. Like the chimera, then, allegory is a phantasm, a cognition, and an image of absence at once. Unlike the analogy of being, whose function it is in *Richard II* to present us with a political ontology, the theory of allegory Benjamin formulates via his reading of Calderón confronts us with a trope whose very objective is to present what is not there. This allegory marks a departure from the structure of analogy and its hierarchical gradations of being explored in *Richard II*. Neither is it akin to the metaphorical transfers and transplants of law in *Measure for Measure*, and the resistances they produce in *Fuenteovejuna*. In both of these plays, despite its deferments and delays, sovereignty remains on the horizon. We are still in relation to sovereignty. In *Life Is a Dream*, however, the situation is different. What the tropes of sovereignty bear in Calderón's *comedia* is not even a suspension of being: it is no thing at all. Sovereignty's signs, the cipher and the image, contain no being. Calderón's sign-system empties out what it presents—above all, the being of power contained in an (earthly) body. Calderón takes sovereignty to a terrain we have not seen until now—hence, perhaps, Benjamin's surprising turn to the seemingly new topic of evil at the end of the *Trauerspiel* book.

As we have seen in different ways, sovereignty's conceptual crux lies with the problem of embodiment. In its seventeenth-century theorists, from James and Suárez, through Shakespeare, Lope, and Calderón, the metaphor of the "body" is given a tremendous role in articulating and overcoming the obvious discrepancy between any particular instantiation of sovereignty in a symbolic body, and the infinite body-of-power that it represents.[122] King James's theory, as we have seen, conceives of this relation in the metaphysical terms of analogy, figuring his own body-of-power through the triple similitudes of "head," "father," and God. Sovereignty, in this view, appears as an idea that, as Gilles Deleuze puts it, "broaden[s] according to a whole network of natural relations." In the case of analogy, these relations are understood in hierarchical ontological and political terms, ascending from lower to higher gradations of being, as we move up from the "body" to the "head." Here, the representational structure of analogy "raises the concept up," as Deleuze puts it, in order to put it into contact with an "Idea" that develops it "morally or esthetically."[123] Not only in this case but in all the case studies we have examined, from *Richard II* through *Life Is A Dream*, the concept of sovereignty is understood through its underlying representational structure. In *Richard II*, the analogical logic of the representation does not reinforce but rather produces our view of the concept. Calderón's play presents us with a different logic. In contrast with the analogical thinking that governs our picture of sovereignty in *Richard II*, *Life Is A Dream* sees sovereignty through a less orderly and more distorted lens. The representational structures the play relies on to figure the concept of sovereignty are more hybrid, complex, and mobile than analogy. Their "logic," as Echevarría has argued, is a logic of the monster. For Echevarría, the visual nature of monstrosity "seems to represent Calderón's zeal for rendering visible a concept of representation that eludes the precision and coherence of logical as well as poetic discourse."[124] Extending Echevarría's account of monstrosity in Calderón specifically to the problem of sovereignty, I would add that Calderón represents the concept of sovereignty itself as a chimera and, indeed, a form of monstrosity.

## Conclusion

After *Richard II*, sovereignty begins to take on a new kind of visibility, one no longer produced as an effect of the analogical correspondences between essences and causes, theorized by the Scholastics, and differently deployed in divine right theory. What now comes into view is a reconfigured representational mode of the cipher. Here, sovereignty appears in the refracted effects of allegory. Allegory corresponds to the changing nature of the new body-of-power, which is now a "body" that is constantly in motion. While monsters in *Life Is a Dream* are indeed creatures that are "so contradictory and multiple that they reenact the clashes of the dynamic reality they represent,"[125] what is crucial is not, as Echevarría argues, that the concept of representation this implies "eludes the precision and coherence of logical as well as poetic discourse," but rather the fact that the new discourse of sovereignty relies on a theory of representation in which the "precision" required assumes an alternative "logic." Replacing an exhausted political-theo-logical discourse of sovereignty based on the king's body, Calderón's visualization of the sovereign-monster in terms of constantly mutating images presents instead a politico-theo-*il*-logical discourse in which the body-of-power appears in the form of moving pictures in space. The concept of representation rendered visible here is one that figures not only the movement of allegory ("one form of non-being into another"), but also the generation of a force that arises from the "empty place" of absolute power, as sovereignty moves into the figural space of the image. Calderón's *comedia* thus confronts and complicates Agamben's structural and topographical analysis of sovereignty in terms of its zones with its own figure of allegory and staging of moving images.[126] It also requires us to modify Echevarría's understanding of the function of monstrosity in Calderón. Against Echevarría's claim that the "changing nature of the monster cannot be adequately conveyed by language," Calderón's monstrous sovereignty stages a nature that can *only* be conveyed in language—in which, as Agamben puts it, language itself "is the sovereign [that], in a permanent state of exception, declares that there is nothing outside language and that language is always beyond itself."[127] Calderón and Agamben converge around this nothingness, in that both find in the structure of language, the very structure—and *paradigm*—of politics in general, and sovereignty, or rather its absence, in particular. Both structures are founded on language. For Agamben,

> [t]he particular structure of law has its foundation in this presuppositional structure of human language. It expresses the bond of inclusive exclusion to which a thing is subject because of the fact of being in language, of being named. To speak [*dire*] is, in this sense, always to "speak the law," *ius dicere*.[128]

Agamben thinks sovereignty through language and through ontology—in other words, through language *as* ontology. Calderón theorizes ontology through theater. For Calderón and Agamben, the figuration of sovereignty itself participates in the conceptual capture of what both call "life." For both, too, "life" is bound up in its representational orders. Literature and theater help us view and understand these orders. Calderón's vision of a life (*la vida*) that appears in the form of moving pictures in space suggests that the "modern logic of sovereignty" is, in the end, a picture logic. It is also a "logic" that empties out the substance of what it presumably presents. Where, for Agamben, that emptying consists of one version of life (*bios*) excluding another (*zoē*), Calderón shows how the presumption of sovereignty is always met with an absence. The movements of Calderón's "ciphers and images"—*cifras y estampas*—capture the emptying-out logics that both thinkers, in different ways, identify at the heart of the concept of sovereignty.

CHAPTER 5

# Return: The "Wrinkles" of Mystery in *The Winter's Tale*

> The word "effect," from the Latin *effectus*, the past participle of *efficere*, "to bring about, to accomplish, to effect, to perform," in effect (that is to say, virtually) comes to stand for any event or action whose structure finds its prime model in the theological, perhaps even theistic concept of God the being that has no cause outside itself (hence the most metaphysical of God's names, *causa sui*). On this reading, not even the most artificial special effect could be possible—that is to say, thought or experienced—without some reference to (or conjuring up) of the miracle and everything for which it stands . . . (Lest we forget, the word miracle comes from Latin *miraculum* and the verb *mirari*, which means "to wonder at.").
>
> —Hent de Vries, "In Media Res"[1]

> It is perhaps altogether questionable whether we have any conscious memories *from* childhood: perhaps we have only memories *of* childhood. These show us the first years of our lives not as they were, but as they appeared to us at later periods, when the memories were aroused. At these times of arousal the memories of childhood did not *emerge*, as one is accustomed to saying, but *were formed*, and a number of motives that were far removed from the aim of historical fidelity had a hand in influencing both the formation and the selection of the memories.
>
> —Sigmund Freud, "Screen Memories"[2]

The representational shift, into the allegorical figures of the cipher and the image (*cifras y estampas*) staged in *Life Is a Dream*, appears to provide us with one form of an ending. By the time we arrive at Calderón's dream play, the effects of sovereignty's rupture from the King's body, staged in Shakespeare's *Richard II*, could be said to be complete. Sovereignty, in *Life Is a Dream*, no longer speaks through—at least the human—body at all. Nor does it even seem to require the law, or that the bodies subject to its force signify its presence, as in *Measure for Measure*. In *Life Is a Dream* sovereignty arrives at what might be considered its late modern representational form: moving images in space. All of the questions of the previous chapters, of sovereignty's origins, derivations, delegations and even delays, would seem at this point to have been successfully redirected from the divided political-theological symbol of the king's body, to the more abstract form of allegory and the disembodied image. As with the de-territorialized flows of information, capital, and military power that move through cyberspace today, sovereignty's representational occupation of spatialized networks of icons and images prefigures the complex media forms through which postmodern global power speaks today.[3] The body-of-power that we have been tracking throughout these pages has, indeed, moved on.

*The Winter's Tale* (1609–11) complicates this story.[4] Shakespeare's hybrid, late play troubles the neat narrative movement of sovereignty's journey "from body-to-space," frequently recounted in political histories and conceptual genealogies, including, in many ways my own. *The Winter's Tale* throws a kink into the machinery of this scheme.[5] Along the way, Shakespeare's experimental play returns us to many of the questions we have been considering in the previous chapters, regarding sovereignty's conceptualization as a "body-of-power," our relation to that "body," and, above all, the effects that the configuration of this relation produces. At the same time, *The Winter's Tale* is not merely a play of returns. As we shall see, Shakespeare's romance represents a synthesizing moment, in which many of the representational operations of sovereignty's embodiment, transference, and resistance we have seen so far come to a point of convergence, only to transform once again. While this claim may strike some as anachronistic, given the fact that the "convergence" in question occurs in a play written two decades before *Life Is a Dream* and is therefore both a logical and a chronological impossibility. As I have suggested throughout these pages, neither logic nor chronology suffice to grasp sovereignty's conceptual movement in a history that includes at least as much generative and degenerative figuration as chronological development and progression.[6]

In this final chapter, I follow both the returns and the syntheses of the sovereignty questions we have been examining so far, by returning myself to the pairing of Shakespeare and Francisco Suárez with which I began. Specifically, I move here from Suárez's political, metaphysical, and juridical writings that we have encountered in the previous chapters to his theological text, *The Mysteries of the Life of Christ* (1592).[7] Reading Suárez's *Mysteries* together with Shakespeare's hybrid play of miracles, *The Winter's Tale* (1609–11), I explore in this chapter one final political-theological reconfiguration, in which playwright and philosopher collaborate to stage the complicated return of an extraordinary body-of-power. I will look at this staging from a slightly different perspective than that through which we have viewed sovereignty so far. Here, the conceptual problem shifts, from a consideration of sovereignty's source and origin in relation to its earthly representative, as in *Richard II*, or from the bodies subject to sovereign force, as in *Measure for Measure* and *Fuenteovejuna*, into a new form of mediation itself. Reading Shakespeare's theatrical work as an "anatomy" of Suárez's theological text and Suárez's *Mysteries* as a form of theater, I focus here specifically on the convergence of affects and effects produced in relation to the staging of an extraordinary body. This time, the body in question is that of a Mother and a Queen. In order to understand the nature of this double effect, it is useful to return to two different perceptions of Truth in relation to politics and theology.

## *Effective History: Theo-Political Returns*

### THE POLITICAL

In the well-known passage that opens the fifteenth chapter of *The Prince* (written in approximately 1513), Niccolò Machiavelli writes, "But since my intention is to say something that will prove of practical use to the inquirer, I have thought it proper to represent things as they are in real truth, rather than as they are imagined" ("Ma sendo l'intento mio scrivere cosa utile a chi la intende, mi è parso più conveniente andare drieto alla verità effettuale della cosa, che alla imaginazione di essa").[8] Proceeding through an array of techniques through which this truth may be produced, Machiavelli suggests that the "real truth" of things ("alla verità effettuale della cosa") is also their "*effective* truth"— the truth that works—i.e., that is effective.[9] A great deal of Machiavelli's advice in *Il Principe* consists of techniques that not only help the prince to see this truth but also, above all, to effectively stage it.

### THE THEOLOGICAL

Roughly a hundred years after Machiavelli's *Prince*, Francisco Suárez published his lengthy refutation of England's King James's Oath of Allegiance, *The Defense of the Catholic and Apostolic Faith* (1613)—the text that, as we have seen, King James had burned. In it, Suárez argues that it would be absurd to imagine that God would have given the Pope the *directive* power to advise princes without also providing him with the *coercive* power to enforce that advice. There are simply certain times and situations when God's representative on earth may be called on to exercise divinely sanctioned force: "[A]ny different system," Suárez insists, would "be imperfect and ineffectual" ("imperfecta et inefficax").¹⁰

For both Machiavelli and Suárez, then, the question of sovereignty is a question of the actual and representational efficacy of power. Still, a wide gulf separates the two thinkers. Between Machiavelli's notion of effective political truth and Suárez's theory of effective political-theological power lie a series of historical and conceptual bifurcations. These include opposing conceptions of temporality, different views of sovereignty's sign-systems, and, not least, competing visions of what each understands by the term "efficiency."¹¹ Given that Machiavelli is a much more familiar figure than Suárez in scholarship on early modern literature and sovereignty, I will restrict my focus in this chapter, as I have throughout this book, to the pairing of Shakespeare and Suárez.¹²

Suárez and Shakespeare illuminate each other in different ways, not only giving us a better picture of the conceptual terrain of early modern sovereignty, but also providing us with terms and tropes through which late modernity continues to think through sovereignty's logics and relations. As we have seen, Suárez's political, philosophical, and juridical, writings present these relations in a variety of ways. While we have had a chance to consider some of these relations and operations, including those of analogy, substitution, and the formation of "impossible beings" in Suárez's *Metaphysical Disputations* (1597) and his treatise *On Laws* (1612), I have not, up to this point, considered Suárez's theological writings.

## Francisco Suárez and the Mysteries of Mary

Responding to an increasingly threatening movement within the Jesuit order itself that was believed to be disseminating "diffuse," "intoxicating," and mystical spiritual texts, Suárez was one of a number of theologians called on, in the late sixteenth and early seventeenth centuries, to publish "more technical, less affective" writings as a corrective. The resulting highly important body of Christian theological texts are, as De Certeau notes, "major works, born of confrontation with the theological and mystic currents of the times; establishing, instancing, justifying what in Rome was called the *via regia* of spirituality, a 'royal road,' henceforth the standard for the entire seventeenth century."[13] As a crucial participant in the construction of this "royal road," Suárez specifically designed his *Mysteries of the Life of Christ* (1592), the second volume of a large commentary on the *Third Part of the Summa Theologica of St. Thomas*, to counter the effects of Christian mysticism. Next to his *Metaphysical Disputations*, "no other work of Suárez has had more editions."[14] Known as the "father of scientific Mariology," Suárez wrote eighteen Mariological disputations.[15] Together, they comprise what is today still considered one of the most comprehensive theological and philosophical considerations of the history, nature, and special properties of the Virgin Mary ever written.[16]

From the Greek word *mysterion* (from *myein*), meaning "to shut" or "to close," the term "mystery" in New Testament theology refers to "the sublime revelation of the Gospel." Catholic *mysteries* are "revealed truths that surpass the power of reason."[17] In contrast to metaphor, which is classically defined in relation to the movement of transfer, the "science" of "mystery" is designed precisely to "shut" down a certain movement, that of reason, and open up an alternative path (*paratur via*) that, with the guidance of faith, leads instead toward revelation.[18] In his Preface to the disputations, Suárez explains that the subject of Mary merits special attention because "after the knowledge of God and Christ, there was for the theologian no knowledge more useful or worthy than that of the Mother of God." For Suárez, the *Mysteries* of Christ cannot be fully understood apart from knowledge of Mary. Following Aristotelian epistemological premises of cause and effect, he argues, in proper Scholastic fashion, that "knowledge of the effect supposes knowledge of the cause":

> Since the Holy Virgin engendered Christ as man, by this reason it is necessary for her to be his cause. Rightly, therefore, ought the way [*paratur via*] for pursuing knowledge about the son be prepared through an understanding of the Mother. For it would not be possible to separate in discourse those [Christ and Mary] who were joined to such an extent by blood and love; nor would it be equitable [*par*] in so long a speech about Christ to be Silent about the Virgin.[19]

Suárez's text promises to, in effect, speak for the Mother—to present Mary's case. His language of equity ("nor would it be equitable [*nec par erat*] for him to be silent") suggests an almost legalistic approach to the theological question of the relation between Mary and the divinity she bears. Suárez's text will thus take upon itself the function not only of explaining the relation but also of staging it, textually. Because Christ and Mary were joined in blood and love, Suárez argues, they must also be combined in discourse. The correlation between Mary's and Christ's historical and physiological relation, on the one hand, and their textual status, on the other, suggests a correspondence model in which the text is transformed from a mere description of the relation into its site and stage.[20] The text, that is, in its very material existence, operates like the bond between Mary and Jesus in their material existence. This bond could be understood in ontological, legal, theological, and even psychoanalytic terms as the site of what psychoanalysis refers to as a "cathexis."[21] This last effect is made possible not only by the structure of the text but above all by the reader-believer's relation to it. Both elements, structure and relation, need to be working at once.

With regard to its structure, Suárez's "testimonial text" is systematically organized into a series of claims, objections, and refutations that collectively function as a fortified "body" of proofs, arranged precisely in order to demonstrate the truth of the mystery without being disrupted by the heteronomy and heresy of metaphorical reading. Suárez's *Mysteries* aspires to a historical and theological precision through the pursuit of a scholastic mode of accumulation, examination, and interrogation. Specifically, Suárez's commentary operates by establishing the text's own relation to a long tradition of sacred writings. As the historian Harro Höpfl points out, the Jesuits' conception of Tradition "was understood as a sort of library or arsenal of doctrines handed down unchanged from the Apostles, but originally unwritten . . ."[22] In its promulgation of this Tradition, commentary moves through an enormous array of hundreds of biblical and other authoritative texts (in a work of "more than a thousand double-column folio pages") on the way to constructing itself as a massive bulwark of systematically presented theology.[23]

The *Mysteries* sets out to explain all of the extraordinary properties of Mary. Proceeding through the statement-objection-reply structure characteristic of the Scholastic method, Suárez responds to the many conceptual, epistemological, and historical challenges that could be raised by his subject by first preparing the reader to understand the ambiguous status of Mary herself. For Mary is the *Mater Dolorosa*, the one who "simultaneously laments the death of Christ, because he is her Son, and welcomes it, because he is her Savior and the Savior of the world."²⁴ The text of the *Mysteries* must strive to contain and define this ambiguity and protect it from potential heretical readings. The task of the exegete is to orchestrate the text's reading by situating it within a framework of authoritative citations and to instruct the reader how to receive them, because the *Mysteries* are truths "found in tradition" ("praesertim habetur haec veritas traditione . . .").²⁵

At the center of all of these challenges is the difficulty posed to dogmatic readings by the problem and subversive potential of metaphor, for the textual construction and interpretive movement of the *Mysteries* continually run on the potentially disruptive tracks of metaphor. In the fifth disputation, Suarez writes,

> It must be said that the Blessed Virgin observed perpetual virginity, and that she never had sexual knowledge of any man. This is an article of Faith. It is proved, first of all, by a single testimonial text from the Old Testament; Ezechiel (44:2): "This gate shall be shut. It shall not be opened and no men shall pass through it: because the Lord the God of Israel hath entered in by it." In this place, even though through a metaphor [*licet sub metaphora*], the discourse is literally about the most holy Virgin, as Jerome attests, and as other Fathers think, who use this testimonial text for confirming this truth [ . . . ]²⁶

This passage—"even though through a metaphor" ("licet sub metaphora")—contains but also stages the mystery of Mary: "This gate shall be shut." Here is where revealed knowledge starts and stops. In all of its syllogistic logic and philological rigor, the *Mysteries* continually runs into the problem of metaphor, even as it equally relies on it. Mary's "shut gate" is part of her complex and paradoxical theological function. Her role, in this respect, is at least double: As Jaroslav Pelikan has shown, she is "at once the way by which the Savior came," and at the same time, the "one through whom we ascend to him who descended through her to us . . . The term Mediatrix referred to both of these aspects of Mary's mediatorial position."²⁷ At the heart of the theological split between Catholics and Protestants, of course, is precisely the question of when a metaphor is more than a metaphor, especially in the ceremony of the Eucharist.²⁸ For Catholics such as Suárez, the priest's language in the Eucharist ceremony is decidedly *not* metaphorical. Rather, it is "representational." To return to Suárez's understanding of representation in the *Defensio fidei* that I discussed in Chapter 2, for Suárez,

> TO REPRESENT IS THE SAME AS MAKING THE THING PRESENT. Let St. Jerome be the third witness who, interpreting Christ's words in Chapter 26 of St. Matthew, says: *after having observed (celebrated) the typical Easter and eaten the flesh of the lamb with the apostles, he takes the bread, which comforts men's heart, and goes on to the true Sacrament of Easter, so that—in a similar way as Melchisedec, priest of the great God, had done by offering bread and wine—He also would represent the reality of his body and blood.*
>
> Perhaps with reference to this some heretic will interpret the word "represent" in a fictitious or metaphorical sense. But the sense and intention of San Jerome are clear: to represent is the same as making a thing present, especially when it deals with something that had been previously promised, or that had been foretold or desired.[29]

Only a heretic would understand the term "representation" here in a metaphorical sense. Real presence is not merely metaphorical. Suárez's text, nevertheless, bears evident signs of anxiety over the threat of heretical, or metaphorical, readings. Perhaps the chief ideological problem at the heart of Counter-Reformation polemics is precisely the status of the sign, a problem, as Peter Goodrich has shown, that links theology to law:

> At one level, the theory of the Eucharist is a theory of signification as such. It is a theory of the sign and of how the sign relates to presence, to an existent or "experiential" thing, to an object, the body of Christ. It is also a theory of interpretation: behind these words, behind these material objects—bread and wine—is hidden the body of the Lord. Only through commentary, through authoritative interpretation, can we have access to that substance, that body and that blood. However, in order to know how to move through this Commentary, we need some instruction. A more specific map as well as guide must be provided to know how to negotiate the specific historical relation between the theory of divine truth that the Eucharist represents and the development of the common law tradition, a tradition also based upon a theory of signs of truth, of law, and the modes of their interpretation. We may note first that the law comes from God and that the nature of God's presence in the flesh is always going to be an essential question of law.[30]

As Protestant and Catholic writers alike stress, the law originates with God. All law—eternal, natural, and human—according to Suárez, is ultimately a branch of theology, given that the *eternal law* is the source of all the others. As Suárez writes in the Preface to *De legibus*, "It ought to seem a wonder [*mirum*] to no one [*Nulli mirum videri debet*] that the discussion of laws should come within the scope of a man professing theology. For theology's eminence, derived from its most eminent subject, excludes every reason for wondering [*admirandi*]."[31] What is the phenomenology of law? In what forms does one not only read and study but also come to know the law? For Suárez, the answer to these questions is directly linked to the practice of theology. Given that God is the source of all law, it falls to the theologian to study law as a branch of theology and to explain the multiple forms through which the law enters the body. This is intended to be comforting, especially in light of the increasing popularity of mysticism, in that "the eminence of theology . . . precludes all reason for *wonder*." Theology is itself figured as a sovereign form: a discipline more than capable of reigning in the potentially disruptive forces of mysticism, heresy, and *wonder* (*mirum*). To the subsequent questions that arise of how, after their origination with God, the different branches of law make themselves felt, Suárez turns directly to the performance of reading and to the labor of exegesis. For as we have seen in my discussion of *Measure for Measure* in Chapter 2, reading, for Suárez, is built into the very definition of law as "lex." "Lex," recall, is a hybrid form, derived from two sources, both the Latin *ligandum* (binding) that Aquinas stresses, and also the *legendum* (that which is to be read) emphasized by Saint Isidore (see Chapter 2). The problem of the reading of law, then, is that of the *right* reading. Like religion, with which, in this view, "lex" shares an etymology (also linking reading and binding), reading and law potentially open themselves up to misuse by unbound, outlaw others. As we have seen in Chapter 2, Suárez underscores the link between reading and binding built into the etymological definition of law ("lex"). For Suárez, one way to understand "law" is to approach it as a text that is both read and that binds. Suárez presents this analysis of a text that binds, not in his theological writings, but rather, in his treatise on law. More recently, scholars, including Emile Benveniste and Jacques Derrida, have debated the question of the binding operation that lies not only at the etymological heart of law, but also of religion.[32] One way of understanding the interlocking relationship among the three terms—

reading, religion, and law—is to see that relationship in the face of what threatens it. In the early modern period, one name for that threat is heresy. Yet if metaphorical reading is heretical reading, as Suárez (and others) will assert, then, in the *Mysteries*, the heretic is always already inside the walls. This is, perhaps, always the case when dealing with sacred texts. As Northrop Frye pointed out long ago:

> [M]any of the central doctrines of traditional Christianity can be grammatically expressed only in the form of metaphor . . . When these doctrines are rationalized by conceptions of a spiritual substance and the like, the metaphor is translated into metonymic language and "explained." But there is a strong smell of intellectual mortality about such explanations, and sooner or later they fade away and the original metaphor reappears, as intransigent as ever . . . The doctrines may be "more" than metaphors: the point is that they can be stated only in a metaphorical this-is-that-form. [T]he Bible belongs to an area of language in which metaphor is functional, and where we have to surrender precision for flexibility.[33]

For Frye, metaphor, within biblical language, is "functional." But *how* does it function? How does metaphor perform its effects and set in motion the type of reading that binds the reader to the biblical text? And how are we to understand the scene of reading as a site of bonding? In what ways does the text function as a "stage" for the double event of reading and binding, or of the being bound of religion? And how, specifically, does metaphor function within this theater of bondage?[34] When and how does metaphor identify itself as being more than metaphorical—as non-metaphorical? Suárez attempts to respond to questions such as these. To begin with, metaphor, according to Suárez, operates differently in the Bible when it's a matter of figuring something that has been "predicted, promised, or desired." As Suárez points out, "metaphor" here is not strictly speaking metaphorical. Rather, it is a representational mode that is required by *mystery* in order to present its truth. As with Hans Blumenberg's "absolute metaphors," biblical metaphors, for Suárez, have a pragmatic, if not a performative function. Biblical metaphors transfer meaning from one realm of life (the temporal) into another, and thus help us to grasp what cannot be directly apprehended (the eternal). Metaphors are only "heretical" when understood in the wrong way. In the tradition of writings that Suárez is following, including especially, that codified by Thomas Aquinas, that means literally. Aquinas's famous passage on the meadow that laughs (*pratum ridet*) says that no matter where you are going, you will never find a meadow that is laughing.[35] Their functions, as Aquinas argues, is to help us widen the grasp—not because they are true, but rather because human intellect is insufficient. Angels don't need them. Metaphors, from this point of view, become a means for humans to overcome intellectual deficiency, nothing more, nothing performative. At the same time, the importance of this overcoming cannot be underestimated. Consequently, what have come to be known as "root metaphors" play a central role in the grounding, organization, and dissemination of many religions. One of the effects of root metaphors in religion, David Tracy suggests, is to form a cluster or "network in which certain sustained metaphors both organize subsidiary metaphors and diffuse new ones. These networks describe the enigma and promise of the human situation and prescribe certain remedies for that situation."[36] The function of root metaphors is particularly important in those Western religions that have come to be known as "religions of the book." As Tracy notes,

> not only is every major religion grounded in certain root metaphors, but Western religions are also "religions of the book"—books that codify root metaphors through various linguistic and generic strategies. For Judaism, Christianity, and Islam certain texts serve not only as charter documents for the religion but as "scripture" in the strict sense: that is, as normative for the religious community's basic understanding and control of its root metaphors and thereby its vision of reality. In the Christian religion, this common situation is intensified.[37]

The nature of this intensification is complex, involving a combination of linguistic, conceptual, and other operations. Built in large part on the effect generated by root metaphors, Christian mystery is (at least) a double genre. It does not merely confront us with questions of a text's rhetoricity but also with those of belief. That is, one only misreads Mary's virginity, or the blood Jesus sweats during the Passion, if one takes these formulations in a metaphorical and not a "mysterious" sense. In distinction from metaphor, mystery presents the reader with what Paul Ricoeur calls a "limit expression," a cut-off point, in which the text marks a border between a space where knowledge ends, and faith begins.[38] In its own terms, its textual status is, thus, different from that of other linguistic assemblages, insofar as its performance consists of "an enigmatic literalness that gets disrupted by metaphorical reading."[39] Mystery is an enigmatic form. The heretic does not believe in this "enigmatic, trans-rational literalness" of the mystery and mistakes it for simple fiction.[40] Tropological reading is heretical reading. Mystery is where metaphor stops.

To fully elaborate the difference between mystery and metaphor would require a more in-depth treatment of each than I can provide here.[41] For the present purposes, my intention is not to present a general theory or concept of metaphor but rather to pause on the question of the relationship between theological events and their tropes as it is formulated by writers such as Shakespeare, Lope de Vega, and Calderón. How does this relationship appear on the baroque stage? The question of whether a theological event can be viewed as a tropological—or a merely tropological one—is, of course, a contentious matter. It is the issue that lies at the heart of Reformation and Counter-Reformation polemics over the status of the sign.[42] Rather than return to these debates here, which other scholars have explored in detail, what I would like to consider is how, within the mode of mystery, the textual "body" it stages can be understood, not only in rhetorical or religious terms, but also in theatrical ones. For what mystery presents us with is an extraordinary body as well as a body that comes with its own form of bonds.

The text of Suárez's *Mysteries* gives us some indication of how these bonds work. Before we can understand that claim, however, we have to return to what might be understood as the media requirements of mystery. These include, to begin with, the establishment of certain framing conditions. In order for the reading of mystery to take place, and take its place, in and between the text and the reader, there must first be a "stage," whether that is in the heart or the mind of the reader, or in the in-between space where the reader-text bond occurs. Second, there are temporal considerations involved in the performance of mystery. Finally, once the first two conditions have been established, on the stage, and in time, there must also always be a readable "body." Otherwise, there is no access to the history and truth of mystery—and mystery is, for Suárez, in the deepest sense of the term, historical. It is historical not only because it "contains" history but also especially because its mode of presentation itself effectively re-attaches us to the historical truth of the event each time it is performed—that is, read. Like metaphor, its presencing effect occurs within a "synchronic structure," in which the real is reactualized upon each new reading. Like the real, or ritual time of the Mass, in which not only Christ's death but also the body of the community is mnemo-technically re-membered through the ritual performance of the Eucharist, mystery is reanimated upon each new reading—*if*, that is, the reading is properly framed, directed, and performed. The being of mystery lies in its systematic presentation. As we shall see, that presentation can be understood as a form of staging, in which what's at stake is the actualization of a relation between reader and text.[43]

The French jurist and psychoanalyst Pierre Legendre describes the stage on which such an actualization occurs as the site of what he (with Scholasticism specifically in mind) refers to as the "Text." "Text," for Legendre, names the symbolic system through which religious and other institutions have, historically, governed forms of life: "Text" is "a system through which society maintains itself through its manipulation of a logic of symbolic transmission."[44] For Legendre, the institutionally generated "Text" becomes the site of an attachment formation that Scholastic thought articulates in terms of "love."[45] The power of sacred texts lies in their capacity to simultaneously figure this love in terms of Truth and also at the same time, *the truth of the Text*: "This is the nature of a sacred text: it is the ineluctable seat of the truth, of a truth which is always genuine, founded as it is in the Great Other, the absolute Other, the imaginary guarantee."[46] For Legendre, the institutional production of knowledge and Truth is always a Text effect. Legendre links this to the space of the Book in general and also to theater: "In the context of scholarship, the amorous relation of a subject to his text necessarily represents itself in a theatrical form: the subject is confronted by a conflation of the object-messenger with the Big Other. It is thus a radical game that the text plays."[47] The concept of sovereignty that begins to emerge in Legendre's account is one in which power is produced in the interaction between subject and Text. As we have seen in different ways throughout this book, one's relation to sovereignty is always a mediated relation. Following Legendre's understanding of Text, one might say with respect to sovereignty that sovereignty's bonds are always media bonds. Legendre turns to the tradition of Scholasticism, in particular, in order to elaborate the function of what he calls "the book" in the production of subjectivity. "A book," he writes, "is a place which eventually has nothing to do with reading." "The book," Legendre argues, "was made to be performed":

> According to the Latin tradition, both before and after the revival of scholasticism and right up until the era of the baroque, the book was understood to be a space for the soul, a prison of the heart where the Absent spoke, it instituted the distance of the divine, an *amour lointain*, or mystical space of love. Without this reference, it is impossible to understand that an essentially juridical conception of absolute power was transposed in the Christian West, onto a certain version of the Vision of the Book.[48]

Legendre links this "Vision" to tradition. Sacred texts, and the authoritative commentaries to which they give rise, not only play a "radical game" in the construction of a tradition, but they also position the subject within a "genealogical structure" in which "the exegetes . . . take their place as a means of accomplishing a precise function: that of explaining how a legal text tells the truth."[49] As we have already seen with Suárez, in scholastic-juridical thought, theology is viewed as "the true matrix of Law." A legal text's truth status, therefore, cannot be understood without linking it to its theological foundations and function.[50] To take just one of many examples Legendre offers of an interpretation and commentary that comes to serve as an authoritative foundation, Legendre refers to St. Jerome's decree on the succession of bishops recorded in Gratian's *Decretals*: "Power must not be deferred to blood but to life." In his commentary, Gratian links succession to genealogy, interpreting the text as a matter of drawing forth Christ's seed.[51] Arguing that sacred texts inscribe their readers in a manner similar to that in which legal texts situate subjects within a "pre-existent discourse of truth," Legendre notes the legal understanding of the term *"succedere,"* "to enter under": "Carrying the etymological meaning a bit further, one discovers a meaning that is usually neglected: working according to plan, succeeding, and so on. This might be summarized in the proposition that belonging to the Text can be defined as a submission that walks."[52] Textual inscription here not only leads one to recognize oneself in response to an institutional "hailing" (as in Althusser's notion of interpellation), it also causes one to walk. The connection between tradition and the training of the body lies at the heart of Legendre's understanding of the "normative function" that is performed by the institutions that govern—biological, social, and subjective—life. Playing a key role in the formation of these institutions are the theological and juridical texts, along with their interpreters, that constitute the "machinery" of modern subjectivity. Textual belonging "captures" the subject and leads him or her to reperform that capture at every renewed encounter with the Text. By establishing such an authoritative genealogy, "text" becomes "Text" and inserts the subject within its "body."

The motor that sets this capture in motion is the activity of exegesis. Jesuit exegetes, in particular, developed a highly sophisticated understanding of the subject's relation to the Text, and they carried this knowledge into their theo-political practice and theory. Guiding both were the forms of thought reproduced in texts such as Suárez's *De legibus* or the *Defensio fidei*. As the historian Harro Höpfl explains ". . . Jesuit theologians for the most part adhered to the *de legibus* and *de iustitia et iure* format . . ." One of the conceptual advantages of this reliance on already existing discursive structures was that it allowed the Society a certain philosophical flexibility at a moment when the practical range of moral, legal, and religious questions it was encountering was expanding in unprecedented ways. In addition to the intellectual advantages it offered, as Höpfl notes, was the fact that "allegiance to a common framework of *topoi*, *loci*, authorities, and arguments was itself an essential bond of unity for this most international, diffuse, and faction-prone of organisations."[53] The political savvy of the Society can be seen, in particular, in its sophisticated approach to textuality. We see this especially in the Society's understanding of metaphor. Returning to one of Christianity's root metaphors, that of "feeding," Höpfl has shown how Jesuit exegesis was particularly effective in reconfiguring the trope in ways that not only furthered its own controversial theory of the pope's *potestas indirecta* but also forged an aspect of its own charter that lies at the heart of the Jesuit mission. As Höpfl notes:

> Particularly ingenious was the exegesis of the apparently innocuous John 21: 15–17: *Pasce oves meas* in the Vulgate, and "Feed my lambs/sheep" in both Douay-Rhemis and the AV. As Bellarmine points out (citing both the Septuagint Greek and the Hebrew), "feed" plainly stood for all the acts pertaining to the office of a shepherd, which include directing, governing, defending, and correcting, and therefore the use of coercion.[54]

Authoritative interpretation thus lies at the heart of the Jesuit understanding of the organization and dissemination of power. Exegetes such as Gratian or Suárez play a crucial role in the formation of a genealogical tradition, not only by explaining and illustrating how a Text tells the truth, but also by constantly reactivating its truth-effects in the subject through its own performance of authoritative commentary. "Exegesis" thus activates a Text that not only marks the presence of an "indirect power," but also ultimately governs the production of the "norms which regulate the body."[55] That seamless textual fabrication lies at the core of genealogical power. A Text acts, and binds "because it refers, by way of an accumulation of texts, to the founding Name."[56] "This scholastic extract suggests," Legendre concludes, "that institutional artifice is without artifice, that the montage is based upon a natural truth: *the discourse of truth is the discourse of the reproduction of truth.*" Thus mediaeval legal formulae, such as that of the *lex animata*, a "Law which breathes," express a "power which incarnates the truth"—makes it flesh, or text, and is reanimated through exegesis.[57] For Legendre, this last operation has the effect of ultimately moving the body through what he describes as a "dance of law."[58]

Suárez's *Mysteries* participates in this dance. Through their influential reproduction and dissemination of the dogmatic Truths, Suárez's Commentaries set the sacred texts in motion, governing their reading, and transforming them from mere "medium" to media-effective event. Here, meaning is actualized in the believer through a precise and technically orchestrated deployment of what Legendre describes as the "elements of montage": identification, accumulation, genealogical reproduction.[59] Each one of these operations plays a role in the performance of exegetical commentary.

In Suárez's 34th *Disputation*, for example, on the question of "Whether the blood Christ sweat on the mount while He prayed was true and natural," Suárez is one of the few commentators who sees this blood non-metaphorically. Of all the gospels, it is only in Luke that Jesus's sweat is said to be "like drops of blood falling to the ground." According to Suárez, it would be a mistake to understand Luke's text as a mere similitude because the truth of the mystery is that Jesus sweated "true and natural blood." In order to demonstrate this, Suárez begins with a consideration of the "proper" (*proprium*) meaning of terms:

I say therefore, first, that Lord Christ emitted true, proper [*proprium*], and natural blood, when he is said to have "sweated blood." This assertion is for me certain, for the words of Luke are explicit; and since those [words] contain the account, they must be understood properly. Wherefore, that which Theophylactus said, that those things are written by hyperbole [*per hyperbolem*]—for just as [in the case of] one who weeps bitterly, we say he weeps blood, so it is that one who sweats greatly for anxiety and inner labor is said to sweat blood, that is, to drip heavily flowing sweat—this interpretation, I say, since it is alienated from the properties of the words, and is not necessary, should by no means be accepted. And Euthymeus, who has the same point at his chap. 64 in his commentary on Matthew, says that Luke does not say that Christ sweated blood, but rather that his sweat was like drops of blood, that is, that his sweat was thick and dense, similar to drops of blood. But certainly, if Luke had wanted only a similitude, he would instead have said, "just like drops of water"; for drops of water seem more similar to drops of sweat than drops of blood. Consider too that the particle "sicut," just like the particle "quasi," does not always signify in Scripture a similitude, but sometimes [signifies] an identity and truth, as at John 1, "We beheld His glory, glory like [*quasi*] that of the only child of the Father." Finally, if in this passage some similitude is conveyed through that particle "sicut" which is lacking in truth, [that deficit of truth] is not in the substance of blood, as if Christ had not sweated true blood, but in the form and figure of drops, perhaps because the drops do not have a completed figure but a simile to it, or, more certainly, because they were not from pure blood, but they had some mixture with sweat. Thus it must simply be said that Christ sweated true blood, as the letter of the Evangelist displays, and was understood by the common sense of the church even from the times of the apostles . . .[60]

It would be erroneous, Suárez explains, to take the text in a figurative sense. As with the mystery of Mary's virginity as a "shut gate," Luke's text contains actual, not rhetorical (*per hyperbolem*) history: It contains, that is, blood. What is ". . . alien to the literal property of the text . . . ," therefore, must be excluded, in order for it to perform its dogmatic function: i.e., to *properly* tie us to the (non)tropological language of mystery.[61] As Suárez proceeds to comment on this passage, he engages in different kinds of arguments, ranging from the physiological ("If the suffering is vehement and lacks the material of sweat, it may happen that the patient expels blood [which] sometimes occurs because of the abundance of blood and a bodily imbalance"), through the linguistic and philological ("'quasi' does not always signify in Scripture a similitude, but sometimes [signifies] an identity"), and, finally, to the strictly theological ("as the letter of the Scriptures carries it within itself," and "as it has been understood in a unanimous sense ever since the time of the apostles"). Combining the three—physiological, linguistic, and theological—modes, Suárez's text moves with the rhythm of a scholastic "dance": authority, objection, its rejection, return, and again. Thus, he begins with the citation of a superior authority ("Saint Luke's words are express on this matter"); considers but then rejects the inferior interpretations of other commentators, such as Teofilo and Eutimio; and, finally, circles back to the position of the original authority ("the letter of the Scriptures"), in order to close his case. Together, the cumulative effects of this choreographical reading lead Suárez to the argument that, in the end, the truth of the mystery lies in properly understanding the effectiveness of Christ's extraordinary will. What defines it, in particular, is its extraordinary capacity to overcome affection:

> And this above all, because even though Christ feared through a natural sentiment, he nevertheless embraced death and all the pain it offered him in an extremely efficacious manner, with a deliberate and effective will, and also with an act of appetite directed by the will, and therefore triumphed over the affection or natural feeling from which the agony came.[62]

Suárez traces the extraordinary physiological effect of sweating blood back to the equally extraordinary nature of Jesus's will. The "extremely efficacious manner" in which Christ embraced death draws on a theological notion of "efficacious grace." What is efficacious is a property of the divine. The term "efficacious"—usually defined in English today as "having the power to produce a desired effect"—appears frequently in Christian theology, often in relation to crucial doctrinal issues.[63] It appears in one of the most important theological debates of the period, the *De Auxiliis* (Of the Helps) controversy between Dominicans and Jesuits over the nature of free will, in which Suárez played a major role. For Suárez and the Jesuits in general, "efficacious grace" (*gratia efficax*) referred to "that mediate knowledge (*scientia media*) whereby God knows, in the objective reality of things what a man, in any circumstances in which he might be placed, would do."⁶⁴ "Efficacious grace," is part of divine knowledge. In addition to its use as a descriptor of grace and God's knowledge, it is also used in other contexts, including to refer to the best form of prayer and to understand the workings of the will.⁶⁵

Related to "efficacious" is the English term "efficacy," from the Latin *efficax*, which refers to the "power or capacity to produce effects."⁶⁶ In Christian theology, "efficacy" is often used in relation to the sacraments—particularly, the salvation gained through the death of Jesus Christ. Christ's death is said to have "efficacy" for those who believe.⁶⁷ Belief is linked to reading and to the knowledge of proper reading. For Suárez, unlike the heretic, only the reader who knows how to move through the Text will be affected by the extraordinary *effect* of Jesus sweating blood, only the reader, that is, who knows how to take the words non-metaphorically. Suárez relies on the literal sense in which Christ's will effectively overcame his natural sentiment—the "*affection* . . . from which the agony came*.*" Historical, performative, and media-theoretical (in Legendre's terms) at once, Suárez's *Mysteries* is a hybrid text. It not only incorporates a massive number of references within its structure, but it also, in effect, teaches its reader how to receive and consume them. It approaches the reader-text relation as if it were preparing itself for a meal. In the course of producing its material and spiritual reality for the believer, the text reveals and conceals its own exegetical procedures, incessantly reiterating the fact that its own "body" consists of the accumulating textual bodies of the authorities it cites. This reminder that the *Mysteries* in fact produces what it purports to merely convey makes it transparent and effective at the same time. Suárez's exegetical performance of reframing, reproducing, and reanimating the Truth of the *Mysteries* lies at the heart of the dogmatic technique of commentary that Legendre describes in terms of a scholastic "dance." Scholastic dance moves according to the Ovidian logic of "art hiding itself in art" (*ars adeo latet arte sua*) in which the art at the same time displays itself as art as it guides its reader through it.⁶⁸ In this sense, Suárez's Mariological writings can be viewed as a media event in which the process of exegesis itself performs a tropological function of "dancing" the Truth—even as it attempts to limit and contain the power of tropes. What Suárez's *Mysteries* demonstrates, beyond its theological, historical, or philological import, is its effectiveness in the forging of a believer's tie to the Text. In this regard, the business of mystery is the construction of a bond. In psychoanalytic terms, Julia Kristeva has shown how a discourse such as Suárez's *Mysteries* participates in the wider historical and cultural construction that psychoanalysis sees as the masculine fantasy of the Mother as "a lost territory." Kristeva links this fantasy to the "idealization of primary narcissism":

> [M]otherhood is the *fantasy* that is nurtured by the adult, man or woman, of a lost territory; what is more, it involves less an idealized archaic mother than the idealization of the *relationship* that binds us to her, one that cannot be localized—an idealization of primary narcissism.[69]

The fantasy of the lost Mother works not by binding its reader/spectator to any real object, but rather to one's own relation to its mode of presentation, its mediation. Following a logic similar to that described in Althusser's definition of "ideology"—in which "it is not their real conditions of existence . . . that 'men' 'represent to themselves' in ideology, but above all . . . their relation to those conditions of existence"[70]— what binds in primary narcissism is not the idealized object itself but one's imaginary relationship to it. Our understanding of this "object" is always, in part, dependent on the manner through which this understanding comes to us, is framed and performed. In each case, whether with primary narcissism, the definition of ideology, or the discourse of political theology, it is the mediating structure itself that not only enables but also *effects* a binding relation. The site of this relation is the mediation itself: political theological bonds are always media bonds.

Shakespeare takes up the question of theo-political bonds and their "legitimacy" in his late romance, *The Winter's Tale* (1611), a play performed for King James one year before the publication of Suárez's treatise *On Laws* (Coimbra 1612), and almost two decades after Suárez's *Mysteries*. *The Winter's Tale* is a play of returns. "Recapitulation," as Walter Cohen has shown, is built into its very form.[71] Additionally, it is a play of thematic and formal divisions: structurally, organized around the relation and separation of two Kings (Leontes and Polixenes), two kingdoms (Sicilia and Bohemia), two seasons (winter and spring), and two distinct dramatic genres (tragedy and comedy). In the course of staging first the divisions and then the reparations, *The Winter's Tale* returns us to many of the sovereignty problems we have encountered throughout these pages, from the questions of allegiance and resistance, with which we entered the scene of sovereignty, through the various figurations of the body-of-power, as divided, destroyed, transferred, transformed, and above all, reconfigured, to the theme of recapitulation itself, as the site of a binding relation. Many of the questions I have been pursuing throughout these pages—of sovereignty's origins, objects, pathways of delegation, bodies, and relations—converge in Shakespeare's hybrid play of "wonder."

*The Winter's Tale* is a play of difference.[72] Like *Life Is a Dream*, the play opens in a climate of uncertainty. Here, however, unlike the disproportion and violence that dramatically introduce Calderón's play, Shakespeare takes as his theme the question of division, as it presents itself in the state, the family, and the body. In the "wintry" territory of Sicilia, Bohemia's King Polixenes is visiting his boyhood friend, Leontes, and his wife, Queen Hermione. The opening lines of the play introduce the themes of belief, "entertainment," and the altered states that the subsequent five acts will develop in novel and dangerous ways. There is "great difference," says one of King Polixenes's men, Lord Archidamus, to Leontes's Lord, Camillo, "betwixt our Bohemia and your Sicilia":

> CAMILLO: I think this coming summer the King of Sicilia means to pay Bohemia the visitation which he justly owes him.
> ARCHIDAMUS: Wherein our entertainment shall shame us; we will be justified in our loves. For indeed—
> CAMILLO: Beseech you—
> ARCHIDAMUS: Verily I speak it in the freedom of my knowledge. We cannot with such magnificence—in so rare—I know not what to say. We will give you sleepy drinks, that your senses, unintelligent of our insufficience, may, though they cannot praise us, as little accuse us.
>
> (1.1.4–15)[73]

Archidamus's anxiety over the "great difference" he fears will be revealed between his Bohemia and Camillo's Sicilia expresses itself as "shame" over what he perceives to be his own country's lack. So overwhelmed is he by the thought of Bohemia's "insufficience" that his language momentarily breaks off ("I know not what to say") before recovering to express the fantasy of drugging Camillo in order to conceal what he would be "shamed" to reveal. Archidamus's solution to compensate for what he hypothesizes to be an insufficient degree of hospitality at home is both humorous and also important, as it introduces a central theme of the play—intoxication: "We will give you sleepy drinks," he says to Camillo.[74] Archidamus's line is both an odd and a fitting beginning to a play of marvelous recoveries and "wondrous" reconciliations. It imagines the solution to a potentially serious social and political problem as one of technique. Like Machiavelli's *verità effettuale della cosa*, Archidamus thinks of the truth in terms of the effects it produces—of the truth, that is, that works, or that, with a little "sleepy drink," can be made to seem to work. With a little technique, one can artificially alter the body to experience something in the absence of the event. Insufficiency is thus a technical problem that can be overcome with the right special effects. The play's "odd" beginning, then, is not really so odd at all, as much as it is an indication of *The Winter's Tale*'s interest in the relationship between the body and the techniques as well as the technologies of "wonder."

On the other hand, *The Winter's Tale* is more than a theatrical foray into the technology of perception. Coexisting with its interest in the relationship between art and science is a powerful exploration of the psychodynamics and, even, "psychotheology," to borrow Eric Santner's term, of sovereignty.[75] Santner defines "psychotheology" as an assemblage that brings together the texts of psychoanalysis and the Judeo-Christian tradition as resources for better understanding "what it means to be answerable to another human being." Particularly novel to the way the question appears, when viewed through the lens of this hybrid construction, is its response to what Santner refers to as "pressure." In addition to the various psychological, political, and social exigencies of the world, "pressure" refers to the way one experiences what Santner refers to as "aliveness," a condition that is understood in both theological and psychoanalytic terms. The highest "pressure" in this reading, then, is that which comes from God: "For in the view I am distilling from the work of Freud and Rosenzweig," Santner writes, "God is above all the name for the pressure to be alive to the world, to open to the too much of pressure generated in large measure by the uncanny presence of my neighbor."[76] *The Winter's Tale* is a rich laboratory for exploring a psychotheological synthesis such as Santner's. Specifically with regard to the concept of sovereignty, the play could be said to be equally interested in the dynamics of breakdown as in the technical and artificial mechanics of forming a sovereign bond. Along the way, it is characterized by a uniquely innovative and occasionally discordant inflection of mood and form.

The presence of shame, for example, runs throughout the play like a leitmotif. From Archidamus's initial fear that Bohemia's insufficient entertainment will "shame" the Bohemians, through Leontes's false accusations of Camillo and his wife ("Camillo is / A federary with her, and one that knows / What she should shame to know herself..." [2.1.89–91]), to his faulty explanation for his son's death ("Conceiving the dishonour of his mother! / [Mamillius] straight declined, drooped, took it deeply, / Fastened and fixed the shame on't in himself..." [2.3.13–15]), shame runs through the play as a recurring source of energy, or perhaps "pressure."[77] In Leontes's case, he will not free himself from shame but merely re-experience it as it returns from his catastrophic errors of the first half of the play, to its renewal before the vision of Hermione's statue, in Act V, where he confesses, "I am ashamed" (5.3.37). The circuit of "shame" is surprisingly central to this play of "wonder."

Initially, however, the play seems to be far removed from considerations of shame. In the opening act, after the exchange we have seen, King Leontes and his wife, Hermione, discuss family, friendship, and childhood with Leontes's boyhood friend, King Polixenes of Bohemia: "We were as twinned lambs that did frisk I'th'sun, / And bleat the one at th' other," Polixenes recalls. "What we changed / Was innocence for innocence—we knew not / The doctrine of ill-doing, nor dreamed / That any did" (1.2.66–70). From this Edenic idyll and the reminiscences it provokes, however, the play abruptly, almost shockingly degenerates, "spiraling," as Christopher Pye puts it, into a psycho-political nightmare of anxiety, madness, and violence.[78] At the heart of this movement lies the question of sexual and political fidelity.

After Leontes tries, unsuccessfully, to persuade Polixenes to prolong his stay in Sicilia, he turns to his wife and asks Hermione to try her hand. When she succeeds at convincing Polixenes to stay, Leontes almost immediately and inexplicably is seized by a stunning paroxysm of jealousy. Viewing Hermione clasp hands with Polixenes, Leontes agonizes: "Too hot, too hot! / To mingle friendship far is mingling blood" (1.2.107–8). As Stephen Orgel points out, Leontes's view of sexual relations is derived from a Scholastic tradition in which sexual intercourse is understood as a "mingling of blood."[79] In *The Winter's Tale*, the stakes of such imaginings are high, directly affecting the body of the sovereign and, consequently, all those subject to his or her power. In this case, Leontes's imaginings of his wife's blood "mingling" with Polixenes's affects not Hermione but his *own* blood, as his heart begins to race: "I have *tremor cordis* on me; my heart dances, / But not for joy, not joy" (1.2.109–10). From this very sudden onset of jealousy, Leontes falls headlong into a rage that nothing short of a complete devastation of his family and his court will be able to cut short. From the moment he starts, like Othello, to imagine his wife's infidelity, Leontes's vision of the world changes, to catastrophic effect. The effects of jealousy lead to an "infected" vision, one of the symptoms of which is that, from this point forward, when Leontes looks out into the world, he sees either only paranoid versions of himself, or conversely, the lack of that self, in others: "Art thou my boy?" he asks his son, Mamillius (1.1.119), suddenly fearing that Hermione (and Polixenes) has "too much blood in him" (2.1.58) and that he himself has not enough.[80] Like Archidamus's fear that this kingdom will not have the capacity to host Sicilia, Leontes's *tremor cordis* thus appears to be the consequence of an imagined lack, of not having enough blood, in his heir. Leontes's mind swings wildly, between the poles of excess ("too much blood") and insufficiency, on the way to naming, in what is one of the play's most notoriously difficult passages, what he takes to be the source of his affliction:

> Affection, thy intention stabs the centre.
> Thou dost make possible things not so held,
> Communicat'st with dreams—how can this be?—
> With what's unreal thou coactive art,
> And fellow'st nothing. Then 'tis very credent
> Thou mayst co-join with something, and thou dost,
> And that beyond commission, and I find it,
> And that to the infection of my brains
> And hard'ning of my brows.
> (1.2.138–42)

Leontes's agony of affection has become one of the most speculated upon conditions in recent Shakespeare criticism. There is something in excess of jealousy here. His lament presents us with a complex network of relations between affect, potentiality, dream, and medium itself. "Affection" may "fellow nothing," but it forges something: a communicative pathway between its bearer and the object of its desire, rage and, perhaps, even self-loathing. It is in this regard the force impelling the construction of a communication network between self and world, as well as the self *as* its own tortured world. His language marks his relation to and, better, breakdown between, self and world.

A staccato outburst of fragments, broken claims and painful questions, Leontes's speech divides into both sign and effect of torn states of feeling and being. It is a famously enigmatic moment: "syntactically and lexically often baffling."[81] Generations of scholars have struggled with the passage, trying to clarify how the term "affection" functions by showing how it must *either* refer to Hermione's lust or to Leontes's jealousy, but not both.[82] As Stephen Orgel points out, some early modern editors have even gone so far as to try to remedy the obscurity of the passage by replacing the word "affection" altogether with the seemingly more domesticatable, "imagination."[83] Yet eliminating the term is hardly a way into the tortured relation between divisions and doublings that are so central to the play and that Shakespeare insists on. As Christopher Pye points out, Leontes's is an extremely complex state of simultaneous suffering and awareness; he is both "in the throes of his delirium and [also able] to recognize it as delirium."[84] It is not, then, a question of replacing the term with "imagination." Imagination presents its own grave problems in the play. Here, the passage refers to exactly what it says it does: to affection, as well as to its powers and effects, including, above all, the effects of division. Leontes divides. From the almost inexplicable and stunningly sudden moment he enters his lethal state of jealousy, he bifurcates into a being for whom feeling and knowing are experienced as forms of acute pain. Affection *acts*. It has autonomy, its own intentions, and desires, most of them, in Leontes's view, not good. Affection wounds. It "stabs the centre" (1.2.137). But *whose* center? Leontes's own "centre"? Hermione's? The center of *what*? Of the body? Of the universe? This is not a completely improbable reading in this play, as Leontes's own association between the "foundations" of his "knowledge" and the universe are later made explicit: "If I mistake / In those foundations which I build upon / The centre is not big enough to bear / A schoolboy's top" (2.1.100–2). The problem, of course, is that he *does* "mistake," and as a result, the "centre" of his knowledge is *not* ample enough to "bear" his false accusations, or even a "schoolboy's top" (unless that image is taken as a figure for Leontes's own immature head at this point). That his nightmare vision of smallness (both the universe's and his own) expresses itself in the language of "toys" prefigures Antigonus's later underestimation of the communicative medium of dreams and his similar dismissal of toys. Shortly before dying, Antigonus sees Hermione, in a dream, returning "in pure white robes / like very sanctity" (3.3.21–2). "Dreams are toys" (3.3.38), he says to himself, trying to dismiss the vision—only to be immediately devoured by a different kind of "bear" than that connected with Leontes's weak foundations.

We see in passages such as these not only an intrusion of the "real," but also *The Winter's Tale*'s real interest in the communicative media through which knowledge and visions of life pass.[85] Like the Virgin's "shut gate," in Suárez's account, Leontes's "affection" has a double, mediating function. On the one hand, it is the source of his affliction, the origin of his torment, and the power that leads to his "knowledge." At the same time, affection is a communicative pathway, a road to what's "unreal." Leontes attributes agency to affection, endowing it with "communicative" powers, and figuring it as a medium or vessel to normally inaccessible states and, above all, *beings*. As Lupton points out, he speaks in "contortedly ontological terms ('unreal,' 'something,' 'nothing') rather than ethical ones."[86] The power of affection bears Leontes beyond normal states of being, consciousness, and reality. As his thought spins out of control (and, paradoxically, into increasing clarity regarding that loss of control), affection becomes figured as a conspirator in his self-betrayal, "co-active" in the art of his own unmaking. Were one to read the lines with the same bewilderment and anxiety that has led so many editors to try to remedy the language's famously enigmatic quality, one might even go so far as to suggest that "art" itself is the passage's ultimate addressee: "co-active art." Art—its power, resistance, and "incoherence" in the face of (or in collaboration with) sovereignty—offers one way of understanding what the "enigma" of the lines might be about. That is, *The Winter's Tale* is a play about the autonomy of the aesthetic sphere in relation to other forms of sovereignty. Thus, as Christopher Pye has shown, putting the question in more theoretical terms, "The aesthetic is the means by which sovereign agency is sustained within the political order of early modernity, the era, that is of autonomous law, on the one hand, and the incipient citizen-subject—the bourgeois domestic subject—on the other."[87] Shakespeare's particular exploration of this "means" in *The Winter's Tale* has to do, in part, with the ways the aesthetic sphere itself can be viewed as a threat to the fantasy of sovereignty, whether of the state or of the self. Thus, in Leontes's case, affection colludes with the king, becoming a "co-active" artist in the forging of a relation "with what's unreal." To support this reading I, like generations of troubled editors, might even simply insert my own punctuation, including commas after "thou" and "co-active," in order to make the line after the question "how can this be?" read not only as yet another fragment, but rather as an accusation: "With what's unreal, *thou*, coactive, *art*!" While, on the one hand, this is, perhaps, an overly "artful" and willful reading, on the other hand, the affective state of being in excessive doubt and willfulness is precisely what the lines themselves are about.

Source and path at once, affection is the "root," as Shakespeare puts it (in another play about sovereignty and disease) of Leontes's affliction. When, after hearing the prophecies of the weird sisters, Banquo asks Macbeth whether they have "eaten on the insane root that takes the reason prisoner?" (1.382–3), he identifies a similar doubling and division between event and mediation. Has the event occurred outside or inside the body (politic)? Has it occurred at all? What are the signs that communicate its significance to the outside? The motif of "eating on the root" is a recurring one in *The Winter's Tale*. It returns at the end of the play, when Leontes's "affection" and "infection" give way to a vision of power so ecstatic that he will wonder not only if it is real, but also especially if it is legitimate. How does one participate in the community of the real? How can one be a part of the real (or, again, in Spanish, "royal") "body-of-power"? What is the legitimacy of the communion? Before arriving at this point, the remainder of the first part of the play will develop the theme of infected affect, describing its consequences as a form of epistemological poisoning. Again, Leontes describes this movement in seemingly self-aware terms:

> There may be in the cup
> A spider steeped, and one may drink, depart,
> And yet partake no venom, for his knowledge
> Is not infected; but if one present
> Th'abhorred ingredient to his eye, make known
> How he hath drunk, he cracks his gorge, his sides
> With violent hefts. I have drunk, and seen the spider.
> (2.1.39–45)

For some critics, the sovereign's splitting in the face of the perceived poison ("he cracks his gorge, his sides / With violent hefts") is part of the play's ongoing critique of the fantasy that is sovereignty. Bradin Cormack sees *The Winter's Tale*'s treatment of division and differentiation as part of its general critique of sovereignty, a critique, that is, of "sovereignty's connection to its own uniqueness."[88] In passages such as these we can see a running critique of a Bodinian vision of the concept of sovereignty as that which is indivisible. "Sovereignty, in Bodin's sense, is the sickness that makes Leontes mad," Cormack observes, highlighting the play's own "erosion" of a the fantasy of autonomy and immunity to difference.[89] The road to recovery from this erosion will require Leontes to recuperate his relation to a certain form of theater, or what, more specifically, he will call "recreation."

### Lead Me to These Sorrows . . .

In Act III, after realizing the depth of his misjudgments, Leontes vows to atone for his errors and their catastrophic effects:

> Once a day I'll visit
> The chapel where they lie, and tears shed there
> Shall be my recreation. So long as nature
> Will bear up with this exercise, so long
> I daily vow to use it. Come,
> And *lead me to these sorrows*.
> (3.2.232–41, my emphasis)

*The Winter's Tale* has received an enormous amount of critical attention in relation to the renewed interest in religion in Renaissance studies in general, and to the question of Shakespeare's Catholic past, in particular.[90] Given such concerns, Leontes's vow to memorialize his dead wife and son at a "chapel" with a daily production of tears could easily be seen to invoke the *Spiritual Exercises* of Ignatius Loyola and his famous "gift of tears."[91] Leontes's promise that tears "shall be [his] recreation." proves to be true in more ways than one. To begin with, the ritualistic ("once a day") performance is linked to the conservation of his loved one's memory. At the same time, it is also clear that his daily visits to the chapel are at least as much a production as they are a conservation of the past: They produce what's lost as much as they recall it. Leontes has lost two loves, but from a certain object-relations point of view, he has also lost his relation to those losses. Or, inversely, all that he has left is that relation. Consequently, it is to the relation that he forms an attachment at the chapel, ritually reproducing his "sorrows." As we have seen, Kristeva understands such an attachment in terms of the processes of "primary narcissism" involved in the idealization of the mother. Leontes's "recreation" of memory (or "mammory," as Jean Howard wittily puts it, given that the lost object's name, Mamillius, from "mamma," links him indissociably with his mother) binds Leontes to mother and son, ritual and "recreation," at once.[92] Like Loyola's exercisant, he performs his sorrow by producing an abundance of tears that enable him to look backward and forward at once. Forming his lens of sorrow, tears become the precondition of Leontes's daily reanimation of mourning. As a "communicative" medium, tears are simultaneously the sign and the consequence, both the product and the performance of "sorrow." Tears are the proof of faith. They come with their own temporality and theatricality. Physiological and affective, Leontes's mourning is a "re-creation" that not only recalls what is past and lost, but also, more accurately, *produces* and re-produces his relationship to that loss, again and again. By theatrically and ritualistically ("daily") "performing sorrow," Leontes also produces what Freud calls a "screen memory" of Hermione, that is, a memory not *from* but *of* Hermione.

The agonized spectacle of Leontes's sorrows leads us to the heart of the play's mystery. As with Suárez's *Mysteries*, Leontes's mediated—or what, following Hent de Vries, I will call "mediatic"—construction of his relation to the past comes with its own structure, stage, and repeated temporality. History and prophecy at once, his repeated exercise and re-creation will position him within the non-linear space-time of theater—that which, as Samuel Weber puts it, "involves a temporal repetition that is suspended in a divided space."[93] In this divided space-time, unlike the time of a developing narrative, there is no "ending." Rather, the ritualized activity of mourning is its own end. The lost object cannot return—at least not normally. Leontes's "recreation," in other words, could be viewed as part of an internal process of recovery and self-transformation, but not an act capable of restoring what is lost.

As the tragic half gives way to the comic recovery, however, Leontes's agony of affection begins to make way for a new form of "recreation," in which affection leads to a different set of special effects. What *The Winter's Tale* at this point will begin to depart from—and in fact rupture—is an entire framework for thinking about sovereignty in relation to the "body-of-power" that we have seen up to this point. From this point forward in the play, no longer will the theoretical question be about the relation between sovereignty's source and its representative, as in *Richard II*, or of the effective functioning of law (*Measure for Measure*). Neither is the play's understanding of temporality similar to *Fuenteovejuna*'s understanding of power as the power to keep one waiting. *The Winter's Tale* will approach the relation between sovereignty and time in a different way than Lope's play. Finally, *The Winter's Tale*, despite its inclusion of an oracle and a chapel, where Leontes pays his daily visits, is not primarily concerned with the sign-system of sacred sovereignty, as in *Life Is a Dream*. Rather, *The Winter's Tale* turns in a new direction, reorienting the sovereignty question back, in a way, to where it has been from the start—to the stage, and its machinery of wonder, without which no sovereignty effects would be possible in the first place.

In the play's famous climactic scene, Paulina presents to the king the lost queen, Hermione, long thought dead, in the form of a statue "performed" by the Italian sculptor Giulio Romano.[94]

> Prepare
> To see the life as lively mocked as ever
> Still sleep mocked death.

At this astonishing reappearance, Leontes, who is stunned and amazed, nevertheless notices one change:

> But yet, Paulina,
> Hermione was not so much wrinkled, nothing
> So agèd as this seems.
> (5.3.27–9)

Hermione returns—but with a difference: She is "wrinkled." Shakespeare's trope introduces a kink in the Ovidian machinery of wonder, representing pagan metamorphosis with a Christian twist. The event of the double miracle—of Hermione's return to the play as "art," and her subsequent movement from art, to life—bears with it what a return in the theater always brings, at least in a temporal sense: a combination of sameness and difference.[95] The figure of the "wrinkle" marks Hermione as both the authentic queen who was "lost," and also as one who is changed. Her reappearance comes with what Lupton calls the "remainders," or reminders of a (material) history that her body, despite all of Paulina's "art," continues to register. Most important to the play is the mysterious effect of these remainders, in that, as Lupton puts it, they both "establish and cancel" the historical relation, moving beyond the normal orders of time and relegating the "unsafe lunes i'th' King" to the wintry past (2.2.29).[96] The figure of the "wrinkle" marks Hermione's return as a performance, in the "mediatic" sense I have been emphasizing throughout these pages. As a metaphor for metaphor itself, as well as the metaphoricity built into the staging of sovereignty's mystery, Hermione's "wrinkles" remind us of the media conditions required for the performance of "wonder." Hermione, the absolute object of the king's desire, is here again, in the representational form of a "statue." At the same time, she is not the same as the queen who was lost. *The Winter's Tale* explores the significance of this difference, and this return of the lost mother—and also emphasizes that the stakes of one's relation to the trope of return itself are high, nothing less than life itself. Like the "affection" that, earlier, had torn the king apart, Hermione's return "transports" Leontes (5.3.68) and, with him, the audience, backward and forward in time at once. Like all media effects, the operation immediately gives rise to questions of legitimacy and, in particular, faith. Thus, Paulina says to Leontes and the audience:

> It is required
> you do awake your faith. Then all stand still;
> Or those that think it is unlawful business
> I am about, let them depart . . .
>
> (5.3.94–7)

Paulina reawakens in Leontes a faith that is both inside and outside life's normal orders of temporality, faith, and knowledge, at once. As the play moves toward its concluding synthesis, of belief and legitimacy, the astonished Leontes responds to the vision of Hermione:

> O, she's warm!
> If this be magic, let it be an art
> Lawful as eating.
>
> (5.3.109–11)

Leontes's exclamation invokes the various discourses, of law, theology, and aesthetics we have been examining throughout. His desire that Hermione's return be legitimate returns *us* to the root: "lawful as eating." Drawing on one of the most important "root metaphors" of Christian theology, Shakespeare concludes his exploration of the relationship between mystery and media with an invocation of the figure that lies at the heart of the performance of Christianity's political-theological notion of community.[97] The metaphor of eating ties together the discussion of affection, biblical language, metaphor, and law. As Peter Goodrich notes, eating is a key sign of recognition:

> At Emmaus the resurrected Christ was recognized not by face or image but by eating . . . The breaking of bread was the sign of divine presence . . . Emmaus signified that what dies can live on, that what passes can be remembered, that what is present is always potentially a reference to some other order of being or to some other text . . . at Emmaus Christ's Eucharistic presence was acted out again.[98]

The theme of recognition presents its own form of return. From *Richard II*'s queen recognizing the significance of her husband's departure, *Fuenteovejuna*'s Commander's anxious questioning of whether his subjects know him, we have encountered the question of recognition in relation to sovereignty—and most often in relation to its absence—before. In the biblical story of Christ at Emmaus, recognition is linked to eating the sign and repeated mark of divine presence, to its staging and re-actualization in and of the community. Crucially, the precondition that allows for all of this transformative action is the presence of commentary:

> Only through commentary, through authoritative interpretation, can we have access to that substance, that body and that blood. . . . The Conceptual apparatus of the Church, the theology of presence in the Eucharist, becomes in law the question of "the spirit of law," of the "living voice of law," of the presence of law as it is disinterred or resurrected through tradition as well as through the legal text, through equity, through the *ecclesia* of the court, through the wisdom of the judges, the sages or holy men (*sacerdotes*) of the common Law.[99]

As in *Measure for Measure*, here, too, the law's desire is satisfied by a body. Unlike in Shakespeare's previous play, however, in which *any* body, or body part, would do, here the Text itself is the "body," and commentary is the spirit that reanimates it—and us along with it. That this body presents itself through the conceptual and poetic operation par excellence, the one that always figures in the question of man's relation to the divine, as well as the divine's relation to art—metamorphosis—is a reminder of the shared media conditions of Mystery and theater.

Yet in *The Winter's Tale*, as we have seen, Shakespeare not only invokes the Ovidian logic of metamorphosis, but he also moves through and beyond it, toward the staging of a media-anatomy of the Christian semiotics of the Eucharist. The lawful and wonder-producing restoration of the "dead" body invokes the sovereign theological event of the miracle itself—the mystery. Shakespeare's romance draws on what Hent de Vries calls the *technicity* of a theological construction, the art (or techné) in which a mediated and also mediating body is fabricated out of a collage of textual authorities: Ovid, Petrarch, and also the book of Revelation.[100] Like Suárez's *Mysteries*, *The Winter's Tale* is a discourse of special effects, of a performance that binds and links the subject to a tradition that is at least as much theatrical as it is theological, and in which what is at stake is, again, less the believer's direct attachment to the desired object as an apprehension of his/her relation to that object: in this case, through the theatrico-Textual mediation and reanimation of the visible body of the Mother. This is not only political theology: It is *psycho*-political theology.[101] *The Winter's Tale* highlights this relation between attachment and mediation by staging its own "dance" of movements and failed transfers between textual and theatrical bodies as *media* events. The play *performs* "the life as lively mocked as ever" (5.3.19) by situating it within a "body" of authorities that prepares us for the "wonder"-producing, sovereign theological event of the *miracle*—the *mystery*. While Hermione does not "mean" the Virgin Mary, as some critics have argued, her staging nevertheless invokes the Virgin's representational history, which hovers over the play in the form of an afterimage.[102] Hermione—and with her the Mariological memory that she reactivates—appears *again*, in a performance that produces "wonder." Like a contemporary media installation, she presents us with a "real virtuality where make-believe is belief in the making."[103] Just as the *Mysteries* both reveal and conceal their truth in metaphor, Hermione both is and is not a special effect. That Shakespeare's play ends with these reminders, and remainders, is not only characteristic of the romances in general, but is also itself a marker of sovereignty's conceptual efficiency as it literally moves into and occupies new media. *The Winter's Tale*'s "wrinkling" of political and theological discourses into an aesthetic framework of the staged return also marks another event. What we see in *The Winter's Tale* are the media effects of "mystery"—a complex historical, representational structure that depends on systematic, interpretive framing and staging. What *The Winter's Tale* anatomizes, unveils, and allows us to understand, in the end, is a structure of "theatricality," in Samuel Weber's terms, upon which modern sovereignty comes increasingly to rest. Depending on repetition and repeatability, this theatricality differs from narrative form, both in its temporality and in its spatiality. This type of theatricality performs a different kind of bond with the individual, a *sovereign bond* that has to be understood as a function of a particular combination of mediation and performance: authentic and artificial at once, metaphorically forged, theatrically structured, physiologically signed.

# After-Image

In lieu of a conclusion, I would like to consider what remains. What, in the end, do the "tears," or tropes of sovereignty, come together to show? Throughout these pages, I have focused on both how the problem of sovereignty has been imagined by the great playwrights of the early modern period, and also on how their visions continue to illuminate the writings of twentieth- and twenty-first century theorists and critics, such as Walter Benjamin, Carl Schmitt, Giorgio Agamben, and Jacques Derrida. For these, and others, while sovereignty may generate a profusion of images, the space from which this generation emerges is itself an "empty" one. Like the goat-stag of the philosophers, sovereignty, at least in theory, has no real being.

On the other hand, we do not need to be reminded of the lethal effects of sovereign power to know that in some sense sovereignty is real enough. Sovereignty may be a fantasy, a chimera, and an "impossible being," in the terms of critical theory or scholasticism—but that does not mean it doesn't *work*. On the contrary, the concept is highly productive. Like religion, with which it has much in common, sovereignty sets the imagination to work, generating an array of fictions and figures. It may be true that sovereignty is an "illusion," as Freud says of religion. But, as Wendy Brown reminds us, "illusion" in Freud does not mean "mistake." It means "wish."[1] It is bound up with fear, and desire, and possibility, which lend it both beautiful and terrifying forms. Sovereignty acts and performs in tremendously creative and troubling ways. In order to understand some of these, I have turned to the language of baroque drama. What I have attempted to trace in these pages are some of the ways the terms reconfigured on the early modern stage continue to govern our manner of thinking about, imagining, fearing, and desiring sovereignty today. The "logics" of this thinking are often less rational than they are poetic and theatrical: they are metaphor-logics borne by the tropes of the stage.

There are many ways of imagining how these tropes move into our time. I have tried to think of this movement in relation to the medium of theater in general, and to the dramatic genre of the "mourning play," as Benjamin describes it, in particular. If, as Fredric Jameson has powerfully argued, modernity "is not a concept but rather a narrative category," then the story told here presents us with a counter image, if not argument regarding our view of that category.[2] How does modernity's narrative move with respect to sovereignty? Is it a movement that "develops"? My response to these questions here has been that the baroque terms and tropes that sovereignty relies on do not "develop," do not, that is, move, in a narrative form—at least not, that is, if we take that term to refer to a form that proceeds from beginning through middle to end.[3] The "*tears* of sovereignty" don't *end*. Rather, they recur. Baroque drama stages returns as much as endings. Unlike Greek tragedy, the *Trauerspiel*, or "tragical history" of modernity is "modern" precisely for its manner of depicting a history that does not develop in a decisive way, but rather decays, reconfigures what remains, and moves on: "Adjourned at the end" is Benjamin's way of putting it, in the juridical-theological language that he, in many ways, learns from the baroque.[4] This view of an "end" in terms of postponement rather than decision throws narrative movement itself into a complicating light. What takes place, for the political-theological "defendant" or "creature" (*Kreatur*) while he or she awaits history's verdict? What does one wait *for*, with regard to sovereignty? For we may be "after" sovereignty, as the title of a recent collection of essays puts it, to refer to the temporal and affective senses in which we "chase" it, but we certainly aren't over it. We are not—to use sovereignty's own spatial metaphor—*beyond* or "above" it.[5]

Following Benjamin's view of the interrupted temporality of the baroque *Trauerspiel*, the consistent account of sovereignty presented in this book suggests that sovereignty's "story" cannot, in the end, be told in narrative form. In the place of narratives, what I have followed on the stages of Shakespeare, Lope, and Calderón, instead, is their production of metaphors. In this light, the image of sovereignty we are presented with is always in some sense a distorted one. That is not to imply that behind the curtain lies the reality. We do not ever, I am suggesting, "see" sovereignty other than through its representational terms, which means that our view of it is always, necessarily at the same time, a mis-view. Sovereignty "speaks" through "tears." Thus, while all of the plays read here do, of course, have their own plots—involving the rise and fall of kings, the restoration of law, the overturning of tyranny, the rectification of paternal error, and the return of the Mother—with regard to the concept of sovereignty, the plots look eerily the same. Sovereignty does not progress in any of them. It does not become "better," more rational, egalitarian, democratic, scientific, fair, or "modern." Again, to repeat what is itself an argument about historical repetition, sovereignty does not *develop*—unless, that is, that term is understood in its photographic sense of coming into view as an image. It certainly doesn't leave its religious layering behind, and move into an autonomous realm of rationality, or secularity. (Rationality itself, as we don't need Hannah Arendt's or Theodor Adorno and Max Horkheimer's analyses of totalitarianism and enlightenment to remind us, can take the most monstrous of forms.[6]) Unlike the position of theorists from Immanuel Kant and Jürgen Habermas, to Richard Rorty and John Rawls, who all in different ways conceive of modernity in terms of a historical break from older models of sovereignty defined in "religious" terms, the view presented here is of a series of image-movements that do not avail themselves of such a break. Phantasm or not, the real chimera that is sovereignty remains with us today, perhaps more than ever.[7] We still view it through our own distorted fears and desires, reanimate it through representational substitutions, witness the resistances these gives rise to, discover it in new forms ("ciphers and images"), and find it back with us again—aged, but effectively the same ("wrinkles"). In this view, sovereignty makes no developmental or narrational sense. It has no "story" to tell.

Perhaps, then, if we have trouble accounting for sovereignty today, it may be that we no longer know how to see or even mis-see it. As one political scientist has recently put it, sovereignty is "like fire." We all know what it is and can feel its effects when it's there, but, from a theoretical point of view, we cannot fully explain it. Sovereignty cannot be made to cohere. It remains "an object of knowledge, yet the accounts of it vary to the point of incommensurability," so much so that it is "no longer a reality for science."[8] There is no right way of looking at sovereignty. If, as some critics have argued, we can no longer "do to our contemporaneity what Bodin, Hobbes and Rousseau did to theirs," this is in some part because *our* contemporaneity, when it comes to sovereignty theory, *is* in many ways theirs—the contemporaneity not only of Bodin and Hobbes, but also of Shakespeare, Lope, Calderón, and Suárez.[9] We are still living in the logics of their terms, seeing sovereignty through the images produced on their stages. "Their" sovereignty is also ours.

This returns me to the tears of *Richard II*. What I have argued throughout these pages is what Shakespeare already knew. The only way to see sovereignty right is to get the "concept" wrong. This is because sovereignty has no single coherent concept, no unified being. The "right" view, in this case, is always the "awry" view, the view of an image, or metaphor. We view sovereignty through "tears"—both in the sense of the distortion and violence involved in viewing such a determining abstraction (Suárez's fire)—but also in the end, as Richard comes to see, as the only sense possible, when the thing itself is ultimately so shape-shifting and empty. Richard may no longer himself be the sovereign of England at the end of the play, as the concept has indeed left his body. But the play allows him to rightly perceive sovereignty's coming form—that of a "well graced actor" moving across the stage.

## Riß

The "tear" has thus been many things for me in this study: a trope, a pun, a trace, the "*trazas*" of Laurencia's curse. Above all, the "tear" has been made to do theoretical work. In tearing Shakespeare's metaphor out of its context to take it as a trope for sovereignty, I am reminded of the German term "*Riss*." Like "tear," *Riß* can mean different things at once. For Marx and Heidegger, it is a word used to refer to their own philosophical and theoretical "designs." "Riß" is part of a plan—a "ground plan," a *Grundriss*. In his essay "The Age of the World Picture," on the emergence of a new world view (which emerges, not coincidentally, in the seventeenth century), Heidegger writes that the "fundamental event" of research, which is the "opening up of a sphere" for thought, is the "projection . . . of a fixed *ground plan*."[10] A "fixed ground plan" is a "*Grundriss*." The translator, William Lovitt, renders the verb *reissen* as "to tear, to rend, to sketch, to design" and the noun "Riss" as "tear," "gap," "outline." "Hence," as Lovitt says, "the noun

*Grundriss* . . . ground plan, design, connotes a fundamental sketching out that is an opening up as well."[11]

Derrida returns to this term, and to Heidegger's use of it, in his analysis of metaphor. Pursuing the question of just how metaphor can be seen to participate in, or on the other hand, be excluded from philosophy and metaphysics, in particular, Derrida pauses to consider the specific language Heidegger uses to think of their relation. As with his analyses of sovereignty, Derrida approaches the problem of the relation between "poetry" (or language) and thought by thinking of it in terms of its *traits*.[12]

Specifically, he asks after the "trait" of each, of poetry (although he warns us about moving too easily from the German word *Dichten* to "poetry") and of thought—as well as the trait of the relation between them. It is at this point that he turns to the term *Riß*:

> Well, the neighboring trait, or as I will say the *approaching* trait, the proper trait that relates (*bezieht*) *Dichten* (which must not be translated, without precaution, as poetry) and thought (*Denken*) one to the other in their neighboring proximity, the trait that sets them *apart* and of which they both *partake*, this common differential trait that attracts them reciprocally, even while signing their irreducible difference, this trait is the *trait*: *Riss*, a tracing-out that breaks a path [*tracement de frayage*], that incises, tears, marks the divergence, the limit, the margin, the mark (at one point, Heidegger names the "march," "*Mark*" as limit, *Grenz-, Grenzland* [171; 67]). And this trait (*Riss*) is a *cut* that the two neighbors, *Denken und Dichten*, make into each other somewhere in infinity.[13]

"Riß" is a "cut" that both separates and connects language to thought, placing them in a "neighborly" relation. Poetry (or literature) and philosophy, metaphor and concept, both come together in the form of a relation figured as a "cut that the two neighbors . . . make into each other." How are we to understand this mutual cutting and neighborly relation that seems at least as violent and marked by separation as connection? And why does Derrida think that thinking about the relation itself, as well as its figuration, is so important to understanding the borderlines of disciplines? While it is not at all clear at first what Derrida is after in dwelling so long on different words and ways to see the relation between language and thought, with the various movements and relations he identifies—the *neighboring*, the *approaching*, the *setting apart*, the *partaking*, the *cutting, tearing, marking* of *divergence*, and, finally, the "march"—it becomes clearer, and also, perhaps, a bit surprising to discover that in the end, what Derrida is interested in here, among other things, is history:[14]

> Now, continues Heidegger, we know *Riss* often only in the "debased" (*abgewerteten*) form that it has in expressions such as "to mark a wall," "to clear and cultivate a field" (*einen Acker auf- und Umreissen*), in order to trace furrows (*Furchen ziehen*) so that the field will shelter, and keep in it (*berge*) the seeds and the crop. The breaching, broaching incision (*Aufriss*) is the totality of the traits (*das Ganze der Zuge*), the *Gefüge* of this *Zeichnung* (inscription, engraving, signature) that throughout *joins* (articulates, spaces, and holds together) the opening of *Sprache*. But this incision remains veiled (*verhüllt*) as long as one does not properly (*eigens*) remark in what sense the spoken and speaking are spoken of. The trait of the incision is therefore veiled, withdrawn, but it is also the trait that brings together and spaces out both the veiling *and* the unveiling, the *withdrawal* and the *withdrawal of the withdrawal*, the *retrait* of the *retrait*.[15]

Heidegger's use of the term "Riß"—which in its "debased" forms means to "cultivate a field," "trace furrows" in the soil, and so on—is also what language does to, with, and in history: It makes marks in the ground, cultivates soil, and "traces furrows" that will shelter seeds for a new crop. Derrida's agricultural view of Heidegger is one that connects his philosophy to the movement, and particularly the withdrawal, of time. Metaphor, in this view, is historical, material, and generative, as both a marker of that movement *and* its withdrawal. It appears, divides, disseminates, and moves on—preparing the ground for the coming term, or trope. Derrida plays with the terms that are central to Heidegger's philosophy of history and its to and from movements of concealing and revealing, drawing and withdrawing. This play is itself part of a larger discourse on the complex interrelations and co-implications of history, metaphor, and thought. Derrida's own relation to this history is not only an "intellectual" one. His objective is not to provide us with a hi-story of ideas. Riß is not a concept. There is no intellectual history of the *Riß*. Rather, in Derrida's discussion it is a performance, in language, and of reading—a term, and a trope, for a relation and for putting language and thought into relation with each other. The reading that produces a relation is itself, in this regard, the point. Reading is an *act* and is in this sense sovereign. (After all, to "read," in English, comes from an etymology that links it to "rule," to "advise," and to "plot"—the very functions of the baroque sovereign, in Benjamin's analysis.[16]) To return to Benjamin's notion of the dialectical image and Haverkamp's account of it as the "image that is read," I would like to conclude this book with the image that has hovered over its pages from the beginning—the image of Francisco Suárez's burning text. It is not the substance of the political debate between James and Suárez that for me lingers (although I am sympathetic to some aspects of Suárez's argument). It is the drama of power itself—and the drama of its resistance. Unlike Francisco Suárez the man, who was averse to political conflict and reluctant to participate in the oath of allegiance controversy, his text has become something of a diva in the opera of early modern sovereignty theory. Its trajectory, once released from the printer, leads us straight to center stage of European political history. And it doesn't disappoint. Its flames return us to where the book began, not only with Walter Benjamin's theory of the "image that is read," but also to a (perhaps surprising) view of Suárez's text itself as a "troublemaker," that which, in Agamben's view, tricks sovereignty to "translate" itself into actuality.[17] What remains, then, is one last trope—the image of sovereignty in flames, on fire, and burning. "Burning" has become an interesting term again. As Peter Goodrich points out, today it means "downloading from the screen, writing to DVD, not destroying text but encoding html—hypertext markup language—onto disk. Burning makes reading possible."[18] As we move from a fire that destroys a text, to a "burning" that makes reading possible, the movement between seventeenth century baroque culture and our own moment with regard to sovereignty might be conceived of in this way: as a transformation in the function of burning. Sovereignty burns its impressions into us in images that are also tropes. The body-of-power no longer appears only on stage but also on such platforms as television, the (movie) theater, the computer, the cell, the iPad, or the Kindle Fire. It has left the king's body behind, but it continues to act on the screen.

# Notes

## INTRODUCTION: THE BODY IS BURNING—SOVEREIGNTY, IMAGE, TROPE

1. The full title of the work (from the 1613 Coimbra edition by Gomez de Loureyro, carried forward verbatim in the only modern edition) is *Defensio fidei Catholicæ apostolicæ adversus Anglicanæ sectæ errores, cum responsione ad apologiam pro juramento fidelitatis, et præfationem monitoriam serenissimi Jacobi Magnæ Britanniæ Regis* (henceforth *DF*). Citations are to the modern edition: *Opera omnia*, ed. Charles Berton (Paris: L. Vivès, 1856), vol. 24.

2. Joseph Henry Fichter, S.J., *Man of Spain: Francis Suarez* (New York: Macmillan, 1940), 300. As Carlos Noreña notes, subsequent to this event, the French Parliament also "ordered in June 1614 the public burning of the *Defensio fidei*, but Papal intervention succeeded in preventing the execution of a decree that seemed intolerable in a Catholic realm." Noreña, "Suárez and the Jesuits," *American Catholic Philosophical Quarterly* 65, no. 3 (Summer 1991): 286.

3. Fichter, *Man of Spain*, 299.

4. On the differences between Catholic and Royalist theory, see J. P. Sommerville, "From Suarez to Filmer: A Reappraisal," *The Historical Journal* 25 (1982): 525–40.

5. Suárez's *Defense of the Faith* was published in 1613 in Coimbra, following the work of Cardinal Robert Bellarmine and others, thus making Suárez and "Suárezian thought" late, but "key," participants in the oath of allegiance controversy. On the historical and conceptual implications of the exchange, see Bernard Bourdin, *The Theological-Political Origins of the Modern State: The Controversy between James I of England & Cardinal Bellarmine*, trans. Susan Pickford (Washington: The Catholic University of America Press, 2010).

6. Suárez's Latin reads, "At Vero in Summo Pontifice est hæc potestas tanquam in superiori habente jurisdictionem ad corripiendum reges, etiam supremos, tanquam sibi subditos, ut supra ostensum est. Unde si crimina sint in materia spirituali, ut est crimen hæresis, potest directe illa punire in rege, etiam usque ad depositionem a regno, si pertinacia regis et providentia communis boni Ecclesiæ ita postulant. Si vero vitia sint in materia temporali, quatenus peccata sunt, etiam potest illa corripere per directam potestatem; quatenus vero fuerint temporaliter nociva reipublicæ Christianæ, indirecte saltem poterit ea punier, quatenus tyrannicum regimen temporalis principis semper etiam est saluti animarum perniciosum." *Opera omnia*, ed. Charles Berton (Paris: L. Vivès 1856), vol. 24, bk. 6, ch. 4, p. 680. For the published English translation, see *Selections from Three Works of Francisco Suárez, S.J.*, trans. Gwladys L. Williams with Ammi Brown and John Waldron (Oxford: Clarendon Press, 1944), vol. II, 719. Subsequent references to this text will appear as *Selections*. While I rely on Williams for most of the English translations, I occasionally modify them, as in this case. I have also consulted the bilingual (Latin-Spanish) editions of books III and VI of the *Defensio fidei*, published separately as *Principatus Politicus* and *De Iuramento Fidelitatis*, by E. Elorduy and L. Pereña, eds., Madrid: Consejo Superior de Investigaciones Científicas, Corpus Hispanorum de Pace, vol. II and XIX, 1965 and 1978: 88.

On Suárez's theory of papal deposing power, see Harro Höpfl, "The Papal *potestas indirecta*," *Jesuit Political Thought: The Society of Jesus and the State, c. 1540–1630* (Cambridge: Cambridge University Press, 2004), ch. 14, esp. 351. As Höpfl points out, the notion of a "potestas indirecta" is "manifestly not scriptural" (352). Against the older expression, "*potestas ex consequenti*, by entailment," the newer term, *potestas indirecta*, "seems to have crept in without anyone noticing," and is a product of the specific historical, political, and theoretical conditions of the Reformation. Its purpose was to mediate between two incompatible and extreme positions that emerged out of Reformation and Counter-Reformation polemics in early modern Europe: the first, that the pope has total supremacy over the secular world; the second, that the pope has *no* authority over this world. As Höpfl points out, it was up to the Jesuits, such as Bellarmine and Suárez, to "produce the Golden Mean" of the *potestas indirecta*. (350).

The distinction between direct and indirect power can be confusing, given that what Suárez refers to as the Pope's "*direct* power" has subsequently come to be known as "*indirect* deposing temporal power"—the papal *potestas indirecta*. The difference is an important one. As the constitutional historian J. N. Figgis notes, the "doctrine of the direct power of the papacy is expressed, e.g., in the *Unam Sanctam* of Boniface VIII, or in the writings of Augustinus Triumphus or Bozius, who asserts that the State is a part of the Church, and that kings are servants of the papacy. The doctrine of the indirect power proclaimed by Bellarmine and Suarez [on the other hand] allows the State an independent existence . . . but [also] claims an indirect power for the Church in cases in which its own interest might be concerned"—that is (to put it in a modern idiom) in states of exception. Unlike the medieval theories, Suárez's thinking "looks forward to the modern separation of Church and State." J. N. Figgis, in James Hastings, *Encyclopedia of Religion and Ethics*, vol. XI, p. 650.

7. "Ratio ergo est, quia tunc non occiditur rex aut princeps, sed hostis reipublicæ." Suárez, *Opera omnia*, ed. Charles Berton (Paris: L. Vivès 1856), vol. 24, bk. 6, ch. 4, p. 677. *Selections*, 711. Suárez is very careful to specify the "limiting conditions" under which this "self-defense" is permitted. *Opera omnia*, vol. 24, bk. 6, ch. 4, pp. 677–8. *Selections*, 712–13.

8. "Certe licet Paulus dixerit: *omnis anima potestatibus sublimioribus subdita sit*, nunquam addidit: Etiam potestatibus excommunicatis vel deprivatis a Papa omnes subditi sint; neque unum ex alio colligi potest, cum sint longe diversa, ne dicam veluti opposita, nam rex deprivatus jam non est sublimior potestas." *Opera omnia*, ed. Charles Berton (Paris: L. Vivès 1856), vol. 24, bk. 6, ch. 4, p. 682. *Selections*, 723. Although Suárez's *Defense* was not published in Coimbra until 1613, reports of its contents reached James beforehand from his English agent in Madrid, Sir John Digby. See Fichter, 293. The full title of James's defense of the Oath was *De triplici nodo, triplex cuneus. Or an Apologie for the Oath of Allegiance*. It was addressed to the Catholic theologian Cardinal Robert Bellarmine and published in 1608. For a discussion of the reception of Suárez's text in France, see Eric Nelson, *The Jesuits and the Monarchy: Catholic Reform and Political Authority in France* (1590–1615).

9. Suárez, *Opera omnia*, vol. 24, bk. 6, ch. 4, p. 679. *Selections*, 717.

10. Harro Höpfl, *Jesuit Political Thought: The Society of Jesus and the State, c. 1540–1630* (Cambridge: Cambridge University Press, 2004), 340.

11. I am grateful to my colleague, Andy Galloway, here and throughout, for helping me with Suárez's Latin and for calling my attention to this crossing of terms in particular.

12. "Triplici nodo," *King James VI and I: Political Writings*, ed. Johann P. Sommerville (Cambridge: Cambridge University Press, 1994), 89.

13. For a discussion, see J. P. Sommerville, *Royalists and Patriots: Politics and Ideology in England, 1603–1640* (New York: Addison Wesley Longman, 1999). On the *Vindiciae contra tyrannos*, see Andrew Hadfield, *Shakespeare and Renaissance Politics* (London: Arden, 2004). On the difference between James's Divine Right theory and Catholic political theory, Annabel Brett points out that against Divine Right, "Catholic political theorists . . . build up the political community from nature and . . . derive the ruler's power from the human community rather than immediately from God, and therefore put a natural limit on legislation and the power of the prince." See Brett, "Scholastic Political Thought and the Modern Concept of the State" in *Rethinking Foundations of Modern Political Thought*, ed. James Tully Brett and Holly Hamilton-Bleakley (Cambridge: Cambridge University Press, 2006), 137.

14. For James's speech, see *The Trew Law of Free Monarchies* (1598) in *King James VI and I: Political Writings*, ed. Johann P. Sommerville (Cambridge: Cambridge University Press, 1994), 72.

For a general overview of resistance theory, see J. P. Sommerville, *Royalists and Patriots: Politics and Ideology in England 1603–1640* (New York: Addison Wesley Longman, 1999), 183–4; and John Neville Figgis, *The Divine Right of Kings* (Gloucester: P. Smith, 1970), 219–55. For the sixteenth century, in particular, see Julian H. Franklin, Francois Hotman, Théodore de Bèze, and Hubert Languet, *Constitutionalism and Resistance: Three Treatises by Hotman, Beza, and Mornay* (New York: Pegasus, 1969). For a representative text of a slightly later articulation of non-resistance theory, see Roger Maynwaring, *Religion and Alegiance: In Two Sermons Preached before the King's Maiestie* (London, Printed by I.H. for Richard Badger, 1627) in Joyce Lee Malcolm's *The Struggle for Sovereignty: Seventeenth-Century English Political Tracts* (Indianapolis: Liberty Fund, 1999).

15. Fichter, *Man of Spain*, 302.

16. Ibid., 302–3.

17. Fichter's is the only English biography to date. It is an abridged and, as Sydney Penner notes, occasionally "hagiographical" version of the definitive biography by Raoul de Scorraille, *François Suárez de la Compagnie de Jesus*, 2 volumes (Paris: Lethielleux, 1912–13). See Sydney Penner, whose website is an excellent resource for material on Suárez and contains reliable and up-to-date links to a wide range of Suárez's texts: http://www.sydneypenner.ca/suarez.shtml. More scholarly discussions in English than Fichter's can be found in Jorge J. E. Gracia, "Francisco Suárez: The Man in History," *American Catholic Philosophical Quarterly*

65 (1991): 259–66; Carlos Noreña, "Suárez and the Jesuits," *American Catholic Philosophical Quarterly* 65, no. 3 (Summer 1991); John Doyle, "Francisco Suárez, His Life, His Works, His Doctrine, and Some of His Influence," *Collected Studies on Francisco Suárez, S.J. (1548–1617),* ed. Victor M. Salas (Leuven: Leuven University Press, 2010); and Daniel Schwartz, ed. *Interpreting Suárez: Critical Essays* (Cambridge: Cambridge University Press, 2012).

18. In hyphenating the phrase, I am following the practice of Louis Marin, whose work on the representation of political-theological sovereignty informs my thinking throughout. See Louis Marin, *Portrait of the King*, trans. Martha M. Houle (Minneapolis: University of Minnesota Press, 1988) as well as "The Body-of-Power and Incarnation at Port Royal and in Pascal—or—Of the Figurability of the Political Absolute" in *Fragments for a History of the Human Body: Part Three*, ed. Michel Feher, Ramona Naddaff, and Nadia Tazi (New York: Zone Books, 1989), 421–47.

19. For a discussion of the priority of resistance to power within the context of modern imperial struggles, see Michael Hardt and Antonio Negri, *Empire* (Cambridge: Harvard University Press, 2000), esp. at 360ff. Hardt and Negri draw on Gilles Deleuze's *Foucault*, trans. Seán Hand (Minneapolis: University of Minnesota Press, 1988).

20. According to the *Oxford English Dictionary* (*OED*), the English word "sovereign" is derived from the thirteenth-century Middle English "*soverain*," from the popular Latin, *superanus*, from Latin, "super," "over," "above." The *OED* provides numerous definitions (including some irrelevant to my purposes, such as a variety of pear); the most pertinent are, "One who has supremacy or rank above or authority over others, a superior; a ruler, governor, lord, or master (first use 1290); Freq. Applied to the Deity in relation to created things" (first use 1297), and "The recognized supreme ruler of a people or country under monarchical government; a monarch; a king or queen" (first use 1297). The term "sovereign" has been used to refer to "a husband in relation to his wife" (first use 1390), "a free citizen or voter of America" (1846), the "superior of a monastery" (1450), and "a gold coin minted in England from the time of Henry VII to Charles I" (1503). The *OED* defines the term "sovereignty" as "Supremacy or pre-eminence in respect of excellence or efficacy" (first use 1340), as well as "Supremacy in respect of power, domination, or rank; supreme dominion, authority, or rule" (1374). In Spanish, the word "soberano" also emphasizes the sovereign's position *above* all others. In what is considered to be the first Spanish-language

dictionary, Sebastián de Covarrubias Horozco's (or Orozco's) *Tesoro de la Lengua Castellana O Española* (1611), the entry for "soberano" reads "el altísimo y poderosísísimo que es sobre todos." See *Tesoro de la Lengua Castellana O Española*, ed. Ignacio Arellano y Rafael Zafra (Madrid: Universidad de Navarra, 2006), 1446. The *Tesoro* is an important source. As Georgina Dopico and Jacques Lezra point out, it is much more than a dictionary. Combining elements of thesaurus, modern lexicon, encyclopedia and "book of wonders," it provides us with a crucial glimpse into the cultural and ideological worlds of early modern Spain. See Dopico's and Lezra's introduction to the *Suplemento al Tesoro de la Lengua Española Castellana*, ed. Georgina Dopico and Jacques Lezra (Madrid: Ediciones Polifemo, 2001), xi–xxviii.

21. For a concise overview of the history and current use of the term "sovereignty," see Richard Falk's entry in the *Oxford Companion to Politics of the World*, ed. Joel Krieger (New York: Oxford University Press, 1993), 851–4.

22. As *The Oxford English Dictionary* (Oxford University Press, 2004) shows, the term "theory," from the late Latin, *theoria* (Jerome in Ezech. XII. xl. 4), refers to a "looking at, viewing, contemplation, speculation, theory, also a sight, a spectacle, abstr. n. f. (:*) spectator, looker on, f. stem—of to look on, view, contemplate. In mod. use prob. from med.L. transl. of Aristotle. Cf. It. teoria (Florio 1598 theoría), F. théorie (15.. in Godefroy. *Compl.*)." "Theory," historically, recurs to visual metaphors to express its operations. As many have pointed out, it shares an etymology with the related terms of *theater* (from Latin *theatrum*, from Greek *theatron*, from *theasthai* [behold]—a structure for viewing)—as well as *theology*, which could be understood as a discourse for viewing God. See, among others, Rainer Nägele, *Theater, Theory, Speculation: Walter Benjamin and the Scenes of Modernity* (Baltimore: Johns Hopkins University Press, 1991).

23. In his famous exchange with Rosencrantz and Guildenstern about the location of Polonius's murdered body, Hamlet invokes the legal theory of the King's Two Bodies:

> ROSENCRANTZ: My lord, you must tell us where the body is, and go with us to the King.
> HAMLET: The King is a thing—
> GUILDENSTERN: A thing, my lord?
> HAMLET: Of nothing.

Hamlet 4.2.23–8 qtd. from *The Norton Shakespeare Based on the Oxford Edition*, 2nd ed., Greenblatt et al, eds.

24. The definitive work on this subject is Ernst Kantorowicz's *The King's Two Bodies: A Study in Medieval Political Theology* (Princeton: Princeton University Press, 1957).

25. "Transposition" is the term Carl Schmitt uses; see *Political Theology II: The Myth of the Closure of Any Political Theology* (Cambridge: Polity, 2008), 117–18. *Tears* follows the movements and figurations of this "body-of-power" through various formations, de-formations, and re-formations. Historically speaking, appearances of the body—at least *some* kind of body—as a figure for sovereignty in religion, philosophy, and law are too numerous to mention. The analytical frameworks of deconstruction, psychoanalysis, and various media theories all approach the problem of sovereign power and political-theological relations via the figure of the "body." The political, as the French jurist and psychoanalyst Pierre Legendre puts it, always "passes by way of the body . . ." *Law and the Unconscious: A Legendre Reader*, ed. Peter Goodrich (New York: St. Martin's Press, 1997), 47.

In addition to Kantorowicz, see Michael Walzer, "On the Role of Symbolism in Political Thought," *Political Science Quarterly* 82, no. 2 (June 1967): 191–204. For a discussion of the metaphor within English history specifically, see David George Hale, *The Body Politic: A Political Metaphor in Renaissance Literature* (The Hague: Mouton, 1971). On the gendering of this body, see Mary Axton, *The Queen's Two Bodies: Drama and the Elizabethan Succession* (London: Royal Historical Society, 1977), as well as Adriana Cavarero, *Stately Bodies: Literature Philosophy, and the Question of Gender* (Ann Arbor: University of Michigan Press, 2002).

26. I've translated Maravall's discussion here. See José Antonio Maravall, *Teoría del Estado en España en el siglo XVII* (Madrid: Centro de Estudios Constitucionales, 1997), 189–90.

27. One could contrast this tradition of understanding sovereignty in terms of its proximity to God with that of the discourse of Republicanism, a strand of which attempts to define political power in terms of its separation from God. Miguel Vatter identifies the beginning of this tradition and its "modern republican attitude toward religion" with Spinoza, who "rejected all attempts at crediting God with sovereignty (on the ground that it is an anthropomorphism) and identified God with Nature." Vatter, "Introduction: Crediting God with Sovereignty," *Crediting God: Sovereignty and Religion in the Age of Global Capitalism* (New York: Fordham University Press, 2011), 15.

28. This return to sovereignty's metaphysical ground coincides with a corresponding insistence on the "resilience of webs of belief." As Miguel Vatter has recently put it, "with the discontent with the modern

project of epistemology, the path is once again being opened for a return to classical and medieval ontology, to Platonism and Aristotelianism in their manifold versions, and with that to a vision of the world that is more compatible with revealed truths." Vatter, *Crediting God*, 2.

29. Giorgio Agamben, *Homo Sacer: Sovereign Power and Bare Life*, trans. Daniel Heller-Roazen (Stanford: Stanford University Press, 1998), 28. My emphasis.

30. Agamben's reading of this history has been the object of much critical discussion. For a dissenting view, particularly regarding Agamben's interpretation of Aristotle, see Jacques Derrida, *Rogues: Two Essays on Reason*, trans. Pascale-Anne Brault and Michael Naas (Stanford: Stanford University Press, 2005), 24. Derrida offers an extended critique of Agamben in the twelfth session of *The Beast and the Sovereign*, ed. Michel-Lisse, Marie-Louise Mallet, and Ginette Michaud, trans. Geoffrey Bennington (Chicago: University of Chicago Press, 2009), 305ff.

31. Sovereignty, as we will see, is thus an eminently paradoxical problem. In addition to Marin's paradox, the paradox I repeatedly underscore throughout these pages is that sovereignty both exceeds and is at the same time entirely dependent upon its representation. In *The Beast and the Sovereign* lectures, Derrida focuses on yet another paradox: that of the inhuman nature of the sovereign and sovereignty.

32. Jean-Luc Nancy, "Complement" in *The Creation of the World or Globalization* (Albany: State University of New York Press, 2007), 103.

33. Nancy continues, "In a rigorous sense, the sovereign foundation is infinite, or rather, sovereignty is never founded. It would, rather, be defined by the absence of foundation or presupposition: Neither in Athens nor in Rome was there a pure absence of presupposition prior to the law. Something of the divine or of destiny remains." "Complement," 103.

34. Ernesto Laclau, "On the Names of God," *Political Theologies, Political Theologies: Public Religions in a Post-Secular World*, ed. Hent de Vries and Lawrence E. Sullivan (New York: Fordham University Press, 2006) 137.

35. Anselm Haverkamp, *Shakespearean Genealogies of Power* (New York: Routledge, 2010), 126ff.

36. The argument that sovereignty arises from an "empty space" has been variously formulated by Agamben ("juridically empty space," *Homo Sacer*, 36–8); Ernesto Laclau ("empty signifier," *Emancipation(s)* 36ff); Louis Marin ("that *empty place* Pascal speaks of precisely with respect to the king, which is satisfaction always deferred" [*Portrait*, 8]); and especially Claude Lefort, *L'Invention démocratique* (Paris: Fayard, 1981).

37. On Schmitt as the "godfather of political theology," see Michael Hollerich, *Blackwell Companion to Political Theology*, ed. Peter Scott and William T. Cavanaugh. Also see Peter M. Stirk, *Carl Schmitt, Crown Jurist of the Third Reich: On Preemptive War, Military Occupation, and orld Empire* (Lewiston, N.Y.: Edwin Mellen Press, 2005). For Schmitt's life and career, see Gopal Balakrishnan, *The Enemy: An Intellectual Portrait of Carl Schmitt* (London: Verso, 2002). On the description of Schmitt as the "Crown Jurist" of the Third Reich, in a newspaper supporting National Socialism, see esp. Balakrishnan's discussion, 182ff.

38. On Schmitt as the "twentieth century's leading theorist of sovereignty," see Paul W. Kahn, *Political Theology: Four New Chapters on the Concept of Sovereignty* (New York: Columbia University Press, 2011), 6.

39. Carl Schmitt, *Hamlet or Hecuba: The Intrusion of the Time into the Play*, trans. David Pan and Jennifer Rust (New York: Telos Press, 2009), 44. Schmitt's account has generated an interesting and important critical response. In addition to the works cited in notes 37–8 above, see the essays collected in a special issue of *Telos* devoted to Schmitt, no. 153 (Winter 2010), "Carl Schmitt's *Hamlet or Hecuba*: The Intrusion of the Time into the Play," and no. 147 (Summer 2009), "Carl Schmitt and the Event." Important discussions include Heinrich Meier's *The Lesson of Carl Schmitt: Four Chapters on the Distinction between Political Theology and Political Philosophy*, trans. Marcus Brainard (Chicago: The University of Chicago Press, 1998); Chantal Mouffe, ed., *The Challenge of Carl Schmitt* (London: Verso, 1999); Raphael Gross, *Carl Schmitt and the Jews: The "Jewish Question," the Holocaust and German Legal Theory*, trans. Joel Golb (Madison: The University of Wisconsin Press, 2007); George Schwab, *The Challenge of the Exception: An Introduction to the Political Ideas of Carl Schmitt between 1921 and 1936* (New York: Greenwood Press, 1989); and Montserrat Herrero López, *El Nomos y lo politico: La filosofía política de Carl Schmitt* (Pamplona: University of Navarra, 1997).

40. For a discussion of the complex interplay of politics and representation in and around James's court, see Jonathan Goldberg, *James I and the Politics of Literature: Jonson, Shakespeare, Donne, and Their Contemporaries* (Stanford: Stanford University Press, 1989), esp. at 116ff.

41. See Jennifer Rust and Julia Reinhard Lupton's analysis in their critical introduction to *Hamlet or Hecuba: The Intrusion of the Time into the Play* (New York: Telos Press, 2009), xxx.

42. Schmitt, *Hamlet or Hecuba*, 44.

43. As Stathis Gourgouris puts it, for Schmitt, it is "reality, not dramatic invention, that brings about the grand innovation Schmitt calls

'the Hamletization of the hero' . . ." For Schmitt, "[t]his gesture does not belong to Shakespeare, it belongs to history." Gourgouris, *Does Literature Think? Literature as Theory for an Antimythical Era* (Stanford: Stanford University Press, 2003).

44. Paul W. Kahn, *Political Theology: Four Chapters on the Concept of Sovereignty* (New York: Columbia University Press, 2011), 6ff. Also see the essays collected in a special edition of *Telos* on *Political Theologies* 148 (Fall 2009).

45. Carl Schmitt, *The* Nomos *of the Earth*, trans. G. L. Ulmen (New York: Telos Press, 2003), 42. My emphasis.

46. For a critique of the "logo- and phallocentric" tradition Schmitt follows here, see Adriana Cavarero, *Stately Bodies: Literature, Philosophy, and the Question of Gender*, trans. Robert de Lucca and Deanna Shemek (Ann Arbor: The University of Michigan Press, 2002). Also see *In Spite of Plato: A Feminist Rewriting of Ancient Philosophy* (New York: Routledge, 1995). For Cavarero, the early modern period, including writers such as Shakespeare and Hobbes, plays a crucial role in the critical formation of this tradition.

47. In *Political Theology*, Schmitt writes that it "would be a distortion of the schematic disjunction between sociology and jurisprudence if one were to say that the exception has no juristic significance and is therefore 'sociology.'" Sociology obfuscates the issue for Schmitt, which is the real necessity of the friend-enemy distinction. In the end, the problem, according to Schmitt, is that sociology pretends that there is no evil. *Political Theology: Four Chapters on the Concept of Sovereignty*, trans. George Schwab (Cambridge: MIT Press, 1985), 22.

48. Howard Caygill, "Non-Messianic Political Theology in Benjamin's 'On the Concept of History,'" in *Walter Benjamin and History*, ed. Andrew Benjamin (London: Continuum, 2005), 224.

49. Schmitt, *Political Theology*, 44–5.

50. Ibid., 45–6.

51. Ibid., 46.

52. As Jacques Lezra has shown, Schmitt's analyses attempt to bridge historical and conceptual accounts of the history and theory of sovereignty. For a discussion of Schmitt's dual (empirical and conceptual) analysis, see Lezra, *Wild Materialism* (New York: Fordham University Press, 2010), 66ff.

53. On Schmitt's "bizarre relationship" with Benjamin, see Horst Bredekamp, "From Walter Benjamin to Carl Schmitt via Thomas Hobbes," *Critical Inquiry* 25, no. 2 (Winter 1999): 247–66, 247.

54. As Samuel Weber has shown, "Benjamin's mode of investigation, his *Forschungsweise*, is indebted to that of Schmitt: both share a certain methodological extremism for which the formation of a concept is paradoxically but necessarily dependent on a contact or an encounter with a singularity that exceeds or eludes the concept." See Samuel Weber, *Benjamin's -abilities* (Cambridge: Harvard University Press, 2008), 179.

55. "Methode ist Umweg. Darstellung als Umweg—das ist denn der methodische Charakter des Traktats. Verzicht auf den unabgesetzten Lauf der Intention ist sein erstes Kennzeichen. Ausdauernd hebt das Denken stets von neuem an, umständlich geht es auf di Sache selbst zurück." Walter Benjamin, *Ursprung des deutschen Trauerspiels* (Suhrkamp Verlag, 1998), 10. (*The Origin of German Tragic Drama*, trans. John Osborne [London: Verso, 2003], 28. Subsequent references to this text will appear as *OGTD*.)

56. Walter Benjamin, *Ursprung des deutschen Trauerspiels*, 10. *OGTD*, 28.

57. Benjamin, *OGTD*, 29.

58. The notion of immanent criticism runs throughout Benjamin's work, from his doctoral dissertation, "The Concept of Criticism in German Romanticism," through various studies of Romanticism and surrealism and his essays "On Language as Such and on Human Language" and "Goethe's Elective Affinities" (published in *Neue Deutsche Beiträge* in 1924). For "The Concept of Criticism in German Romanticism" and "Goethe's Elective Affinities," see *Selected Writings, Vol. 1, 1913–1926*, ed. Marcus Paul Bullock, Michael William Jennings, Howard Eiland, and Gary Smith (Cambridge: Harvard University Press, 1996).

59. On the notion of interpretation as staging, Samuel Weber writes, "Interpretation is not something added to the idea: it is its mode of 'staging' a world of phenomena selectively and tendentiously." See Weber, *Benjamin's-abilities*, 199 and 140. Other Benjamin scholars, including Andrew Benjamin and Rainer Nägele, have also highlighted the importance of staging to Benjamin's thought.

60. I am following Anselm Haverkamp's preferred translation of the German term *Trauerspiel*, "mourning play." See *Shakespearean Genealogies of Power: A Whispering of Nothing in* Hamlet, Richard II, Julius Caesar, Macbeth, The Merchant of Venice, *and* The Winter's Tale (New York: Routledge 2011).

61. Walter Benjamin, *Das Passagen-Werk. Gesammelte Schriften*, vol. 5, no. 1 (Frankfurt am Main: Suhrkamp Verlag, 1991), note [N2a,3], 576–7. Subsequent references to this text will appear as *GS*. For the

English translation of this note entry, see Walter Benjamin, *The Arcades Project*, trans. Howard Eiland and Kevin McLaughlin (Cambridge, Mass.: Belknap Press, 1999), 462. On Carl Schmitt's (mis)understanding of Marxist dialectics, in general, and Benjamin's dialectical image, in particular, see Stathis Gourgouris, *Does Literature Think? Literature as Theory for an Antimythical Era* (Stanford: Stanford University Press, 2003), 90ff.

62. The phrase "semi-concept" is Gerhard Richter's, in *Thought-Images: Frankfurt School Writers' Reflection from Damaged Life* (Stanford: Stanford University Press, 2007), 61.

63. Benjamin makes his opposition to Heidegger and Hegel explicit in a subsequent entry to *The Arcades Project*:

> What distinguishes images from the "essences" of phenomenology is their historical index. (Heidegger seeks in vain to rescue history for phenomenology abstractly through "historicity.") These images are to be thought of entirely apart from the categories of the "human sciences," from so-called habitus, from style, and the like. For the historical index of the images not only says that they belong to a particular time; it says, above all, that they attain to legibility only at a particular time. [N3,1]
> *The Arcades Project*, trans. Howard Eiland and Kevin McLaughlin (Cambridge, Mass.: Belknap Press, 1999), 462.
> (*GS* vol. 5, no. 1, 577; [N3,1])

For an informative discussion of this passage, see Samuel Weber, *Benjamin's -abilities*, 48–9. On the contrast between Benjamin's dialectical image and Heidegger's historicity, see Beatrice Hanssen, *Walter Benjamin's Other History: Of Stones, Animals, Human Beings, and Angels* (Berkeley: University of California Press, 2000) and Howard Caygill, "Benjamin, Heidegger and the Destruction of Tradition," *Walter Benjamin's Philosophy: Destruction and Experience*, ed. Andrew Benjamin and Peter Osborne (New York: Routledge, 1994), 1–31. Regarding Benjamin's relation to Hegel, Max Pensky writes that "[e]ven if Hegel does not figure prominently in Benjamin's philosophical speculation on the nature of historical time and historical experience, his figure looms large in the background, and his version of 'dialectical images' (not a term Hegel would have used, naturally), and the philosophy of history and the dialectic they rest upon, are the foil against which Benjamin developed his own views." See Pensky, "Method and Time in Benjamin's Dialectical Images," *Cambridge Companion to Walter Benjamin*, ed. David S. Ferris (Cambridge: Cambridge University Press, 2004), 190.

64. Anselm Haverkamp, "Notes on the 'Dialectical Image,' (How Deconstructive Is it?)," *Diacritics* 22, no. 3–4 (Fall-Winter 1992): 71. Haverkamp develops the discussion by focusing on the term "schema," the Greek word for the Latin "figura":

> Against the more popular uses of the term, Benjamin's image insists on being a schema, but a schema of reading . . . What makes these images real images for Benjamin is that they are decidedly not archaic images—implying that archaic images are anything but true. The dialectics of these images manifests itself in a schema whose effect rather than whose archaic cause is decisive; the notorious "aura" attests to that, even though Benjamin's use of the term seems not always free from nostalgia. Ernst Robert Curtius, whose conception of "topos-research" offers an interesting parallel, falls for what Benjamin seeks to avoid: a confusion of "place" in language with an "archetypal" content whose identity the tradition of *topoi* is meant to guarantee. (72–3)

Haverkamp's discussion of the "dialectical image" has been largely developed in *Figura cryptica. Theorie der literarischen Latenz* (Suhrkamp, 2002). An English translation is forthcoming from State University of New York Press.

65. In this regard, as we shall see in my discussion in Chapter 4 on *Life is a Dream*, the dialectical image is connected to what Benjamin calls "Natural history" (*NaturGeschichte*), produced, in Benjamin's view, by the violent effects of the Counter-Reformation.

66. For a discussion of Benjamin's notion of language as an "archive and resonance chamber," see Eric Santner, *The Royal Remains: The People's Two Bodies and the Endgames of Sovereignty* (Chicago: The University of Chicago Press, 2011), xx. Where Santner reads Benjamin to theorize theo-political community in terms of "flesh," I draw on Benjamin's work to better understand baroque drama's construction of sovereignty as a "body" of power. While my reading is not, strictly speaking, a historicist one, its focus on baroque drama's production of tropes for sovereignty is nevertheless meant to complement socio-historicist studies such as Walter Cohen's *Drama of a Nation* (Ithaca: Cornell University Press, 1985) by examining sovereignty's meta-phorological grounds as these are conditioned by the theater. As I hope is clear, such a view is not limited to an understanding of theater merely as a space for conceptualization; it also provides opportunities for a historically and philosophically informed *critique* of the concept of sovereignty.

67. Book-length studies of Benjamin's dialectical images include Michael W. Jennings, *Dialectical Images: Walter Benjamin's Theory of Literary Criticism* (Ithaca: Cornell University Press, 1987) and Susan Buck-Morss, *The Dialectics of Seeing: Walter Benjamin and the Arcades Project* (Cambridge: MIT Press, 1995). I am particularly indebted to Anselm Haverkamp's "Notes on the 'Dialectical Image' (How Deconstructive Is It?)"; Samuel Weber's *Benjamin's -abilities*, esp. 48–50; Gerhard Richter's *Thought-Images*, 61ff; Margaret Cohen's *Profane Illumination: Walter Benjamin and the Paris of Surrealist Revolution* (Berkeley: University of California Press, 1993), esp. 46–55; Rainer Nägele's *Theater, Theory, Speculation*, 63; and Beatrice Hanssen, *Walter Benjamin's Other History: Of Stones, Animals, Human Beings, and Angels* (Berkeley: University of California Press, 2000).

68. As Paul Kahn notes, world-destroying violence and sacrifice are two key reasons for the resurgence of political theology today, not solely as a discourse of belief, but rather as one of critique. For many legal and political theorists, the resurgence of political theology as a form of critique is in part the consequence of failures on both the right and the left to confront the problem of total destruction. In both cases, the suggestion is that "theory" hasn't caught up with the times. As Russell Berman puts it, "The theological turn can be as consistent with Foucault's exhortation to defend society against the state as it is with Adorno's insistence on considering all things from the standpoint of redemption. Yet those positions belong to an era of theory and society increasingly distant. What we need now is a political theology of the new bureaucratic regime." See Berman, "Introduction," *Telos* (Special issue on Political Theologies), 148 (Fall 2009): 4. I take up Berman's surprising call in my next project, "Baroque Files," which considers what such a political theology might look like, from the standpoint of the seventeenth century. Both Kahn and Berman link political theology to violence and to inadequacies of the left to confront it. See Kahn, *Political Theology: Four New Chapters on the New Concept of Sovereignty* (New York: Columbia University Press, 2011), 6–7. As Jean-Luc Nancy reminds us, "all theologicopolitics, including its 'secularization,' is and can be nothing other than sacrificial." For Nancy, "To have to do with the world, which is not a 'Cause'—and which is itself without any Cause—is to have to do with sacrifice no longer." Until then, we remain in the world of political theology. See Nancy, *The Sense of the World*, trans. Jeffrey S. Librett (Minneapolis: University of Minnesota Press, 1997), 9.

69. See William Egginton, *The Theater of Truth: The Ideology of (Neo)Baroque Aesthetics* (Stanford: Stanford University Press, 2010).

70. See Hent de Vries, "In Media Res: Global Religion, Public Spheres, and the Task of Contemporary Comparative Religious Studies," in *Religion and Media* (Stanford: Stanford University Press, 2001), 3–42.

71. As Gregg Lambert, succinctly puts it, the "frequent analogy between the baroque and the postmodern" designates not so much a historical period so much as an "effect that results from the composition of specific traits . . . a manner of style of composition." I pursue these "effects" back into their theatrical mediation, focusing in particular on the metaphor-logics produced on the baroque stage. See Lambert, *The Return of the Baroque in Modern Culture* (London: Continuum, 2006), 9.

72. The passage reads:

> [T]he duetie, and alleageance of the people to their lawfull king, their obedience, I say, ought to be to him, as to Gods Lieutenant in earth, obeying his commands in all thing, except directly against God, as the commands of Gods Minister, acknowledging him a Iudge set by God ouer them, hauing power to iudge them, but to be iudged onely by God, whom to onely hee must giue count of his iudgement; fearing him as their iudge, louing him as their father; praying for him as their protectour; for his continuance, if he be good; for his amendement, if he be wicked; following and obeying his lawfull commands, eschewing and flying his fury in his vnlawfull, without resistance, but by sobbes and teares to God, according to that sentence vsed in the primitiue Church in the time of the persecution.
>
> *Preces, & Lachrymæ sunt arma Ecclesiæ* (Prayers and tears are the weapons of the church)
>
> <div align="right">James I, <i>The Trew Law of Free Monarchies. Political Writings</i>, ed. Johann P. Sommerville (Cambridge: Cambridge University Press, 1994), 72.</div>

73. Identifying the birth of "modern subjectivity" in writers of the early modern period, from Petrarch through Shakespeare, Cervantes, and Montaigne, has become a critical commonplace. For pioneering studies, see Joel Fineman's *The Subjectivity Effect in Western Literary Tradition* (MIT Press, 1991), and Katherine Mauss, *Inwardness and Theater in the English Renaissance* (Chicago: University of Chicago Press, 1995).

74. Derrida writes of tears and vision: "Now if tears *come to the eyes*, if they *well up in them*, and if they can also veil sight, perhaps they reveal, in the very course of this experience, in this coursing of water, an essence of the eye, of man's eye. . . . For at the very moment they veil sight, tears would unveil what is proper to the eye—." See Derrida,

*Memoirs of the Blind: The Self-Portrait and Other Ruins*, trans. Pascale-Anne Brault and Michael Nass (Chicago: University of Chicago Press, 1993), 126. Here, the trope of the *tear* could be taken as a figure for metaphor itself—the history of which, in Derrida's view, revolves around attempts to define and distinguish that which is proper to the eye/I. On the crux of the proprietary criterion of metaphor, see Derrida's "*Retrait* of Metaphor" and "White Mythology" in *Margins of Philosophy* (Chicago: Chicago University Press, 1982).

75. Puttenham writes, "the learned clerks who have written methodically of this art in the two master languages Greek and Latin have sorted all their figures into three ranks, and the first they bestowed upon the poet only . . . and that first sort of figures doth serve the ear only and may be therefore called *Auricular* . . . Thus then I say that auricular figures be those which work alteration in the ear by sound, accent, time, and slipper volubility in utterance . . . And not only the whole body of a tale in poem or history may be made in such sort pleasant and agreeable to the ear, but also every clause by itself, and every single word carried in a clause, may have their pleasant sweetness apart." *The Art of English Poesy by George Puttenham: A Critical Edition*, ed. Frank Whigham and Wayne A. Rebhorn (Ithaca: Cornell University Press, 2007), 244–5. Coincidentally, one of the words Puttenham offers to illustrate the "wrong ranging [of] the accent of a syllable" in his discussion of *auricular figures* is the word "sovereign": "as to say *sovéreign* for *sovéreign*, *gracíous* for *grácious*, *endúre* for *endúre*, *Solómon* for *Sólomon*" (246).

76. Leonard Barkan, "The Heritage of Zeuxis: Painting, Rhetoric, History" in *Antiquity and Its Interpreters*, ed. Alina Payne, Ann Kuttner, Rebekah Smick (Cambridge: Cambridge University Press, 2000), 100.

77. Studies that *do* present such intellectual or conceptual histories include Jean Bethke Elshtain's *Sovereignty: God, State, and Self* (New York: Perseus, 2008); Robert Jackson's *Sovereignty: Evolution of an Idea* (Cambridge: Polity Press, 2011); and Jens Bartelson's *A Genealogy of Sovereignty* (Cambridge: Cambridge University Press, 1995).

78. On the historical migration of sovereignty's signs from the physical symbolism of the king's body into space, see Mikhail Iampolski, *Fiziologia Simvolicheskoso. Book 1. Vozurachshenie. Leviafana. Politicheskaia Teologia, Reprezentatsia Vlasti I konets Starogo rezhima* (Moscow: NLO, 2004). I am indebted to Professor Iampolski for his presentation of much of this material in his graduate seminars on sovereignty at New York University (in 2000 and 2001). See also Christopher Pye, who, focusing on the early modern period in particular, writes of a "process of political disincorporation . . ." Pye, *The Vanishing: Shakespeare, the*

*Subject, and Early Modern Culture* (Durham: Duke University Press, 2000), 16

79. Ernst Cassirer credits Suárez in particular for his role in this development. According to Cassirer, Suárez's text marks this movement even as it conceals and "congeals" it within the language of scholasticism. See Cassirer, *Substance and Function and Einstein's Theory of Relativity*, trans. William Curtis Swabey and Marie Collins Swabey (Chicago: The Open Publishing Co., 1923), 283. On the movement toward disembodiment in early modern science and philosophy, see Alexandre Koyré, *From the Closed World to the Infinite Universe* (Baltimore: Johns Hopkins University Press, 1968).

On sovereignty's movement toward decorporealization, see Jacques Derrida, in Giovanna Borradori, *Philosophy in a Time of Terror: Dialogues with Jürgen Habermas and Jacques Derrida* (Chicago: University of Chicago Press, 2003), 257. Also, see especially Derrida's discussion of religion in "Faith and Knowledge," *Acts of Religion*, ed. and intro. Gil Anidjar (New York: Routledge, 2002), 40–101.

80. For such readings, see on the Spanish side, among others, Jonathan Thacker, *Role-Play and the World* as *Stage in the "Comedia"* (Liverpool: Liverpool University Press, 2002). Where Thacker analyzes dramatic characters as "social actors," I focus instead on the figuration of power as a historical and conceptual "event" in terms similar to those Jacques Lezra has articulated in *Unspeakable Subjects: The Genealogy of the Event in Early Modern Europe* (Stanford: Stanford University Press, 1997).

81. Jodi Campbell provides a useful summary of modern trends in *comedia* criticism, noting in particular that "for the period spanning roughly 1950–1980, there were two approaches to studying the *comedia*: that of studying the characteristics of the genre, and that of studying the works of either Lope or Calderón." As Campbell points out, this second group focused almost exclusively on *Fuenteovejuna* and *Life is a Dream* "at the expense of lesser known works by Lope or Calderón and of lesser known playwrights." See *Monarchy, Political Culture, and Drama in Seventeenth-Century Madrid: Theater of Negotiation* (Aldershot, Hampshire: Ashgate, 2006), 10–12. The present study falls squarely within this second group, precisely for the paradigmatic place these plays continue to occupy in the critical imagination with regard to sovereignty.

82. For psychoanalytic criticism of seventeenth-century drama in relation to absolutism, including the French theater, see Mitchell Greenberg, *Baroque Bodies: Psychoanalysis and the Culture of French Absolutism* (Ithaca: Cornell University Press, 2001), and *Canonical States/Canonical*

*Stages: Oedipus, Othering, and Seventeenth-Century Drama* (Minneapolis: University of Minnesota Press, 1994).

83. I take up this question in my next project, on "Baroque Files." For a general treatment of these theorists in Spain, see Bernice Hamilton's *Political Thought in Sixteenth-Century Spain* (Oxford: Clarendon Press, 1963) as well as J. A. Fernández-Santamaria, *The State, War and Peace: Spanish Political Thought in the Renaissance 1516–1559* (Cambridge: Cambridge University Press, 1977). Particularly informative is Annabel Brett's discussion of scholastic political thought in the Counter-Reformation in *Rethinking the Foundations of Modern Political Thought*, ed. Annabel Brett and James Tully (Cambridge: Cambridge University Press, 2006), 130–48.

84. Lezra, *Wild Materialism*, esp. 66–7.

85. For a discussion of the ongoing "haunting" of these logics, which draws on works such as Derrida's *Spectres of Marx* but also moves into new territory, see Mark Lewis Taylor, "Thinking the Theological: A Haunting," in *The Theological and the Political: On the Weight of the World* (Minneapolis: Fortress Press, 2011).

86. For a general synopsis of Blumenberg's metaphorology, see David Adams, "Metaphors for Mankind: The Development of Hans Blumenberg's Anthropological Metaphorology," *Journal of the History of Ideas* 52, no. 1 (Jan.–Mar., 1991): 152–66.

More specifically, as Anthony Reynolds explains, "Blumenberg's own methodological point of departure is Heidegger's history of Being, *Seinsgeschichte*, whose very *epoché* (corresponding to Vico's *ricorso*), *Seinsvergessenheit*, Blumenberg reinterprets in the rhetorical terms of his metaphorology. In this way, the project of metaphorology displaces Heidegger's metaphysics of history and reduces it to the pragmatism of a meta-rhetoric of deconstruction" (Reynolds 20, quoting Anselm Haverkamp).

87. See Hans Blumenberg, "Prospect for a Theory of Nonconceptuality," *Shipwreck with Spectator: Paradigm of a Metaphor for Existence*, trans. Steven Rendall (Cambridge: MIT Press, 1997), 85. See also Blumenberg, *Paradigms for a Metaphorology*, trans. Robert Savage (Ithaca: Cornell University Press, 2010).

88. Hans Blumenberg, *Paradigms for a Metaphorology*, trans. Robert Savage (Ithaca: Cornell University Press, 2010), 14.

89. See Dirk Mende, "Histories of Technicization: On the Relation of Conceptual History and Metaphorology" in "Hans Blumenberg," special issue, *Telos* 158 (Spring 2012): 59–79.

90. Blumenberg, *Paradigms*, 3.

91. Ibid., 5.

92. Blumenberg, *Spectator*, 81. Blumenberg includes "aesthetic" phenomena among the areas in which these forms manifest themselves (*Shipwreck*, 89). Yet, as Derrida has shown, these phenomena also appear in philosophy and are arguably the motor of philosophical discourse itself. See Derrida, "White Mythology," *Margins of Philosophy*, trans. Alan Bass (Chicago: University of Chicago Press, 1982).

93. Blumenberg, *Shipwreck*, 82.

94. For a reading of early modern theater's, and particularly Shakespeare's, contributions to political theory in terms of "scenes," see Paul Kottman, *A Politics of the Scene* (Stanford: Stanford University Press, 2008).

95. For Foucault's understanding of "archaeology," see *The Archaeology of Knowledge and the Discourse on Language*, trans. Sheridan Smith (New York: Pantheon Books, 1972). In making the claim that theater "stages tropes," I am building on both older and more recent scholarship. On the staging of Latin tropes in medieval Spanish drama, for example, see Margaret Wilson, *Spanish Drama of the Golden Age* (Oxford: Pergamom Press, 1969). For a reading of Shakespeare's theater as a machinery for the production of tropes of history, see Anselm Haverkamp, *Shakespearean Genealogies of Power* (New York: Routledge, 2011). My specific focus, however, is on the different ways that this staging of tropes participates in a wider conceptual history. One of the primary objectives of this book is to follow how the language produced in early modern theater continues to inform our understanding of the concept of sovereignty.

96. On the question of the "event" in early modern Europe, see Jacques Lezra, *Unspeakable Subjects: The Genealogy of the Event in Early Modern Europe* (Stanford: Stanford University Press, 1997). The notion of the "event" is often associated with the philosophy of Martin Heidegger. See *Contributions to Philosophy (From Enowning)*, trans. Parvis Emad and Kenneth Maly; *Identity and Difference*, trans. Joan Stambaugh; and the Introduction to "What Is Metaphysics?" in *Pathmarks*, trans. David Farrell Krell, ed. William McNeill (Cambridge: Cambridge University Press), 82–96. For Heidegger, "genuine (historical) events involve a change in mentality and understanding of the world, so that they cannot be considered mere happenstances." See Giovanni Borradori, *Philosophy in a Time of Terror, Philosophy in a Time of Terror: Dialogues with Jürgen Habermas and Jacques Derrida* (Chicago: University of Chicago Press, 2003), 194 n.14. Jacques Derrida often returns to Heidegger's discussions of the event (*Ereignis*). See Jacques Derrida, "Structure, Sign and Play in

the Discourse of the Human Sciences," in *Writing and Difference* (Chicago: University of Chicago Press, 1980), 278; and "A Certain Impossible Possibility of Saying the Event," trans. Gila Walker, *Critical Inquiry* 33.2 (Winter 2007), 441–61.

97. As William Lafleur writes of the connection between religion and metaphor, "as long as we have bodies we will have metaphors and as long as we have metaphors we will have religion." See Lafleur, "Body," in *Critical Terms for Religious Studies* (Chicago: University of Chicago Press, 1998 ), 51.

98. Once again, I am drawing on the work of Benjamin, although I take the term "archive," in this instance, from Eric Santner's description of language as a medium in Benjamin. See *The Royal Remains*, xx.

99. Linking this aspect of his work, methodologically, to that of Foucault, and arguing that an *archaeology* is always in some ways also a "paradigmatology," Agamben writes that, "To be sure my investigations, like those of Foucault, have an archaeological character ... Nevertheless, the *archē* they reach—and this perhaps holds for all historical inquiry—is not an origin presupposed in time. Rather, locating itself at the crossing of diachrony and synchrony, it makes the inquirer's present intelligible as much as the past of his or her object." See Giorgio Agamben, *The Signature of All Things: On Method*, trans. Luca di Santo (New York: Zone Books, 2009), 31–2.

100. See Agamben, *What Is an Apparatus? and Other Essays*, trans. David Kishik and Stefan Pedatella (Stanford: Stanford University Press, 2009).

101. For his informative discussion of Agamben's relation not only to Benjamin but also Foucault, see Leland de la Durantaye, *Giorgio Agamben: A Critical Introduction*, esp. 243–6.

102. Interview with Abu Bakr Rieger, qtd. in de la Durantaye, *Giorgio Agamben*, 243, my emphasis.

103. The argument that texts are "governed by controlling figures" was probably most famously developed by Paul de Man. See, among other works, *Allegories of Reading Allegories of Reading: Figural Language in Rousseau, Nietzsche, Rilke, and Proust* (New Haven: Yale University Press, 1979).

104. It was not uncommon, for example, during the years following the Clarence Thomas–Anita Hill incident, to view the hearings as, in some sense, a re-troping of *Measure for Measure*. See, for example, Wendy Doniger, *The Bedtrick: Tales of Sex and Masquerade* (Chicago, University of Chicago Press, 2000), 274. While much critical attention was, rightly, given to the various aspects of the racial and sexual conflicts

of the cultural production and reception of the media-spectacle, less was paid to the concept of justice itself that gradually emerged throughout the hearings.

105. In addition to the works of Austen and Almodóvar, a recent Summer Institutes in Literary Studies seminar of the National Humanities Center directed by Sarah Beckwith focuses on the play's "afterlives" in George Eliot (*Daniel Deronda*), Eric Rohmer (*Contes d'Hiver*), Isak Dinesen (*Winter's Tales*), Jill Paton Walsh (*A Desert in Bohemia*), and Elizabeth Taylor (*A Game of Hide and Seek*). Professor Beckwith's seminar is titled, "Versions of *The Winter's Tale*: Theater, Literature, Film and Philosophy," announced in *The New York Review of Books*, vol. 59, no. 18 (November 22, 2012), 9.

106. I am grateful to Jacques Lezra for his suggestion of this term as a way of thinking about the tropes viewed here. In grammar, syncategoremata are "words that cannot serve by themselves as subjects or predicates of categorical propositions." *Cambridge Dictionary of Philosophy* (Cambridge: Cambridge University Press, 1999), 896ff. In scholastic logic, a syncategorematic term is a word that cannot alone serve as the subject of a proposition but that, together with others, can. See Norman Kretzmann, "Syncategoremata, Exponibilia, Sophismata," in *The Cambridge History of Later Medieval Philosophy* (Cambridge: Cambridge University Press, 1982), 211–45.

107. For the strongest theoretical elaboration of this claim, see Louis Marin's work on the crossing of sovereignty and representation in French absolutism: *Portrait of the King* (Minneapolis: University of Minnesota Press, 1988) and "The Body-of-Power and Incarnation at Port Royal and in Pascal" in *Fragments for a History of the Human Body* (New York: Zone, 1989).

108. As Walter Cohen has shown, although "many of the same components went into the absolutist crisis in Spain as in England ... their structural and historical significance differed because of the absence of capitalism and radical Protestantism" in Spain. See Cohen, *Drama of a Nation* (Ithaca: Cornell University Press, 1985), 260. For a discussion of the importance of the institution of theater to the development of the public sphere in England and Spain, see, in addition to Cohen's *Drama of a Nation*, Jean-Christophe Agnew, *Worlds Apart: The Market and the Theater in Anglo-American Thought 1550–1750* (Cambridge, Cambridge University Press, 1986); Anthony B. Dawson and Paul Yachnin, *The Culture of Playgoing in Shakespeare's England: A Collaborative Debate* (Cambridge: Cambridge University Press, 2001); Melveena McKendrick, *Theatre in Spain: 1490–1700* (Cambridge: Cambridge University Press,

1989); Thomas Austin O'Connor, *Love in the "Corral": Conjugal Spirituality and Anti-Theatrical Polemic in Early Modern Spain* (New York: Peter Lang, 2000); and Jonathan Thacker, *A Companion to Golden Age Theatre* (Woodbridge: Tamesis, 2007).

109. Vatter, *Crediting God*, 3.

110. See Heinrich Meier's, "What Is Political Theology?" in *Leo Strauss and the Theologico-Political Problem*, trans. Marcus Brainard (Cambridge: Cambridge University Press, 2006), 77–87. Also see the diverse collection of essays in Hent de Vries and Lawrence E. Sullivan, *Political Theologies: Public Religions in a Post-Secular World* (New York: Fordham University Press, 2006).

111. Heinrich Meier, "What Is Political Theology?" 79.

112. Schmitt, *Political Theology*, 4–15. On medieval political theology in general, and the "semi-religious terminology," Elizabethan lawyers used to describe the nature of royalty in particular, see Kantorowicz, *The King's Two Bodies*, esp. 16–17.

See Hans Blumenberg's pointed response to Schmitt in which he counters that Schmitt's political theology is really a "theology as politics" and a "metaphorical theology." Blumenberg, *The Legitimacy of the Modern Age*, trans. Robert M. Wallace (Cambridge: MIT Press, 1983), 98, 101.

Louis Marin describes this transfer as a *transpositio* between the "remarkable structure of the theological body into the juridical and political domain—a transposition that brings to light the historical gesture of absolutism." See Marin, *Portrait of the King*, 12. On the distinction between the powers that constitute theo-political sovereignty, Francis Oakley points out:

> The distinction between the absolute and ordinary powers of the King was essentially a piece of political theology, and from this fact—so often underlined in the seventeenth-century literature itself—it drew much of its authority and its power to convince. Its history was longer, richer, more dense, and more intricate than has heretofore been supposed, and it is against the background of this long history that the English appeals to the distinction should be viewed. If this is done, they (or the majority of them) will be seen to have postulated the existence, not of two parallel or coordinate powers each confined by law to its own proper sphere, but rather of two powers, one of which was in essence superior to the other, and which in time of necessity or for reason of state could transcend the other and encroach upon its domain.
>
> Oakley, "Jacobean Political Theology," *Journal of the History of Ideas* 29, no. 3 (July–Sept. 1968): 343.

The question of sovereignty, then, becomes *how* to decide, or *who* decides *when* it is a "time of necessity."

113. In his important study of early modern English literature and law, *A Power to Do Justice*, Bradin Cormack, for example, warns against the "almost irresistible tendency to make sovereignty have meaning only as political theology." The danger is that by doing so, sovereignty is made to appear "more stable than it is, even in so sophisticated an account of structure as that which Agamben gives." Forcefully assimilating sovereignty to political theology threatens to undermine a critique of power by focusing on origins rather than the "more mundane process of administrative, distribution and management." By concentrating on jurisdiction as the real locus of sovereignty, *A Power to Do Justice* attempts to rectify this imbalance. Cormack's focus on jurisdiction as the site of sovereignty also identifies one of sovereignty's futures, as the concept moves away from the dualities of the king's two bodies theory and into increasingly abstract forms, as I argue throughout this book. See Bradin Cormack, *A Power to Do Justice: Jurisdiction, English Literature, and the Rise of Common Law, 1509–1625* (Chicago: University of Chicago Press, 2007), 9.

114. Perhaps *the* representative study from a psychoanalytic point of view is Freud's major essay, *Moses and Monotheism*, in *The Standard Edition of the Complete Psychological Works of Sigmund Freud*, Vol. XXIII (1937–39), trans. James Strachey (London: Vintage, 2001), 3–137. On the relationship between psychoanalysis and Judaism in relation to sovereignty, see also Eric Santner, *On the Psychotheology of Everyday Life: Reflections on Freud and Rosenzweig* (Chicago: University of Chicago Press, 2001). On deconstruction, see the essays collected in Jean-Luc Nancy's *Dis-Enclosure: The Deconstruction of Christianity*, trans. Bettina Bergo, Gabriel Malenfant, and Michael B. Smith (New York: Fordham University Press, 2008). For a recent discussion of the Hebrew Bible from a political theory perspective, see Michael Walzer, *In God's Shadow: Politics in the Hebrew Bible* (New Haven: Yale University Press, 2012).

115. I borrow the felicitous metaphor of "thinking as a search for siblings" from Gerhard Richter. See Richter, "A Matter of Distance: Benjamin's One-Way Street Through the Arcades," in *Thought-Images: Frankfurt School Writer's Reflections from Damaged Life* (Stanford: Stanford University Press, 2007), 43.

116. Illustrations of political theology's continued presence in public political discourse are too numerous to mention. Recent examples in the United States include, what Mark Lewis Taylor refers to as the almost "too easy example" of George W. Bush citing scripture before embarking

on the Iraq war. One might additionally refer to arguments over the use of public space in and around "ground zero" in New York after September 11, the ongoing debate over prayer in public schools and the teaching of "intelligent design," or the legal and political battles that continue to rage over same sex marriage. See Mark Lewis Taylor, *The Theological and the Political: On the Weight of the World* (Minneapolis: Fortress Press, 2011). At the international level, recourse to an authority "outside" that of the state to justify political or military action occurs regularly over the question of Sharia law, as well as that of the legality and constitutionalism of international operations of "protection." For a discussion, see Anne Orford, *International Authority and the Responsibility to Protect* (Cambridge: Cambridge University Press, 2011). A major resource for a consideration of the problem of political theology from a range of disciplinary perspectives is *Political Theologies*, ed. Hent de Vries and Lawrence E. Sullivan. See especially de Vries's excellent "Introduction: Before, Around, and Beyond the Theologico-Political," 1–90.

117. See Blumenberg, *The Legitimacy of the Modern Age*, 89–102.

118. See de Vries, "In Media Res." For Louis Althusser's famous, and important, definition of ideology reads: "it is not their real conditions of existence, their real world, that 'men' 'represent to themselves' in ideology, but above all it is their relation to those conditions of existence which is represented to them . . . it is the *imaginary nature of this relation* which underlies all the imaginary distortion that we can observe (if we do not live in its truth) in all ideology." See Althusser, "Ideology and Ideological State Apparatuses" in *Lenin and Philosophy and Other Essays*, trans. Ben Brewster (New York: Monthly Review Press, 1971), 164.

119. For a discussion of Shakespeare's theater as the place where the "logic" of this "positioning is discovered and exposed," see Anselm Haverkamp, *Shakespearean Genealogies of Power*, 2ff. Haverkamp's own term for what he calls the "'eventuality'—not to call it the event-character—of Shakespeare reception," is "*latency*."

120. On the notion of a social imaginary, see the seminal work of Cornelius Castoriadis, *The Imaginary Institution of Society*, trans. Kathleen Blamey (Cambridge: MIT Press, 1998), and Michèle Le Doeuff, *The Philosophical Imaginary*, trans. Colin Gordon (London: Athlone Press, 1989).

121. See the special issue of *Representations* devoted to the work of Kantorowicz, including Greenblatt's Introduction, cited here. Greenblatt describes the *King's Two Bodies* as "a vast *archive* of the materials out of which figures as various as Hans Blumenberg, Carl Schmitt, and Giorgio Agamben have constructed fiercely conflicting theories of secularization"

and writes that "... under Kantorowicz's gaze fantastic creatures—half-bodily, half institutional—being to emerge from bureaucratic formulas." See Greenblatt, "Introduction: Fifty Years of *The King's Two Bodies*," *Representations* 106 (Spring 2009): 64–5.

122. See Lezra, *Wild Materialism*, 41.

123. James Brown Scott, Introduction to *Selections from Three Works*, trans. by Gwladys L. Williams, Ammi Brown, and John Waldron. 2 vols. (Oxford: Clarendon Press London, 1944), 6a. Regarding the reservations surrounding Suárez's early admission to the Society, there is some question whether this may also have had to do with suspicions regarding his family's converso background. For a discussion, see Robert A. Maryks, *The Jesuit Order as a Synagogue of Jews: Jesuits of Jewish Ancestry and Purity-of-Blood Laws in the Early Society of Jesus* (Leiden: Brill, 2010).

124. In addition to De Scorraille, see John Doyle, "Francisco Suárez, His Life, His Works, His Doctrine," *Collected Studies on Francisco Suárez, S.J. (1548–1617)*, ed. Victor M. Salas (Leuven: Leuven University Press, 2010), 1–20.

125. The honorific title given to Suárez by Pope Paul V, "*Doctor eximius ac pius*," means "Eminent and pious teacher."

126. On the notion of a "baroque modernity" see the collection of essays in *Hispanic Baroques*, edited by Nicholas Spadaccini and Luis Martin-Estudillo (Vanderbilt University Press, 2005). On Suárez in particular, see *Interpreting Suárez*, ed. Daniel Schwartz (Cambridge: Cambridge University Press, 2012); Daniel D. Novotny, "In Defense of Baroque scholasticism," *Studia Neoaristotelia* 6 (2009), 209–33. José Pereira's *Suárez: Between Scholasticism & Modernity* (Milwaukee: Marquette University Press, 2007) is a suggestive but occasionally erratic book-length study. The bibliography on Hobbes and Bodin is enormous and too big to reproduce here. For a particularly useful study of sovereignty in relation to Hobbes and Shakespeare, see Paul Kottman, *A Politics of the Scene* (Stanford: Stanford University Press, 2008). On Hobbes, sovereignty, and rhetoric, see Patricia Lawler, *Exemplary Figures: Hobbes's Political Aesthetics of Subjection* (New York: Fordham University Press, forthcoming). On Shakespeare and Bodin, see Jacques Lezra, "Phares, or, Divisible Sovereignty," in *Wild Materialism* (New York: Fordham University Press, 2011), 63–87, as well as Bradin Cormack, "Shakespeare's Other Sovereignty: On Particularity and Violence in *The Winter's Tale* and the Sonnets," *Shakespeare Quarterly* 62.4 (2011), 485–513. On political theology in the early modern period, see *Political Theology and Early Modernity*, ed. Graham Hammill and Julia Reinhard Lupton, with a Postscript by Étienne Balibar (Chicago: University of

Chicago Press, 2012). On Shakespeare and political theology, see Julia Reinhard Lupton, *Citizen-Saints: Shakespeare and Political Theology* (Chicago: University of Chicago Press, 2005). On political theology specifically in the context of early modern English literature, see Jennifer Rust, *The Body in Mystery: the Political Theology of the Corpus Mysticum in Post-Reformation English Literature* (Chicago: Northwestern University Press, forthcoming). On Machiavelli, see Graham Hammill, *The Mosaic Constitution: Political Theology and Imagination from Machiavelli to Milton* (Chicago: The University of Chicago Press, 2012). For recent work comparing Hobbes's political theory to Suárez's, see Lorella Cedroni, *La comunità perfecta: il pensiero politico di Francisco Suárez* (Roma: edizioni Studium, 1996).

127. See Jean-François Courtine, "Le project suarézien de la métaphysique," *Archives de Philosophie* 42 (1979): 236. The American scholar John P. Doyle has published a number of translations, articles, and books on Suárez, including, most recently, *Collected Studies on Francisco Suárez, S.J. (1548–1617)*, ed. Victor M. Salas (Leuven, Belgium: Leuven University Press, 2010).

128. Reijo Wilenius, *The Social and Political Theory of Francisco Suárez* (Helsinki: Acta Philosophica Fennica, 1963), 22.

129. John Doyle cites Joaquín Iriarte on the extraordinary diffusion of Suárez's text in the seventeenth century, particularly in comparison with the mere four editions of Descartes' *Meditationes*. See Doyle, *Collected Studies on Francisco Suárez, S.J. (1548–1617)*, ed. Victor M. Salas (Leuven, Belgium: Leuven University Press, 2010), 7.

130. Martin Heidegger, *The Basic Problems of Phenomenology*, trans., intro., and lexicon Albert Hofstadter (Bloomington: Indiana University Press, 1988), 80. The problem, Heidegger continues, is one of defining the "ontological interconnection of reality and existence" (77–8): "[W]e are not now dealing so much with the question of the knowability and demonstrability of God's existence as with the still more original problem of the distinctness of the concept of God as an infinite being, *ens infinitum*, over against the being that is not God, the *ens finitum*" (79).

131. At least as far as I have been able to discover, in this age of electronic searches.

132. Julia Reinhard Lupton and Graham Hammill have highlighted various aspects of these bifurcations of sovereignty in early modern literature. See, Lupton, *Afterlives of the Saints* (Stanford: Stanford University Press, 1996) and *Citizen-Saints: Shakespeare and Political Theology* (2005) and Graham Hammill, *The Mosaic Constitution: Political Theology and Imagination from Machiavelli to Milton* (2012).

133. In using the term "apparatus," I am specifically gesturing toward the "archaeological" function of what Michel Foucault refers to as a *dipositif*. Where for Foucault, the *dispositif* attempts to describe a series of connections between linguistic formations and relations of power, for Agamben the modern apparatus is specifically a "machine that produces subjectifications." For Agamben, the apparatus of *confession*, for example, is instrumental to the formation of Western subjectivity. What distinguishes modern apparatuses, in the age of capitalism, on the other hand, is that they no longer subjectify but rather *desubjectify*. The apparatus of the cell phone does not lead to "a new subjectivity, but only a number through which he can, eventually be controlled." "It is impossible," Agamben argues, "for the subject of an apparatus to use [the cell phone] 'in the right way.'" Agamben, *What Is an Apparatus? and Other Essays*, trans. David Kishik and Stefan Pedatella (Stanford: Stanford University Press, 2009), 21. I read Suárez's texts with Agamben's notion of the "apparatus" in mind. Despite what is often considered to be their supersession in the seventeenth century by thinkers such as Bacon, Hobbes, Descartes, and Leibniz, writers of the "Second Scholasticism," such as Suárez, along with those from the Spanish school of Salamanca, played an extremely important role in the development of modern economic theory, human rights thinking, and the discipline that would come to be known as international law. In this regard, not only Suárez, but also the earlier Spanish writers associated with the School, including especially Francisco de Vitoria, Domingo de Soto, and Luis de Molina, provides us with an important critical lens, if not "apparatus," through which to view the modern formation of sovereignty.

134. Jean-Luc Marion, "Outline of a History of Definitions of God in the Cartesian Epoch," in *On the Ego and on God: Further Cartesian Questions*, trans. Christina M. Gschwandtner (New York: Fordham University Press, 2007), 161–92.

## 1. BREAKDOWN: ANALOGY AND ONTOTHEOLOGY IN *RICHARD II*

1. Rodolphe Gasché, *The Tain of the Mirror: Derrida and the Philosophy of Reflection* (Cambridge: Harvard University Press, 1986), 302, 306.

2. Laurence Sterne, *The Life and Opinions of Tristram Shandy, Gentleman*, ed. Tim Parnell (London: Everyman, 2000), 84.

3. Jacques Derrida, *The Beast and the Sovereign*, ed. Michel-Lisse, Marie-Louise Mallet, and Ginette Michaud, trans. Geoffrey Bennington (Chicago: University of Chicago Press, 2009), 20.

4. Antonio Negri, *Insurgencies: Constituent Power and the Modern State*, trans. Maurizia Boscagli (Minneapolis: University of Minnesota Press, 1999). Originally published as *Il potere constituente: saggio sulle alternative del moderno* (Carnago [Varese]: Sugar Co., 1992).

5. Charles Howard McIlwain, *The Political Works of James I* (Cambridge: Harvard University Press, 1918), lvi.

6. My understanding of the term "event" is largely informed by the work of Jacques Lezra. As Lezra points out, genealogies of concepts "must always also be genealogies of the *event* . . ." (Lezra 5). I do not pursue sovereignty's conceptual genealogy so much as attempt to understand how early modern theater provides the concept with a tropology or archaeo-tropology in which the production of the tropes themselves can be understood, in Lezra's terms, as "thought-events" and "practice-events." For Lezra, "the theatrical 'event' is always and constitutively double, it always and necessarily is already a 'reading' or a 'performance' of a script that remains both infinitely separate from and intimately represented within it." See Jacques Lezra, *Unspeakable Subjects: The Genealogy of the Event in Early Modern Europe* (Stanford: Stanford University Press, 1997), 10.

7. "Speech to parliament of 21 March 1610" in Johann P. Sommerville, *King James VI and I: Political Writings* (Cambridge: Cambridge University Press, 1994), 179. The title page of the speech lists the date as 1609 according to the old (Julian) calendar.

8. Louis Marin, "The Body-of-Power and Incarnation at Port Royal and in Pascal—or—Of the Figurability of the Political Absolute," *Fragments for a History of the Human Body—Part Three*, ed. Michel Feher with Ramona Naddaff and Nadia Tazi (New York: Zone, 1989), 420–47.

9. James I, "Speech to parliament of 21 March 1610" in Johann P. Sommerville, *King James VI and I: Political Writings* (Cambridge: Cambridge University Press, 1994), 179.

10. Ibid., 181.

11. Barbara Stafford, *Visual Analogy: Consciousness as the Art of Connecting* (Cambridge: MIT Press, 1999), 23–4.

12. Ibid., 24.

13. Hampus Lyttkens, *The Analogy Between God and the World: An Investigation of Its Background and Interpretation of Its Use by Thomas of Aquino* (Uppsala: Almquist & Wiksells, 1953), 47.

14. Paul Ricoeur, *The Rule of Metaphor: Multi-disciplinary Studies of the Creation of Meaning in Language*, trans. Robert Czerny with Kathleen McLaughlin and John Costello, S.J. (Toronto: University of Toronto Press, 1997), 273.

In terms of drama theory, we might think of this philosophical attempt to find a "third modality" in relation to genre, authority, and in particular to what the Italian Renaissance theorist Giovanni Battista Guarini referred to as the "third thing" that is *tragi-comedy*. This is not only an attempt to find a way out of a critical impasse, or to synthesize what is often understood to be the antithetical philosophies of life represented by comedy and tragedy, but also especially (if we think of the problem in relation to sovereign authority) related to what Victoria Kahn has described, in a different context, as the "structural necessity of an external authority or third term in any scene of self-authorization." See Giovanni Battista Guarini, *Il Pastor Fido* (1590), and Victoria Kahn, "Political Theology and Fiction in *The King's Two Bodies*," *Representations* 106, no. 1 (May 2009): 100n.39.

15. This question is inevitably linked to the genre of theodicy, which, as Paul Ricoeur writes, is the "flagship of onto-theology." *Evil: A Challenge to Philosophy and Theology*, trans. John Bowden (London: Continuum, 2004), 49.

16. For Heidegger's discussion of analogy see *Aristotle's Metaphysics* [theta] *1–3: On the Essence and Actuality of Force*, trans. Walter Brogan and Peter Warnek (Bloomington: Indiana University Press, 1995), 38.

17. Heidegger, *Aristotle's Metaphysics*, 38. Aristotle's categories include: a quantity, a quality, a relative, a place, a time, a position, a having, a doing, or a being affected. See Aristotle, *Categoriae (Categories)*, *The Basic Works of Aristotle*, ed. Richard McKeon (New York: Random House, 1941), 7–39.

18. Thomas Aquinas, *Summa Theologiae* Ia, qu. 13, art. 5, in *Basic Writings of Saint Thomas Aquinas*, vol. I, ed. Anton C. Pegis (New York: Random House, 1945), 120.

19. Jean-Luc Marion, "Outline of a History of Definitions of God in the Cartesian Epoch" in *On the Ego and on God: Further Cartesian Questions*, trans. Christina M. Gschwandtner (New York: Fordham University Press, 2007), 162.

20. Marion, citing Thomas Aquinas, *Summa contra gentiles*, 3, 49 in *On the Ego and on God: Further Cartesian Questions*, trans. Christina M. Gschwandtner (New York: Fordham University Press, 2007), 162.

21. Johann P. Sommerville, *Royalists and Patriots: Politics and Ideology in England 1603–1640*, 2nd edition (New York: Addison Wesley Longman, 1999), 53.

22. Of the centrality of analogy in the "Classical Age" (roughly from Descartes through Kant), Foucault writes:

The relation of languages to the world is one of analogy rather than of signification; or rather, their value as signs and their duplicating function are superimposed; they speak the heaven and the earth of which they are the image; they reproduce in their most material architecture the cross whose coming they announce—that coming which establishes its existence in its own turn through the Scriptures and the Word.

*The Order of Things: An Archaeology of the Human Sciences* (New York: Random House, 1973), 37–8.

23. Suárez is frequently cited as an important figure in the development of modern legal and political theory. George Keeton, for example, devotes several pages to Suárez's crucial role in the formulation of the *ius gentium* in Suárez's *De Legibus* (published in 1612, not 1513, as is misprinted in the text). Similarly, Paul Cefalu discusses Suárez's conception of *ius* in his chapter on *King Lear*, "The Early Modern Veil of Ignorance: Natural Rights Theory in *King Lear*." See *Revisionist Shakespeare: Transitional Ideologies in Texts and Contexts* (New York: Palgrave Macmillan, 2004). What is generally neglected, however, is the opportunity Suárez's diverse writings offers *to historicize* the bi- or even tri-furcated nature of sovereignty as it is being conceptually formulated in the early seventeenth century. Along with Shakespeare, Calderón, and Lope, Suárez is a key participant in the formation of sovereignty's conceptual ground.

24. See James Brown Scott's Introduction to *Selections from Three Works of Francisco Suárez, S.J.*, trans. Gwladys L. Williams et. al (Oxford: Clarendon Press, 1922), 2a.

25. On the correspondence between Sir John Digby and James, see Raúl de Scorraille, S.J., *El P. Francisco Suárez de la Compañia de Jesús*, trans. Pablo Hernández, S.J. (Barcelona: Subirana, 1917), 178–85; Roger Lockyer, *James VI and I* (London: Longman, 1998), 150; and John Michael Archer, *Sovereignty and Intelligence: Spying and Court Culture in the English Renaissance* (Stanford: Stanford University Press, 1993).

26. Because this is so central to what will later become known as "resistance theory," it is worth reading what Suárez writes in detail. In addition to the passage cited in the introduction to this book, Suárez describes the pope's indirect power over kings in Book 3 of the *Defense* as follows:

> Et tunc, quamvis temporalis princeps ejusque potestas in suis actibus directe non pendeat ab alia potestate ejusdem ordinis, et quæ eumdem finem tantum respiciat, nihilominus fieri potest ut necesse sit ipsum

dirigi, adjuvari, vel corrigi in sua materia, superiori potestate gubernante homines in ordine ad excellentiorem finem et æternum, et tunc illa dependentia vocatur indirecta, quia illa superior potestas, circa temporalis non per se, aut propeter se, sed quasi indirecte, et propter sliud interdum versatur.

Opera omnia vol. 24, p. 225.

Under such circumstances, even though the temporal prince and his power may not be directly subject, in regard to his own acts, to any other power within the same order and serving solely the same [civil] end, nevertheless it may become necessary for this prince to be directed, aided, or corrected in his own field of activity by a higher power that governs men in relation to a more excellent and an eternal end. In that case, the dependence in question is called indirect dependence, since such a superior power is concerned with temporal affairs, not in themselves nor for their own sake, but (as it were) indirectly, and often on account of some other factor.

William, *Selections*, 668.

27. "Probatur consequentia, nam quæ a Deo sunt, ordinata sunt, et optime instituta; ergo si Pontifici dedit potestatem directivam, dedit coactivam, quon institutio aliter facta esset imperfecta et inefficax." *Opera omnia* vol. 24, p. 315. I return to Suárez's description of power's efficiency in Chapter 5, on Shakespeare's *The Winter's Tale*.

28. Niccolò Machiavelli, *Il principe* (Mondadori: Milan, 1994), 67; English translation by George Bull, *The Prince* (New York: Penguin Books, 1995), 48.

29. James Brown Scott, Preface to *Selections from Three Works of Francisco Suárez, S.J.* (Oxford: Clarendon Press, 1944), vol. 1, a3.

30. For a discussion of the significance of the Peace of Westphalia, see Richard Falk, "Revisiting Westphalia, Discovering Post-Westphalia," *The Journal of Ethics* 6, no. 4 (2002): 311–52, and Stephen D. Krasner, *Sovereignty: Organized Hypocrisy* (Princeton: Princeton University Press, 1999).

31. See James Brown Scott's introduction to the English *Selections from Three Works of Francisco Suárez, S.J.*, vol. 2, (Oxford: Clarendon Press, 1944), 17a.

32. Gerhard von Glahn, *Law Among the Nations: An Introduction to Public International Law*, 2nd edition (London: Macmillan, 1970), 38–9, cited in Doyle, *Collected Studies on Francisco Suárez, S.J. (1548–1617)* (Leuven: Leuven University Press, 2010), 315.

33. On Suárez and the University of Coimbra, see Hampus Lyttkens, *The Analogy Between God and the World: An Investigation of Its Background and Interpretation of Its Use by Thomas of Aquino* (Uppsala: Almquist & Wiksells, 1953), 234. Jorge Gracia argues that the *Disputationes* is "the first systematic and comprehensive treatise on metaphysics composed in the West that is not a commentary on Aristotle's metaphysics . . . [and] is to this day the most complete and comprehensive exposition of scholastic and Aristotelian metaphysics . . . [going through] at least seventeen editions outside the Iberian peninsula. By comparison, Descartes' *Meditations on First Philosophy* were edited only nine times in the sixty years that followed their publication in 1641." Gracia, "Francisco Suárez: The Man in History," *The American Catholic Philosophical Quarterly* 65.3 (Summer 1991): 261, 265.

34. Jean-Francois Courtine, "Le project suarézien de la métaphysique," *Archives de Philosophie*, No. 42 (1979): 236. Cited in Gracia, "Suárez," 264.

35. Martin Heidegger, *The Basic Problems of Phenomenology*, trans., intro., and lexicon Albert Hofstadter (Bloomington: Indiana University Press, 1988), 80. The problem, Heidegger continues, is one of defining the "ontological interconnection of reality and existence" (77–8). "[W]e are not now dealing so much with the question of the knowability and demonstrability of God's existence as with the still more original problem of the distinctness of the concept of God as an infinite being, *ens infinitum*, over against the being that is not God, the *ens finitum*" (79).

36. *Disputationes metaphysicae* 28, s. 3, n. 11, trans. John P. Doyle, *The Metaphysical Demonstration of the Existence of God* (South Bend, Ind.: St. Augustine's Press, 2004), 37–8. *Opera omnia* vol. 26, p. 16.

37. *Disputationes metaphysicae*, 28, s. 3, n. 1. The Latin text reads:

*Analogia proportionalitatis propria non est inter Deum et creaturas.*—Ad hanc ergo analogiam necesse est ut unum membrum sit absolute tale per suam formam, aliud vero non absolute, sed ut substat tali proportioni vel comparationi ad aliud. At vero in praesenti hoc non intercedit, sive rem ipsam, sive nominis impositionem consideremus. Creatura enim esset ens ratione sui esse absolute et sine tali proportionalitate considerati, quia nimirum per illud est extra nihil et aliquid actualitatis habet; nomen etiam entis non ideo est impositum creaturae, quia servat illam proportionem seu proportionalitatem ad Deum, sed simpliciter quia in se aliquid est et non omnino nihil; immo, ut infra dicemus, prius intelligi potest tale nomen impositum enti creato quam increato.

> Denique omnis vera analogia proportionalitatis includit aliquid metaphorae et improprietatis, sicut ridere dicitur de prato per translationem metaphoricam; at vero in hac analogia entis nulla est metaphora aut improprietas, nam creatura vere, proprie ac simpliciter est ens; non est ergo haec analogia attributionis; restat ergo ut si est aliqua analogia, illa sit alicuius attributionis; atque ita tandem docuit D. Thom., I, q. 13 a.5 et 6, et I cont. Gent., c. 34, q.7, et In I, in prolog., q.1 a. 2, ad 2.
>
> Opera omnia vol. 26, p. 16.

38. On the question of this equivocation, E. J. Ashworth explains that to understand why Suárez thinks analogies of proportionality are metaphorical while his own analogy of "intrinsic attribution" is not, we have to "go back to the key passage in Aristotle's *Sophistic Elenchi* 166a 15–20, where Aristotle distinguished three varieties of equivocation: one when either the phrase or the name primarily signifies more than one thing, e.g. 'piscis' and 'canis'; another when we are accustomed to speak in that way; a third when words put together signify more than one thing, but taken alone <signify> simply, e.g. 'scil saeculum.'" Ashworth cites Aristotle, *Sophistici Elenchi* 166a 15–20, quoted from Boethius's translation in *Aristoteles Latinus* VI 1–3: *De Sophisticis Elenchis*, ed. B. G. Dod (Leiden-Brussels 1975).

39. Ashworth, 62.

40. Suárez, *Disputationes metaphysicae*, 28, s 3, n. 15:

> *In creaturis attributio ad Deum non est ut non habentis intrinsece formam ad id quod habet.*—Ex his igitur constat attributionem inventam inter Deum et creaturam non posse esse prioris generis, scilicet, in qua forma ad quam fit attributio in uno tantum est intrinsece et proprie, in aliis extrinsece ente per translationem; nam constat creaturam non denominari ens extrinsece ab entitate aut esse quod est in Deo, sed a proprio et intrinseco esse, ideoque non per tropum, sed per veritatem et proprietatem ens appellari.
>
> Doyle, trans., 41, Opera omnia vol. 26, p. 18.

41. See especially the different views of the American Suárez authority, John Doyle, and the French philosophers, Jean-Luc Marion and Jean Francois Courtine, who both look to Suárez, in particular, in order to rethink political theology and ontology.

42. See Marion, "Outline of a History of Definitions of God in the Cartesian Epoch," *On the Ego and on God: Further Cartesian Questions*, trans. Christina M. Gschwandtner (New York: Fordham University Press, 2007), 164.

43. I am taking this summary of the overall problem from Martin Heidegger's "The Thesis of Medieval Ontology Derived form Aristotle," in *The Basic Problems of Phenomenology*, trans., intro., and lexicon Albert Hofstadter (Bloomington: Indiana University Press, 1988), 83ff.

44. Ibid., 81.

45. For Scholastics such as Suárez, as Heidegger explains, the problem of the relationship between essentia and existentia is a theological and particularly Christological one. As Heidegger writes, "The ens infinitum is necessarium; it cannot not be; it is per essentiam, actuality belongs to its essence; it is actus purus, pure actuality without any possibility. Its essentia is its existentia. Existence and essence coincide in this being. God's essence is his existence." Heidegger, *Basic Problems*, 82.

46. Marion, *On the Ego and on God: Further Cartesian Questions* (New York: Fordham University Press, 2007), 164.

47. Ibid., Marion is quoting Suárez, *Disputationes metaphysicae* 31. s.12, n.40: "Rursus neque illae enuntiationes sunt verae quia cognoscuntur a Deo, sed potius ideo cognoscuntur, quia verae sunt, alioqui nulla redid posset ratio, cur Deus necessario cognosceret illas esse versa." *Opera omnia* vol. 26, p. 295.

48. Marion, *On the Ego and on God: Further Cartesian Questions* (New York: Fordham University Press), 164. My emphasis.

49. "Suarez, ultime représentant de la scolastique pour Descartes, a d'une part tangentiellement annihilé l'analogie par le concept objectif d'ens jusqu'à la rendre quasi inutile, et d'autre part conduit tangentiellement toute l'analogie à l'univocité jusqu'à la rendre suspecte d'inefficacité; ce double tournant rend, aux yeux de Descartes, l'analogie à la fois vaine et funeste." See Jean-Luc Marion, *Sur la theologie blanche de Descartes* (Paris: Presses Universitaires de France, 1981), 139.

50. Marion, *On the Ego and on God*, 163.

51. Antonio Negri, "Constituent Power: The Concept of a Crisis" in *Insurgencies: Constituent Power and the Modern State*, trans. Maurizia Boscagli (Minneapolis: University of Minnesota Press, 1999), 22.

52. For a discussion, see Bruno Bosteels, "Afterword: Thinking, Being, Acting, or, On the Uses and Disadvantages of Ontology for Politics," in the essays collected in *A Leftist Ontology: Beyond Relativism and Identity Politics*, ed. Carsten Strathausen (Minneapolis: University of Minnesota Press, 2009), 235–52.

53. Giorgio Agamben, *Homo Sacer: Sovereign Power and Bare Life*, trans. Daniel Heller-Roazen (Stanford: Stanford University Press, 1998).

54. In his reading of *Richard II*, Anselm Haverkamp ties the new sovereignty to the "linguistic latency" of the phrase, "In God's name."

Along the way, he exposes a "substitutional pattern of God's necessary exception" built into Carl Schmitt's concept of the sovereign exception. See "*Richard II*, Bracton, and the End of Political Theology," in *Shakespearean Genealogies of Power* (New York: Routledge, 2011), 56.

55. The precondition for such a development, as Negri and Hardt point out is crisis. "Crisis," they write, "is the sign of an alternative possibility on the plane of immanence." *Empire* (Cambridge: Harvard University Press), 374.

56. Antonio Negri, *The Savage Anomaly: The Power of Spinoza's Metaphysics and Politics*, trans. Michael Hardt (Minneapolis: University of Minnesota Press, 1991), 43.

57. Antonio Negri, "*Reliqua Desiderantur:* A Conjecture for a Definition of the Concept of Democracy in the Final Spinoza," *The New Spinoza*, ed. Warren Montag and Ted Stolze (Minneapolis: University of Minnesota Press, 1997), 223.

58. See David Norbrook, "The Emperor's New Body? *Richard II*, Ernst Kantorowicz, and the Politics of Shakespeare Criticism," *Textual Practice* 10 (2), 1996, 329–57; Lorna Hutson, "Imagining Justice: Kantorowicz and Shakespeare," *Representations* 106 (Spring 2009): 118–42; and "'Not the King's Two Bodies'": Reading the Body Politic in Shakespeare's *Henry IV*," in *Rhetoric and Law in Early Modern Europe*, ed. Lorna Hutson and Victoria Kahn (New Haven: Yale University Press, 2001), 166–98.

59. Specifically, Kahn reads Kantorowicz in relation to Schmitt's political theology and Ernst Cassirer's understanding of myth. "Positioning Kantorowicz between Schmitt and Cassirer," she writes, "will in turn help us understand the importance of fiction—both legal and literary—to the model of political theology advanced by *The King's Two Bodies*." Victoria Kahn, "Political Theology and Fiction in *The King's Two Bodies*," *Representations* 106 (2009): 78.

60. "In fact," Kahn writes, "one could even argue that *TKTB* was influential not only because of the centrality of myth, literature, and representation but also because *TKTB* is essentially about the power of *metaphor*." Kahn, "Political Theology and Fiction in *The King's Two Bodies*," *Representations* 106 (2009): 96, n.5.

61. Lezra, *Wild Materialism*, 66–7.

62. Negri, *Insurgencies*, 21.

63. Agamben, *Homo Sacer*, 43.

64. Important discussions of the perspective glass passage include Claudio Guillen, "On the Concept and Metaphor of Perspective," *Comparatists at Work*, ed. Stephen G. Nichols and Richard B. Vowles

(Waltham, Mass.: Blaisdell Publishing, 1968); and Ernest B. Gilman, *The Curious Perspective: Literary and Pictorial Wit in the Seventeenth Century* (New Haven: Yale University Press, 1978).

65. Scott McMillin reads the Queen's tears in relation to the representation of identity and interiority on-stage. "Shakespeare's *Richard II*: Eyes of Sorrow, Eyes of Desire," *Shakespeare Quarterly* 35 (1984): 40–52. For a treatment of sovereignty in the play, see Christopher's Pye's path-breaking "The Betrayal of the Gaze: *Richard II*" in *The Regal Phantasm: Shakespeare and the Politics of Spectacle* (London: Routledge, 1990), 82–105.

66. Pye, "The Betrayal of the Gaze," 82–105.

67. As Scott McMillin has shown, the Queen is, in some ways, still present in the deposition scene. "The Queen does not appear in it—no women do—but her influence is felt" ("Shakespeare's *Richard II*" 44). In this regard, Richard's Queen is part of a series of Shakespeare's Queens, including Katherine of Aragón, in *Henry VIII* and Hermione in *The Winter's Tale*, whose presence-absence in trial scenes is inseparable from Shakespeare's conceptualization of sovereignty. As I hope to show elsewhere, Shakespeare's most philosophical treatment of sovereignty-on-trial works itself out precisely through these present-absent Queens.

68. In a brilliant reading of this passage, Richard Halpern writes that "here, we might say, the king's two bodies have been replaced by the king's two buckets, as the seemingly horizontal opposition of forces between the kinsmen Richard and Bolingbroke is shown to be mediated by a vertical gravitational pull." "The King's Two Buckets: Kantorowicz, *Richard II* and Fiscal *Trauerspiel*," *Representations* 106 (Spring 2009), 69. Halpern likens the exchange to that between Ernst Kantorowicz and Carl Schmitt, describing Richard's "rhetorical jujitsu" as a kind of model "for Kantorowicz, whose victorious bucket will be filled with footnotes rather than tears," 69.

69. See *Richard II*, ed. Peter Ure (London: Thomson Learning, 2001), 136 n.184. The metaphor of the buckets also appears, curiously, in a description of the diplomatic activity between England and Spain during the period of the so-called "Spanish match": the failed negotiations for a marriage between Prince Charles and the Infanta, María of Spain. John Chamberlain describes the "constant flow of messengers between Madrid and London," that "goes up and down like a well with two buckets." Roger Lockyer, *King James VI and I* (London: Addison-Wesley, 1998), 150.

70. In John Cowell's 1607 popular legal dictionary, *The Interpreter: Or Booke Containing the Signification of Words*, famous for its argument

that the monarch is not subject to human laws, the entry under "fate" reads,

> *Fate or Fat*: is a great wooden vessel, which among brewers in *London*, is ordinarily used at this day, to measure malt by, containing a quarter, which they have for expedition in measuring. This word is read *anno* I. *H.5. cap. 10. & anno* II. *H.6. cap. 8.*

Brought down to the level of beer-maker's instrument, *Fate* would hardly seem to occupy a central position in common law thinking. Yet, ironically, the conflation of "fate" and "vat," which reduces the former to a beer-making vessel, turns out to be an apt figure for the play's treatment of the force so central to classical tragedy. I am grateful to Peter Goodrich for pointing out this odd entry. For the problem of Cowell's bringing the king's prerogative "within the purview of the language of common-law," see Glenn Burgess, *The Politics of the Ancient Constitution: An Introduction to English Political Thought 1603–1642* (University Park: Pennsylvania State University Press, 1992), 150–56.

71. Benjamin, *Origin of German Tragic Drama*, 92.

72. Walter Benjamin, "N [Re the Theory of Knowledge, theory of Progress]," trans. Leigh Hafrey and Richard Sieburth, in *Benjamin: Philosophy, Aesthetics, History*, ed. Gary Smith (Chicago: University of Chicago Press, 1989), 50.

73. Qtd. in Ernst Kantorowicz, *The King's Two Bodies: A Study in Mediaeval Political Theology* (Princeton, N.J: Princeton University Press, 1997), 36.

74. For discussions of this analogical world order, see Arthur O. Lovejoy, *The Great Chain of Being: A Study of the History of an Idea* (Cambridge: Harvard University Press, 1936); Martin Heidegger's "The Question Concerning Technology" in *Basic Writings* (New York: Harper & Row, 1977); and especially in the context of Shakespeare studies, E. M. W. Tillyard's canonical *The Elizabethan World Picture* (London: Chatto & Windus, 1943).

75. Well-known arguments for Shakespeare's construction or even "discovery" of modern interiority include Harold Bloom's *Shakespeare: The Invention of the Human* (New York: Riverhead Books, 1998); Katharine Eisaman Maus's more subtle *Inwardness and Theater in the English Renaissance* (Chicago: University of Chicago Press, 1993); and Joel Fineman's seminal, "Shakespeare's 'Perjur'd Eye,'" in *The Subjectivity Effect in Western Literary Tradition: Essays Toward the Release of Shakespeare's Will* (Cambridge: MIT Press, 1991).

76. *Hamlet*, 4.3.28.

77. For Negri, social contract theory is the hegemonic figure of political theory in the seventeenth century. Negri opposes contractarian theory, which he sees as "immediately juridical," legitimating the transfer of power from civil society to state, and, finally, upholding the theory of the absolutist state, to republican traditions, which exclude the idea of a transfer of power, and which oppose the transcendence of the contract with the *immanence* of a constitutive, dynamic, and participatory conception of power. *Reliqua Desiderantur* 222–3.

78. Anselm Haverkamp writes that "'In weeping after [the murdered King's] untimely bier' (last line of the entire play), the new king makes and declares the dead king's imitation of Christ a theatrical *arcanum*: a state secret to be exposed as such, comparable *cum grano salis* to the semiotic paradox of the Eucharist in France, not in reformed England, in the public realm of princely representations." *Shakespearean Genealogies of Power* (New York: Routledge, 2011), 55.

79. On the shift from substance to function, see Ernst Cassirer, *Substance to Function and Einstein's Theory of Relativity*, trans. William Curtis Swabey and Marie Collins Swabey (Chicago: The Open Court Publishing Co., 1923). For Negri's analysis of sovereignty's relationship to time, see "Virtue and Fortune: the Machiavellian Paradigm," in *Insurgencies: Constituent Power and the Modern State* (Minneapolis: University of Minnesota Press, 1999), 37–81.

80. Benjamin, "*Trauerspiel* and Tragedy" in *Selected Writings Volume I, 1913–1926*, eds. Marcus Bullock and Michael W. Jennings (Cambridge: Harvard University Press, 1997), 55–8.

81. Regarding analogy's "decomposition," my reading agrees with Howard Caygill's argument that "Richard experiences the decomposition of the metaphysics of Kingship." John J. Joughin, ed. *Philosophical Shakespeares* (London: Routledge, 2000), 112. In his influential reading of *Hamlet* and *Macbeth*, Franco Moretti, too, argues that "the image of the sovereign has been decomposed." See Moretti, "The Great Eclipse: Tragic Form as the Deconsecration of Sovereignty," in *Signs Taken for Wonders: On the Sociology of Literary Forms* (London: Verso, 2005), 68. Most pertinent to my discussion, Anselm Haverkamp has argued that in the mirror scene of *Richard II*, Shakespeare "decomposes" the analogy linking king to God. For Haverkamp, "Shakespeare's point is that Bracton's juridical pragmatism . . . provoked with the deposition of Richard an afterimage of what this king could not *be*, but, as king, could very well elucidate and expose through his deposition, the law's supra-legal foundation." *Shakespearean Genealogies* 51.

82. William Shakespeare, *The Life of Henry the Fifth*, in *The Norton Shakespeare Based on the Oxford Edition*, 2nd edition, Stephen Greenblatt, Walter Cohen, Jean E. Howard, and Katharine Eisaman Maus, eds. (New York: Norton, 2008), 1524.

83. Louis Marin, "The Body-of-Power and Incarnation at Port Royal and in Pascal," 440. On "mediatic," see Hent de Vries, "In Media Res: Global Religion, Public Spheres, and the Task of Contemporary Comparative Religious Studies," in *Religion and Media* (Stanford: Stanford University Press, 2001), 3–42.

84. On the "empty place" of power, see Claude Lefort, *L'Invention démocratique* (Paris: Fayard, 1981).

85. Benjamin, *Origin of German Tragic Drama*, 66. Benjamin's German reads, "die verzögernde Überspannung der Transzendenz." The "over-straining" leads to a paradox. It means that, in the end, there is no transcendence. The desire for it is extended so far that it is finally forced to reveal itself—as radical immanence. This leads to Benjamin's absorption in dead things as markers of a melancholia that "from a theological perspective," as Rainer Nägele puts it, "is hopelessly entangled in the satanic materiality of the world, with no redemption in sight." *Theater, Theory, Speculation: Walter Benjamin and the Scenes of Modernity* (Baltimore: Johns Hopkins Press, 1991), 167–206. In Benjamin, however, this "theological perspective" is inverted, and the fallen, "satanic realm" of materiality is now endowed with the "potentiality of revelation." Nägele, 168–9.

86. As Kantorowicz shows in his discussion of the Norman Anonymous, the ontological being of the king does not exist; rather, it *becomes*. It is something produced through a performance at the altar: "The King as *persona geminata* is ontological and, as an effluence of a sacramental and liturgical action performed at the altar, it is liturgical as well." *The King's Two Bodies*, 59. In other words, the king's essence is actualized on-stage, in theater. For a discussion, see Haverkamp, *Shakespearean Genealogies of Power*, 54ff and *Hamlet: Hypothek der Macht*, ed. Dirk Baecker and Elmar Lampson (Berlin: Kadmos Verlag, 2001).

## 2. REANIMATION: THE LOGIC OF TRANSFER IN *MEASURE FOR MEASURE*

1. Jacques Derrida, *The Beast and the Sovereign Volume I*, trans. Geoffrey Bennington, ed. Michel Lisse, Marie-Louise Mallet, and Ginette Michaud (Chicago: University of Chicago Press, 2009), 33n2. The Translator's note tells us that "French readers would immediately

recognize the reference to Pascal's *Pensée* that reads, "L'homme n'est ni ange ni bête, et le malheur veut que qui veut faire l'ange fait la bête." ("Man is neither angel not beast, and the misery of it is that whoever tries to act the angel acts the beast.")

2. *All About My Mother* (*Todo Sobre Mi Madre*), written and directed by Pedro Almodóvar (Sony Pictures Classics, 1999). I borrow the description "brain-dead trilogy" from Marsha Kinder's "Reinventing the Motherland: Almodóvar's Brain-Dead Trilogy," *Film Quarterly* 58, no. 2 (Winter 2004): 9–25.

3. Almodóvar 1999. My translation.

4. On "subjective assemblage," see Antonio Negri and Michael Hardt, "The Social Bases of the Postmodern State and the Existing Prerequisites of Communism," in *Labor of Dionysius: A Critique of the State Form* (Minneapolis: University of Minnesota Press, 1994), 286ff.

5. For as Marcel Gauchet has shown, the Counter-Reformation subject of the seventeenth century could be defined in relation to a "constitutive split" between the conflicting demands of inward isolation from the world, and outward subjection to it. It is a problem, for Gauchet, made particularly acute by the developments of contortions within Christianity during and after the Reformation. *The Disenchantment of the World: A Political History of Religion*, trans. Oscar Burge (Princeton: Princeton University Press, 1999), 131.

6. All references are to the Arden edition of *Measure for Measure*, second series, ed. J. W. Lever (Surrey: Thomas Nelson & Sons, 1965).

7. The words "terror" and "love" are not Bodin's terms. Bodin, "On the true marks of sovereignty." *On Sovereignty*, ed. Julian H. Franklin (Cambridge: Cambridge University Press, 1992), 46–88.

8. Among the various meanings, *The Oxford English Dictionary* (*OED*) lists for the noun, "angel" (from "Latin angel-us, or Greek ἄγγελ-ος a messenger, used by the LXX to translate Hebrew *mal'āk*, in full *mal'āk-yĕhōwāh* 'messenger of Jehovah'") are "divine messenger" (c950), 6. "An old English gold coin, called more fully at first the angel-noble" (1488), and 8. slang. "A financial backer of an enterprise, esp. one who supports a theatrical production. orig. U.S. (1891)" ("angel, n." OED Online, September 2012. Oxford University Press. http://www.oed.com/view/Entry/7458?rskey=RTMzrC&result=1 (accessed October 27, 2012).

On the sovereign as a "character angelicus," Ernst H. Kantorowicz writes that "he is the perpetual actualization of all royal potencies and therefore owns the character angelicus which the political theorists tried to understand, sometimes in terms of the two-natured God, sometimes in the sense of Justice and Law, and sometimes on the basis of People and Polity." *The King's Two Bodies—A Study in Medieval Political Theology* (Princeton: Princeton University Press, 1957), 495. Future references to this text will appear as *TKTB*.

9. See Leonard Barkan, "Cosmas and Damian: Of Medicine, Miracles, and the Economies of the Body," in *Organ Transplantation: Meanings and Realities*, ed. Stuart J. Youngner, Renée C. Fox, and Laurence J. O'Connell (Madison: University of Wisconsin Press, 1996), 221–51.

10. Jacobus de Voragine, *The Golden Legend*, trans. Granger Ryan and Helmut Ripperger (New York: Longmans, 1941), 577–8. Quoted in Barkan, 225.

11. Barkan, "Cosmas and Damian," 236.

12. Ibid.," 243.

13. Nancy S. Leonard, "Substitution in Shakespeare's Problem Comedies," *English Literary Renaissance* 9.2 (Spring 1979): 281–301; Alexander Leggatt, "Substitution in Measure for Measure," *Shakespeare Quarterly* 39.3 (Fall 1988): 342–59; and William Empson, "Sense in Measure for Measure," *The Structure of Complex Words* (Cambridge: Harvard University Press, 1989), 270–88. What Empson introduces is developed in Jean-Luc Nancy's analysis of the "theologico-political," which also pursues a particular construction of "sense." See *The Sense of the World*, trans. Jeffrey S. Librett (Minneapolis: University of Minnesota Press, 1997).

14. *Law and the Unconscious: A Legendre Reader*, edited and translated by Peter Goodrich with Alain Pottage and Anton Schütz (New York: St. Martin's Press, 1997), 20.

15. Louis Martz, "'Of Government': Theme and Action in Measure for Measure," in *Classical, Renaissance and Postmodernist Acts of the Imagination: Essays Commemorating O. B. Hardison, Jr.*, ed. Arthur Kinney (Newark: University of Delaware Press, 1996), 212, quoted in Debora Kuller Shuger, *Political Theologies in Shakespeare's England: The Sacred and the State in Measure for Measure* (New York: Palgrave, 2001), 1.

16. James I, "Basilicon Doron," *Political Writings*, ed. J. P. Sommerville (Cambridge: Cambridge University Press, 1994), 34.

17. Suárez, "The Meaning of the Term 'Law' (Lex)," *On Laws and God the Lawgiver*, Williams translation, 26. Suárez's Latin reads:

*Legis etymologia.*—Atque hinc intulit D. Thomas in illo art. 1, quæst. 90, etymologiam legis; putat enim a ligando sumptam esse, quia proprius effectus legis est ligare, seu obligare, quod secutus est Gabriel in 3, dist. 37, art.1, et Clichtove, in Damas., lib. 4 Fidei, cap. 23, eamdem etymologiam legis ex Cassiodoro refert, et probat. Consonatque Scriptura, quæ leges appellat vincula, Jerem. 2: *Fregisti jugum, rupisti vincula.* Isidorus autem, lib. 2 Etymol., cap. 10, et lib. 5, cap. 3, a legendo putat legem esse dictam, quod inde colligit, quia lex debet esse scripta, et ideo legenda est. Sed quia nunc latius de lege loquimur, ut illa etymologia possit in omnem legem convenire, oportet *legendi* verbum ad interiorem lectionem, seu recogitationem ampliare, ut notavit Alensis, 3 p., q. 26, memb. 1. Nam sicut lex naturalis dicitur a Paulo scripta in cordibus, ad Roman. 2, ita in eis mente legi potest et debet, id est, meditari et recogitari, ut secundum illam mores dirigantur, juxta illud Psalm. 118: *Lucerna pedibus meis verbum tuum.* Et huic etymologiæ consonant nomen hebraicum, quo lex *Tora* dicitur, id est, instructio.

*Opera omnia* vol. 5, p. 3.

18. The operation of law's seizure here coincides with what Pierre Legendre describes in terms of a subjective "capture." *Law and the Unconscious*, 17–19.

19. Virpi Mäkinen points out that in the work of philosophers like Descartes, the term "precise" refers to a "cutting away from a thing's complete metaphysical structure to some mere part of it." "Self-Preservation and Natural Rights in Late Medieval and Early Modern Political Thought," in *The Nature of Rights: Moral and Political Aspects of Rights in Late Medieval and Early Modern Philosophy*, ed. Virpi Mäkinen (Helsinki: The Philosophical Society of Finland, 2010), 173, n.26. Also see John Michael Archer, *Citizen Shakespeare* (New York: Palgrave, 2005), 67–8.

20. On anti-Puritan satire, see Shuger, *Political Theologies*. Also see especially Peter Lake, whom Shuger cites and whose concluding chapter, "*Measure for Measure*, Anti-Puritanism and 'Order' in Early Stuart England," links English anti-Puritanism to the accession of James I specifically. *The Antichrist's Lewd Hat: Protestants, Papists and Players in Post-Reformation England* (New Haven: Yale University Press, 2002), 621–700.

21. The term "hypocrite" itself comes from the Greek *hupokritēs*, meaning "actor."

22. At 1.2.157, Claudio complains of "enrolled penalties/Which have, like unscour'd armour, hung by th'wall/So long, that nineteen zodiacs have gone round/And none of them been worn;" But at 1.3.21, the Duke refers to the "needful bit and curbs to headstrong

jades, / Which for this fourteen years we have let slip." On this discrepancy, Lever writes that it "may be due to a confusing of the figures 4 and 9; or Shakespeare may simply have forgotten what he wrote." Lever, Introduction to *Measure for Measure*, 17n157.

23. See, respectively, Jonathan Dollimore, "Transgression and Surveillance in *Measure for Measure*," in *Political Shakespeares: Essays in Cultural Materialism*, ed. Jonathan Dollimore and Alan Sinfield (Cornell: Cornell University Press, 1994), 72–87; and Marc Shell, *The End of Kinship: Measure for Measure, Incest, and the Ideal of Universal Siblinghood* (Baltimore: Johns Hopkins University Press, 1988).

24. Aristotle, *Poetics, with the Tractatus Coislinianus, Reconstruction of Poetics II, and the Fragments of the On Poets*, trans. Richard Janko (Indianapolis: Hackett, 1987), p. 28, section 57b, lines 7–9.

25. George Puttenham, *The Arte of English Poesy: A Critical Edition*, ed. Frank Whigham and Wayne A. Rebhorn (Ithaca: Cornell University Press, 2007), 227.

26. Carl Schmitt, *Political Theology: Four Chapters on the Concept of Sovereignty*, trans. George Schwab (Cambridge: MIT Press, 1988), 24. Suárez, too, uses the term "organ" (*organo*) to describe the constituent members of the body politic. In his discussion of the conditions under which it is licit to kill a king ruling tyrannically in the *Defensio fidei*, for example, he writes that "Thus it is indeed true, strictly speaking, that this [killing] is committed, under the circumstance described, not by private but by public authority; or rather, by the authority either of a kingdom willing to be defended by any citizen whomsoever as by its own members or organ [*a* membro et organo], or else by the authority of God, the Author of nature, Who gives to every individual the power of defending the innocent." (Unde etiam in rigore, verum est id non fieri tunc auctoritate privata, sed public, vel potius regni volentis a quolibet cive tanquam a membro et organo suo defendi, vel Dei auctoris naturae dantis cuicumque homini potestatem defendi innocentem.) *Opera omnia* vol. 24, p. 679.

27. Jacques Lezra, *Wild Materialism: The Ethic of Terror and the Modern Republic* (New York: Fordham University Press, 2010), 246n8.

28. "PODER. Del verbo latino possum, potes. Poder, nombre, la facultad que uno da a otro para que en lugar de su persona haga alguna cosa. Poder es lo mismo que poderío, latine potestas. De dos exércitos, quando enviste uno con otro peleando todos, dezimos darse la batalla de poder a poder. Poderoso, latine potens." Sebastián de Covarrubias Orozco, *Tesoro de la Lengua Castellana o Española*, ed. by

Ignacio Arellano and Rafael Zafra (Madrid: University of Navarra, 2006), 1368.

29. *Representare idem est quod rem præsentem facere.*—Tertius testis sit Hieronymus, exponens verba Christi, Matt. 26, ubi sic inquit: *Postquam typicum pascha fuerat impletum, et agni carnes cum Apostolis comederat, assumit panem, qui confortat cor hominis, et ad verum Paschæ transgreditur sacraentum, ut quomodo in figuratione ejus Melchisedech, summi Dei sacerdos, panem et vinum offerens fecerat, ipse quoque veritatem sui corporis et sanguinis repræsentaret.* Ubi etiam fortasse prodibit hæreticus, qui verbum *repræsentaret,* in aliquam fictionem vel metaphoram intrepretetur. Vis vero verbi, et mens Hieronymi perspicua est: idem enim est repræsentare, quod rem præsentem, facere, præsertim quæ antea promissa erat, vel futura prædicta, aut desiderata. (*Opera omnia* vol. 24, p. 128.)

30. On theatrical representation and "actualization" in relation to psychoanalysis, see Samuel Weber, "Psychoanalysis and Theatricality," *Theatricality as Medium* (New York: Fordham University Press, 2004), 251–76.

31. Jonathan Goldberg, *James I and the Politics of Literature* (Stanford: Stanford University Press, 1989), 234.

32. Goldberg, *James I*, 153.

33. Goldberg's playful and rigorous readings of Shakespeare would generally support this point, I believe. Goldberg's Shakespeare criticism is indebted in different ways to the work of Derrida. See especially *Shakespeare's Hand* (Minneapolis: University of Minnesota Press, 2002). On language's duality in relation to power, see Derrida, "The Retrait of Metaphor," in *Psyche: Inventions of the Other, Volume I*, ed. Peggy Kamuf and Elizabeth Rottenberg (Stanford: Stanford University Press, 2007), 1–47.

34. Agamben, *Homo Sacer: Sovereign Power and Bare Life*, trans. Daniel Heller-Roazen (Stanford: Stanford University Press, 1998), 47.

35. Agamben, *Homo Sacer*, 45.

36. For metaphor theorists this is a contentious point. Paul Ricoeur, for example, argues that simile is not a subset of metaphor, referring to Aristotle's *Rhetoric*; Ricoeur, *The Rule of Metaphor: Multi-disciplinary Studies of the Creation of Meaning in Language*, trans. Robert Czerny with Kathleen McLaughlin and John Costello, S.J. (Toronto: University of Toronto Press, 1997), 25.

37. Puttenham, *Arte of English Poesie*, 189.

38. Ibid., 190.

39. Citing Angelo's 2.2.143 soliloquy: "She speaks, and 'tis such sense / that my sense breeds with it," Empson argues that it is Isabella's

words (her "sense") that produce Angelo's desire (sensuality) to possess her body. The error both the Duke and Isabella make is to think they can avoid the pitfalls of sense and somehow "get outside the world and above justice." They believe that their bodies are not bound to the body politic and its principal sense-making machine, the law, in the same way as others'. "Sense in *Measure for Measure*" in *Structure of Complex Words*, 284.

40. Schmitt, quoted in Agamben, *Homo Sacer*, 26.
41. Empson, *Structure of Complex Words*, 284.
42. Agamben, *Homo Sacer*, 26.
43. Agamben, *Homo Sacer*, 8–9.
44. Hans Blumenberg, *Paradigms for a Metaphorology*, trans. Robert Savage (Ithaca: Cornell University Press, 2010), 14.
45. Paul de Man, "The Epistemology of Metaphor," *Aesthetic Ideology*, ed. and intro. Andrzej Warminski (Minneapolis: University of Minnesota Press, 1996), 45.
46. Stanley Fish, "The Law Wishes to Have a Formal Existence," in *The Fate of Law*, ed. Austin Sarat and Thomas R. Kearns (Ann Arbor: University of Michigan Press, 1993), 178–9.
47. Ibid., 195.
48. Ibid., 196.
49. Ibid., 207–8.
50. Ibid., 207–8.
51. Ibid., 159.
52. Ibid., 162.
53. Anselm Haverkamp counters with a different understanding of the relationship between law and form. Haverkamp emphasizes the deconstructibility of rhetoric by poetics: "Poetics is built upon, and therefore insists on, the pure difference that had to be excluded from the figurative practice of rhetoric." "Rhetoric, Law, and the Poetics of Memory," *Cardozo Law Review* 13, no. 5 (March 1992): 1652. What Haverkamp suspects is that Fish's denial of any legal essence ultimately translates to "a state where violence has been monopolized by the stronger law" ("Rhetoric," 1652).
54. Walter Benjamin, *Origin of German Tragic Drama*, trans. John Osborne (London: Verso, 1994), 95.
55. Ibid., 96.
56. Michel Foucault, *Discipline and Punish: The Birth of the Pri*son, trans. Alan Sheridan (New York: Vintage Books, 1995), 55. Samuel Weber quotes Schmitt's *Political Theology*, "For the reality of juridical life, what is decisive is who decides":

[This] requires embodiment ... in a subject whose singularity is the necessary correlative of the decision. The decision ... has to be "formal," since it proceeds from a divergence of general from particular ... that positive law ... can never bridge. It is by virtue of ... the decisional intervention of a singular subject that "law" can be endowed with "life," even though from the point of view of normative legality it is a life born out of "nothing," created ex nihilo ... this model ... will assume ... decisive important in Schmitt's elaboration of the "principle of representation."

Samuel Weber, *Targets of Opportunity: On the Militarization of Thinking* (New York: Fordham University Press, 2005), 35.

57. Jonathan Goldberg, *James I and the Politics of Literature: Jonson, Shakespeare, Donne, and Their Contemporaries* (Stanford: Stanford University Press, 1989), 149.

58. See Ricoeur, *Rule of Metaphor*, 17.

59. On the image as a substitute in Roman funeral ceremonies, Agamben cites Elias Bickermann, "Die römische Kaiserapotheose," *Archiv für Religionswissenschaft* 27 (1929). *Homo Sacer*, 95. On the relationship between religion and magic in sixteenth- and seventeenth-century England, see Keith Thomas, *Religion and the Decline of Magic*: "men and women sought a substitute for the metaphysical aid of the medieval church in a welter of occult practices," qtd. in Montrose, *The Purpose of Playing: Shakespeare and the Cultural Politics of the Elizabeth Theatre* (Chicago: University of Chicago Press, 1996), 31.

60. Foucault, *Discipline and Punish*, 55.

61. Michel Foucault, "Governmentality," *Essential Works of Foucault 1954–1984, Volume Three: Power*, ed. James D. Faubion, trans. Robert Hurley et al (New York: The New Press, 2000), 210.

62. Cornelia Vismann and Anselm Haverkamp, "Habeas Corpus: The Law's Desire to Have the Body," in *Shakespearean Genealogies of Power* (New York: Routledge, 2011), 124–5.

63. Ibid., 128.

64. Shell, *End of Kinship*, and Shuger, *Political Theologies*.

65. See Julia Reinhard Lupton, "Antigone in Vienna," in *Citizen-Saints: Shakespeare and Political Theology* (Chicago: University of Chicago Press, 2005), 140.

66. For the most developed elaboration of this argument, see Julia Reinhard Lupton, *Citizen-Saints: Shakespeare and Political Theology* (Chicago: University of Chicago Press, 2005).

On the constitutive split of the believer's body between the demands of the "here-below and the beyond," see Marcel Gauchet, *The Disenchantment of the World: A Political History of Religion*, trans. Oscar Burge (Princeton: Princeton University Press, 1997), 131. The believer is torn apart, in yet another "tear" that distinguishes the political-theological subject's body from the oneness of the body of the citizen, which becomes one by entering into a "politics of the norm." See Lupton, *Citizen-Saints*, 21. For Lupton, *Measure for Measure*, and Isabella's choice, in particular, leave us with the "startling spectacle of consent in reverse," (*Citizen-Saints*, 140).

67. Louis Marin, *Portrait of the King*, trans. Martha M. Houle (Minneapolis: University of Minnesota Press, 1988), 6.

68. Ibid., 6–7.

69. Ibid., 7.

70. Ibid., 7–8.

71. Ibid, 7.

72. Jacques Lezra, "The Appearance of History in Measure for Measure," in *Unspeakable Subjects: The Genealogy of the Event in Early Modern Europe* (Stanford: Stanford University Press, 1997), 260.

73. Ibid., 288.

74. On the term "order" rather than "power" or "law," see my discussion of Pierre Legendre's concept of the "normative function" in this chapter.

75. *TKTB*, 48.

76. Again, Kantorowicz: "[T]he jurists salvaged much of the mediaeval inheritance by transferring certain peculiarly ecclesiastical properties of kingship to the legal stage setting, thereby preparing the new halo of the rising national states and, for good or evil, of the absolute monarchies. *TKTB*, 126.

77. See Jacques Derrida, "Faith and Knowledge—The Two Sources of 'Religion' at the Limits of Reason Alone," in *Acts of Religion*, ed. and intro. Gil Anidjar (New York: Routledge, 2002), 65.

78. Or rather, according to Marin, three bodies. Seeing in the Eucharist ceremony the representational ratio of political absolutism, Marin argues that the priest's utterance of the liturgical formula "This is my body" produces not one but three bodies: *a "sacramental body visible as the real presence of Jesus Christ* on the altar . . . *the absent historical body of Jesus Christ as narrative representation,"* and, finally, an *"eccesiastical body as symbolic fictive society at once visible and invisible"* (*Portrait of the King*, 12).

79. Jacques Lezra compares Barnadine to the pirate, "the figure of interruption." Barnadine could equally be viewed as a figure of

resistance—one who plays a role not unlike that of Melville's Bartleby in Agamben's analysis of the impotentia of sovereignty. See *Unspeakable Subjects*, 257–94.

80. We do not hear Isabella's reply to the Duke's request for her hand at 5.1.490. Her last words are, "Thoughts are no subjects; / Intents, but merely thoughts" (5.1.451). After this, she does not speak again, which could be taken to mean that neither her thoughts nor her body will be subjected to the Duke's desire to marry her—or that intention itself does not rise to the level of thought. In either case, the response remains enigmatic. What is certain is that Isabella does not say "yes."

81. J. W. Lever cites the reaction of Samuel Johnson, who "found the light or comick part very natural and pleasing," but objected that the "grave scenes" in general showed "more labour than elegance." Coleridge "viewed the whole play as profoundly disturbing." Lever, ed. and intro. *Measure for Measure* (London: Methuen, 1965), lv–lvi.

82. On selfhood in the comedies, see Nancy S. Leonard, "Substitution in Shakespeare's Problem Comedies," *English Literary Renaissance*, vol. 9, no. 2 (March 1979), 281–301.

83. Shuger, *Political Theologies*, 107.

84. Haverkamp and Vismann:

> From the seventeenth century onwards, the time gained by the procedure is used for preliminary investigations. The law no longer takes an interest in the body as such, it focuses on the surrounding network of environment, contact and movement. Written deposits allows for the deposition of witnesses before the actual trial; they are taken down in order to perpetuate testimony . . . Whatever there is to be put in depositions serves to make them independent from the witnesses' actual performance in court. Thus the depositions function in the same way as the deposits; they conserve the body wanted by written or pecuniary surrogates.
>
> *Shakespearean Genealogies of Power*, 123.

85. See Peter Brook, *The Empty Space* (New York: Touchstone, 1996).

On the relationship between sovereignty and "sense," see Jean-Luc Nancy:

> The women and men of our time have, indeed, a rather sovereign way of losing their footing without anxiety, of walking on the waters of the drowning of sense. A way of knowing precisely that sovereignty is nothing, that it is this nothing in which sense always exceeds itself.

That which resists everything—and perhaps always, in every epoch—is not a mediocre species instinct or survival instinct, but this very sense.
And later:
Sovereignty has no doubt lost the sense it had, reducing itself to a kind of "black hole" of the political. But this does not mean that the sense of being-in-common, inasmuch as sense itself is in common, does not have to make itself sovereign in a new way.

Jean-Luc Nancy, The Logic of Sense: The Sense of the World,<br>trans. Jeffrey S. Librett (Minneapolis: University of<br>Minnesota Press, 1997), 2, 91.

Also see *Globalization* (103) where Nancy again describes sovereignty in terms of "nothing." How does the "sense of being-in-common . . . make itself sovereign" in *Measure?* For Marc Shell it is, above all, a family sense, the sense that universal siblinghood makes / does not make. If all men are brothers, then I am my son's brother, there is universal incest, and men who are not my brothers are not men (human). This is one implication of *Measure,* one kind of (non)sense, one way of "configuring the political space," as Nancy puts it.

## 3. RESISTANCE: WAITING FOR POWER IN *FUENTEOVEJUNA*

1. Kristeva, *The Sense and Non-Sense of Revolt* (New York: Columbia University Press, 2001), 8.
2. Giorgio Agamben, *Homo Sacer*, trans. Daniel Heller-Roazen (Stanford: Stanford University Press, 1998), 11.
3. On the historical context, see Emilio Cabrera Andrés Moros, *Fuentovejuna: La Violencia Antiseñorial en el Siglo XV* (Barcelona: Editorial Crítica, 1991), 145, as well as Francisco López Estrada ed., *Fuente Ovejuna* (Madrid: Clásicos Castalia, 1996).
4. For an analysis of political theology in *Measure for Measure* in relation to English Puritanism, see Debora Kuller Shuger, *Political Theologies in Shakespeare's England: The Sacred and the State in Measure for Measure* (New York: Palgrave, 2001). More generally, on the role of religious politics in early modern English theater, see Peter Lake and Michael Questier, *The Antichrist's Lewd Hat: Protestants, Papists and Players in Post-Reformation England* (New Haven: Yale University Press, 2002).
5. Most scholars date the writing of the play to 1612–14. *Measure for Measure* was performed in 1604, the same year James signed a peace treaty with Spain. By the time *Fuenteovejuna* emerged, Anglo-Spanish

relations had taken a bellicose turn. Domestic and international intrigues surrounding James's court in 1612–14 include James's complicated relation with the Howard faction and the spectacular Overbury scandal, in which James's support of the pro-Spanish Howards would further alienate the king from the House of Commons. This was also the time (1613) when James's daughter, Elizabeth, married Frederick V, the Elector Palatine, who would later lead the German Protestant Union against Hapsburg attempts to reestablish Catholicism throughout the Holy Roman Empire, thus starting the Thirty Years War (1618–48). See J. P. Sommerville, *Royalists and Patriots: Politics and Ideology in England, 1603–1640* (Longman 1999).

6. Two years prior to this event, Spain had experienced one of those events in a country's history that decidedly alters its future. In 1474, the death of the Spanish king Henry IV, known as "the impotent," produces a power vacuum, leading to rival claims to the throne. While one sector of the Castilian nobility supported the king's daughter, Doña Juana, known pejoratively by her enemies as "la Beltraneja" (for their belief that she descended from one of Henry's courtiers, Don Beltrán de la Cueva), the remaining nobility defended the king's half-sister, Isabel, who, together with her husband, Ferdinand of Aragón, would later become known as the "Catholic Kings." Between the claims of a "daughter" and those of a sister, these conflicts and their inherent questions regarding succession, family politics, and above all the imminent threat of civil war provide the thematic and historical framework for what is probably Lope de Vega's most well-known play, *Fuenteovejuna*. As critics have pointed out, Lope manipulates his historical sources, emphasizing the Comendador's crimes and downplaying the violence of the villagers. For a discussion of the historical background, see López Estrada, as well as Donald Larson, *The Honor Plays of Lope de Vega* (Cambridge: Harvard University Press, 1977), 83.

7. Donald McGrady, ed., *Fuente Ovejuna* (Barcelona: Crítica, 1993), 5.

8. Lope probably gave his speech to the academy at the end of 1607 or in early 1608. See Enrique García Santo-Tomás, *Arte nuevo de hacer comedias* (Madrid: Cátedra, 2009), 43.

9. Victor Dixon, trans. "*New Rules for Writing Plays At This Time*, Addressed to the Academy of Madrid," *Lope de Vega, Arte Nuevo de Hacer Comedias en Este Tiempo* (Madrid: Festival de Teatro Clásico de Almagro), 181; *Arte Nuevo de Hacer Comedias*, ed. Enrique García Santo-Tomás (Madrid: Cátedra, 2009), 144.

10. Santo-Tomás, ed., 144, my emphasis.

11. Dixon, 181–2.
12. Ibid., 181.
13. Among the definitions offered by the 2010 *Spanish Royal Academy Dictionary* are 1. to courteously refuse an invitation [Rechazar cortésmente una invitación]; 2. (in grammar) to show the different linguistic forms of a word according to different grammatical cases; 3) [*Gram*. En las lenguas con flexión casual, enunciar las formas que presenta una palabra como manifestación de los diferentes casos]; 3. to lean downwards or toward one side or another [inclinarse hacia abajo o hacia un lado u otro]; 4. to diminish in health, intelligence, or wealth, etc. [Decaer, menguar, ir perdiendo en salud, inteligencia, riqueza, lozanía, etc.]; 5. what is said of a thing when it reaches its end: the decline of the sun [Dicho de una cosa: Caminar o aproximarse a su fin y término. *Declinar el Sol, el día*.]; 6. to change the nature or custom of something until it reaches its extreme opposite: for example to decline from virtue to vice, strength to weakness. [Ir cambiando de naturaleza o de costumbres hasta tocar en extremo contrario. *Declinar de la virtud en el vicio del rigor, en la debilidad.*] See http://buscon.rae.es/draeI/.
14. Sebastián de Covarrubias Horozco, *Tesoro de la Lengua Castellana O Española*, ed. Ignacio Arellano and Rafael Zafra (Navarra: Editorial Iberoamericana, 2006), 669.
15. That "declinar" in Spanish, or "decline" in English, were words to play with, insofar as they associate linguistic and other events in productive, often humorous ways was not lost on Lope's contemporary, Shakespeare, who has Polonius attempt to describe, *succinctly*, Hamlet's fall into madness as a "declension": "And he, repulsèd,—a short tale to make—Fell into a sadness, then into a fast, / Thence to a watch, thence into a weakness, / Thence to a lightness, and, by this *declension*, Into the madness wherein now he raves, And all we wail for" (*Hamlet* 2.2.146–9). Polonius's "short tale" of Hamlet's "declension" is one way of accounting for, and ending, events. *The Norton Shakespeare Based on the Oxford Edition*. Second edition, ed. Stephen Greenblatt, Walter Cohen, Jean E. Howard, and Katharine Eisaman Maus (New York: Norton, 2008), 1722.
16. Anthony Cascardi, *Ideologies of History in the Spanish Golden Age* (University Park: Pennsylvania State University Press, 1997), 40, 46. Cascardi links the play's outcome, in which the peasants call *not* for self-rule, but rather for a renewed subjection to the Catholic Kings—to the history of Spain's own historical resistance to the processes of modernization. For Cascardi, the Spanish *comedia*, on the whole, is engaged in a collective project of political and historical resistance to these processes, a resistance for which *Fuenteovejuna*, in particular, is

exemplary. Figuring authority in terms of the "hierarchies of the past," the play demonstrates an "imaginary means through which Spanish society was able simultaneously to confront and to resist" the transformations toward modernity occurring in the rest of early modern Europe (21). For a reading of *Hamlet* in terms of recognition and as a construction of the subject "before the law," see Thomas Keenan, "Left to Our Own Devices: On the Impossibility of Justice," in *Fables of Responsibility: Aberrations and Predicaments in Ethics and Politics* (Stanford: Stanford University Press, 1997), 7–42.

17. Peter W. Evans, "Civilisation and its Discontents in *Fuenteovejuna*," in *Conflicts of Discourse: Spanish Literature in the Golden Age* (Manchester: Manchester University Press, 1990), 122. As Evans explains: "Through its depiction of the *Comendador* the play shows an extreme case of women's sexual objectification by a man whose behavior is partially sanctioned by a contradictory ideology that simultaneously denounces sexual harassment while also using it as one of the yardsticks by which to judge standards of masculinity" (Evans, *Conflicts of Discourse*, 127).

18. Ibid., 114.

19. Mitchell Greenberg, *Canonical States, Canonical Stages: Oedipus, Othering, and Seventeenth-Century Drama* (Minneapolis: University of Minnesota Press, 1994), 38.

20. Ibid., 41.

21. Ibid., 40.

22. Ibid., 38.

23. Agamben, *Homo Sacer*, 8.

24. Ibid., 8.

25. Ibid., 9. My emphasis.

26. Agamben's structural device of the *homo sacer* has produced vast amounts of commentary. Good collections of essays include Andrew Norris, ed., *Politics, Metaphysics, and Death: Essays on Giorgio Agamben's* Homo Sacer (Durham: Duke University Press, 2005), as well as *The Agamben Effect*, Alison Ross, ed., *South Atlantic Quarterly* (2008), and Leland de la Durantaye's comprehensive study, *Giorgio Agamben: A Critical Introduction* (Stanford: Stanford University Press, 2009).

27. This can be linked to Derrida's analysis of metaphor and metaphysics in Heidegger. See my discussion of the German term *Riß* in relation to metaphor in the conclusion.

28. Spitzer, "A Central Theme," 402.

29. Ibid., 409.

30. "El idioma distinguía entre la noción ideal y objetiva del 'honor,' y el funcionamiento de esa misma noción, vitalmente realizada en un proceso de vida." Américo Castro, *De la edad conflictiva: Crisis de la Cultura Española en el Siglo XVII* (Madrid: Taurus Ediciones, S.A., 1976), 57–8. For a discussion, see Georgina Dopico Black, *Perfect Wives: Adultery and Inquisition in Early Modern Spain* (Durham: Duke University Press, 2001), 129ff.

31. This description comes from Robert Savage, in Blumenberg's *Paradigms*.

32. "El honor *es*, pero la honra pertenece a alguien, actúa y se está moviendo en una vida." Castro, *De la edad conflictiva*, 57–8.

33. Castro writes that "la palabra *honra* parece más adherida al alma de quien siente derruido o mermado lo que antes existía con plenitud y seguridad. . . . Y la comedia prosperó grandemente presentando casos de fractura y de compostura de honras maltrechas." *De la edad conflictive* 58–9.

34. Ibid., 56.

35. For an interesting discussion of these anxieties (including whether they should even be considered as such) in the context of early modern English drama, see Anthony Dawson and Paul Yachnin, *The Culture of Playgoing in Shakespeare's England: A Collaborative Debate* (Cambridge: Cambridge University Press, 2001).

36. Diego Saavedra Fajardo, *Empresas Políticas*, ed. Sagrario López (Madrid: Cátedra, 1999), 677.

37. Melveena McKendrick points out that the terms were often "used interchangeably." McKendrick, "Communicating the Past" in *Approaches to Teaching Early Modern Spanish Drama*, ed. Laura R. Bass and Margaret R. Greer (New York: The Modern Language Association of America, 2006), 31. Geraint Evans refers to Sebastián de Covarrubias's *Tesoro de la Lengua Castellana o Española*, in which Covarrubias writes that "Honor vale le mesmo que honra." "Masculinities and Honour in *Los Comendadores de Córdoba*," in *A Companion to Lope de Vega*, ed. Alexander Samson and Jonathan Thacker (Woodbridge: Tamesis, 2008), 201.

38. Lope de Vega, *Arte Nuevo de Hacer Comedia*, ed. Enrique García Santo-Tomás (Madrid: Cátedra, 2009), 149.

39. Benjamin, *Origin of German Tragic Drama*, 86–7. Future references to this text will appear as *OGTD*.

40. Dopico Black, *Perfect Wives*, 39.

41. Ibid., 40.

42. Covarrubias, *Tesoro*, 1436–7.

43. Louis Marin, *Portrait*, 31.

44. As Dopico Black points out, the problem of the interpretation of signs in the early seventeenth century is intimately connected with Counter Reformation polemics regarding interpretation, in particular those having to do with that all-important Christian event: the ceremony of the Eucharist. See *Perfect Wives, Other Women: Adultery and Inquisition in Early Modern Spain* (Durham: Duke University Press, 2001).

45. On the "violence" of inscription in the play, see Catherine Larson, "'Violent Hierarchies': The Deconstructive Voice and Writing Undone in *Fuenteovejuna*," in *Language and the Comedia* (Lewisburg: Bucknell University Press, 1991), 109–65.

46. Georgina Dopico Black, *Perfect Wives*, 8.

47. Peter Goodrich, introduction to *Law and the Unconscious: A Legendre Reader* (New York: St. Martin's Press, 1997), 19–20.

48. Ibid., 31.

49. Ibid., 32. As Goodrich points out, In Sir John Fortescue's English common law formulation, "To fear God is the effect of the law." Introduction, *Law and the Unconscious*, 33.

50. See Laplanche and Pontalis's entry, "Resistance," in *The Language of Psycho-Analysis* (New York: Norton, 1973), 394–7.

51. Goodrich, Introduction to *Law and the Unconscious*, 32.

52. There is much critical debate over the nature of Laurencia's violation. Where for critics such as Donald McGrady, for example, "La transformación de la cara de Laurencia refleja su pérdida de virginidad," Victor Dixon, Marc Vitse, and others insist that *Fuenteovejuna* is more coherent once it is understood—in a surprise—at the end that Laurencia has indeed managed to successfully resist her aggressor. In this case, the revolt and subsequent violence is in *defense* of her honor, and *not* an act of revenge. See Victor Dixon 1988: 161–3 and 1989: 22–3.

53. This line has been variously translated as, "Yes, I am Laurencia, but so changed that looking at me you still doubt it" (Flores 66); "I'm in such a state / that the change in me makes you / unsure who I am" (Appelbaum); and Victor Dixon's, perhaps best approximation: "I see I'm so much changed / you can't be certain who I am." See Flores, 66; Appelbaum, 107; and Dixon, 167.

54. See McGrady, *Fuente Ovejuna*, 188.

55. See *Diccionario Espasa términos jurídicos* (Madrid: Espasa Calpe, 2007).

56. Laurencia's disheveled hair could be seen to participate in a developing tradition of Marian theology and iconography in the early

seventeenth century, in which a connection is suggested between the Virgin and "the 'wild woman' or 'Amazon' in archetypal theory." This tradition, including well-known paintings by Rubens, Velázquez, Zuburán, Valdés Leal, and Cano, perhaps reaches its culminating moment later in the century, with Bartolomé Esteban Murillo's *Virgin of the Immaculate Conception* (1678). See Anthony M. Stevens-Arroyo, "The Evolution of Marian Devotionalism within Christianity and the Ibero-Mediterranean Polity," *Journal for the Scientific Study of Religion*, 37:1 (March 1998): 66.

57. Where Juan María Marín, Rinaldo Froldi, López Estrada, and Dixon all insert a comma between "golpes" at the end of line 1751 and "de la sangre" at the beginning of line 1752, Donald McGrady omits it in his critical edition of the play. This is the version I am following here. McGrady, *Fuente Ovejuna* (Barcelona: Crítica, 1993), 123.

58. I am grateful to Jacques Lezra for pointing this out to me.

59. De Man took as an example of a literal statement undoing a figurative one Archie Bunker's exasperated question to his wife, Edith, about the right way to lace up bowling shoes: "What's the difference?!" meaning, as De Man points out, *not* that he wants to *know* whether there is any difference between one technique of lacing and another, but rather that he wants to *say* that "there *is no difference!*" Paul de Man, "Semiology and Rhetoric," in *Allegories of Reading* (New Haven: Yale University Press, 1982).

60. See, for example, *Discipline and Punish: The Birth of the Prison*, trans. Alan Sheridan (New York: Vintage Books, 1995).

61. For a discussion, see Michael Hardt and Antonio Negri, *Empire* (Cambridge: Harvard University Press, 2000), esp. at 360ff.

62. The notion of "pastoral power" lies at the center of the debate between Catholic theorists, such as Suárez, who support the Pope's "indirect" or "coercive" power, and King James who, as we've seen, reject it. For Suárez, "it falls to the Pope not only to correct wandering sheep and bring them back to the fold, but also to chase away wolves and defend his flock against its enemies" (*Defense* I. p. 286, qtd. in Skinner II. 180). Where that argument pits the English as wolves not protecting their subjects/sheep, Laurencia, characteristically, doubles and inverts the analogy, attacking the men for having failed in their pastoral duties to protect her against wolves, such as Férnan Gómez—and then turning *them* into sheep unworthy of protection. The men are thus *both* in the position of an incompetent shepherd/Pope, *and also* (as a result) unworthy of shepherding. For a discussion of Foucault's notion of "pastoral power" in the context of Counter-Reformation

Spain, see Cascardi, *Ideologies*, 118ff. Cascardi focuses, in particular, on subject formation and the different "mechanisms of control," developed in Spain and countries such as England and France. Cascardi argues that the difference between the "disciplinary techniques" that emerge in Spain can be understood as part of a general resistance and reaction to the latter country's emerging "progressive philosophical rationalism." Cascardi, *Ideologies*, 120.

63. Laurencia's curse is also a call—a call and a turn, or return, which has to do with tropes, in this case, one of Lope's favorites: the trope of the Amazon. That the call is made in the subjunctive mode is important in that it is precisely that mode that is shared by law, proverbs, and a certain, complex notion of the future, or futurity.

64. On the structure of the curse and its bio-political implications, especially in the work of Shakespeare, see Björn Quiring, *Shakespeares Fluch. Die Aporien der rituellen Verstoßung in Königsdramen der englischen Renaissance* [Shakespeare's Curse. The Aporias of Ritual Exclusion in History Dramas of the English Renaissance] (Munich: Wilhelm Fink Verlag, 2009).

65. The Spanish term "trazar" itself, here translated as "I swear that," can be understood in contemporary Spanish to mean, "to sign," "to trace," "to draw," "to plan," and "to set in stone." From the Latin *tractiare*, from *tractus*, the dictionary of the *Real Academia Española* defines it as follows:

tr. Hacer trazos.

tr. Delinear o diseñar la traza que se ha de seguir en un edificio u otra obra.

tr. Discurrir y disponer los medios oportunos para el logro de algo.

tr. Describir, dibujar, exponer por medio del lenguaje los rasgos característicos de una persona o de un asunto. [To *write*, to make it real or legally binding like a swearing.]

66. Again, for some critics, it is important to understand that Laurencia "had not succumbed" to the Commander's attempt to violate her. The significance of this is that it transforms the denouement of the play into a case of *defense* (of honor) rather than vengeance. See Victor Dixon, *Fuente Ovejuna*, 22–3. For me, what is important is that Laurencia is questioning—and for a moment effectively overturning—the premises of the honor code themselves, including its presumption to assign value to life.

67. Benjamin, *OGTD*, 86–7.

68. Legendre, *Law and the Unconscious*, xiii–xiv.

69. In emphasizing the term "responsibility," I am intentionally foregrounding both the play's *response* to *Measure for Measure*'s representation of sovereignty in terms of the "organ-transplant" logic, as well as its treatment of what would become known in the twentieth century as the international law concept of the *responsibility to protect*. *Fuenteovejuna* could be seen as an early thematization of the political and philosophical question, so familiar today, of when and how to intervene in another polity's affairs in order to protect a civilian population. For a lucid and compelling discussion, see Anne Orford, *International Authority and the Responsibility to Protect* (Cambridge: Cambridge University Press, 2011).

70. Melveena McKendrick, "The Amazon, the Leader, the Warrior," in *Woman and Society in the Spanish Drama of the Golden Age: A Study of the* Mujer Varonil (Cambridge: Cambridge University Press, 1974), 175–6.

71. The future subjunctive emerged from the Latin future perfect and was largely used to express a future contingency (a certain condition had to be met for another event to follow). It is typically used in legal documents as well as older literary texts. In Spanish, proverbs are often expressed in this mode—for example, "venga lo que viniere," "sea lo que fuere," and so on. Its use began to fall off markedly in the sixteenth century. A historical overview with bibliography can be found at http://descargas.cervantesvirtual.com/servlet/SirveObras/12159284227989301865402/019785.pdf?incr=1. I am grateful to Michael Armstrong-Roche for directing me to this information.

72. Cascardi, *Ideologies of History*, 21.

73. Drawing on the work of Emile Benveniste, Derrida reminds us that the term "*ipseity*" (self-sameness) is both a (presumed) quality of the subject and also of the concept of sovereignty. The non-contradiction of being one's self is related to autonomy and to the ability to act. Derrida links the term to notions of the *proper, property* and mastery:

> I thus wish to suggest the oneself [*soi-même*] the "self-same [*même*]" of the "self [*soi*]" (that is, the same *meisme*, which comes from *metipse*), as well as the power, potency, sovereignty, or possibility implied in every "I can," the *pse* of *ipse* (*ipissimus*) referring always, through a complicated set of relations, as Benveniste shows quite well, to possession, property, and power, to the authority of the lord or seignior, of the sovereign, and most often the host (*hospites*), the master of the house or the husband. So much so that *ipse* alone, like *autos* in Greek, which *ipse*

can actually translate (*ipse* is *autos*, and the Latin translation of "know thyself," of *gnothi seauton*, is in fact *cognosce te* ipsum), designates the oneself as master in the masculine: the father, husband, son or brother, the proprietor, owner, or seignior, indeed the sovereign. Before any sovereignty of the state, of the nation-state, of the monarch, or, in democracy, of the people, ipseity names a principle of legitimate sovereignty, the accredited or recognized supremacy of a power or a force, a *kratos* or a *cracy*. (*Rogues* 11–12)

Derrida's passage is as clear a philosophical expression of sovereignty as one can find. The sovereign is the *one*—the undivided, self-same one who "can." Sovereignty is an "I can" business and sovereigns are "can do" people—at least conceptually. What Derrida is showing, on the other hand, is that every "I can" is already divided. The "proper" divides and depends on what is not proper.

74. See the article version, "The Politics of Friendship," 642.

75. Derrida, *Politics of Friendship*, trans. George Collins (London: Verso, 2006), ix.

76. Ibid., 13.

77. Ibid., 14.

78. For an influential instance of this argument, see José Antonio Maravall, *Teatro y Literature en la Sociedad Barroca* (Barcelona: Crítica, 1990). More recently, David R. Castillo sees Laurencia's speech as a "reification of the masculinist ideals encoded in the call of honor." *(A) wry Views: Anamorphosis, Cervantes, and the Early Picaresque* (West Lafayette: Purdue University Press, 2001), 116.

79. For a clear and illuminating exposition of the political in Derrida, see Martin Hägglund, *Radical Atheism: Derrida and the Time of Life* (Stanford: Stanford University Press), 2008.

80. I am invoking methodologically different analyses by Julia Kristeva, *The Sense and Non-Sense of Revolt* (New York: Columbia University Press, 2001), and Antonio Negri, *Time for Revolution* (Continuum, 2005). Where Kristeva discusses revolution from the perspective of psychoanalytic theory, Negri provides a materialist critique in relation to theories of temporality. From the perspective of the present study, his discussion of spatial metaphors is particularly suggestive.

81. Line numbers refer to the McGrady edition (Barcelona: Crítica, 1993).

82. Derrida, "The Politics of Friendship," *Journal of Philosophy* 85, no. 11, November 1988, 642.

83. Derrida, *Politics of Friendship*, 15.

84. Ibid., 149.

85. Ibid., ix.

86. Ibid.

87. This section title is not only borrowed from Isaac Bashevis Singer's novel but, more specifically, from Gil Anidjar's discussion of the enemy in *The Jew, the Arab: A History of the Enemy* (Stanford: Stanford University Press, 2003).

88. Anselm Haverkamp, "The Enemy Has No Future," *Cardozo Law Review* 26 (2004–5).

89. See Carl Schmitt, *The Concept of the Political*, trans. and intro. George Schwab (Chicago: University of Chicago Press, 1996), 26.

90. Schmitt, *The Concept of the Political*, 27, my emphasis. The German reads, "Er ist eben der andere, der Fremde, und es genügt zu seinem Wesen, daß er in einem besonders intensiven Sinne existenziell etwas anderes und Fremdes ist, so daß im extremen Fall Konflikte mit ihm möglich sind . . ." (2002:27).

91. Ibid., 28–9.

92. *Futures Past: On the Semantics of Historical Time*, trans. Keith Tribe (New York: Columbia University Press, 2004).

93. Haverkamp, "The Enemy Has No Future," *Cardozo Law Review* 26, no. 6, (2005): 2553–62.

94. Schmitt, *Political Theology*, 45.

95. Haverkamp, "The Enemy," 2556.

96. Jacques Lezra describes "weak concepts" in terms of an "ungovernable semantic excess"—an ungovernability (I would add) that can be linked to the turning of tropes. See Lezra, *Wild Materialism*, 63ff.

97. Ibid., 27.

98. Or *attempted* rape. Again, Victor Dixon writes that "This late-minute revelation that Laurencia had not, as Lope may have meant us to surmise, been raped, is seen by some critics as utterly unrealistic, a sentimental sop to the popular taste of his time." Dixon argues that "on the contrary . . . this 'happy ending,' as well as poetically 'right,' is consistent with all that precedes it, and in particular with the characterisation of Laurencia as a woman of wit, resourcefulness and resolution, in all ways more than a match for the Commander." Dixon, Introduction to *Fuente Ovejuna*, trans. Victor Dixon (Warminster: Aris and Phillips, 1991), 22–3.

99. Dopico Black, *Perfect Wives*, 129.

100. See Flores, 70, and Dixon, 179.

101. See Peter Evans, "Civilisation and Its Discontents in *Fuenteovejuna*," in *Conflicts of Discourse: Spanish Literature in the Golden Age*, ed. Peter Evans (Manchester: Manchester University Press, 1990), 121.

102. Contra Arendt, the public space of the law court will become precisely the site of a friendship that breaks away from the play's previous *orders* of "love."

103. On "love" in the public sphere, see Hanna Arendt, *The Human Condition* (Chicago: University of Chicago Press, 1958), 51–2.

104. Legendre, *Law and the Unconscious* (New York: St. Martin's Press, 1997), xiii–xiv.

105. Ibid., xiii.

106. See Jacques Lacan, Séminaire 16, "D'un autre à l'Autre," sessions of March 12 and March 26, 1969, where he writes, "c'est en tant qu'il est ici une place que nous pouvons designer du terme conjoignant l'intime à la radicale extériorité, c'est en tant que l'object a est extime." *Le Séminaire de Jacques Lacan, Livre XVI, D'un Autre à l'autre 1968–1969*, ed. Jacques-Alain Miller (Paris: Seuil, 2006).

107. For a discussion, see Jacques-Alain Miller, "Extimité" in *Lacanian Theory of Discourse: Subject, Structure, and Society*, eds. Mark Bracher, et al. (New York: New York University Press, 1994).

108. For a lucid and rigorous discussion of the philosophical underpinnings of theories of subjection in Hegel, Nietzsche, Freud, Foucault, and Althusser, see Judith Butler, *The Psychic Life of Power: Theories in Subjection* (Stanford: Stanford University Press, 1997).

109. See Legendre, *Law and the Unconscious*, 39.

110. Ibid., 37.

111. Ibid.

112. For psychoanalysis, resistance is decisive. As Laplanche and Pontalis point out, "the forces to be seen at work in resistance and in repression were one and the same." *The Language of Psycho-Analysis*, trans. Donald Nicholson-Smith (New York: Norton, 1973), 395. Translated into the terms of psychoanalysis, the events of *Fuenteovejuna*—and, specifically, the villagers' "resistance" to political and sexual oppression—would draw its force from the same pool as the oppression itself. Resistance and repression, in this light, are the same.

113. For *Fuenteovejuna's* fascinating reception history, see López-Estrada, Kirschner, Parker, and Wheeler.

114. The Commander's intervention illustrates one of the central tenets of the performance of authority. As Agamben points out, the notion of authority itself, which comes from the Latin word *auctor*, "originally designates the person who intervenes in the case of a minor

(or the person who, for whatever reason, does not have the capacity to posit a legally valid act), in order to grant him the valid title that he requires." Agamben, *Remnants of Auschwitz*, trans. Daniel Heller-Roazen (Zone Books, 2002), 148. Eric Santner adds to this that "[w]hat Agamben leaves out of his discussion of the *auctor* are the ways in which his acts, which certify or validate, which grant life 'to what could not live alone' [Agamben, *Remnants*, 150], implant, as it were, a surplus life in the one thereby authorized." See Santner, *On the Psychotheology of Everyday Life* (Chicago: Chicago University Press, 2001), 27 n.3. My own discussion begins with, or returns to, this notion of "surplus," particularly as it emerges in the interplay of sovereignty's body, including its conceptual *implants* or transplants, and the resistances these provoke. Sovereign power is always, in some representational (not "logical") sense, "prosthetic power."

115. On love as "feudal loyalty" and "harmony" in the play overall, see Leo Spitzer, "A Central Theme and Its Structural Equivalent in Lope's *Fuenteovejuna*," in *Representative Essays*, ed. Alban K. Forcione, Herbert Lindenberger, and Madeline Sutherland (Stanford: Stanford University Press, 1988), 397–420; and Everett Hesse, "Los conceptos del amor in *Fuenteovejuna*," *Revista de Archivos, Bibliotecas y Museos* LXXV (1968–72). Derrida argues that there is an "essential link" between protection and obligation built into sovereignty:

> Between protecting and obliging to obey there is an essential link. "I protect you" means, for the state, I oblige you, you are my subject, I subject you [ . . . ] I oblige you by forcing you to obey [ . . . ] I oblige you to have gratitude, I oblige you to recognition [*reconnaissance:* recognition and gratitude]: to recognize the state and the law, and to recognize them for obliging you (in both senses of the word: constraining and doing a service by protecting, obliging to recognize). It is in this sense that Schmitt [ . . . ] will say that "*Protego ergo obligo* is the *cogito ergo sum* of the state." In the paragraph of the *Leviathan* that I am going to read, I emphasize the lexicon of *protection*, where this lexicon and its logic explain the paradox of the mortal immortality of sovereignty. Sovereignty—the soul, and therefore the life of the state, the artificial respiration of the state—is posited, instituted, promised, contracted, *artificially, as immortal* only because it is *naturally mortal*. It is prosthetic and artificial technique that immortalizes it or in any case guarantees it an indefinite survival.
>
> *The Beast and the Sovereign*, trans. Geoffrey Bennington (Chicago: University of Chicago Press, 2009), 43.

116. Angel Flores, trans., *Fuente Ovejuna* in *Great Spanish Plays in English Translation* (New York: Dover Publications, 1962).

117. Bodin, 74. Later, Hegel will argue that

> The right to pardon criminals arises from the sovereignty of the monarch, since it is this alone which is empowered to actualize mind's power of making undone what has been done and wiping out a crime by forgiving and forgetting it. The right of pardon is one of the highest recognitions of the majesty of mind. Moreover it is one of those cases where a category which belongs to a higher sphere is applied to or reflected in the sphere below.
>
> *Philosophy of Right*, trans. Knox, 186.

118. Loraux, *Mothers in Mourning with the Essay of Amnesty and Its Opposite*, trans. Corinne Pache (Ithaca: Cornell University Press, 1998), 84.

119. See Derrida, "To Forgive: The Unforgivable and the Imprescriptible." *Questioning God*, ed. John D. Caputo, Mark Dooley, and Michael J. Scanlon (Bloomington: Indiana University Press, 2001), 21–51. The link between the pardon and time is thus crucial. The problem also has to do with divisions. As Peter Krapp writes,

> One obvious problem with the institutionalization of memory and forgetting and with the institutionalization of forgiveness in particular, is that it seems to undermine and undo what Derrida calls the "solitude of two, in the sense of forgiveness," which "would seem to deprive any forgiveness of sense or authenticity that was asked for collectively." "Making a public spectacle of it," would seem to pre-empt the possibility of this scene being sincere. Instead, it becomes a display, it appears as a mere immodesty, it is taken for a distraction.
>
> Peter Krapp, "Between Forgiveness and Forgetting," *Derrida and Legal Philosophy*, ed. Peter Gooodrich, Florian Hofmann, et al (New York: Palgrave, 2008), 167.

120. On early modern "theaters of pardon," see Bernadette Meyler, *Theaters of Pardoning: Sovereignty and Judgment from Shakespeare to Kant* (unpublished manuscript).

121. Among the meanings included in the transitive and pronominal forms of "valer" (with preposition de), from the Latin, *valēre*, are "to shelter," "to protect" (amparar, proteger) and in a more juridical sense "to resort to a favor or intervention of someone else for a legal matter or request" [*recurrir al favor o interposición de otro para un intento*]. Diccio-

*nario de la Lengua Española*. Vigésima segunda edición. http://buscon.rae.es/drael/?type=3&val=a&val_aux=&origen=REDRAE.

122. Marin writes, "A force is force only through annihilation, and in this sense all force is, in its very essence, absolute, since it is such only to annihilate all *other* forces, to be without exterior and incomparable." See *Portrait of the King*, trans. Martha M. Houle (Minneapolis: University of Minnesota Press, 1981), 7.

123. Ibid., 290. My emphasis.

124. What is the relationship between example and exception here? While Agamben himself does not refer to theater in his analysis of the relation between example and exception, the stage, I believe, is a medium that effectively marks the paradoxical relation of (non) belonging he is trying to elucidate. For Agamben, the example and the exception are not antithetical terms. Drawing on set theory, Agamben writes in the *Homo Sacer* that

> The example shows its belonging to a class. But for this very reason the example steps out of its class. It does this the very moment it exhibits its class. The example is thus excluded from the normal case not because it does not belong to it but, on the contrary, because it exhibits its own belonging to it. The example is truly a paradigm, in the etymological sense: it is what is "shown beside" and a class can contain everything except its own paradigm. (*Homo Sacer* 22)

What makes it both a representative of the class and also *excluded* from that class is its performance of "stepping out" of and exhibiting its paradoxical non-belonging. The exception is different: "The exception is included in the normal case precisely because it does not belong to it . . . Non-belonging can be shown only at the center of the class, by an exception" (*Homo Sacer* 22). Agamben's terms present us not only with a paradox but also a conceptual and representational crux: where the example is excluded, the exception is included in the set: "Exception and example are correlative concepts that are ultimately indistinguishable and that come into play every time the very sense of the belonging and commonality of individuals is to be defined" (*Homo Sacer* 22). This "com[ing] into play" both unites and distinguishes exception and example. Moving from example to exception, Agamben arrives, finally, at the merger of the two in his definition of a *paradigm*—a "showing beside." Read in Agamben's terms, *Fuenteovejuna* is exemplary and paradigmatic at once. It is both a "state-of-exception" play, and also posited as "exemplary" of different ideals, including revolutionary courage, natural virtue, and the benefits of divinely sanctioned monarchy.

I see the play, above all, as an example of art's resistance to political appropriation.

125. Cascardi is referring to Michel Foucault's phrase "the fascism in us all, in our heads and in our everyday behavior, the fascism that causes us to love power, to desire the very thing that dominates and exploits us" in his Preface to Gilles Deleuze and Felix Guattari's *Anti-Oedipus: Capitalism and Schizophrenia* (University of Minnesota Press, 1985), xi–xiv. *Ideologies of History in the Spanish Golden Age* (University Park: Pennsylvania State University Press, 1997), 46.

126. Jacques Derrida has written a book length study of the term. *Aporias*, trans. Thomas Dutoit (Stanford: Stanford University Press, 1993).

127. *Law and the Unconscious* (New York: St. Martin's Press, 1997), xiii–xiv. Derrida's most sustained discussions of autoimmunity appear in "Faith and Knowledge," in *Acts of Religion*, ed. and intro. Gil Anidjar (New York: Routledge, 2002), 80 n.27; Giovanna Borradori, *Philosophy in a Time of Terror* (Chicago: University of Chicago Press, 2003). For helpful discussions, see Michael Naas, *Derrida from Now On* (New York: Fordham University Press, 2008), esp. 124ff.; and Martin Hägglund, *Radical Atheism*.

On the history of legal immunity in the European Middle Ages, see Barbara H. Rosenwein, *Negotiating Space: Power, Restraint, and Privileges of Immunity in Early Medieval Europe* (Ithaca: Cornell University Press, 1999).

128. The question of whether a political community transfers or merely delegates power to the ruler lies at the heart of many political debates of the sixteenth and seventeenth centuries. For Counter-Reformation theorists, such as Suárez, it was crucial to refute the popular claim, upon which much popular sovereignty thinking rests, that the political community merely *delegates* civil power to the ruler—which it can subsequently revoke. For Suárez, the argument "that the kingdom may, if it shall so choose, depose or change its king . . . is *altogether false*" (Williams 386, my emphasis). While this might seem confusing given the fact that Suárez also justifies tyrannicide, as we have seen, the difference, as is often the case with scholastic thought, has to do with distinctions. The problem of tyrannicide [or resistance] is a special case, and Suárez arrives at his conclusion only after an extended consideration of conditions and requirements and movement through an array of arguments and opinions, which he reviews in his *Defense of the Faith*. The question of delegation versus transfer is different.

129. For Suárez, "such power, in the nature of things, resides immediately in the community; and therefore, in order that it may justly come to reside in a given individual, as in a sovereign prince, it must necessarily be bestowed upon him by the consent of the community." See *A Treatise on Laws and God the Lawgiver: Selections from Three Works*, ed., James Brown Scott, trans., Gwladys L. Williams, Ammi Brown, and John Waldron (Oxford: Clarendon Press, 1944), 384.

For different ways of understanding this "alienation," see Negri and Hardt, *Labor of Dionysus: A Critique of the State Form*, ed. Buckley, Massumi, Hardt (Minneapolis: University of Minnesota Press, 1994).

130. Running through the work of all of the "theorists" I have been discussing—from Suárez through Marin—is the problem of an "empty place." For Benjamin, the fall into spatialization staged by the baroque plays of mourning represents the mechanized time of modernity, which he calls an "empty form," which remains unfulfilled (as opposed to "Messianic time," which will, someday, be fulfilled). For Agamben, the space that his theory of sovereignty opens up between the exception and the norm is (quoting Schmitt), a "juridically empty space" (*HS* 36–8). For Marin, following Pascal, ". . . the reflection of presence always accuses more intensely, in the subject of representation that is its effect, the desire for the absolute of being a lack to fill, of being that *empty place* Pascal speaks of precisely with respect to the king, which is satisfaction always deferred" (*Portrait* 8). For Schmitt himself, on the other hand, as Friedrich Balke has pointed out, sovereignty is a "borderline concept" (*PT* 5). What this means, specifically, is that it has neither a first (natural), nor a second (political) body. Rather, the concept presents us (again) with an "empty space." Friedrich Balke, "'The War Has Not Ended': Thomas Hobbes, Carl Schmitt, and the Paradoxes of Countersovereignty." *Crediting God: Sovereignty and Religion in the Age of Global Capitalism*, ed. Miguel Vatter (New York: Fordham University Press, 2011), 179–89. All of these theorists (and one could add to the list Claude Lefort, Ernesto Laclau, Jean-Luc Nancy, and others) share a notion of sovereignty as fundamentally either itself or emerging out of an *emptiness*, a "nowhere," a nothing. (In Derrida's article on Marin, another name for this *empty space* is "death.") The danger of sovereignty's empty place, as Suárez understood and tried to avoid, has to do with metaphor. Suárez's ontology strives to reign in the wildness that metaphorical readings can lead to. He goes to great pains in the *Metaphysical Disputations* to describe the concept of being in a "non-metaphorical" way.

131. The Italian philosopher Gianni Vattimo has coined the term "weak thought" (*il pensiero debole*) to refer to a thinking of metaphysics

and religion that does not focus on God's power but rather his love. "Weak thought" Vattimo writes, "is thus certainly a metaphor and, to some extent a paradox . . . It points out a path, it indicates a direction of the route; it is a way that forks from the no matter how masked hegemonic rationality [*ragione-dominio*] from which, nevertheless, we all know a definitive farewell is impossible." Gianni Vattimo and Pier Aldo Rovatti, Foreword, *Il pensiero debole*. For a discussion, see Giovanna Borradori, "'Weak Thought' and Postmodernism: The Italian Departure from Deconstruction," *Social Text* 18 (Winter 1987–88): 39–49.

132. See "Autoimmunity: Real and Symbolic Suicides: A Dialogue with Jacques Derrida," in *Philosophy in a Time of Terror*, ed. Giovanna Borradori (Chicago: University of Chicago Press, 2003), 120. On "democracy to come," also see Derrida, *The Politics of Friendship*, 306:

> For democracy remains to come; this is its essence in so far as it remains: not only will it remain indefinitely perfectible, hence always insufficient and future, but, belonging to the time of the promise, it will always remain, in each of its future times, to come: even when there is democracy, it never exists, it is never present, it remains the theme of a non-presentable concept.

133. Reijo Wilenius's description of the Jesuits as the "radical left" of the period.

134. As critics have noted, the honor plays are almost always projected back in time, invoking mythic origins. They are *not* mirrors of contemporary moments—at least not directly. I am grateful to Michael Armstrong-Roche for pointing this out to me, and for discussions with him about the play, from which I have greatly profited.

135. Lorca's productions stressed the democratic and anti-monarchical aspects of the play, cutting out the appearance of the Catholic Kings in the final scene altogether. The anti-monarchical interpretation is taken up by Marxists in the sixties and seventies. See Jason T. Parker, "Recruiting the Literary Tradition: Lope de Vega's *Fuenteovejuna* as Cultural Weapon during the Spanish Civil War," *Bulletin of the Comediantes* 66, no. 1 (2010). I am grateful to Michael Armstrong-Roche for posing this question regarding *Fuenteovejuna*'s "futures" to me at a meeting of the *Theater Without Borders* Comparative Renaissance Drama workshop in Madrid, May 2011.

136. Wheeler, 126.

137. Wheeler notes that "Of all the Golden Age dramatists treated during the almost three years of the Seville *ABC*, Lope de Vega attracted

the most attention. The Falangists found in him their concept of the state, nation, and religion, and his *Fuenteovejuna* came to be a symbol of their ideology" (119). For the reception of the play, in addition to Wheeler and Parker, see Kirschner, López Estrada, Duncan, Thacker (*Companion*), Fiore (*Hispanic Essays in Honor of Frank P. Casa*), and Stanley Appelbaum, who points out that the Bolshoi Ballet staged a revolutionary production of "Laurencia" in 1939. For a representative reading that argues that the play is "certainly not democratic," see Javier Herrero, "The New Monarchy: A Structural Reinterpretation of *Fuenteovejuna*," *Revista Hispánica Moderna* 36.4 (1970–71): 174. Herrero is responding to tradition marked in the nineteenth century by Menéndez y Pelayo's argument that it is the "*demos*" who are the play's true protagonist and that "No hay obra más democrática en el Teatro castellano." [*There is no more democratic work in the Castilian theater.*]

138. Agamben, *Homo Sacer*, 11.

139. The name "*Fuente Ovejuna*" is the product of a popular etymology: "fuente de las ovejas" ("fountain of the sheep"). More acceptable, however, is the etymology: "Fuente" Abejuna" for being the place where there was (and there still is) an abundant production of honey. See Rinaldo Froldi, *Fuente Ovejuna* (Madrid: Espasa Calpe, S.A. 1998), 111. Although they ultimately reject the preference for "Fuente *abejuna*," Moros and Cabrera nevertheless write that the invitation to think of the village in relation to the classical topos of the Roman *Mellaria* "resultaría, en cierto modo, defendible, el nombre de *Fuente-abejuna*, el cual podía parecer más elegante desde el punto de vista semántico, sin olvidar que al hacerlo así se añadía a la villa el prestigio que tradicionalmente suele asociarse a toda vinculación con lo clásico" (Andrés-Moros and Emilio Cabrera, *Fuenteovejuna: La Violencia Antiseñorial en el Siglo XV* [Barcelona: Editorial Crítica, 1991], 45).

140. Of the eventual replacement of the military orders by the absolutist power of the Crown, J. H. Elliott writes that "[w]hen the Grand Masterships of Calatrava and Alacántara fell vacant in 1487 and 1494 respectively, they duly went to Ferdinand; and a papal bull of 1523 definitively incorporated all three Orders into the Crown." As Elliott points out, "[t]here is still no study of the resources of the Military Orders and of their role in the history of sixteenth- and seventeenth-century Spain, but it would be hard to overestimate the importance of their contribution to the reassertion of royal power." Their financial value to the Crown is obvious enough. *Imperial Spain 1469–1716* (Harmondsworth: Penguin, 1990), 89.

## 4. TRANSFORMATION: THE BODY MOVES OUT IN *LIFE IS A DREAM*

1. The phrase is William Egginton's. *The Theater of Truth: The Ideology of (Neo) Baroque Aesthetics* (Stanford: Stanford University Press, 2010), 85. Regarding the play's date, Ciriaco Morón (following Albert Sloman) proposes 1635 for its composition and 1636 for its publication. Fausta Antonucci, on the other hand, suggests an earlier composition date of 1629. Morón, Introduction to *La vida es sueño* (Madrid: Cátedra, 1995), 68. Antonucci, *La vida es sueño* (Barcelona: Crítica, 2008), 11. Unless otherwise indicated, the line numbers in the text refer to Morón's (Cátedra) edition. I have consulted English translations by Gregary J. Racz, *Life Is a Dream* (New York: Penguin Books, 2007); Stanley Appelbaum, *Life Is a Dream: A Dual Language Book* (Minneola: Dover Publications, 2002); Michael Kidd, *Life's a Dream: A Prose Translation* (Boulder: University of Colorado Press, 2004); and Edwin Honig, *Life Is a Dream* (New York: Hill and Wang, 1970).
2. Courtine, Jean-Francois, "Le project suarézien de la métaphysique," *Archives de Philosophie* 42 (1979): 236. On the view of Calderón as a conservative playwright, see Duncan Wheeler, "The Performance History of Golden-Age Drama in Spain (1939–2006)," *Bulletin of the Comediantes* 60, no. 2 (2008): 119–55.
3. Egginton, *Theater of Truth*, 85.
4. On Calderón's life, see Don W. Cruickshank, *Don Pedro Calderón* (Cambridge: Cambridge University Press, 2009).
5. Jonathan Thacker, *A Companion to Golden Age Theatre* (Woodbridge: Tamesis, 2010), 112–15.
6. Ibid., 114.
7. Ibid., 115.
8. Antonio Feros, "'Sacred and Terrifying Gazes': Languages and Images of Power in Early Modern Spain," *The Cambridge Companion to Velázquez*, ed. Suzanne L. Stratton-Pruitt (Cambridge: Cambridge University Press, 2002), 71.
9. Ibid., 73.
10. Ibid.
11. Lope de Vega, cited in Feros, "'Sacred and Terrifying Gazes,'" 74.
12. I am alluding to Mitchell Greenberg's felicitous title, "baroque bodies," to refer to a similar question within the context of French absolutism. Greenberg, *Baroque Bodies: Psychoanalysis and the Culture of French Absolutism* (Ithaca: Cornell University Press, 2001). Greenberg's psychoanalytic readings of seventeenth-century French absolutism

informs much of my thinking about the theatrically productive nature of the fantasy of absolute power. It is "capable of generating a proliferation of both conscious and unconscious associations by which and through which our culture constantly reinvents itself" (p. 1). Greenberg's understanding of the "protean" nature of absolutism's imaginary body, which includes a sense of plurality and emptiness at once, corresponds to my view of sovereignty as a "body" that is both determining and empty.

13. All of these theorists circumscribe the king's power within the jurisdictional and temporal limits of the civil sphere. Key representatives of the School of Salamanca include Francisco de Vitoria (1483–1546); Domingo de Soto (1494–1560); the Jesuits Luis de Molina (1535–1600) and Juan de Mariana (1536–1624); and the writer most addressed here, in the polemic with England during the Oath of Allegiance controversy, Francisco Suárez himself (1548–1617). On the "Catholic theory of civil society," see J. P. Sommerville, "From Suárez to Filmer: A Reappraisal," *The Historical Journal* 25, no. 3 (1982): 525.

14. Here, I draw on Walter Benjamin's understanding of the difference between "mechanical time" and "historical time," which can also mean "biblical" or "religious" time. For a discussion, see Beatrice Hanssen, *Walter Benjamin's Other History: Of Stones, Animals, Human Beings, and Angels* (Berkeley: University of California Press, 2000), 58ff.

15. Walter Benjamin, *The Origin of German Tragic Drama*, trans. John Osborne (London: Verso, 1994), 62, my emphasis. Subsequent references to this text will appear as *OGTD*.

16. Ibid., 81.

17. Jane Newman, *Benjamin's Library: Modernity, Nation, and the Baroque* (Ithaca: Cornell University Press, 2011), xiii.

18. *The Correspondence of Walter Benjamin*, ed. Gershom Scholem and Theodor W. Adorno, trans. Manfred R. Jacobson and Evelyn M. Jacobson (Chicago: University of Chicago Press, 1994), 286.

19. Benjamin, *OGTD*, 81.

20. Regarding Calderón's decision to set a play about a potential tyrannicide in "Poland," Henry W. Sullivan explains that Calderón's choice was potentially dangerous, as ". . . the example of Poland came too close to the mark for comfort. This was the phase of the Counter-Reformation (1635) when the Jesuits were successfully drawing the Polish nation away from their sixteenth-century experiment with Protestantism and back to the Catholic fold. The last thing Calderón would have wished to suggest was the political murder of the king's 'other Body' as the Catholic solution to a constitutional dilemma." Henry W. Sullivan, "The Political Murder of the King's Other Body: 1562–1649," in *Conflicts*

*of Discourse: Spanish Literature in the Golden Age*, ed. Peter W. Evans (Manchester: Manchester University Press, 1990), 142–3.

21. Rosaura's warrior guise reminds us of the figure of the Amazon, introduced but abandoned by Lope de Vega's Laurencia in *Fuenteovejuna*. More pointedly, with regard to sovereignty, it offers a counter-image to the official court portraits of Philip IV painted by Velázquez, "that so imposingly represent his sovereign body controlling, dominating, and ordering the chaos of the political and instinctual worlds with royal skill, courage, power, and charisma." Alban Forcione, *Majesty and Humanity: Kings and Their Doubles in the Political Drama of the Spanish Golden Age* (New Haven: Yale University Press, 2009), 2. This counter-image is made more complex by the fact that (unlike the transvestite early modern English theater) in Spain, the "role would have been played by a professional female actress." For a discussion, see Ivan Cañadas, *Public Theater in Golden Age Madrid and Tudor-Stuart London: Class, Gender and Festive Community* (Aldershot: Ashgate, 2005), 40–75.

22. Recall that in the earlier play, the Bishop of Carlisle warns the English of the consequences to the realm if they take Bolingbroke as their king:

> And if you crown him, let me prophesy—
> The blood of English shall manure the ground,
> And future ages groan for this foul act,
> Peace shall go sleep with Turks and infidels,
> And, in this seat of peace, tumultuous wars
> Shall kin with kin, and kind with kind, confound.
> (*Richard II*, 4.1.136–41)

*Life Is a Dream* returns us, in a sense, to Carlisle's vision, which has now become the play's "reality." As it is also in *Hamlet* (1.2.64), the confounding of "kin" with "kind" is one of *Life Is a Dream*'s recurring preoccupations, as is the imminent danger of its principal cause: civil war.

23. Yet another "rupture" one could identify in the opening of *Life Is a Dream* is that between Calderón himself and Lope, who in his *Arte nuevo*, as Jonathan Thacker points out, "had explicitly listed the term 'hipogrifo' . . . as an offensive 'vocablo exquisito' to be avoided by dramatic poets." Thacker, *A Companion to Golden Age Theatre* (Woodbridge: Tamesis, 2010), 113.

24. Morón, Introduction, *La vida es sueño*, 23.

25. On Suárez's theory of non-contradiction, see *On Beings of Reason (De Entibus Rationis) Metaphysical Disputation LIV*, trans. and intro. John P. Doyle (Milwaukee: Marquette University Press, 1995), 38–43.

26. Reijo Wilenius, *The Social and Political Theory of Francisco Suárez* (Helsinki: Acta Philosophica Fennica, 1963), 113.

27. Again, the phrase is Mitchell Greenberg's. See *Baroque Bodies: Psychoanalysis and the Culture of French Absolutism* (Ithaca: Cornell University Press, 2001).

28. Suárez, *On Laws, Selections from Three Works*, ed. James Brown Scott, trans. Gwladys L. Williams, Ammi Brown, and John Waldron (Oxford: Clarendon Press, 1944), 13.

29. Williams, 14. On Catholic theories of sovereignty theory, see J. P. Sommerville, *Royalists and Patriots: Politics and Ideology in England 1603–1640*, 2nd edition (New York: Addison Wesley Longman, 1999). See also James Brown Scott, *The Catholic Conception of International Law* (Washington: Georgetown University Press, 1934).

30. The relation of power (what Benjamin refers to as "*Gewalt*") to representation is one of the central problems of the baroque. A wealth of recent studies on the baroque as a critical problem marks a veritable "baroque turn." Representative examples include Lois Parkinson Zamora's *The Inordinate Eye: New World Baroque and Latin American Fiction* (Chicago: University of Chicago Press, 2006); and *Baroque New Worlds: Representation, Transculturation, Counterconquest*, ed. Lois Parkinson Zamora and Monika Kaup (Durham: Duke University Press, 2010). For an analysis of the baroque in relation to digital media, see Tim Murray, *Digital Perspective: New Media Art and Cinematic Folds* (Minneapolis: University of Minnesota Press, 2008). See also the essays compiled by José Ramón Jouve Martín and Renée Soulodre-LaFrance in a special issue of the *Revista Canadiense de Estudios Hispánicos* 33, no. 1 (Autumn 2008) on "La Constitución del Barroco Hispánicao Problemas y Acercamientos," as well as the essays on "The Neobaroque and the Americas" in *PMLA* 124, no. 1 (January 2009): 127–88. All of these follow in the wake of such seminal works as Heinrich Wölfflin's, *Renaissance and Baroque*, trans. Kathrin Simon (Ithaca: Cornell University Press, 1992); Jose Antonio Maravall's *Culture of the Baroque: Analysis of a Historical Structure*; Gilles Deleuze's *The Fold: Leibniz and the Baroque*, trans. Tom Conley (Minneapolis: University of Minnesota Press, 1993); and Roberto González Echevarría's *Celestina's Brood: Continuities of the Baroque in Spanish and Latin American Literature* (Durham: Duke University Press, 1993). For an excellent overview of influential theoretical statements on the baroque, see Gregg Lambert, *The Return of the Baroque in Modern Culture* (London: Continuum, 2006). Much of this work remains indebted to Benjamin's understanding of the baroque as a philosophical and theo-political problem.

31. Quoted in Agamben, *Homo Sacer: Sovereign Power and Bare Life*, trans. Daniel Heller-Roazen (Stanford: Stanford University Press, 1998), 31.

32. Ibid., 31.

33. Ibid., 36–7.

34. Ibid., 37.

35. Ibid., 38.

36. Niccolò Machiavelli, *The Prince*, trans. George Bull (Harmondsworth: Penguin, 1981), 130–1. *Il principe* (Milan: Mondadori, 1994), 111.

37. Recall that, as we saw in Chapter 1 in the *Trauerspiel* book, Benjamin quotes Schmitt's theory that "sovereign is he who *decides* on the exception," even as his own view is that it is the task of the baroque sovereign to "avert" this. *OGTD*, 65. See Samuel Weber's discussion, "Taking Exception to Decision: Walter Benjamin and Carl Schmitt," in *Benjamin's -abilities* (Cambridge: Harvard University Press, 2008), 176–94.

38. Lezra, *Wild Materialism*, 93.

39. Lezra shows how Agamben "inherits [the topological zone of indistinction] from the classic problem of future contingents." *Wild Materialism*, 91.

40. Marcel Gauchet, *The Disenchantment of the World: A Political History of Religion*, trans. Oscar Burge (Princeton: Princeton University Press, 1999), 131.

41. Gauchet, *Disenchantment*, 215.

42. Benjamin, *OGTD*, 79.

43. To return to Chapter 1 and the problems that opened this study, one can understand this prospective mode as directly related to the historical framework created by the structure of the *analogia entis*. See William R. LaFleur, "Body," in *Critical Terms for Religious Studies*, ed. Mark C. Taylor (Chicago: University of Chicago Press, 1998).

44. For an excellent discussion of the image in relation to historical evidence in the seventeenth century, see Peter Burke, "Images as Evidence in Seventeenth-Century Europe," *Journal of the History of Ideas* 64, no. 2 (April 2003): 273–96. On the problem of images in relation to legal theory and history, see Costas Douzinas and Lynda Nead, *Law and the Image: The Authority of Art and the Aesthetics of Law* (Chicago: University of Chicago Press, 1999). On the image in relation to the political, theological, and art historical developments of the Reformation, see Joseph Leo Koerner, *The Reformation of the Image* (Chicago: University of Chicago Press, 2008). For an excellent overview of the pre-history of the Reformation debates, see Jaroslav Pelikan, *Imago Dei:*

*The Byzantine apologia for Icons* (Princeton: Princeton University Press, 2011). Finally, for a philosophical discussion of the movement of thinking about the image from the Renaissance through Kant and Heidegger, see Jean-Luc Nancy, "Masked Image," in *The Ground of the Image*, trans. Jeff Fort (New York: Fordham University Press, 2005), 80–99.

45. Peter Goodrich, "The Iconography of Nothing: Blank Spaces and the Representation of Law in *Edward VI and the Pope*," *Law and the Image: The Authority of Art and the Aesthetics of Law*, ed. Costas Douzinas and Lynda Nead (Chicago: University of Chicago Press, 1999), 105.

46. Ibid., 100.

47. James South, "Francisco Suárez on Imagination," *Vivarium* 39, no. 1, p. 119.

48. Ibid., 156.

49. Ibid., 120.

50. Ibid., 123.

51. Ibid.

52. Ibid., 156.

53. Ibid.

54. Roberto González Echevarría, *Celestina's Brood: Continuities of the Baroque in Spanish and Latin American Literatures* (Durham: Duke University Press, 1993), 81.

55. Ibid., 83.

56. Morón, "Introduction," 23.

57. Ibid.

58. Georgina Dopico, "*Lengua e Imperio*: Sueños de la Nación en los *Tesoros* de Covarrubias," in *Suplemento al Tesoro de la Lengua Española Castellana*, eds. Georgina Dopico and Jacques Lezra (Madrid: Polifemo, 2001), CCXLVII [p. 247].

59. See especially Agamben's chapter, "The Ambivalence of the Sacred," in *Homo Sacer*, 75–80. According to Eva Geulen, these "few pages in *Homo Sacer* amount to one of Agamben's most convincing achievements." For Geulen, "[t]he significance of [Agamben's] courageous exposure of ambivalence as a 'scientific mythologeme' (75) cannot be overestimated for any attempt to understand the relationship of religion and law in modernity." Eva Geulen, "The Function of Ambivalence in Agamben's Reontologization of Politics," trans. Roland Végso, in *A Leftist Ontology: Beyond Relativism and Identity Politics*, ed. Carsten Strathausen (Minneapolis: University of Minnesota Press, 2009), 27.

60. For a discussion of the complex topology of Agamben's Möbius strip, see Jacques Lezra, *Wild Materialism: The Ethic of Terror and the Modern Republic* (New York: Fordham University Press, 2010), 92–7.

61. Agamben, *Homo Sacer*, 38.

62. Schmitt's "law void" (qtd. in *Homo Sacer*, 38), Ernesto Laclau's "empty signifier" (*Emancipation(s)* 36ff), Louis Marin's "empty place" of the king (*Portrait* 8), and Jean-Luc Nancy's "nothingness" (*The Creation of the World or Globalization* 103) all point to the recurring paradox of sovereignty: that it is both everything and nothing, supreme power and absolute cipher at once.

63. See John Doyle, "Another God, Chimerae, Goat-Stags, and Man-Lions: A Seventeenth-Century Debate about Impossible Objects," *The Review of Metaphysics* 48, no. 4 (June 1995): 772.

64. Francisco Suárez, *On Beings of Reason (De Entibus Rationis), Metaphysical Disputation LIV*, trans. John P. Doyle (Milwaukee: Marquette University Press, 1995), 63.

65. Agamben, *Homo Sacer*, 64.

66. Suárez, *On Beings of Reason*, trans. Doyle, 64.

67. Francis Bacon, *The Advancement of Learning, Book One* in *Francis Bacon: A Critical Edition of The Major Works*, ed. Brian Vickers (Oxford: Oxford University Press, 1996), 141.

68. See Francis Bacon, *The Advancement of Learning, Book Two*, in *Francis Bacon: A Critical Edition of The Major Works*, ed. Brian Vickers (Oxford: Oxford University Press, 1996), 217.

69. Antonio Feros, "'Sacred and Terrifying Gazes': Languages and Images of Power in Early Modern Spain," *The Cambridge Companion to Velázquez*, ed. Suzanne L. Stratton-Pruitt (Cambridge: Cambridge University Press, 2002), 72–3.

70. On this withdrawal as well as the complex theoretical movement of the body's fading in and out of sacredness, see, in addition to Feros, Alban Forcione, *Majesty and Humanity: Kings and Their Doubles in the Political Drama of the Spanish Golden Age* (New Haven: Yale University Press, 2009).

71. *Richard II* (5.5.41–54), ed. Peter Ure (London: Thomson Learning, 2001), 171–2. (First published 1956 by Methuen & Co.)

72. *Life Is a Dream*, trans. and introduction Gregory J. Racz (New York: Penguin Books, 2007), 22.

73. See Negri's essay on Machiavelli in "Virtue and Fortune: the Machiavellian Paradigm," in *Insurgencies: Constituent Power and the Modern State* (Minneapolis: University of Minnesota Press, 1999), 37–81.

74. Stanley Appelbaum, *Life Is a Dream / La vida es sueño: A Dual-Language Book* (Minneola: Dover Publications, 2002), 38–9.

75. Benjamin, *OGTD*, 69–74, 85, and 95–100. For a discussion of Benjamin's theory of the splitting of the sovereign in relation to

modernity and theories of subjectivity, see Samuel Weber, "Taking Exception," in *Benjamin's -abilities*, 176–94. Rainer Nägele summarizes the challenges Benjamin's book poses to at least one familiar Enlightenment narrative, the "story of modern self-consciousness":

> The Baroque as a cultural and stylistic phenomenon, the *Trauerspiel* as its theatrical form, and the drama of fate as a subgenre, which found its most sublime expression in Calderón's plays, are all marked by the traces of an otherness that radically resists integration in the (hi-)story of individuation, autonomy, and secularization.
>
> *Theater, Theory, Speculation: Walter Benjamin and the Scenes of Modernity* (Baltimore: Johns Hopkins Press, 1991), 176–7.

76. Deleuze, *The Fold*, 3.
77. Ibid., 3.
78. Deleuze writes that "A labyrinth is said, etymologically, to be multiple because it contains many folds. A labyrinth corresponds exactly to each level: the continuous labyrinth in matter and its parts, the labyrinth of freedom in the soul and its predicates." *The Fold*, 3.
79. Ibid., 3.
80. Regarding the "doubtful light" of Segismundo's crypt, along with the general problem of seeing in play, I would here complicate Echevarría's discussion of "species" as image by returning to Suárez. Where Echeverría invokes the Scholastic background of discussion of the image, by referring to the crucial role Thomistic thought plays in its conceptualization, his argument can now be extended by turning toward the highly influential ways Suárez modifies Aquinas's theory. As South has shown, Suárez reduces this gap between human and animal cognition preparing the way for certain theoretical work on the question of the animal.
81. "Morbidly thirsty" is Stanley Appelbaum's translation.
82. *Faerie Queene*, Book II, canto xiii, line 69, in *Edmund Spenser's Poetry*, 2nd edition, ed. Hugh Maclean (New York: Norton, 1982), 185–95.
83. See Augustine, *On Christian Doctrine*, III.5: "There is a miserable servitude of the spirit in this habit of taking signs for things, so that one is not able to raise the eye of the mind above things that are corporal and created to drink in eternal light." *On Christian Doctrine*, trans. D. W. Robertson, Jr. (Upper Saddle River, N.J.: Prentice-Hall, 1958), 84.
84. Leo Spitzer, "A Central Theme and Its Structural Equivalent in Lope's *Fuenteovejuna*," in *Representative Essays*, edited by Alban K.

Forcione, Herbert Lindenberger, and Madeline Sutherland (Stanford: Stanford University Press, 1988), 397–420.

85. In his edition of the play, Ciriaco Morón argues that, "It is easy to perceive in the encounter between Rosaura and Segismundo a Platonic view of the woman. Above all, Rosaura has the civilizing power of beauty." ("Por eso es fácil percibir en el encuentro de Rosaura y Segismundo la visión platónica de la mujer. Rosaura tiene, sobre todo, el poder civilizador de la belleza.") See Pedro Calderón de la Barca, *La vida es sueño*, ed. Ciriaco Morón (Madrid: Catedra, S.A., 1995), 19.

86. See "Calderón's *La vida es sueño:* Mixed-(Up) Monsters," in Roberto González Echevarría, *Celestina's Brood*, 86–7.

87. Leonard Barkan has discussed their interdependence in the Renaissance in terms of the relationship between theories of painting and poetry. See *Mute Poetry Speaking Pictures* (Princeton: Princeton University Press, 2013).

88. Ciriaco Morón notes that the two terms of sovereign prerogative, mercy and justice, are frequently used in Cervantes, Lope, and Calderón: "Clemency (or piety in this sense) is an adornment of justice. In their administration of justice, kings had to distinguish between clemency and piety more than by force." ["La clemencia (o piedad en ese sentido) era un adorno de la justicia. En la administración de la justicia los reyes debían distinguirse por la clemencia / piedad, más que por el rigor."] See Morón, *LVS*, 88.

89. "Contrahecho" can mean both something imitated (from "contrahacer," "to imitate some thing"), and something deformed, that has a (particularly bodily) deformity or "a body that is twisted or hunchbacked" ("Que tiene torcido o corcovado el cuerpo"). *Diccionario de la Lengua Española, Volume I* (Madrid: Espasa Calpe, 1992), 557. Covarrubias's entry reads "Contrahazer. Imitar alguna cosa de lo natural o artifical" (*to imitate some thing . . .* ). Sebastián de Covarrubias Horozco, *Tesoro de la Lengua Castellana o Española*, ed. Ignacio Arellano and Rafael Zafra (Madrid: Iberoamericana, 2006), 601.

90. Morón, Introduction, *La vida es sueño*, 24.

91. Juan de Mariana, *Del rey y la institución real*, libro II, cap 14, quoted in Morón, *LVS*, 25.

92. Antonio Regalado, *Calderón: Los Orígenes de la modernidad en la España del Siglo de Oro* (Barcelona: Ediciones Destino, S.A., 1995), II, 54.

93. Diego Saavedra Fajardo, *Empresas Políticas*, ed. Sagrario López Poza (Madrid: Ediciones Cátedra, S.A., 1999), 415.

94. Ibid., 423.

95. As Dian Fox writes, "[A]ll Spanish political commentators, from Mariana to Quevedo, essentially agreed with Saavedra's rendition of the characteristics of the ideal ruler. The *príncipe político-cristiano* possesses the cardinal virtues, temperance, fortitude, justice, and the foremost, prudence. Able to rule over his own passions, he is an example for his subjects to emulate. He loves his people, favors the poor, exalts the Christian faith, and strives for spiritual glory." See Fox, *Kings in Calderón: A Study in Characterization and Political Theory* (London: Tamesis, 1986), 14.

96. Covarrubias, *Tesoro*, 531.

97. Covarrubias defines "estampa" (print, portrait, image) as the "writing or drawing that is printed" and links this directly to the development of the printing press in France: "La escritura o dibujo que se imprime con la invención de la imprenta; la cual se experimentó antes que en otra parte en cierto estado en Francia, dicho Estampes, que fue antiguamente de los condes de Alansón, y el lugar principal se llama Estampes, de donde tomó el nombre la estampa." *Tesoro de la Lengua Castellana O Española*, 843–4. The *Royal Academy of Spanish* dictionary, too, emphasizes the materiality of the "estampa" (engraving or print): "Reproducción de un dibujo, pintura, fotografía, etc., traslada al papel o a otra materia, por medio del tórculo o prensa, desde la lamina de metal o madera en que está grabada, o desde la piedra litográfica en que está dibujado." Figuratively, "estampa" can refer to the "figure of a person or animal" [7. a *Figura total de una persona o animal*], as well as "trace or footprint" [8. *huella del pie del hombre o de los animales en la tierra*.] *Diccionario de la Lengua Española* (Madrid: Real Academia Española, 1992), 907.

98. Ernst Cassirer neatly summarizes this view: "From the Christian point of view the only master, not only the master of human conduct but also the master of human thoughts, is God. In him, and in him alone, we find the true *magisterium*. All knowledge whatever [*sic*], the knowledge of the sensible world as well as mathematical or dialectic knowledge, is based upon an illumination by this eternal source of light." Cassirer, *The Myth of the State* (New Haven: Yale University Press, 1974), 84.

99. See Benjamin, *OGTD*, 92.

100. Benjamin describes allegory as a "schema"—an "object of knowledge." "But," he continues, qualifying his subject, "it is not securely possessed until it becomes a fixed schema: at one and the same time a fixed image and a fixing sign" (*OGTD* 184). "Schema" is the Greek word for the Latin term "figura." On the relationship between "schema" and Benjamin's dialectical image, Anselm Haverkamp writes:

> Against the more popular uses of the term, Benjamin's image insists on being a schema, but a schema of reading ... What makes these images real images for Benjamin is that they are decidedly not archaic images—implying that archaic images are anything but true. The dialectics of these images manifests itself in a schema whose effect rather than whose archaic cause is decisive; the notorious "aura" attests to that, even though Benjamin's use of the term seems not always free from nostalgia. Ernst Robert Curtius, whose conception of "topos-research" offers an interesting parallel, falls for what Benjamin seeks to avoid: a confusion of "place" in language with an "archetypal" content whose identity the tradition of *topoi* is meant to guarantee.
>
> Anselm Haverkamp, "Notes on the 'Dialectical Image' (How Deconstructive Is It?)," *Diacritics: A Review of Contemporary Criticism* 22, no. 3–4 (1992): 72–3.

A revised version of this discussion appears in *Figura cryptica. Theorie der literarischen Latenz* (Frankfurt am Main: Suhrkamp, 2002).

101. Benjamin, *OGTD*, 166.

102. Ibid., 188. The translation is Samuel Weber's. See Weber, *Mass Mediauras: Form, Technics Media* (Stanford: Stanford University Press, 1996), 93.

103. Benjamin, *OGTD*, 188.

104. The philosopher representing the Baroque's "metaphysical tendency" here is Leibniz, inventor of calculus, and avid reader of Suárez.

105. Benjamin, *OGTD*, 80.

106. Ibid., 66.

107. Weber, "Taking Exception," in *Benjamin's -abilities*, 187.

108. *Diccionario de la Lengua Española, Tomo II* (Madrid: Espasa Calpe, 2002), 1749.

109. Although he, too, sees the play's "Poland" in terms of divided space, Mitchell Greenberg goes further. Confirming the play's emphasis on space even more than time, Greenberg sees *Life Is a Dream* as "a universe of impossible contradictions in which internal conflicts can be resolved only by and through their projection on to *another scene* ... a mythic scene in which the monstrous that is brought forth upon the stage of representation must, in an ambivalent ceremony of guilt and retribution, be sacrificed to the very society that produces what according to its own underlying codes of political and sexual propriety it cannot accept." *Canonical States, Canonical Stages: Oedipus, Othering, and Seventeenth-Century Drama* (Minneapolis: University of Minnesota Press, 1994), 64.

110. Benjamin, *OGTD*, 233. ("Und zwar bedeutet es genau das Nichtsein dessen, was es vorstellt.") *Ursprung des deutschen Trauerspiels*, ed. Rolf Tiedemann (Frankfurt am Main: Suhrkamp, 1996), 233.

111. I borrow the phrase "perpetuum mobile" from Anselm Haverkamp. "The whole of Shakespeare," Haverkamp writes, "is a *perpetuum mobile*, it runs as if from itself and produces ever anew the matter that it needs: History, the ever-same old story." See Haverkamp, "*Perpetuum Mobile*: Shakespeare's Perpetual Renaissance," *Shakespearean Genealogies of Power* (New York: Routledge, 2011), 7–15.

112. Greenberg, *Canonical Stages*, 233.

113. Benjamin, *OGTD*, 80.

114. Ibid., 66.

115. Ibid., 216.

116. On political theology in Benjamin, see Eric Jacobson, *Metaphysics of the Profane: The Political Theology of Walter Benjamin and Gershom Scholem* (New York: Columbia University Press, 2003); and Marc De Wilde, "Violence in the State of Exception: Reflections on Theologico-Political Motifs in Benjamin and Schmitt," *Political Theologies: Public Religions in a Post-Secular World* (New York: Fordham University Press, 2006), 188–201.

117. The relation between theology and language in Benjamin is an immense and extremely complex topic and requires a fuller treatment than I can give here. See, to begin with, Benjamin's essay, "On Language as Such and on the Language of Men." For a discussion, see Peter Fenves, *The Messianic Reduction: Walter Benjamin and the Shape of Time* (Stanford: Stanford University Press, 2010).

118. Samuel Weber, *Benjamin's -abilities* (Cambridge: Harvard University Press, 2008), 134.

119. For Augustine's understanding of the non-being of evil, see *Confessions*, bk. VII, trans. Henry Chadwick (Oxford: Oxford University Press, 1998), 111–16.

120. Benjamin, *OGTD*, 233.

121. I am grateful to Margherita Pascucci for her illuminating discussions of Benjamin's work in general and his notion of allegory in particular. See Pascucci, *Il pensiero di Walter Benjamin. Un'introduzione* (Trieste: Parnaso, 2002).

122. On the "logical relation" between a concept and its object, see Deleuze, *The Fold*, 125.

123. Deleuze, *The Fold*, 125.

124. Echevarría, *Celestina's Brood*, 112.

125. Ibid., 112–13.

126. On literature's capacity to provide this figure in general, and on allegory in particular, see Paul de Man:

> The paradigm for all texts consists of a figure (or a system of figures) and its deconstruction. But since this model cannot be closed off by a final reading, it engenders, in its turn, a supplementary figural superposition which narrates the unreadability of the prior narration. As distinguished from primary deconstructive narratives centered on figures and ultimately always on metaphor, we can call such narratives to the second (or the third) degree *allegories*."
> *Allegories of Reading: Figural Language in Rousseau, Nietzsche, Rilke, and Proust* (New Haven: Yale University Press, 1979), 305.

If, for de Man, allegory operates like a narrative, then for Benjamin it is more spatial and imagistic. Its mobility is different, corresponding, or perhaps better illustrating the particular mode of theatricality Samuel Weber develops, largely by returning to Benjamin and his primary baroque examples, such as *Hamlet*. See Weber, *Theatricality as Medium* (New York: Fordham University Press, 2004).

127. Agamben, *Homo Sacer*, 21.

128. Ibid., 21.

## 5. RETURN: THE "WRINKLES" OF MYSTERY IN *THE WINTER'S TALE*

1. Hent de Vries, "In Media Res: Global Religion, Public Spheres, and the Task of Contemporary Comparative Religious Studies," in *Religion and Media*, ed. Hent de Vries and Samuel Weber (Stanford: Stanford University Press, 2001), 24, 25.

2. Sigmund Freud, "Screen Memories" in *The Uncanny*, trans. David Mclintock (New York: Penguin Books, 2003), 21.

3. On the symbolic space of war, see Jean-Luc Nancy, "War, Law, Sovereignty—*Techné*," trans. Jeffrey S. Librett, in *Rethinking Technologies*, ed. Verena Andermatt Conley (Minneapolis: University of Minnesota Press, 1993), 28–58. On sovereignty and the media, see Samuel Weber, *Targets of Opportunity: On the Militarization of Thinking* (New York: Fordham University Press, 2005). The function of the image in relation to sovereignty is a complex one. As Weber notes, in recent "wartime," it is precisely the "absence of images" of the enemy that becomes one of the "enabling conditions" of modern terrorism as well as the responses it generates. Weber, "Wartime," in *Targets*, 42–62.

4. Regarding the play's date, a known 1611 first performance at the Globe is often referred to, although the play was, of course, composed

before, perhaps, according to the Oxford editors, even as early as 1609. Shakespeare's primary source was Robert Greene's prose romance, *Pandosto* (1588). For a discussion, see Stephen Orgel, Introduction, *The Winter's Tale* (Oxford: Oxford University Press, 1996).

5. Different versions of this narrative of sovereignty's historical movement into increasingly disembodied representational forms appear in writers as diverse as Otto von Gierke, *Political Theories of the Middle Age*, trans. F. W. Maitland (Bristol: Thoemmes Press, 1996), 61–73; Alexander Koyré, *From the Closed World to the Infinite Universe* (Baltimore: Johns Hopkins University Press, 1968); Jean Bethke Elshtain, *Sovereignty: God, State, and Self* (New York: Basic Books, 2008); Jeans Bartelson, *A Genealogy of Sovereignty* (Cambridge: Cambridge University Press, 1995); Marcel Gauchet, *The Disenchantment of the World: A Political History of Religion*, trans. Oscar Burge (Princeton: Princeton University Press, 1999); Adriana Cavarero, *Stately Bodies: Literature, Philosophy and the Question of Gender*, trans. Robert de Lucca and Deanna Shemek (Ann Arbor: The University of Michigan Press, 2002); Jacques Derrida, "Faith and Knowledge: The Two Sources of 'Religion' at the Limits of Reason Alone" in *Acts of Religion*, ed. Gil Anidjar, trans. Samuel Weber (New York: Routledge, 2002), 40–101; Christopher Pye, *The Vanishing: Shakespeare, the Subject and Early Modern Culture* (Durham: Duke University Press, 2000); Eric Santner, *The Psychotheology of Everyday Life* (Chicago: The University of Chicago Press, 2001); and Giorgio Agamben, *Homo Sacer: Sovereign Power and Bare Life*, trans. Daniel Heller-Roazen (Stanford: Stanford University Press, 1998).

6. On the question of anachronism in Shakespeare, see Richard Halpern, *Shakespeare Among the Moderns* (Ithaca: Cornell University Press, 1997), esp. 3–10, and Jonathan Gil Harris, *Untimely Matter in the Time of Shakespeare* (Philadelphia: University of Pennsylvania Press, 2009), esp. 6–10 and 49–50.

7. The full title is *Commentariorum ac disputationum in tertiam partem Divi Thomae tomus secundus* (*Second Tome of the Commentaries and Disputations on the Third Part of the Summa Theologica of Saint Thomas Aquinas*), published at Alcalá in 1592. Henceforth Suárez, *Mysteries*, *Opera omnia*, vol. 19 (Paris: 1856).

8. Niccolò Machiavelli, *Il principe* (Mondadori: Milan, 1994), 67; English translation, *The Prince*, by George Bull (New York: Penguin Books, 1995), 48.

9. There is some overlap between what I am referring to as "effective history" and Hans-Georg Gadamer's notion of "wirkungsgeschichtliches Bewusstsein," sometimes translated as a linguistically conditioned

formation of "historically effected consciousness." For Gadamer's concept, see "The Principle of History of Effect (Wirkungsgeschichte)," in *Truth and Method*, trans. Joel Weinsheimer and Donald G. Marshall (New York: Continuum 1996), 300–7.

10. Suárez, *Defensio fidei*, bk 3, ch. 23; *Opera omnia* vol. 24, p. 315.

11. On the dividing effect of the Reformation on the Christian believer's subjectivity between a commitment to the beyond and to the here-below, see Marcel Gauchet, *The Disenchantment of the World: A Political History of Religion*, trans. Oscar Burge (Princeton: Princeton University Press, 1997), 131. The difference between Machiavelli and the "reason of state" political theory that comes to be associated with him, and Suárez, could further be understood as that between an incipient rationality of statecraft, and an older, Augustinian view of the relationship between the origin and proper exercise of temporal power. Key names associated with "reason of state" include Francesco Guicciardini, one of the first to use the phrase, as well as Giovannni Botero, whose 1589 treatise, *Della ragion di stato* (ed. L. Firpo, Turin: Unione Tipografico, 1948) was called *The Reason of State [Ragione de Stato]*. For the Spanish response to both Machiavelli and reason of state, see Pedro Ribadeneira, *Tratado de la Religion y Virtudes que deve tener el Principe Christiano, para governar y conservar sus Estados. Contra lo que N Machiavelo y los Politicos deste tiempo enseñan* (1595).

12. Machiavelli's work continues to generate an enormous amount of theoretical and critical writing on early- and late-modern sovereignty. Antonio Negri and Michael Hardt have shown how Machiavelli's thought informs contemporary theories of power. Hardt and Negri, *Empire* (Cambridge: Harvard University Press, 2000). On Machiavelli and political theology, see Graham Hammill, "Machiavelli and Hebrew Scripture," *The Mosaic Constitution* (Chicago: University of Chicago Press, 2012), 31–66. Suárez is much less known in English-language scholarship. While he is occasionally acknowledged by Shakespeare scholars as an important figure in early modern intellectual history, few of these discuss specific aspects of his work. For an exception, see Paul Cefalu, *Revisionist Shakespeare: Transitional Ideologies in Texts and Contexts* (New York: Palgrave, 2004), 112ff.

13. Michel de Certeau, *The Mystic Fable, Volume One: The Sixteenth and Seventeenth Centuries*, trans. Michael B. Smith (Chicago: University of Chicago Press, 1995), 250–1.

14. Richard J. O'Brien, S.J., Introduction to *The Mysteries of the Life of Christ*, trans. Richard J. O'Brien, S.J. (West Baden Springs: Edwards Brothers, 1954), vii.

15. See *New Catholic Encyclopedia*, Vol. 9, 2nd edition (Detroit: Gale, 2003), 171.

16. Suárez's text is "the first attempt in Scholastic theology to give a separate and comprehensive treatment based on theological sources of the questions about Mary" (O'Brien, viii). For discussions, see Sara Jane Boss, ed., *Mary: The Complete Resource* (Oxford: Oxford University Press, 2007), as well as *Mary* (London: Continuum, 2003), and Marina Warner, *Alone of All Her Sex: The Myth and the Cult of the Virgin Mary* (New York: Knopf, 1976).

17. See *Catholic Encyclopedia* online: http://www.newadvent.org/cathen/10662a.htm.

18. On metaphor as movement, see Paul Ricoeur, *The Rule of Metaphor: Multi-Disciplinary Studies of the Creation of Meaning in Language*, trans. Robert Czerny with Kathleen McLaughlin and John Costello, S.J. (Toronto: University of Toronto Press, 1997), 17.

19. Suárez's Latin reads, "ejusdem Deiparae cognitione comparari non poterat. Cognitio enim effectus cognitionem causae supponit; cum autem B. Virgo Christum ut hominem genuerit, sub hac ratione causam illius esse necesse est. Recte igitur ad scientiam de filio consequendam permatris cognitionem paratur via; neque enim poterant, qui et sanguine et dilectione adeo conjuncti sunt, disputatione sejungi, nec par erat in tam longo de Christo sermone, de Virgine tacere. See Suárez, *Commentarii et Disputationes in Tertiam Partem D. Thomae a quaestione vigesima septima ad quinquagesimam nonan*." Praefatio, sec.1; *Opera omnia* vol. 19, p. 1.

20. Peter Goodrich points out that "The legal concept of Text and of textual system was initially mystical and required comparably initiate forms of reading and interpretation." One of the historical consequences of this genealogy is its latent association of text, territory, and even terror: "In a surprisingly literal sense, the Text was the body of the social, it was in one etymology the terror and territory of the social, the space and conceptual geography that a culture inhabited." Goodrich, "Introduction: Psychoanalysis and Law," in *Law and the Unconscious: A Legendre Reader*, ed. Peter Goodrich (New York: St. Martin's, 1997), 23.

21. Here and throughout, I am extremely grateful to my colleague Andy Galloway for his advice on the translation of these passages. The English term "cathexis," which is often associated with "investment," refers to the subject's act of "investing" psycho-sexual energy into a representative object. As Donald Nicholson-Smith points out, James Strachey coined the term from the Greek (κάθεξις in Greek). See the translator's note to Jean Laplanche and J. B. Pontalis, *The Language of*

*Psychoanalysis*, trans. Donald Nicholson-Smith (New York: Norton, 1973), 65. Although it is initially modeled on various ways of understanding physical and physical energy, as Laplanche and Pontalis explain, the "concept is generally taken in a metaphorical sense, in which case it does no more than express an analogy between psychical operations and the working of a nervous apparatus conceived of in terms of energy" (63). Nicolson-Smith notes that Freud himself preferred the more idiomatic, German term, "Besetzung," from the verb, "besetzen," to occupy (e.g., in a military context, to occupy a town, a territory). Samuel Weber has argued that Besetzung "can also signify a theatrical 'cast.'" What the military and the theatrical senses have in common is that the place "occupied" is not originally linked to "its occupiers" (whether military or theatrical) any more than the object is to the drive that "occupies" it. Weber, *Targets of Opportunity: On the Militarization of Thinking* (New York: Fordham University Press, 2005), 48.

22. Harro Höpfl, *Jesuit Political Thought: The Society of Jesus and the State, c. 1540–1630* (Cambridge: Cambridge University Press, 2004), 46.

23. See Suárez, *Mysteries*, trans. O'Brien, v.

24. See Jaroslav Pelikan, *Mary Through the Centuries: Her Place in the History of Culture* (New Haven: Yale University Press, 1996), 125–6.

25. "praesertim habetur haec veritas traditione . . ." Suárez, *Mysteries*, *Opera omnia* vol. 19, p. 88. Following Eric Santner, who has shown how biblical texts can be read to both structure our "fantasmatic organizations" and at the same time open up alternative ways of imagining social, sexual, political, and theological relations, the task of the exegete, in this view, is to structure something like a controlled fantasy. Santner, *The Psychotheology of Everyday Life* (Chicago: University of Chicago Press, 2001), 5.

26. "*Maria post partum virgo permansit.*—Dicendum vero est B. Virginem perpetuam virginitatem coluisse, neque virum unquam cognovisse. Est de fide. Et primo probatur unico testimonio Veteris Testamenti, Ezech. 44: *Porta haec clausa erit, et vir non transibit per eam, quoniam Dominus Deus Israel ingressus est per eam.* Quo loco, licet sub metaphora, ad litteram sermo est de Virgine sanctissima, ut ibi testator Hieronymus, et sentient alii Patres, qui ad hanc veritatem confirmandam hoc utuntur testimonio . . ." (Suárez, *Mysteries*, *Opera omnia*, vol. 19, p. 88).

27. Pelikan, 131.

28. On the difference between Catholic and Protestant interpretations of the Eucharist ceremony, in the context of the English reformers, see Judith Anderson, *Translating Investments: Metaphor and the Dynamic*

*of Cultural Change in Tudor-Stuart England* (New York: Fordham University Press, 2005). As Anderson points out, "[p]erhaps the crucial difference is that for the conservatives, the translation [of the Latin substantive verb *est*] is objective and real, whereas for the reformers, transubstantiation occurs merely in language . . . While both sides assert spiritual presence, the conservatives crucially in the elements of bread and wine, the reformers definitively in the believer, what finally and most fundamentally separates them is the spiritual status of the material realm, and what joins them is a fear of mere language—language unmoored to a material or spiritual reality outside it—which is precisely and ironically the linguistic condition their arguments and counterarguments work to expose." *Translating Investments*, 44–5. Anderson shows how early modern debates over the semiotics of the Eucharist anticipate later discussions, such as those between Paul Ricoeur and Jacques Derrida, on "dead metaphors" and Ernst Cassirer and Emile Benveniste over "whether language is timeless or temporal, essential or existential, *langue* or *parole* . . ." (41).

29. "*Representare idem est quod rem præsentem facere.*—Tertius testis sit Hieronymus, exponens verba Christi, Matt. 26, ubi sic inquit: *Postquam typicum pascha fuerat impletum, et agni carnes cum Apostolis comederat, assumit panem, qui confortat cor hominis, et ad verum Paschæ transgreditur sacraentum, ut quomodo in figuratione ejus Melchisedech, summi Dei sacerdos, panem et vinum offerens fecerat, ipse quoque veritatem sui corporis et sanguinis repræsentaret.* Ubi etiam fortasse prodibit hæreticus, qui verbum *repræsentaret*, in aliquam fictionem vel metaphoram intrepretetur. Vis vero verbi, et mens Hieronymi perspicua est: idem enim est repræsentare, quod rem præsentem, facere, præsertim quæ antea promissa erat, vel futura prædicta, aut desiderata." *Defensio fidei* in *Opera omnia*, vol. 24, p. 128.

30. Peter Goodrich, *Languages of Law: From Logics of Memory to Nomadic Masks* (London: Weidenfeld and Nicolson, 1990), 55.

31. Suárez, *De legibus seu de Deo legislatore* Proœmium, *Opera omnia*, vol. 5, p. ix. *On Laws*, Preface, trans. Williams, 13.

32. While Benveniste argues against the derivation of the Latin *religio* from the verb *ligare* (to bind), Derrida stresses the connection. Derrida, *Acts of Religion*, esp. at 71–4. Also see Legendre, *Law and the Unconscious*, 234.

33. Northrop Frye, *The Great Code: The Bible and Literature* (New York: Harcourt Brace Jovanovich, 1982), 55–6.

34. David Tracy has shown that in religion certain texts become "normative for the religious community's basic understanding and

control of its root metaphors and thereby its vision of reality." "Root metaphors" that are central to Christianity's understanding of community include those having to do with "eating" and "feeding." Tracy, "Metaphor and Religion: The Test Case of Christian Texts," in *On Metaphor*, ed. Sheldon Sacks (Chicago: University of Chicago Press, 1981), 89. These tropes take us straight to the heart of the Jesuit understanding of their institution as a worldly one. For Suárez, in particular, the Eucharist is "one of the principle acts of feeding [the faithful]." Paul V. Murphy, "'God's Porters': the Jesuit Vocation According to Francisco Suárez," *Archivum Historicum Societatis Iesu* 70 (Jan.–June 2001): 18.

35. The locus classicus for this discussion is Thomas Aquinas's *The Summa Theologica*, Part I, where he writes that "all names applied metaphorically to God are applied to creatures primarily rather than to God, because when said of God they mean only similitudes to such creatures. For as *smiling* applied to a field means only that the field in the beauty of its flowering is like to the beauty of the human smile by proportionate likeness, so the name of *lion* applied to God means only that God manifests strength in His works, as a lion in his. Thus, it is clear that applied to God the signification of these names can be defined only from what is said of creatures." Aquinas, "On the Names of God," *Summa Theologica*, Part I, Question 13, art. 6, in *Basic Writings of Saint Thomas Aquinas, Volume One*, ed. Anton C. Pegis (New York: Random House, 1945), 122. See also *Summa Contra Gentiles Book One: God*, trans. Anton C. Pegis (Notre Dame: University of Notre Dame Press, 1975), 143–7.

36. David Tracy, "Metaphor and Religion: The Test Case of Christian Texts," in *On Metaphor*, ed. Sheldon Sacks (Chicago: University of Chicago Press, 1981), 89. Paul Ricoeur traces the term "root metaphors" to the work of Stephen C. Pepper, who Max Black cites in *Models and Metaphors*. Ricoeur, *The Rule of Metaphor*, 352 n40.

37. Tracy, "Metaphor and Religion," 90.

38. Ricoeur, *Figuring the Sacred: Religion, Narrative, and Imagination*, trans. David Pellauer, ed. Mark I. Wallace (Minneapolis: Fortress Press, 1995), 228–32. For Ricoeur, the significance of biblical language, and specifically the naming of God, does not lie in its capacity to produce knowledge. Biblical language cannot be distinguished from other forms of language in terms of knowledge alone. The uniquely performative effect of the biblical text has to do with the framing conditions that govern the believer's relation to it. These are what lead the text *not* to a knowing but rather to a *showing* of the Truth. What is effective about a dogmatic text is its dual performance of revealing and

concealing its meaning at once. At this performative level, the mystery of what it reveals always lies somewhere beyond or to the side of mere knowledge. Ricoeur cites Ludwig Wittgenstein's description of the relation between religious experience and a language, in which "What is said is only this; whatever ultimately may be the nature of the so-called religious experience, it comes to language, it is articulated in a language, and the most appropriate place to interpret it on its own terms is to inquire into its linguistic expression." *Figuring the Sacred*, at 16 and 35. For Ricoeur, the "logic of meaning" in religious discourse, "depends on the use of *limit-expressions* that bring about the rupturing of ordinary speech . . . The kingdom of God is polarly opposed to paradise, not only as the future is opposed to the past but as every limit-expression is opposed to the whole of interplay of correspondence. And in this regard, the expression 'kingdom of God' may be understood as the *index* that points limit-expressions in the direction of *limit-experiences* that are the ultimate reference of our modes of speaking." Ricoeur's notion of a limit-expression that is neither representational nor referential but indicative—showing nothing but itself—is akin to Blumenberg's absolute metaphor in that both indicate that which is ultimately inaccessible. Ricoeur, *Figuring the Sacred*, 60–1.

39. See Dirk Mende, *Metapher: Zwischen Metaphysik und Archäologie: Schelling, Heidegger, Derrida Blumenberg* (München: Fink Verlag, 2013).

40. Ibid., 222.

41. The question of whether there is a "specifically religious and theological use of metaphor" has been taken up by a range of scholars in theology, philosophy, linguistics, and literary studies, from Friedrich Schleiermacher and Immanuel Kant through Northrop Frye, Harold Bloom, and Jacques Derrida. The bibliography is immense. David Tracy lists some of the most important arguments in existentialist, phenomenological, and analytical philosophies and theologies, including the work of Soren Kierkegaard, Paul Tillich, and Karl Jaspers. Other philosophers who have approached the question from the analytical tradition include Ian Ramsey, Frederick Ferre, and Stepehen Toulmin. See Tracy, "Metaphor and Religion," 92.

42. For an excellent discussion, see Anderson, *Translating Investments*.

43. On this synchronic structure, see Anderson, *Translating Investments*, 47.

44. Legendre, *Law and the Unconscious*, 152.

45. Ibid., 152.

46. Ibid., 87.
47. Ibid.
48. Ibid., 73.
49. Ibid., 155–6.
50. On theology as the "matrix of law," see Legendre, *Law and the Unconscious*, 53. See also Suárez's discussion of the relationship between natural law and eternal law that opens *De legibus, Opera omnia* vol. 5, pp. ix–xi. *A Treatise on Laws and God the Lawgiver*, trans. Williams, 13–17.
51. Legendre, *Law and the Unconscious*, 155.
52. Ibid., 154–5.
53. Höpfl, *Jesuit Political Thought*, 182–3.
54. Ibid., 352.
55. Legendre, *Law and the Unconscious*, 55.
56. Ibid., 155.
57. Ibid., 156.
58. Legendre's understanding of "dance" is fascinating. Ranging from anthropological considerations to treatment of modern systems of management and advertising, dance, he writes, "has always been of particular interest to those who control the norms which regulate the body because dance has to do with the basic order of things, that is, with the division of society or the order of enjoyment. Dance plays a vital role on the political stage . . . *Dance is a medium which disseminates a Text.*" *Law and the Unconscious*, 55.
59. Legendre summarizes what he calls the "elements of the montage":

> (i) The author of the compilation which records this text identifies himself as a messenger or transmitter; the commentator only exists to give value to the text, whose political author is the text itself. (ii) The express content of the technical legal rule . . . counts as legal only because it refers, by way of an accumulation of other texts, to the founding Name (Christ). (iii) The truth status of the Reference is defined as founded upon a genealogical reproduction (hence the metaphor of Christ's seed).
>
> Legendre, *Law and the Unconscious*, 155.

60. Suárez, *CD*, disp. 34, sec. 2, par. 3. *Opera omnia* vol. 19, pp. 543–4.
61. See Judith Anderson's discussion of Derrida's pun, "proper-ties," in *White Mythology*, in *Translating Investments*, esp. at 49. Here, and elsewhere in the book, Anderson discusses in illuminating detail the

complexities of sacred exegesis and the problem of metaphor, in particular, in Reformation polemics.

62. My translation. Suárez's Latin reads:

> Eo vel maxime quod, licet Christus naturali affectu timeret, tamen deliberata voluntate et efficaci, et actu appetitus a voluntate imperato, mortem et omnes dolores, qui efficacissime proponebantur, amplectebatur, et naturalem affectum superabat, et hinc agonia proveniebat.
>
> *Mysteries, Opera Omnia* vol. 19, p. 544

63. The *New Oxford American Dictionary*, for example, defines "efficacious" as "successful in producing a desired or intended result."

64. The *Catholic Encyclopedia* summarizes the different positions taken by the Jesuits and Dominicans as follows: "The Dominicans declared that the Jesuits conceded too much to free will, and so tended toward Pelagianism. In turn, the Jesuits complained that the Dominicans did not sufficiently safeguard human liberty, and seemed in consequence to lean towards Calvinism." See *"Congregatio de Auxiliis"* in the *Catholic Encyclopedia* online: http://www.newadvent.org/cathen/04238a.htm.

65. Under the term, "voluntary," the *Catholic Encyclopedia* includes the following description:

> It is requisite that the thing be an effect of the will consequent upon actual knowledge, either formal or virtual, in the rational agent. It is not quite the same as free; for a free act supposes self-determination proceeding from an agent capable, at the time, of determining himself or not at his choice. However, as every specific voluntary act in this life is also free (except those rare will-impulses, when man is swept to sudden action without time to perceive in non-action the element of good requisite for determination not to act) the moralist commonly uses the terms voluntary and free interchangeably. A thing may be voluntary in itself, as when in its own proper concept it falls under the efficacious determination of the agent, or voluntary in something else, as in its cause.... Voluntary in cause requires foreknowledge of the effect, at least virtual, viz. under a general concept of effects to follow; and production thereof by virtue of the will's efficiency exercised in the willing of its cause.
>
> *Catholic Encyclopedia* online: http://www.newadvent.org/cathen/15506a.htm

On prayer—including especially on the efficacy of prayers for the dead—see the *Catholic Encyclopedia* online on "prayer" (Greek *euchesthai*,

Latin *precari*, French *prier*, to plead, to beg, to ask earnestly): http://www.newadvent.org/cathen/12345b.htm.

66. See "efficacy" in the *Oxford English Dictionary*. http://www.oed.com.proxy.library.cornell.edu/view/Entry/59736?redirectedFrom=efficacy#eid.

67. Donald K. McKim, *Westminster Dictionary of Theological Terms* (Louisville: John Knox Press, 1996), 87.

68. Ovid, *Metamorphoses Books IX–XV*, trans. Frank Justus Miller (Cambridge: Harvard University Press, 1984), 82–3.

69. Julia Kristeva, "Stabat Mater The Paradox: Mother or Primary Narcissism," in *Tales of Love*, trans. Leon S. Roudiez (New York: Columbia University Press, 1987), 234.

70. Louis Althusser, "Ideology and Ideological State Apparatuses," in *Lenin and Philosophy and Other Essays*, trans. Ben Brewster (New York: Monthly Review Press, 1971), 164.

71. Discussing the play's tragicomic romance form, Cohen writes that the "distinctive sense of recapitulation produced by the form, particularly in its pastoral manifestations, makes it the appropriate end point for a history of Renaissance public theater. Especially in the plays of Shakespeare and Calderón, long periods of suffering ultimately issue in the triumphant reconciliation of family and nation." Cohen, *Drama of Nation* (Ithaca: Cornell University Press, 1985), 384.

72. Bradin Cormack argues that "*The Winter's Tale* is about the threat of difference to indivisible sovereignty and, in reverse, the absurdity of indivisibility as a starting point for thinking about power in a world in which power simply is differentiated, and in which meaning simply is distributed." Cormack, "Shakespeare's Other Sovereignty: On Particularity and Violence in *The Winter's Tale* and the Sonnets," *Shakespeare Quarterly* 62.4 (2011), 490.

73. All passages from *The Winter's Tale* are cited from the Oxford edition, ed. Stephen Orel (Oxford University Press, 1998).

74. That *The Winter's Tale* is a play of sovereignty is already indicated by this opening exchange. As Bradin Cormack has pointed out, Archidamus's name, although never pronounced in the play, is related to the Greek term for sovereignty, *arche*, "first cause," "supreme power," "sovereignty," and, through a diminutive form, to office (*archidion*, "minor office"). Cormack, "Shakespeare's Other Sovereignty: On Particularity and Violence in *The Winter's Tale* and the Sonnets," *Shakespeare Quarterly* 62.4 (2011), 496. For a discussion of the play in relation to hospitality, see Julia Reinhard Lupton, "Hospitality and Risk in *The*

*Winter's Tale*," in *Thinking with Shakespeare* (Chicago: University of Chicago Press, 2011), 161–86.

75. Eric L. Santner, *On the Psychotheology of Everyday Life: Reflections on Freud and Rosenzweig* (Chicago: University of Chicago Press, 2001).

76. Ibid., 9.

77. Further instances dealing with "shame" include Leontes's accusation of Hermione: "As you were past all shame . . ." (3.2.82); his own rapid assumption of shame at the end of the same scene: "unto / Our shame perpetual" (3.2.236); the shepherdess, Mopsa's line, "maybe he has paid you more, which will shame you to give him again" (4.4.239); and Autolycus, the rogue's "for I am proof against that title [of rogue] and what shame else belongs to't." (4.4.833).

78. On *The Winter's Tale*'s invocations of a prelapsarian past, it is worth noting that the notion of Eden itself is itself linked to an excess of pleasure. The English word "Eden" is related to the Hebrew word "ednah," which is usually translated as "bliss." Eden and ednah are cognates. Eden is thus related to the pleasure of the apple, or even to sexual pleasure. "Shall I know pleasure [*ednah*]?" (i.e. "shall I know bliss?") Sarah asks, in response to the declaration of the angels, that she and Abraham will have a son. I am grateful to Tracy McNulty for pointing this out to me. See Robert Alter, ed. *Genesis: Translation and Commentary* (New York: Norton, 1997). On the "spiraling relation" of the play, see Christopher Pye, "Against Schmitt," 202.

79. Orgel, 100.

80. "Art" is a conjugation of "to be." The question of Mamillius's being is for Leontes the same as the question of his own condition. From these early ontological questions, the play will move increasingly toward a different sense of "art," as aesthetics, on the way toward a resolution of its crises that hinges on the complex reconciliations of art. (On *The Winter's Tale*'s formulation of an early modern aesthetic sphere, see Christopher Pye, "Against Schmitt," *South Atlantic Quarterly* 108:1 (Winter 2009): 197–217.

81. For a discussion of some of the editorial attempts to render the play's "syntactically and lexically often baffling" language more comprehensible, see Stephen Orgel's excellent introduction to the play, *The Winter's Tale*, ed. Orgel (Oxford: Oxford University Press, 1998), 7–10. "What does it mean," Orgel asks, "that a play speaks incomprehensibly?" (Orgel 10)

82. Some scholars have argued that "affection" is "not the technical philosophical term but the normal vernacular word for love, passion, or lust." (See Maurice Hunt, qtd. in Orgel, p. 9.) At the same time, the

word *does* still bear its older "technical" and philosophical history. Scholasticism, for example, understands "affectio" in relation to its older, Aristotelian legacy that links the term to the will, and to love. In *De voluntate, et intentione, actibusque intellectus praeviis* (*Concerning the Will, Intention, and prior Acts of the Intellect*), Suárez writes that "love can be used more generally and can sometimes signify an affection of the will, either concerning a means or concerning an end" (Penner 4). Suárez also uses the term "affectio" in relation to religion. As Michael J. Buckley has shown in his 1608–9 text on the nature of the Christian state, the *Virtue and Status of Religion*, written at the request of Pope Paul V, Suárez "contended that the term *religio*—like '*fides*' and '*votum*'—was legitimately and 'customarily applied (*tribui solere*) not only to internal affect, but also to the *external actions* and, indeed, to the *things* (rebus) by which God was worshipped as also to the *doctrina* that teaches such worship or ceremony.' Religion in this sense is no longer simply a virtue; it is also both things such as external ritual and ceremonial objects and the teachings and the beliefs that instruct about their appropriate use." In this way, Buckley points out, "Suárez subsumes what Aquinas had called the acts or objects of religion into religion itself, and in doing so, he opens up *religio* to the cultural and anthropological meaning and inquiries that will constitute its character in modernity." Buckley, "The Study of Religion and the Rise of Atheism: Conflict or Confirmation?" in *Fields of Faith: Theology and Religious Studies for the Twenty-First Century*, ed. David F. Ford, Ben Quash, and Janet Martin Soskice (Cambridge: Cambridge University Press, 2005), 8–9.

Later in the century, Spinoza re-theorizes "affect," defining it as an intellectual, productive capacity. Affect thinks, has ideas, acts, and produces images: The "affections of the human body whose ideas set forth external bodies as if they were present to us we shall call images (imagines), although they do not reproduce the shape of things. And when the mind regards bodies in this way, we shall say that it 'imagines' (imaginari)." Spinoza, *Ethics: Treatise on the Emendation of the Intellect and Selected Letters*, trans. Samuel Shirley (Indianapolis: Hackett Publishing, 1992), 78. For Spinoza, an affect is an empowerment and not a simple change or modification. (See *Ethics* III, 3, defn. 3.)

83. Orgel recounts the case of Nicholas Rowe, "normally [the] most tolerant of editors," who "felt moved to [this] radical revision," (Orgel 9).

84. See Christopher Pye, "Against Schmitt: Law, Aesthetics, and Absolutism in Shakespeare's *Winter's Tale*," *South Atlantic Quarterly* 108:1 (Winter 2009): 197–217. Pye dates the rise of an autonomous aesthetic sphere earlier than many critics, locating it in the early modern period in

general, and with *The Winter's Tale*, specifically. Such an aesthetic autonomy, according to Pye, interrupts a Schmittian conception of sovereignty, predicated on the relation between sovereign and law. I am indebted to this reading and follow it throughout, shifting only in emphasis, from the aesthetic to what Hent de Vries refers to as the "mediatic."

85. By "intrusion of the real," I have in mind something closer to Jacques Lacan's understanding of the relationship between imagination, symbolization, and "reality" than Carl Schmitt's notion of an "irruption" [*Einbruch*] of historical time into "the time of the play" that I discuss in the Introduction.

86. Lupton, *Afterlives*, 187.

87. Pye, "Against Schmitt," 198.

88. For Cormack *The Winter's Tale* "is a jurisdictional play because it disperses its action across kingdoms and along coasts, but also because it uses jurisdiction, a principle of *distribution* across territory and office, to explore the relation of common terms (including language) to the particular identities that participate in those terms." (See "Shakespeare's Other Sovereignty," 486.)

89. Cormack, 490. For a philosophical reading of the play's exploration of the fantasy of autonomy and the anxieties of human separateness, see Stanley Cavell, "Recounting Gains, Showing Losses: Reading *The Winter's Tale*," in *Disowning Knowledge in Six Plays of Shakespeare* (Cambridge: Cambridge University Press, 1999), 193–222.

90. See especially Ken Jackson, "'Grace to boot': St. Paul, Messianic Time, and Shakespeare's *The Winter's Tale*" in *The Return of Theory in Early Modern Studies: Tarrying with the Subjunctive*, ed. Paul Cefalu and Bryan Reynolds (New York: Palgrave, 2011), 102–210); Richard Wilson, "The Statue of Our Queen: Shakespeare's Open Secret," in *Secret Shakespeare: Studies in Theatre, Religion and Resistance* (Manchester: Manchester University Press, 2004), 246–70; Huston Diehl, "'Strike All That Look Upon with Marvel': Theatrical and Theological Wonder in *The Winter's Tale*," in *Rematerializing Shakespeare: Authority and Representation on the Early Modern English Stage*, ed. Bryan Reynolds and William N. West (New York: Palgrave, 2005), 19–34; Julia Reinhard Lupton, "'*The Winter's Tale*' and the Gods: Iconographies of Idolatry," in *Afterlives of the Saints: Hagiography, Typology and Renaissance Literature* (Stanford: Stanford University Press, 1996), 175–218; and Anselm Haverkamp, "A Whispering of Nothing: *The Winter's Tale*," *Shakespearean Genealogies of Power* (New York: Routledge 2011), 87–106.

91. "I felt within me that I approached, or was taken before, the Father, and with this movement my hair rose and I felt what seemed a very remarkable burning in every part of my body, followed by tears and the most intense devotion." Saint Ignatius of Loyola, *Personal Writings*, trans. Joseph A. Munitiz and Philip Endean (London: Penguin Books, 1996), 74.

92. See Jean Howard's introduction to the play in *The Norton Shakespeare*, ed. Stephen Greenblatt (New York: Norton, 1997), 2877.

93. See Samuel Weber, *Theatricality as Medium* (New York: Fordham University Press, 2004), 259.

94. On the significance of this name, see Leonard Barkan, "'Living Sculptures': Ovid, Michelangelo, and the *Winter's* Tale," *ELH* 48:4 (Winter, 1981): 656–8. For a discussion of the reanimated statue, not only in *The Winter's Tale* but as a much wider recurring fantasy, see Kenneth Gross, *The Dream of the Moving Statue* (Ithaca: Cornell University Press, 1992). Gross links the fantasy to the myth of the golem in the Jewish Kabbalistic tradition and to the text of the Torah scroll itself:

> The golem, which has been described as an "artificial anthropoid," is a man-shaped figure of kneaded clay which is "animated" by its learned maker. There is some debate over how figurative or how literal such a process of animation was in Kabbalistic writing and ritual praxis, but it is clear from medieval and Renaissance commentaries that the making of such a creature ideally entailed a repossession of the creative power of God, in particular a reactivation of the generative potency embodied in the sacred letters of the torah scroll itself. (10)

95. It is interesting, in this regard, to note Sam Mendes's excision altogether of the "wrinkles" line in his production of *The Winter's Tale* at the Brooklyn Academy of Music, Brooklyn, New York, February 10–March 7, 2009.

96. Julia Reinhard Lupton, *Afterlives of the Saints: Hagiography, Typology, and Renaissance Literature* (Stanford: Stanford University Press, 1996), 217.

97. On the centrality of the figure to the Jesuit conception of pastorship, see Paul V. Murphy, "God's Porters."

98. Peter Goodrich, *Languages of Law*, 54.

99. Ibid., 55.

100. For a discussion of the play's invocations of these writers see Leonard Barkan, "'Living Sculptures': Ovid, Michelangelo, and *The Winter's Tale*," *ELH* 48, no. 4 (Winter 1981), 639–67; and Lynn Enterline "'You Speak a Language That I Understand Not': The Rhetoric of

Animation in *The Winter's Tale*," *Shakespeare Quarterly* 48, no. 1 (Spring 1997): 17–44.

101. Here I am modifying the title of Eric Santner's study of sovereignty, in relation to the crossing of Judaism and psychoanalysis. See Santner, *On the Psychotheology of Everyday Life: Reflections on Freud and Rosenzweig* (Chicago: University of Chicago Press, 2001). On the play's desubjectifying effect, see Pye, "Against Schmitt," 204ff.

102. Velma Bourgeois Richmond, for example, writes that "[i]n the context of Catholicism the statue, a clothed female form, *means* the Blessed Virgin Mary, Mother of God and Queen of Heaven, certainly the most famous and frequently sculptured female figure in Europe" (199; my emphasis). Richmond reads Paulina's line, "It is required / You do awake your faith" (5.2.93), as a direct expression of Christian mysticism: "What is not required are many words. The deepest spiritual understanding, mysticism, is beyond the verbal because full contemplation of God means no-thing, and words explain things" (200–1). But Paulina is staging Hermione, hardly a "full contemplation of God." Are we only to attribute Hermione's sixteen-year absence to divine intervention? Must *The Winter's Tale* be read as Catholic theology? It is, in part, against this dogmatic reading that the present analysis is directed.

On the term "afterimage," see Augustine, *On the Trinity*, 64. Julia Reinhard Lupton refers to Aby Warburg's use of the term "afterimage" to refer to "both the dessication [*sic*] and the reanimation of classical myths in what he called their *Nachleben* or 'afterlife.'" See Lupton, *Afterlives of the Saints: Hagiography, Typology, and Renaissance Literature* (Stanford: Stanford University Press, 1996), 176. A simultaneous "desiccation" and "reanimation" of his own relation to Hermione is precisely what Leonte's ritualistic production of *tears* performs.

103. "Thinking about miracles," writes Hent de Vries, "has never been possible without introducing a certain *technicity* and, quite literally, manipulation . . ." De Vries, *Religion and Media*, 13 and 24.

AFTER-IMAGE

1. Wendy Brown, *Walled States, Waning Sovereignty* (New York: Zone, 2010), 131.

2. Fredric Jameson, *A Singular Modernity: Essay on the Ontology of the Present* (London: Verso, 2002), 94.

3. The contrast between baroque theatricality and narrative form in general that I am developing here is based on Samuel Weber's analysis of

the relationship between early modern theater and the Reformation. As a consequence of the Reformation's critique of the Church, "Theater," Weber argues, "emerges as the paradigmatic worldly institution in a world where *meaning*—which, in the Christian framework at least, is structured as a completed and self-contained narrative, with beginning, middle, and end—is subverted by the deprecation of *works*." Weber, *Theatricality as Medium* (New York: Fordham University Press, 2004), 172.

4. Benjamin's German reads, "Man darf wohl den Exkurs in das Juristische noch weiter treiben und im Sinne der mittelalterlichen Klageliteratur von dem Prozeß der Kreatur sprechen, deren Klage gegen den Tod—oder gegen wen sonst sie ergehen mag—am Ende des Trauerspiels halb nur bearbeitet zu den Akten gelegt wird. Die Wiederaufnahme ist im Trauerspiel angelegt und bisweilen aus herer Latenz getreten." This is very different from the *clearing* of the soil in preparation for a new epoch that we see (according to Florens Christian Rang, Benjamin's principal source) at the end of tragedy. In the *Trauerspiel* of modernity, there is no "resolution," merely a legal delay. "Zu den Akten legen" means to lay aside a file. "Akte" means "file." In addition to the legal connotations, the term *Akten* ("Files"), of course, also resonates with theater, in English, *to act*. See Benjamin, *Ursprung de deutschen Trauerspiels*, 117–18. See Cornelia Vismann, *Files: Law and Media Technology*, trans. Geoffrey Winthrop-Young (Stanford: Stanford University Press, 2008).

5. *After Sovereignty: On the Question of Political Beginnings*, ed. Charles Barbour and George Pavlich (New York: Routledge, 2010), 1. On "sovereignty's" English etymology, see the Introduction, note xxiv.

6. Hannah Arendt, *The Origins of Totalitarianism* (New York: Harcourt, Brace, Jovanovich, 1976). Max Horkheimer and Theodor W. Adorno, *The Dialectic of Enlightenment*, trans. John Cumming (New York: Continuum, 1972).

7. Against the more optimistic and innovative forms of power theorized by Negri, Hardt, and others, sovereignty, according to Roberto Esposito, is very much here to stay:

> Anything but destined to weaken as some had rashly forecast (at least with regard to the world's greatest power), sovereignty seems to have extended and intensified its range of action—beyond a repertoire that for centuries had characterized its relation to both citizens and other state structures. With the clear distinction between inside and outside weakened (and therefore also the distinction between war and peace that had characterized sovereign power for so long), sovereignty finds itself

directly engaged with questions of life and death that no longer have to do with single areas, but with the world in all of its extensions.

> Esposito, *Bíos: Biopolitics and Philosophy*, trans. Timothy Campbell (Minneapolis: University of Minnesota Press, 2008), 13–14.

8. Jens Bartelson, *A Genealogy of Sovereignty* (Cambridge: Cambridge University Press, 1995), 3.

9. Ibid., 1.

10. See Martin Heidegger, "The Age of the World Picture," *The Question Concerning Technology and Other Essays*, trans. William Lovitt (New York: Harper & Row, 1977), 118.

11. See Lovitt, in Heidegger, *The Question Concerning Technology*, trans. Lovitt, 118 n.6.

12. For Derrida's discussion of sovereignty in terms of its *traits*, see *Without Alibi*, trans. Peggy Kamuf (Stanford: Stanford University Press, 2002).

13. See Jacques Derrida, "The *Retrait* of Metaphor," *Psyche: Inventions of the Other, Volume I*, trans. Peggy Kamuf (Stanford: Stanford University Press, 2007), 73.

14. This might be especially surprising to those critics who have argued that Derrida is often *not* interested in providing a history of his concepts. Friedrich Balke, for example, has shown that Derrida's understanding of sovereignty is "metaphysical" and has "no real history" and can therefore be analyzed "as another variant of the deconstruction of the metaphysical heritage." At the same time, Balke is sympathetic to the contributions Derrida does have to make to our understanding of sovereignty. His point here is to contrast Derrida's understanding with Foucault's. See Balke, "Derrida and Foucault on Sovereignty," *Derrida and Legal Philosophy* (New York: Palgrave/Macmillan), 101.

15. Derrida, "Retrait," *Psyche*, 77.

16. On the Old and Middle English history of "to read," see the *Oxford English Dictionary*.

17. Agamben, *Homo Sacer*, 47.

18. See Peter Goodrich, "Screening Law," *Law and Literature* 26, no.1 (2009), 1–2.

# Works Cited

Adams, David. "Metaphors for Mankind: The Development of Hans Blumenberg's Anthropological Metaphorology." *Journal of the History of Ideas* 52, no. 1 (January–March, 1991): 152–66.
Agamben, Giorgio. *The Signature of All Things: On Method.* Translated by Luca D'Isanto with Kevin Attell. New York: Zone Books, 2009.
———. *What Is an Apparatus? and Other Essays.* Translated by David Kishik and Stefan Pedatella. Stanford: Stanford University Press, 2009.
———. *State of Exception.* Translated by Kevin Attell. Chicago: University of Chicago Press, 2005.
———. *The Time That Remains: A Commentary on the Letter to the Romans.* Translated by Patricia Dailey. Stanford: Stanford University Press, 2005.
———. *Homo Sacer: Sovereign Power and Bare Life.* Translated by Daniel Heller-Roazen. Stanford: Stanford University Press, 1998.
Agnew, Jean-Christophe. *Worlds Apart: The Market and the Theater in Anglo-American Thought, 1550–1750.* Cambridge: Cambridge University Press, 1986.
Almodóvar, Pedro. *All About My Mother* [*Todo Sobre Mi Madre*]. Screenplay and Dir. Pedro Almodóvar. Perf. Cecilia Roth, Marisa Paredes, Candela Peña, Antonia San Juan, Penelope Cruz. Sony Pictures Classics, 1999.
Althusser, Louis. "Ideology and Ideological State Apparatuses." In *Lenin and Philosophy and Other Essays*, translated by Ben Brewster. New York: Monthly Review Press, 1971.
Anderson, Judith. *Translating Investments: Metaphor and the Dynamic of Cultural Change in Tudor-Stuart England.* New York: Fordham University Press, 2005.

Andrés-Moros, Emilio Cabrera. *Fuenteovejuna: La Violencia Antiseñorial en el Siglo XV.* Barcelona: Editorial Crítica, 1991.

Anidjar, Gil. *The Jew, the Arab: A History of the Enemy.* Stanford: Stanford University Press, 2003.

Antonucci, Fausta, ed. *La vida es sueño.* Barcelona: Crítica, 2008.

Appelbaum, Stanley. Introduction to *Fuenteovejuna: A Dual-Language Book.* Minneola: Dover, 2002.

Aquinas, Thomas. *Summa contra Gentiles. Book One: God.* Translated by Anton C. Pegis. Notre Dame: University of Notre Dame, 1975.

———. *Basic Writings.* Edited by Anton C. Pegis. New York: Random House, 1945.

Archer, John Michael. *Sovereignty and Intelligence: Spying and Court Culture in the English Renaissance.* Stanford: Stanford University Press, 1993.

Arendt, Hannah. *The Human Condition.* Chicago: University of Chicago Press, 1958.

Aristotle. *Poetics, with the Tractatus Coislinianus, reconstruction of poetics II, and the fragments of the On Poets.* Translated by Richard Janko. Indianapolis: Hackett, 1987.

Ashworth, E. J. "Suárez on the Analogy of Being: Some Historical Background." *Vivarium* 33 (1995): 50–75.

Augustine of Hippo. *On the Trinity: Books 8–15.* Edited by Gareth B. Matthews. Translated by Stephen McKenna. Cambridge: Cambridge University Press, 2002.

———. *Confessions.* Translated by Henry Chadwick. Oxford: Oxford University Press, 1991.

———. *On Christian Doctrine.* Translated by D. W. Robertson, Jr. Upper Saddle River, N.J.: Prentice-Hall, 1958.

Axton, Mary. *The Queen's Two Bodies: Drama and the Elizabethan Succession.* London: Royal Historical Society, 1977.

Bacon, Francis. *The Advancement of Learning, Book Two, Francis Bacon: A Critical Edition of The Major Works.* Edited by Brian Vickers. Oxford: Oxford University Press, 1996.

Balakrishnan, Gopal. *The Enemy: An Intellectual Portrait of Carl Schmitt.* London: Verso, 2002.

Balke, Friedrich. "'The War Has Not Ended': Thomas Hobbes, Carl Schmitt, and the Paradoxes of Countersovereignty." In *Crediting God: Sovereignty and Religion in the Age of Global Capitalism*, edited by Miguel Vatter, 179–89. New York: Fordham University Press, 2011.

Barkan, Leonard. *Mute Poetry Speaking Pictures.* Princeton: Princeton University Press, 2013.

———. "The Heritage of Zeuxis—Painting, Rhetoric, History." In *Antiquity and Its Interpreters*, edited by Alina Payne, Ann Kuttner, and Rebekah Smick. Cambridge: Cambridge University Press, 2000.

———. "Cosmas and Damian: Of Medicine, Miracles, and the Economies of the Body." In *Organ Transplantation: Meanings and Realities*, edited by Stuart J. Youngner, Renée C. Fox, and Laurence J. O'Connell, 221–51. Madison: University of Wisconsin Press, 1996.

———. "'Living Sculptures': Ovid, Michelangelo, and the *Winter's Tale*." *ELH* 48, no. 4 (Winter 1981): 639–67.

Bartelson, Jens. *A Genealogy of Sovereignty*. Cambridge: Cambridge University Press, 1995.

Benjamin, Walter. *The Arcades Project*. Translated by Howard Eiland and Kevin McLaughlin. Cambridge, Mass.: Belknap Press, 1999.

———. "Short Shadows II." In *Selected Writings, Volume II, 1927–1934*, edited by Michael W. Jennings, Howard Eiland, and Gary Smith, 700–2. Cambridge: Harvard University Press, 1997.

———. "*Trauerspiel* and Tragedy." In *Selected Writings, Volume I, 1913–1926*, edited by Marcus Bullock and Michael W. Jennings, 55–8. Cambridge: Harvard University Press, 1997.

———. *The Origin of German Tragic Drama*. Translated by John Osborne. London: Verso, 1994.

Berman, Russell A. Introduction. "Political Theologies." *Telos* 148 (Fall 2009): 3–6.

Bertelli, Sergio. *The King's Body: Sacred Rituals of Power in Medieval and Early Modern Europe*. Translated by R. Burr Litchfield. University Park: Pennsylvania State University Press, 2001.

Beverley, John. *Essays on the Literary Baroque in Spain and Spanish America*. Woodbridge, Suffolk, U.K.: Tamesis, 2008.

Blue, William. "The Politics of Lope's *Fuenteovejuna*." *Hispanic Review* 59, no. 3 (Summer 1991): 295–315.

Blumenberg, Hans. *Paradigms for a Metaphorology*. Translated by Robert Savage. Ithaca: Cornell University Press, 2010.

———. "Prospect for a Theory of Nonconceptuality." In *Shipwreck with Spectator: Paradigm of a Metaphor for Existence*, translated by Steven Rendall. Cambridge, Mass.: MIT Press, 1997.

———. *The Legitimacy of the Modern Age*. Translated by Robert M. Wallace. Cambridge, Mass.: MIT Press, 1983.

Borradori, Giovanna. *Philosophy in a Time of Terror: Dialogues with Jürgen Habermas and Jacques Derrida*. Chicago: University of Chicago Press, 2003.

Bosteels, Bruno. "Afterword: Thinking, Being, Acting, or, On the Uses and Disadvantages of Ontology for Politics." In *A Leftist*

*Ontology: Beyond Relativism and Identity Politics*, edited by Carsten Strathausen, 235–52. Minneapolis: University of Minnesota Press, 2009.

Bourdin, Bernard. *The Theological-Political Origins of the Modern State: The Controversy Between James I of England and Cardinal Bellarmine*. Translated by Susan Pickford. Washington, D.C.: The Catholic University of America Press, 2010.

Bourgeois Richmond, Velma. *Shakespeare, Catholicism, and Romance*. New York: Continuum, 2000.

Braun, Harald E. *Juan de Mariana and Early Modern Spanish Political Thought*. Aldershot: Ashgate, 2007.

Brett, Annabel. "Individual and Community in the 'Second Scholastic': Subjective rights in Domingo de Soto and Francisco Suárez." In *Philosophy in the Sixteenth and Seventeenth Centuries: Conversations with Aristotle*, edited by Constance Blackwell and Sachiko Kusukawa, 146–68. Aldershot, Hampshire: Ashgate, 1999.

Brett, Annabel, James Tully, and Holly Hamilton-Bleakley, eds. *Rethinking Foundations of Modern Political Thought*. Cambridge: Cambridge University Press, 2006.

Brook, Peter. *The Empty Space: A Book about the Theatre: Deadly, Holy, Rough, Immediate*. New York: Touchstone, 1996.

Brown Scott, James. *The Catholic Conception of International Law*. The Lawbook Exchange, 2007.

Brown, Wendy. *Walled States, Waning Sovereignty*. New York: Zone, 2010.

Buccola, Regina and Lisa Hopkins, eds. *Marian Moments in Early Modern British Drama*. Aldershot: Ashgate, 2007.

Burgess, Glenn. *The Politics of the Ancient Constitution: An Introduction to English Political Thought 1603–1642*. University Park: Pennsylvania State University Press, 1992.

Butler, Judith. *The Psychic Life of Power: Theories in Subjection*. Stanford: Stanford University Press, 1997.

Calderón de la Barca, Pedro. *La Vida es Sueño*. Edited by Fausta Antonucci. Barcelona: Crítica, 2008.

———. *La Vida es Sueño*. Edited by Ciriaco Morón. Madrid: Cátedra, 1995.

———. *La Cisma de Inglaterra*. Translated by Kenneth Muir and Ann L. Mackenzie. Warminster: Arist & Phillips, 1990.

Campbell, Jodi. *Monarchy, Political Culture and Drama in Seventeenth-Century Madrid: Theater of Negotiation*. Hampshire: Ashgate, 2006.

Cascardi, Anthony J. *Ideologies of History in the Spanish Golden Age*. University Park: Pennsylvania State University Press, 1997.

Cassirer, Ernst. *The Myth of the State*. New Haven: Yale University Press, 1974.

———. *Substance to Function and Einstein's Theory of Relativity*. Translated by William Curtis Swabey and Marie Collins Swabey. Chicago: The Open Court Publishing Co., 1923.

Castillo, David R. *(A)wry Views: Anamorphosis, Cervantes, and the Early Picaresque*. West Lafayette: Purdue University Press, 2001.

Castro, Américo. *De la edadconflictiva: Crisis de la Cultura Española en el Siglo XVII*. Madrid: Taurus Ediciones, S.A., 1976.

Cavanaugh, William T. *Theopolitical Imagination*. Edinburgh: T&T Clark Ltd., 2002.

Cavarero, Adriana. *Stately Bodies: Literature, Philosophy, and the Question of Gender*. Translated by Robert de Lucca and Deanna Shemek. Ann Arbor: University of Michigan Press, 2002.

Cavell, Stanley, *Pursuits of happiness: the Hollywood comedy of remarriage*. Cambridge: Harvard University Press, 1981.

Caygill, Howard. "Non-Messianic Political Theology in Benjamin's 'On the concept of History.'" In *Walter Benjamin and History*, edited by Andrew Benjamin. London: Continuum, 2005.

———. "Shakespeare's Monster of Nothing." In *Philosophical Shakespeares*, edited by John J. Joughin, 105–14. London: Routledge, 2000.

———. "Benjamin, Heidegger and the Destruction of Tradition." In *Walter Benjamin's Philosophy; Destruction and Experience*, edited by Andrew Benjamin and Peter Osborne, 1–31. London: Routledge, 1994.

Cedroni, Lorella. *La comunità perfecta: ilpensiero politico di Francisco Suárez*. Rome: Edizioni Studium, 1996.

Cohen, Walter. *Drama of a Nation: Public Theater in Renaissance England and Spain*. Ithaca: Cornell University Press, 1985.

Collins, Stephen L. *From Divine Cosmos to Sovereign State: An Intellectual History of Consciousness and the Idea of Order in Renaissance England*. Oxford: Oxford University Press, 1989.

Cormack, Bradin. "Shakespeare's Other Sovereignty: On Particularity and Violence in *The Winter's Tale* and the Sonnets." *Shakespeare Quarterly* 62.4 (2011): 485–513.

———. *A Power to Do Justice: Jurisdiction, English Literature, and the Rise of Common Law, 1509–1625*. Chicago: University of Chicago Press, 2007.

Courtine, Jean-Francois. *Nature et empire de la loi: études suaréziennes*. Paris: Vrin, 1999.

———. "Le project suarézien de la métaphysique." *Archives de Philosophie* 42 (1979): 236.

Covarrubias Orozco, Sebastián de. *Tesoro de la Lengua Castellana O Española*. Edited by Ignacio Arellano y Rafael Zafra. Madrid: Iberoamericana, 2006.

———. *Suplemento al Tesoro de la Lengua Española Castellana*. Edited by Georgina Dopico and Jacques Lezra. Madrid: Ediciones Polifemo, 2001.

———. *Emblemas Morales*. Edited by Carmen Bravo-Villasante. Madrid: Fundación Universitaria Española, 1978.

Cowell, John. *The Interpreter* (1607). Menston: The Scolar Press Limited, 1972.

Curtius, Ernst Robert. *European Literature in the Late Middle Ages*. Translated by Willard R. Trask. Princeton: Princeton University Press, 1991.

Dawson, Anthony B. and Paul Yachnin. *The Culture of Playgoing in Shakespeare's England: A Collaborative Debate*. Cambridge: Cambridge University Press, 2001.

De Armas, Frederick A. "A Woman Hunted, a City Besieged: Spanish Emblems and Italian Art in *Fuenteovejuna*." In *Approaches to Teaching Early Modern Spanish Drama*, edited by Laura R. Bass and Margaret R. Greer, 45–52. New York: MLA, 2006.

De Certeau, Michel. *The Mystic Fable. Volume One: The Sixteenth and Seventeenth Centuries*. Translated by Michael B. Smith. Chicago: University of Chicago Press, 1995.

De la Durantaye, Leland. *Giorgio Agamben: A Critical Introduction*. Stanford: Stanford University Press, 2009.

Deleuze, Gilles. *The Fold: Leibniz and the Baroque*. Translated by Tom Conley. Minneapolis: University of Minnesota Press, 1993.

De Man, Paul. *The Resistance to Theory*. Foreword by Wlad Godzich. Minneapolis: University of Minnesota Press, 2002.

———. "The Epistemology of Metaphor." In *Aesthetic Ideology*, edited and introduction by Andrzej Warminski. Minneapolis: University of Minnesota Press, 1996.

———. *Allegories of Reading: Figural Language in Rousseau, Nietzsche, Rilke, and Proust*. New Haven: Yale University Press, 1979.

Derrida, Jacques. *The Beast and the Sovereign*. Edited by Michel-Lisse, Marie-Louise Mallet, and Ginette Michaud. Translated by Geoffrey Bennington. Chicago: University of Chicago Press, 2009.

———. "The Retrait of Metaphor." *Psyche. Inventions of the Other. Vol. I*. Stanford: Stanford University Press, 2007.

———. *Paper Machines*. Stanford: Stanford University Press, 2005.

———. *Rogues*. Translated by Michael Naas. Stanford: Stanford University Press, 2004.

———. "Faith and Knowledge." In *Acts of Religion*, edited and introduction by Gil Anidjar, 40–101. New York: Routledge, 2002.

———. *Without Alibi*. Translated by Peggy Kamuf. Stanford: Stanford University Press, 2002.

———. "To Forgive: The Unforgivable and the Imprescriptible." In *Questioning God*, edited by John D. Caputo, Mark Dooley, and Michael J. Scanlon, 21–51. Bloomington: Indiana University Press, 2001.

———. *The Politics of Friendship*. Translated by George Collins. New York: Verso, 1997.

———. *The Gift of Death*. Translated by David Wills. Chicago: University of Chicago Press, 1995.

———. "The Force of Law: The 'Mystical Foundation of Authority.'" Translated by Mary Quaintance. *Cardozo Law Review* 11, nos. 5–6 (July/August 1990): 919–1046.

———. *Limited Inc*. Evanston: Northwestern University Press, 1988.

———. "The Politics of Friendship." *Journal of Philosophy* 85, no. 11 (November 1988): 642.

———. "White Mythology: Metaphor in the Text of Philosophy." In *Margins of Philosophy*, translated by Alan Bass. Chicago: University of Chicago Press, 1985.

de Vries, Hent. "Introduction: Before, Around, and Beyond the Theologico-Political." In *Political Theologies: Public Religions in a Post-Secular World*, edited by Hent de Vries and Lawrence E. Sullivan. New York: Fordham University Press, 2006.

———. "In Media Res: Global Religion, Public Spheres, and the Task of Contemporary Comparative Religious Studies." In *Religion and Media*, edited by Hent de Vries and Samuel Weber. Stanford: Stanford University Press, 2001.

Diehl, Huston. "'Strike All That Look Upon with Marvel': Theatrical and Theological Wonder in *The Winter's Tale*." In *Rematerializing Shakespeare: Authority and Representation on the Early Modern Stage*, edited by Bryan Reynolds and William N. West, 19–34. New York: Palgrave, 2005.

Dixon, Victor, ed. and introduction to *Fuente Ovejuna* by Lope de Vega Carpio. Warminster: Aris and Phillips, 1991.

———. "'Su Majestad Habla, En Fin, Como Quien Tanto Ha Acertado.' La Conclusión Ejemplar de *Fuente Ovejuna*." *Criticón* 42 (1988): 155–68.

Dollimore, Jonathan. "Transgression and Surveillance in *Measure for Measure*." In *Political Shakespeares: Essays in Cultural Materialism*, edited by Jonathan Dollimore and Alan Sinfield. Cornell: Cornell University Press, 1994.

Dopico, Georgina. "Sueños de la nación: los Tesoros de Covarrubias." *Suplemento al Tesoro de Covarrubias*. Edited by Georgina Dopico and Jacques Lezra. Madrid: Polifemo, 2001.

Dopico Black, Georgina. *Perfect Wives, Other Women: Adultery and Inquisition in Early Modern Spain*. Durham: Duke University Press, 2001.

Doyle, John P. "Another God, Chimerae, Goat-Stags, and Man-Lions: A Seventeenth-Century Debate about Impossible Objects." *The Review of Metaphysics* 48, no. 4 (June 1995): 771–808.

Echevarría, Roberto González. "Calderón's *La vidaessueño*: Mixed-(Up) Monsters." In *Celestina's Brood: Continuities of the Baroque in Spanish and Latin American Literature*. Durham: Duke University Press, 1993.

Egginton, William. *In Defense of Religious Moderation*. New York: Columbia University Press, 2011.

Eire, Carlos M. N. *From Madrid to Purgatory: The Art and Craft of Dying in Sixteenth-Century Spain*. Cambridge: Cambridge University Press, 1995.

Elliott, J. H. *Spain, Europe and the Wider World 1500–1800*. New Haven: Yale University Press, 2009.

———. *Empires of the Atlantic World: Britain and Spain in America 1492–1830*. New Haven: Yale University Press, 2006.

———. *Imperial Spain 1469–1716*. Harmondsworth: Penguin, 1990.

———. *Spain and Its World 1500–1700: Selected Essays*. New Haven: Yale University Press, 1989.

Elshtain, Jean Bethke. *Sovereignty: God, State, and Self*. New York: Basic Books, 2008.

Empson, William. *The Structure of Complex Words*. Cambridge: Harvard University Press, 1989.

Enterline, Lynn. "'You Speak a Language That I Understand Not': The Rhetoric of Animation in *The Winter's Tale*." *Shakespeare Quarterly* 48, no. 1 (Spring 1997): 17–44.

Evans, Peter W. "Civilisation and Its Discontents in *Fuenteovejuna*." In *Conflicts of Discourse: Spanish Literature in the Golden Age*, edited by Peter Evans. Manchester: Manchester University Press, 1990.

Falk, Richard. "Revisiting Westphalia, Discovering Post-Westphalia." *The Journal of Ethics* 6, no. 4 (2002): 311–52.

———. "Sovereignty." In *The Oxford Companion to Politics of the World*, edited by Joel Krieger, 851–4. New York: Oxford University Press, 1993.
Feros, Antonio. "'Sacred and Terrifying Gazes': Languages and Images of Power in Early Modern Spain." In *The Cambridge Companion to Velázquez*, edited by Suzanne L. Stratton-Pruitt, 68–86. Cambridge: Cambridge University Press, 2002.
———. *Kingship and Favoritism in the Spain of Philip III, 1598–1621*. Cambridge: Cambridge University Press, 2000.
———. "'Vicedioses, perohumanos': el drama del Rey." *Cuadernos de Historia Moderna* 14. Editorial Complutense (Madrid, 1993): 103–31.
Ferris, David S. Editor, ed. *The Cambridge Companion to Walter Benjamin*. Cambridge: Cambridge University Press, 2004.
———, ed. *Walter Benjamin: Theoretical Questions*. Stanford: Stanford University Press, 1996.
Fiore, Robert L. "*Fuenteovejuna*: Philosophical Views on the State and Revolution." In *Hispanic Essays in Honor of Frank P. Casa*, edited by A. Robert Lauer and Henry W. Sullivan, 103–11. New York: Peter Lang, 1997.
Fish, Stanley. "The Law Wishes to Have a Formal Existence." In *The Fate of Law*, edited by Austin Sarat and Thomas R. Kearns, 159–208. Ann Arbor: University of Michigan Press, 1991.
———. "Wrong Again." In *Doing What Comes Naturally: Change, Rhetoric, and the Practice of Theory in Literary and Legal Studies*, 103–19. Duke University Press, 1990.
Forcione, Alban K. *Majesty and Humanity: Kings and Their Doubles in the Political Drama of the Spanish Golden Age*. New Haven: Yale University Press, 2009.
Foucault, Michel. "Governmentality." In *Essential Works of Foucault 1954–1984, Volume Three: Power*, edited by James D. Faubion. Translated by Robert Hurley et al. New York: The New Press, 2000.
———. *Discipline and Punish: The Birth of the Prison*. Translated by Alan Sheridan. New York: Vintage Books, 1995.
———. "The Subject and Power." In *Michel Foucault: Beyond Structuralism and Hermeneutics*, edited by Hubert L. Dreyfus and Paul Rabinow, 208–28. Chicago: University of Chicago Press, 1983.
———. *The Order of Things—An Archaeology of the Human Sciences*. A translation of *Les Mots et les choses*. New York: Pantheon Books, 1973.
Fox, Dian. *Kings in Calderón: A Study in Characterization and Political Theory*. London: Tamesis, 1986.

Franklin, Julian H. *Constitutionalism and Resistance: Three Treatises by Hotman Beza, and Mornay.* Translated by Julian H. Franklin. New York: Pegasus, 1969.

Freinkel, Lisa. *Reading Shakespeare's Will: the Theology of the Figure from Augustine to the Sonnets.* New York: Columbia University Press, 2002.

Freud, Sigmund. "Screen Memories." In *The Uncanny.* Translated by David Mclintock, 1–22. New York: Penguin Books, 2003.

———. *Moses and Monotheism: Three Essays (1939 [1934–38]).* In *The Standard Edition of the Complete Psychological Works of Sigmund Freud, Vol. XXIII,* 3–137. London: Vintage, 2001.

———. *The Origins of Religion: Totem and Taboo, Moses and Monotheism and Other Works.* Translated by James Strachey. New York: Penguin, 1990.

Froldi, Rinaldo. *Fuente Ovejuna.* Madrid: Espasa Calpe, S.A., 1998.

Galli, Carlo. *Political Spaces and Global War.* Edited by Adam Sitze. Translated by Elisabeth Fay. Minneapolis: University of Minnesota Press, 2010.

Gasché, Rodolphe. *The Tain of the Mirror.* Cambridge: Harvard University Press, 1994.

Gauchet, Marcel. *The Disenchantment of the World: A Political History of Religion.* Translated by Oscar Burge. Princeton: Princeton University Press, 1997.

Geulen, Eva. "The Function of Ambivalence in Agamben's Reontologization of Politics." In *A Leftist Ontology: Beyond Relativism and Identity Politics,* edited by Carsten Strathausen, 19–32. Minneapolis: University of Minnesota Press, 2009.

———. "Under Construction: Walter Benjamin's 'The Work of Art in the Age of Mechanical Reproduction.'" In *Benjamin's Ghosts: Interventions in Contemporary Literary and Cultural Theory,* 121–41. Stanford: Stanford University Press, 2002.

Gierke, Otto von. *Political Theories of the Middle Ages.* Translated and introduction by Frederic William Maitland. Bristol: Thoemmes Press, 1996.

Gil Harris, Jonathan. *Untimely Matter in the Time of Shakespeare.* Philadelphia: University of Pennsylvania Press, 2008.

Gilman, Ernest. *The Curious Perspective: Literary and Pictorial Wit in the Seventeenth Century.* New Haven: Yale University Press, 1978.

Goldberg, Jonathan. *James I and the Politics of Literature: Jonson, Shakespeare, Donne, and Their Contemporaries.* Stanford: Stanford University Press, 1989.

Goodrich, Peter. "Screening Law." *Law and Literature* 21:1. 2009.
———. "The Iconography of Nothing: Blank Spaces and the Representation of Law in *Edward VI and the Pope*." In *Law and the Image: The Authority of Art and the Aesthetics of Law*, edited by Costas Douzinas and Lynda Nead, 89–116. Chicago: University of Chicago Press, 1999.
———. *Law and the Unconscious: A Legendre Reader*. Translated by Peter Goodrich, Alain Pottage, and Anton Schütz. New York: St. Martin's Press, 1997.
———. *Languages of Law: From Logics of Memory to Nomadic Masks*. London: Weidenfeld and Nicolson, 1990.
Gourgouris, Stathis. *Does Literature Think? Literature as Theory for an Antimythical Era*. Stanford: Stanford University Press, 2003.
Gracia, Jorge J. E. *Suárez on Individuation*. Milwaukee: Marquette University Press, 2000.
———. "Francisco Suárez: The Man in History." *The American Catholic Philosophical Quarterly*, formerly the *New Scholasticism* 65, no. 3 (Summer 1991): 259–66.
Gratton, Peter. "Derrida and the Limits of Sovereign Reason: Freedom, Equality, but Not Fraternity." Telos 148 (Fall 2009): 141–60.
Greenberg, Mitchell. *Baroque Bodies. Psychoanalysis and the Culture of French Absolutism*. Ithaca: Cornell University Press, 2001.
———. *Canonical States, Canonical Stages: Oedipus, Othering, and Seventeenth-Century Drama*. Minneapolis: University of Minnesota Press, 1994.
Greenblatt, Stephen. "Introduction: Fifty Years of *The King's Two Bodies*." *Representations* 106, no. 1. (May 2009): 63–6.
Greene, Roland. "Not Works but Networks: *Colonial Worlds in Comparative Literature*." In *Comparative Literature in an Age of Globalization*, edited by Haun Saussy. Baltimore: Johns Hopkins University Press, 2006.
Griffin, Eric J. *English Renaissance Drama and the Specter of Spain: Ethnopoetics and Empire*. Philadelphia: University of Pennsylvania Press, 2009.
Gross, Kenneth. *The Dream of the Moving Statue*. Ithaca: Cornell University Press, 1992.
Guillen, Claudio. "On the Concept and Metaphor of Perspective." In *Comparatists at Work*, edited by Stephen G. Nichols and Richard B. Vowles. Waltham, Mass.: Blaisdell Publishing, 1968.
Hägglund, Martin. *Radical Atheism: Derrida and the Time of Life*. Stanford: Stanford University Press, 2008.

Hale, David George. *The Body Politic: A Political Metaphor in Renaissance English Literature*. Paris: Mouton, 1971.
Halpern, Richard. "The King's Two Buckets: Kantorowicz, *Richard II*, and Fiscal *Trauerspiel*." *Representations* 106 (Spring 2009).
Hammill, Graham. *The Mosaic Constitution: Political Theology and Imagination from Machiavelli to Milton*. Chicago: University of Chicago Press, 2012.
———. *Shakespeare Among the Moderns*: Ithaca: Cornell University Press, 1997.
Hanssen, Beatrice. *Walter Benjamin's Other History: Of Stones, Animals, Human Beings, and Angels*. Berkeley: University of California Press, 2000.
Harrison, Bernard. "'White Mythology' Revisited: Derrida and His Critics on Reason and Rhetoric." *Critical Inquiry* 25, no. 3 (Spring 1999).
Hastings, James, ed. *Encyclopaedia of Religion and Ethics*, Volume XI. New York: Charles Scribner's Sons, 1919.
Haverkamp, Anselm. *Shakespearean Genealogies of Power: A Whispering of Nothing in* Hamlet, Richard II, Julius Caesar, Macbeth, The Merchant of Venice, *and* The Winter's Tale. Oxford: Routledge, 2011.
———. "The Enemy Has No Future: Figure of the Political." *Cardozo Law Review* 26, no. 6 (2005): 2553–62.
———. "*Richard II*, Bracton, and the End of Political Theology." *Law and Literature* 16, no. 3 (Fall 2004): 313–26.
———. *Hamlet: Hypothek der Macht*. Edited by Dirk Baecker and Elmar Lampson. Berlin: KadmosVerlag, 2001.
———, with Cornelia Vismann. "Habeas Corpus: The Law's Desire to Have the Body." In *Violence, Identity, and Self-Determination*, edited by Hent de Vries and Samuel Weber. Stanford: Stanford University Press, 1997.
———. "Notes on the 'Dialectical Image' (How Deconstructive Is it?)." *Diacritics* 22, nos. 3–4 (1992): 70–80.
———. "Rhetoric, Law, and the Poetics of Memory." *Cardozo Law Review* 13, no. 5 (March 1992): 1639–53.
Hegel, Georg Wilhelm Friedrich. *Philosophy of Right*. Translated by T. M. Knox. London: Oxford University Press, 1967.
Heidegger, Martin. *Aristotle's Metaphysics 1–3, On the Essence and Actuality of Force*. Translated by Walter Brogan and Peter Warnek, p. 38. Bloomington: Indiana University Press, 1995.
———. *The Basic Problems of Phenomenology*. Translated by Albert Hofstadter. Bloomington: Indiana University Press, 1988.

———. *The Question Concerning Technology and Other Essays.* Translated by William Lovitt. New York: Garland Publishing, 1977.
Herrero, Javier. "The New Monarchy: A Structural Reinterpretation of *Fuenteovejuna.*" *Revista Hispánica Moderna* 36.4 (1970–71): 174–85.
Hesse, Everett. "Los conceptos del amor in *Fuenteovejuna.*" *Revista de Archivos, Bibliotecas y Museos.* LXXV (1968–72).
Honig, Bonnie. *Democracy and the Foreigner.* Princeton: Princeton University Press, 2003.
Höpfl, Harro. *Jesuit Political Thought: The Society of Jesus and the State, c. 1540–1630.* Cambridge: Cambridge University Press, 2004.
Horkheimer, Max, and Adorno, Theodor. *Dialectic of Enlightenment.* Translated by John Cumming. New York: Continuum, 1998.
Hutson, Lorna. "Imagining Justice: Kantorowicz and Shakespeare." *Representations* 106 (Spring 2009): 118–42.
———. "Not the King's Two Bodies: Reading the 'Body Politic' in Shakespeare's *Henry IV.*" In *Rhetoric and Law in Early Modern Europe*, edited by Lorna Hutson and Victoria Kahn, 166–98. New Haven: Yale University Press, 2001.
Iampolski, Mikhail. *Fiziologia Simvolicheskoso. Book 1. Vozurachshenie Leviafana. Politicheskaia Teologia, Reprezentatsia Vlasti I konets Starogorezhima.* Moscow: NLO, 2004.
Jameson, Fredric. *A Singular Modernity: Essay on the Ontology of the Present.* London: Verso, 2002.
Jauss, Hans Robert. *Toward an Aesthetic of Reception.* Translated by Timothy Bahti. Minneapolis: University of Minnesota Press, 1982.
Kahn, Paul W. *Political Theology: Four New Chapters on the Concept of Sovereignty.* New York: Columbia University Press, 2011.
Kahn, Victoria. "Political Theology and Fiction in *The King's Two Bodies.*" *Representations* 106, no. 1 (May 2009): 77–101.
Kamen, Henry. *The Spanish Inquisition: A Historical Revision.* London: Weidenfeld and Nicolson, 1997.
Kantorowicz, Ernst H. *The King's Two Bodies—A Study in Medieval Political Theology.* Princeton: Princeton University Press, 1957.
Kasl, Ronda, ed. *Sacred Spain: Art and Belief in the Spanish World.* New Haven: Yale University Press, 2009.
Keenan, Thomas. *Fables of Responsibility: Aberrations and Predicaments in Ethics and Politics.* Stanford: Stanford University Press, 1997.
Kinder, Marsha. "Reinventing the Motherland: Almodóvar's Brain-Dead Trilogy." *Film Quarterly* 58.2 (Winter 2004): 9–25.
Kirschner, Teresa J. *El Protagonistacolectivo en* Fuenteovejuna. Salamanca: Ediciones Universidad de Salamanca, 1979.

Koselleck, Reinhart. *Futures Past: On the Semantics of Historical Time.* Translated by Keith Tribe. New York: Columbia University Press, 2004.

Kottman, Paul A. *A Politics of the Scene.* Stanford: Stanford University Press, 2008.

Koyré, Alexandre. *From the Closed World to the Infinite Universe.* Baltimore: Johns Hopkins University Press, 1974.

Krapp, Peter. "Between Forgiveness and Forgetting." In *Derrida and Legal Philosophy*, edited by Peter Goodrich, Florian Hoffmann, Michel Rosenfeld, and Cornelia Vismann, 167–76. New York: Palgrave, 2008.

Krasner, Stephen D. *Sovereignty: Organized Hypocrisy.* Princeton: Princeton University Press, 1999.

Kristeva, Julia. *The Sense and Non-Sense of Revolt.* Translated by Jeanine Herman. New York: Columbia University Press, 2000.

———. "Stabat Mater." In *Tales of Love*, translated by Leon S. Roudiez. New York: Columbia University Press, 1987.

Küpper, Joachim, "*La cisma de Inglaterra* y la concepción calderoniana de la historia." In *Hacia Calderón*, edited by Hans Flasche, 184–201. Stuttgart: Franz Steiner, 1988.

Laclau, Ernesto. *Emancipation(s).* London: Verso, 2007.

———. "On the Names of God." In *Political Theologies: Public Religions in a Post-Secular World*, edited by Hent de Vries and Lawrence E. Sullivan, 137–47. New York: Fordham University Press, 2006.

Lake, Peter, and Michael Questier. *The Antichrist's Lewd Hat: Protestants, Papists and Players in Post-Reformation England.* New Haven: Yale University Press, 2002.

Lange, Marjory E. *Telling Tears in the English Renaissance.* Leiden: E. J. Brill, 1996.

Larrainzar, Carlos. *Una Introducción a Francisco Suárez.* Pamplona: Ediciones Universidad de Navarra, 1976.

Larson, Catherine. "'Violent Hierarchies': The Deconstructive Voice and Writing Undone in *Fuenteovejuna.*" In *Language and the Comedia: Theory and Practice.* Lewisburg: Bucknell University Press, 1991.

Larson, Donald R. *The Honor Plays of Lope de Vega.* Cambridge: Harvard University Press, 1977.

Le Doeuff, Michèle. *The Philosophical Imaginary.* Translated by Colin Gordon. London: Athlone Press, 1989.

Lefort, Claude. *Democracy and Political Theory.* Translated by David Macey. Minneapolis: University of Minnesota Press: 1988.

Legendre, Pierre. *Law and the Unconscious: A Legendre Reader*. Translated by Peter Goodrich, Alain Pottage, and Anton Schütz. New York: St. Martin's Press, 1997.
Leonard, Nancy S. "Substitution in Shakespeare's Problem Comedies." *English Literary Renaissance* 9, no. 2 (March 1979): 281–301.
Lezra, Jacques. *Wild Materialism: The Ethic of Terror and the Modern Republic*. New York: Fordham University Press, 2010.
———. "The Appearance of History in *Measure for Measure*." In *Unspeakable Subjects: The Genealogy of the Event in Early Modern Europe*. Stanford: Stanford University Press, 1997.
Lockyer, Roger. *King James VI and I*. London: Addison-Wesley, 1998.
Loftis, John, *Renaissance Drama in England & Spain: Topical Allusion and History Plays*. Princeton: Princeton University Press, 1987.
López Estrada, Francisco. Critical introduction to *Fuente Ovejuna*, by Lope de Vega. Madrid: Castalia, 1996. 5–50.
Lorenz, Philip. "'Christall Mirrors,' Analogy and Onto-Theology in Shakespeare and Francisco Suárez." *Religion and Literature* 38, no. 3 (Autumn 2006): 101–20.
———. "Notes on the 'Religious Turn': Mystery, Metaphor, Medium," in "Literary History and the Religious Turn." Special issue, *English Language Notes* 44, no. 1 (Spring 2006): 163–72.
Luis-Martínez, Zenón. "Shakespeare's Historical Drama as *Trauerspiel*: *Richard II* and After." *ELH* 75 (2008): 673–705.
Lupton, Julia Reinhard. *Thinking with Shakespeare*. Chicago: University of Chicago Press, 2011.
———. *Citizen-Saints: Shakespeare and Political Theology*. Chicago: University of Chicago Press, 2005
———. *Afterlives of the Saints: Hagiography, Typology, and Renaissance Literature*. Stanford: Stanford University Press, 1996.
Lupton, Julia Reinhard, and Kenneth Reinhard. *After Oedipus: Shakespeare in Psychoanalysis*. Ithaca: Cornell University Press, 1993.
Lyttkens, Hampus. *The Analogy Between God and the World—An Investigation of Its Background and Interpretation of Its Use by Thomas Aquino*. Wiesbaden : Harrassowitz, 1953.
Machiavelli, Niccolò. *The Prince*. Translated and introduction by George Bull. New York: Penguin Books, 1995.
———. *Il principe*. Mondadori: Milan, 1994.
Malcolm, Joyce Lee. *The Struggle for Sovereignty: Seventeenth-Century English Political Tracts*. Indianapolis: Liberty Fund, 1999.
Maravall, José Antonio. *Teoría del Estado en España en el Siglo XVII*. Madrid: Centro de Estudios Constitucionales, 1997.

———. *Culture of the Baroque: Analysis of a Historical Structure.* Translated by Terry Cochran. Minneapolis: University of Minnesota Press, 1986.

Mariana, Juan de. *The King and the Education of the King.* Translated by George Albert Moore. Chevy Chase, Md.: Country Dollar Press, 1948.

Marin, Louis. "The Body-of-Power and Incarnation at Port Royal and in Pascal—or—Of the Figurability of the Political Absolute." In *Fragments for a History of the Human Body*, Part Three, edited by Michel Feher with Ramona Naddaff and Nadia Tazi. New York: Zone, 1989.

———. *Food for Thought.* Translated by Mette Hjort. Baltimore: Johns Hopkins University Press, 1989.

———. *Portrait of the King.* Translated by Martha M. Houle. Minneapolis: University of Minnesota Press, 1988.

Marín, Juan María. Introduction to *Fuente Ovejuna*, by Lope de Vega, 11–71. Madrid: Cátedra, 2002.

Marion, Jean-Luc. "Outline of a History of Definitions of God in the Cartesian Epoch." In *On the Ego and on God: Further Cartesian Questions*, translated by Christina M. Gschwandtner, 161–92. New York: Fordham University Press, 2007.

———. *Sur la theologie blanche de Descartes.* Paris: Presses Universitaires de France, 1981.

Marthaler, Berard, L., O.F.M. Conv. *New Catholic Encyclopedia.* 2nd ed. Vol. 10. New York: Thomson-Gale, 2003.

Martz, Louis. "'Of Government': Theme and Action in *Measure for Measure*." In *Classical, Renaissance and Postmodernist Acts of the Imagination: Essays Commemorating O. B. Hardison, Jr.*, edited by Arthur Kinney. Newark: University of Delaware Press, 1996.

Maryks, Robert A. *The Jesuit Order as a Synagogue of Jews: Jesuits of Jewish Ancestry and Purity-of-Blood Laws in the Early Society of Jesus.* Leiden: Brill, 2010.

Mazzio, Carla, and Douglas Trevor, eds. *Historicism, Psychoanalysis, and Early Modern Culture.* New York: Routledge, 2000.

McIlwain, Charles Howard. *The Political Works of James I.* Cambridge: Harvard University Press, 1918.

McKendrick, Melveena. "Communicating the Past." In *Approaches to Teaching Early Modern Spanish Drama*, edited by Laura R. Bass and Margaret R. Greer, 29–38. New York: Modern Language Association, 2006.

———. *Identities in Crisis: Essays on Honour, Gender and Women in the Comedia.* Kassel: Edition Reichenberger, 2002.

———. *Playing the King: Lope de Vega and the Limits of Conformity*. London: Tamesis, 2000.

———. *Theatre in Spain 1490–1700*. Cambridge: Cambridge University Press, 1992.

McKim, Donald, K. *Westminster Dictionary of Theological Terms*. Louisville: John Knox Press, 1996.

McMillin, Scott. "Shakespeare's *Richard II:* Eyes of Sorrow, Eyes of Desire." *Shakespeare Quarterly* 35 (1984): 40–52.

Meier, Heinrich. "What Is Political Theology?" In *Leo Strauss and the Theologico Political Problem*, translated by Marcus Brainard, 75–88. Cambridge: Cambridge University Press, 2006.

———. *The Lesson of Carl Schmitt: Four Chapters on the Distinction between Political Theology and Political Philosophy*. Translated by Marcus Brainard. Chicago: University of Chicago Press, 1998.

Mende, Dirk. "Histories of Technicization: On the Relation of Conceptual History and Metaphorology in Hans Blumenberg" in "Hans Blumenberg," special issue, *Telos* 158 (Spring 2012): 59–79.

———. *Metapher: Zwischen Metaphysik und Archäologie: Schelling, Heidegger, Derrida Blumenberg* (München: Fink Verlag, 2013).

Menon, Madhavi. *Wanton Words: Rhetoric and Sexuality in English Renaissance Drama*. Toronto: University of Toronto Press, 2004.

Meyler, Bernadette. *Theaters of Pardoning: Sovereignty and Judgment from Shakespeare to Kant*. Unpublished manuscript.

Miller, Jacques-Alain. "*Extimité.*" In *Lacanian Theory of Discourse: Subject, Structure, and Society*. Edited by Mark Bracher, et al. New York: New York University Press, 1994.

Monod, Paul Kléber. *The Power of Kings: Monarchy and Religion in Europe, 1589–1715*. New Haven: Yale University Press, 1999.

Montrose, Louis. *The Purpose of Playing: Shakespeare and the Cultural Politics of the Elizabethan Theatre*. Chicago: University of Chicago Press, 1996.

Moretti, Franco. "The Great Eclipse: Tragic Form and the Deconsecration of Sovereignty." In *Signs Taken for Wonders: Essays in the Sociology of Literary Forms*, 42–82. London: Verso, 2005.

Morón, Ciriaco. Introduction to *La vida es sueño*, by Calderón de la Barca. Madrid: Cátedra, 1995.

Mouffe, Chantal, ed. *The Challenge of Carl Schmitt*. London: Verso, 1999.

Murphy, Paul V. "'God's Porters': the Jesuit Vocation According to Francisco Suárez." *Archivum Historicum Societatis Iesu* 70 (January–June 2001): 3–28.

Naas, Michael. *Derrida From Now On*. New York: Fordham University Press, 2008.

Nägele, Rainer. *Theater, Theory, Speculation: Walter Benjamin and the Scenes of Modernity.* Baltimore: Johns Hopkins Press, 1991.

Nancarrow, Mindy. "Francisco Suárez's Bienaventurada Virgen and the Iconography of the Immaculate Conception." In *Imagery, Spirituality and Ideology in Baroque Spain and Latin America*, edited by Jeremy Roe and Marta Bustillo, 3–14. Cambridge: Cambridge University Press, 2010.

Nancy, Jean-Luc. *Dis-Enclosure: The Deconstruction of Christianity.* Translated by Bettina Bergo, Gabriel Malenfant, and Michael B. Smith. New York: Fordham University Press, 2008.

———. "Complement." In *The Creation of the World or Globalization.* Translated by François Raffoul and David Pettigrew. Albany: State University of New York Press, 2007.

———. *The Sense of the World.* Translated by Jeffrey S. Librett. Minneapolis: University of Minnesota Press, 1997.

———. "War, Law, Sovereignty—*Techné.*" Translated by Jeffrey S. Librett. In *Rethinking Technologies*, edited by Verena Andermatt Conley, 28–58. Minneapolis: University of Minnesota, 1993.

Negri, Antonio. *Negri on Negri: Antonio Negri in Conversation with Anne Dufourmantelle.* Translated by M. B. DeVevoise. New York: Routledge, 2004.

———. "The Machiavellian Paradigm." In *Insurgencies: Constituent Power and the Modern State*, translated by Maurizia Boscagli. Minneapolis: University of Minnesota Press, 1999.

———. "*Reliqua Desiderantur:* A Conjecture for a Definition of the Concept of Democracy in the Final Spinoza." In *The New Spinoza*, edited by Warren Montag and Ted Stolze. Minneapolis: University of Minnesota Press, 1997.

———. *Savage Anomaly: The Power of Spinoza's Metaphysics and Politics.* Translated by Michael Hardt. Minneapolis: University of Minnesota Press, 1991.

Newman, Jane O. *Benjamin's Library: Modernity, Nation, and the Baroque.* Ithaca: Cornell University Press, 2011.

Norbrook, David. "The Emperor's New Body?" *Richard II*, Ernst Kantorowicz, and the Politics of Shakespeare Criticism." *Textual Practice* 10, no. 2 (1996): 329–57.

Noreña, Carlos. "Suárez and the Jesuits." *American Catholic Philosophical Quarterly* 65, no. 3 (Summer 1991): 286.

Norris, Andrew, ed. *Politics, Metaphysics, and Death: Essays on Giorgio Agamben's* Homo Sacer. Durham: Duke University Press, 2005.

Oakley, Francis. *Kingship: The Politics of Enchantment.* Malden, Mass.: Wiley–Blackwell, 2006.

———. "Jacobean Political Theology." *Journal of the History of Ideas* 29, no. 3 (1968): 323–46.
O'Connor, Thomas Austin. *Love in the "Corral": Conjugal Spirituality and Anti-theatrical Polemic in Early Modern Spain*. New York: Peter Lang, 2000.
Ong, Walter J. S.J. *Ramus: Method and the Decay of Dialogue from the Art of Discourse to the Art of Reason*. Chicago: University of Chicago Press, 2004.
Orford, Anne. *International Authority and the Responsibility to Protect*. Cambridge: Cambridge University Press, 2011.
Orgel, Stephen. Introduction to *The Winter's Tale*, by William Shakespeare. Oxford: Oxford University Press, 1998.
Parker, Alexander. *The Mind and Art of Calderón. Essays on the Comedias*. Cambridge: Cambridge University Press, 1988.
Parker, Jason T. "Recruiting the Literary Tradition: Lope de Vega's *Fuenteovejuna* as Cultural Weapon during the Spanish Civil War." *Bulletin of the Comediantes* 66, no. 1 (2010).
Pascal, Blaise. *Pensées*. Translated by A. J. Krailsheimer. London: Penguin Books, 1995.
Pelikan, Jaroslav. *Mary Through the Centuries: Her Place in the History of Culture*. New Haven: Yale University Press, 1996.
Preuss, Ulrich K. "Political Order and Democracy: Carl Schmitt and His Influence." In *The Challenge of Carl Schmitt*, edited by Chantal Mouffe, 155–79. London: Verso, 1999.
Puttenham, George. *The Art of English Poesy. A Critical Edition*. Edited by Frank Whigham and Wayne A. Rebhorn. Ithaca: Cornell University Press, 2007.
Pye, Christopher. "Against Schmitt: Law, Aesthetics, and Absolutism in Shakespeare's *Winter's Tale*." *South Atlantic Quarterly* 108, no. 1 (Winter 2009): 197–217.
———. *The Vanishing Subject: Shakespeare, the Subject, and Early Modern Culture*. Durham: Duke University Press, 2000.
———. *The Regal Phantasm: Shakespeare and the Politics of Spectacle*. London: Routledge, 1990.
Quintero, María Cristina. "English Queens and the Body Politic in Calderón's *La cisma de Inglaterra* and Rivadeneira's *Historia Eclesiástica del Scisma del Reino de Inglaterra*." *MLN* 113, no. 2 (March 1998): 259–82.
Rasmussen, Ulrik Houlind. "The Memory of God: Hans Blumenberg's Philosophy of Religion." Ph.D Diss. University of Copenhagen, July 2009.
Regalado, Antonio. *Calderón: Los Orígenes de la modernidad en la España del Siglo de Oro*. Barcelona: Ediciones Destino, S.A., 1995.

Richter, Gerhard, *Thought-Images: Frankfurt School Writers' Reflections from Damaged Life*. Stanford: Stanford University Press, 2007.

Ricoeur, Paul. *Evil: A Challenge to Philosophy and Theology*. Translated by John Bowden. London: Continuum, 2004.

———. *The Rule of Metaphor: Multi-Disciplinary Studies of the Creation of Meaning in Language*. Translated by Robert Czerny with Kathleen McLaughlin and John Costello, S.J. Toronto: University of Toronto Press, 1997.

———. *Figuring the Sacred: Religion, Narrative, and Imagination*. Translated by David Pellauer. Edited by Mark I. Wallace. Minneapolis: Fortress Press, 1995.

———. "The Specificity of Religious Language." *Semeia: An Experimental Journal for Biblical Criticism* 4 (1975): 107–45.

Rosenwein, Barbara H. *Negotiating Space: Power, Restraint, and Privileges of Immunity in Early Medieval Europe*. Ithaca: Cornell University Press, 1999.

Ross, Alison, ed. *The Agamben Effect*. Special Issue of *South Atlantic Quarterly*, 107, no. 1 (Winter 2008). Durham: Duke University Press, 2008.

Rust, Jennifer. "Political Theology and Shakespeare Studies." *Literature Compass* 5 (2008).

Saavedra Fajardo, Diego. *Empresas Políticas*. Edited by Sagrario López Poza. Madrid: Ediciones Cátedra, 1999.

Samson, Alexander, and Jonathan Thacker. *A Companion to Lope de Vega*. Woodbridge: Tamesis, 2008.

Santner, Eric L. *The Royal Remains: The People's Two Bodies and the Endgames of Sovereignty*. Chicago: University of Chicago Press, 2011.

———. *On the Psychotheology of Everyday Life: Reflections on Freud and Rosenzweig*. Chicago: University of Chicago Press, 2001.

Schmitt, Carl. *Hamlet or Hecuba: The Intrusion of the Time into the Play*. Translated by David Pan and Jennifer Rust. New York: Telos Press, 2009.

———. *Political Theology II: The Myth of the Closure of Any Political Theology*. Translated by Michael Hoelzl and Graham Ward. Cambridge: Polity Press, 2008.

———. *The Nomos of the Earth in the International Law of the Just Publicum Europaeum*. Translated by G. L. Ulmen. New York: Telos Press, 2003.

———. *Der Begriff des Politischen: Text von 1932 Mit Einem Vorwort und Drei Corollarien*. Berlin: Duncker & Humblot, 2002.

———. *The Concept of the Political*. Translated and introduction by George Schwab. Chicago: University of Chicago Press, 1996.

———. *Roman Catholicism and Political Form*. Translated by G. L. Ulmen. Westport: Greenwood Press, 1996.

———. *Political Theology: Four Chapters on the Concept of Sovereignty*. Translated by George Schwab. Cambridge, Mass.: MIT Press, 1988.

Scorraille, Raoul de. *Francois Suarez, de la Compagnie de Jésus, d'après ses lettres, ses autres écrits inédits et un grand nombre de documents nouveaux*. 2 volumes. Paris: Lethielleux, 1912–13.

Scott, James Brown. *The Catholic Conception of International Law; Francisco de Vitoria, Founder of the Modern Law of Nations; Francisco Suárez, Founder of the Modern Philosophy of Law in General and in Particular of the Law of Nations; A Critical Examination and a Justified Appreciation*. Washington, D.C.: Georgetown University Press, 1934.

Shakespeare, William. *King Richard II*. Edited by Peter Ure. London: Thomson Learning, 2001.

———. *The Norton Shakespeare Based on the Oxford Edition*. 2nd ed. Edited by Stephen Greenblatt, Walter Cohen, Jean E. Howard, Katherine Eisaman Maus. New York: Norton, 1997.

———. *The Winter's Tale*. Edited by Ernest Schanzer. London: Penguin Books, 1986.

———. *Measure for Measure*. Edited by J. W. Lever. Walton-on-Thames Surrey: Methuen & Co. Ltd., 1965.

Shell, Marc. *The End of Kinship: "Measure for Measure," Incest and the Ideal of Universal Siblinghood*. Baltimore: Johns Hopkins University Press, 1988.

Shuger, Debora Kuller. *Political Theologies in Shakespeare's England: The Sacred and the State in* Measure for Measure. New York: Palgrave, 2001.

Simay, Philippe. "Tradition as Injunction: Benjamin and the Critique of Historicism." In *Walter Benjamin and History*, by Andrew Benjamin. London: Continuum, 2005.

Sitze, Adam. Editor's Introduction to *Political Spaces and Global War*, by Carlo Galli. Minneapolis: University of Minnesota Press, 2010. xi–lxxxv.

Sommerville, J. P. *Royalists and Patriots: Politics and Ideology in England 1603–1640*. 2nd ed. New York: Addison Wesley Longman, 1999.

———. *King James VI and I: Political Writings*. Cambridge: Cambridge University Press, 1994.

———. "From Suárez to Filmer: A Reappraisal." *The Historical Journal* 25, no. 3 (1982): 525–40.

South, James B. "Francisco Suárez on Imagination." *Vivarium* 39, no. 1, 119–58. Leiden: Brill, 2001.

Spitzer, Leo. "A Central Theme and Its Structural Equivalent in Lope's *Fuenteovejuna.*" In *Representative Essays*, edited by Alban K. Forcione, Herbert Lindenberger, and Madeline Sutherland, 397–420. Stanford: Stanford University Press, 1988.

Stafford, Barbara. *Visual Analogy: Consciousness as the Art of Connecting.* Cambridge: MIT Press, 1999.

Stellardi, Giuseppe. *Heidegger and Derrida on Philosophy and Metaphor: Imperfect Thought.* Amherst, New York: Humanity Books, 2000.

Stevens-Arroyo, Anthony. "The Evolution of Marian Devotionalism within Christianity and the Ibero-Mediterranean Polity." *Journal for the Scientific Study of Religion* 37, no. 1 (March 1998): 50–73.

Stirk, Peter M. *Carl Schmitt, Crown Jurist of the Third Reich: On Preemptive War, Military Occupation, and World Empire.* Edwin Mellen Press, 2005.

Stroud, Matthew D. "The Lessons of Calderón's *La cisma de Inglaterra.*" In *Hispanic Essays in Honor of Frank P. Casa*, edited by Robert A. Lauer and Henry W. Sullivan, 253–63. New York: Peter Lang, 1997.

Suárez, Francisco. *The Metaphysical Demonstration of the Existence of God: Metaphysical Disputations 28–29.* Translated by John P. Doyle. South Bend, Indiana: St. Augustine's Press, 2004.

———. *On Beings of Reason (De Entibus Rationis) Metaphysical Disputation LIV.* Translated and Introduction by John P. Doyle. Milwaukee: Marquette University Press, 1995.

———. *The Dignity and Virginity of the Mother of God: Disputations I, V, VI from The Mysteries of the Life of Christ.* Translated by Richard J. O'Brien, S.J. West Baden Springs, Indiana: Edwards Brothers, 1954.

———. *Misterios de la Vida de Cristo.* [*De Mysteriis Vitae Christi*] (1592). Translated by Romualdo Galdos, S.I. Madrid: Editorial Católica, 1948.

———. *Selections from Three Works.* Edited by James Brown Scott. Translated by Gwladys L. Williams, Ammi Brown, and John Waldron. 2 volumes. Oxford: Clarendon Press London, 1944.

———. *Metaphysicarum disputationum.* Salamanca, 1597. In *Opera omnia*, vols. 25–26. Edited by Charles Berton. Paris: Vives, 1856–61. Available at http://cdigital.dgb.uanl.mx/la/1080042136_C/1080042136_C.html.

———. *Tractatus de legibus ac Deo legislatore.* Coimbra, 1612. In *Opera omnia*, vols. 5–6. Edited by Charles Berton. Paris: Vives, 1856–61. Available online via Universidad Autonoma de Nuevo Leon's Coleccion Digital: http://cdigital.dgb.uanl.mx/la/1080042136_C/1080042136_C.html.

———. *Commentariorum ac disputationum in tertiam partem Divi Thomae tomus secundus* [*Second Tome of the Commentaries and Disputations on the Third Part of the Summa Theologica of Saint Thomas Aquinas*] published at Alcalá in 1592. In *Opera omnia*, vol. 19 (Paris: 1856). Available online at http://www.archive.org/stream/rpfranciscisuare19suar#page/n19/mode/2up

———. *De Voluntario Et Involuntario*. Disputation 6, Section 1. Translated by Sydney Penner. http://www.sydneypenner.ca/SuarTr.shtml#dvi.

Swiffen, Amy. "Giorgio Agamben: Thought Between Two Revolutions." In *After Sovereignty: On the Question of Political Beginnings*, edited by Charles Barbour and George Pavlich, 166–79. New York: Routledge, 2010.

Tanner, J. R. *English Constitutional Conflicts of the Seventeenth Century 1603–1689*. Cambridge: Cambridge University Press, 1962.

Taubes, Jacob. *The Political Theology of Paul*. Translated by Dana Hollander. Stanford: Stanford University Press, 2003.

Taylor, Mark Lewis. *The Theological and the Political: On the Weight of the World*. Minneapolis: Fortress Press, 2011.

Terada, Rei. "Scruples or Faith in Derrida." *Late Derrida: Special Issue*. Edited by Ian Balfour. *South Atlantic Quarterly* 106, no. 2 (Spring 2007): 237–64.

Thacker, Jonathan and Alexander Samson. *A Companion to Lope de Vega*. Woodbridge: Tamesis, 2008.

———. *A Companion to Golden Age Theatre*. Woodbridge: Tamesis, 2010.

Tierney, Brian. *The Idea of Natural Rights: Studies on Natural Rights, Natural Law, and Church Law 1150–1625*. Grand Rapids: Eerdmans, 1997.

Tillyard, E. M. W. *The Elizabethan World Picture*. New York: Vintage, 1959.

Tracy, David. "Metaphor and Religion: The Test Case of Christian Texts." In *On Metaphor*, edited by Sheldon Sacks, 89–104. Chicago: University of Chicago Press, 1981.

Vanita, Ruth. "Mariological Memory in *The Winter's Tale* and *Henry VIII*." *SEL* 40, no. 2 (Spring 2000).

Varela, Javier. *La Muerte del Rey: El Ceremonial Funerario de la Monarquía Española 1500–1885*. Madrid: Turner, 1990.

Vatter, Miguel, ed. *Crediting God: Sovereignty and Religion in the Age of Global Capitalism*. New York: Fordham University Press, 2011.

Vega Carpio, Lope de. *Arte Nuevo de Hacer Comedias*. Edited by Enrique García Santo-Tomás. Madrid: Cátedra, 2009.

———. *Fuente Ovejuna*. Edited by Juan María Marín. Madrid: Cátedra, 2002.

———. *Fuente Ovejuna*. Edited by Rinaldo Froldi. Madrid: Espasa Calpe, S.A., 1998.

———. *Fuente Ovejuna*. Edited by Francisco López Estrada. Madrid: Castalia, 1996.

———. *Fuente Ovejuna*. Edited by Donald McGrady. Barcelona: Crítica, 1993.

———. *Fuente Ovejuna*. Edited and translated by Victor Dixon. Warminster: Aris & Phillips, 1991.

———. *Fuente Ovejuna*. In *Great Spanish Plays in English Translation*, edited by Angel Flores. New York: Dover, 1991.

Walzer, Michael. *In God's Shadow: Politics in the Hebrew Bible*. New Haven: Yale University Press, 2012.

———. "On the Role of Symbolism in Political Thought." *Political Science Quarterly* 82, no. 2 (June 1967): 191–204.

Weber, Samuel. *Benjamin's -abilities*. Cambridge: Harvard University Press, 2008.

———. *Targets of Opportunity: On the Militarization of Thinking*. New York: Fordham University Press, 2005.

———. *Theatricality as Medium*. New York: Fordham University Press, 2004.

———. *Mass Mediauras: Form, Technics, Media*. Stanford: Stanford University Press, 1996.

———. "Taking Exception to the Decision: Walter Benjamin and Carl Schmitt." *Diacritics* 22, nos. 3–4 (Fall–Winter 1992): 5–34.

———. "Genealogy of Modernity: History, Myth and Allegory in Benjamin's *Origin of the German Mourning Play*." *MLN* 106, no. 5 (April 1991).

———. "Religion, Repetition, Media." In *Religion and Media*, edited by Hent de Vries and Samuel Weber. Stanford: Stanford University Press, 2001.

West, William N. "Humanism and the Resistance to Theology." In *The Return of Theory in Early Modern English Studies: Tarrying with the Subjunctive*, edited by Paul Cefalu and Bryan Reynolds, 167–91. New York: Palgrave, 2011.

Wheeler, Duncan. "The Performance History of Golden-Age Drama in Spain (1939–2006)." Bulletin of the *Comediantes* 60, no. 2 (2008): 119–103.

Wilenius, Reijo. *The Social and Political Theory of Francisco Suárez.* Helsinki: *Acta Philosophica Fennica,* 1963.

Wilson, Richard. *Secret Shakespeare: Studies in Theatre, Religion and Resistance.* Manchester: Manchester University Press, 2004.

# Index

1606 Oath of Allegiance: James I, 2–3; modern politics and, 34

absolute metaphors, 21–2
abstractions, human intellect and, 169
aesthetics, *The Winter's Tale* (Shakespeare), 229–30
affection, 227–9
Agamben, Giorgio: being of sovereignty, 76; constituent power and sovereignty, 49; genealogy of modernity, 160–2; *Homo Sacer: Sovereign Power and Bare Life*, 97; metaphor, 79–80; paradox of sovereignty, 8; potentiality, 75–6; power and violence relationship, 159–60; sovereignty, space of, 103–4, 167–8; sovereignty theories, 7–8, 79; spatiality, 162–3; state of exception, 161–2
*All About My Mother* (*Todo Sobre Mi Madre*) (Almodóvar), 59–61
allegory: evil, 200; *Life Is a Dream* (Calderón), 187; non-existence of what it presents, 198; *El Palacio Confuso* (Lope), 193; sovereignty and, 195
Almodóvar, Pedro, *All About My Mother* (*Todo Sobre Mi Madre*), 59–61
Althusser, Louis, ideology definition, 103
Amazons, *Fuenteovejuna* (Lope), 124–7

*analogia entis*, 37
analogical gap of finite and infinite, 45–6
analogy: Aristotle, 36; Foucault, Michel, 38; Greek, 35; Middle Ages, 36; proportional, 41–2; religious discourse and, 35–6; Ricoeur, Paul, 36; Sommerville, J. P., 38; Stafford, Barbara, 35
appearance of sovereignty, 34–5
Aristotle, analogy, 36
*El Arte Nuevo de Hacer Comedias* (Lope), 99
association theory, 72

Bacon, Sir Francis, Scholasticism, 170
Barkan, Leonard: bodily exchange trope, 63–4; figure of rhetoric/figure of history, 18
baroque culture, Benjamin, Walter, 16–17
baroque drama, confusion, 83–4
being: categories, 43–4; of sovereignty, 76
beings of reason, 168–9
Benjamin, Walter: allegory, re-theorization, 199–200; baroque culture, 16–17; Calderón and, 156–7; confusion, 83–4; contemplative necessities, 157, 199; evil, 198, 200; history, 15–16; honor, 109; image, 14–15; metaphor, 84; method as digression, 14; mourning play, 14;

Benjamin, Walter (cont.)
    *The Origin of German Tragic Drama*,
    14–15; sovereign as history's
    representative, 192–3; twentieth-
    century modernity, 16–17;
    violability, 122–3
Black, Georgina Dopico, Inquisition,
    109–10
Bloom, Harold, humanist subject in
    Shakespeare, 54
Blumenberg, Hans: absolute metaphors,
    21–2; history, representation, 22;
    *Paradigms for a Metaphorology*, 21
bodily exchange trope, 63–4
body metaphor, 23–4; *Life Is a Dream*
    (Calderón), 172–4; *The Winter's
    Tale* (Shakespeare), 205. See also
    embodied sovereignty
body of law, *Measure for Measure*
    (Shakespeare), 66
body's relation to sovereignty,
    *Fuenteovejuna* (Lope), 140–1

Calderón de la Barca, Pedro: allegory,
    187; Benjamin, Walter, and, 156–7;
    body-of-power, 172–4; Christianity,
    164; ciphers and images, 189–91;
    language style, 153–4; modernity
    and, 153; monster, 166–7; rhetorical
    style, 153–4; *Richard II*
    (Shakespeare) and, 155–6; royal
    propaganda, 154; sign-system of
    sovereignty, 174–7; temporal power
    as loaned power, 191–2. See also *Life
    Is a Dream* (Calderón)
Cascardi, Anthony, on *Fuenteovejuna*
    (Lope), 102, 113, 124–5, 129, 146–7,
    149, 151
Castro, Américo: honor, being and
    movement distinction, 108–9; honor
    in Spanish Golden Age drama,
    106–7; process of life, 107
categories of being, 43–4
Catholic Kings' dilemma,
    *Fuenteovejuna* (Lope), 144–5

chimera, 168–9
Christianity: Calderón, 164; efficacy in
    Christian theology, 222; Gauchet,
    Marcel, 163–4; politics of war and,
    131
ciphers and images, 189–91; what God
    determines, 196–7
circularity of sovereignty, 87
conception, language and, 37
confusion, Benjamin, Walter, 83–4
conjection *versus* divination, 189
constituent power, 45; and sovereignty, 49
contemplative necessities, 157, 199
Covarrubias Horozco, Sebastián de,
    110–11

*De legibus* (Suárez), 40; definition of
    law, 69
De Man, Paul, epistemology of
    metaphor, 80
*A Defense of the Catholic Faith against
    the Errors of the Anglican Sect*
    (Suárez). See *Defensio fidei*
*Defensio fidei* (Suárez), 1–4; Pope's
    power, 206–7; representation, 211;
    Thirty Years War and, 5
democracy: Derrida, Jacques, 150–1;
    temporality, 127–8
Derrida, Jacques: auto-immunity,
    147–8; democracy to come, 150–1;
    pardon, 143–4; *Politics of Friendship*,
    126–8; tears, 118
divination *versus* conjecture, 189
drama, baroque, Walter Benjamin on,
    83–4

earth, relation to law, 11–12
ecclesiastical jurisdiction, 3
efficacy: Christian theology and, 222; of
    power, 207
embodied sovereignty, 47–8; law and,
    78; new historicism, 84–5
*Empresa* (Fajardo), 108
Empson, William, on *Measure for
    Measure* (Shakespeare), 65–6, 77

the enemy, 130–1; *Fuenteovejuna* (Lope), 132; political enemy, 131
enigmatic writing, 190. *See also* ciphers and images
epistemology of metaphor, 80
essences: existences and statements, 43–4; *versus* reflections, 50
Eucharist and metaphor, 73–4
evil, Walter Benjamin on, 198, 200
exegesis, 218–19; *Mysteries of the Life of Christ* (Suárez) and, 222–3
existences, essences and statements, 43–4

Fajardo, Diego Saavedra, *Empresa,* 108
fantasy: of absolute power, 315; controlled (Suarez), 315; of sovereignty, 150, 229–31, 239
Fichter, Joseph: hagiographic description, 4–5; side effects of Suárez's text, 4
fidelity, *The Winter's Tale* (Shakespeare), 226
figurative speech, metaphor as sovereign figure, 85
figure of transport, 77
fire analogy for sovereignty, 241
Fish, Stanley: formalism, 82; metaphor and law, 80–2
fold trope, 177–8
forgetting, *Fuenteovejuna* (Lope), 144
formalism, 82
Foucault, Michel: analogy, 38; penal practice and torture, signs of sovereignty on the body, 86–7
friendship, Derrida, Jacques, 126–7
Frye, Northrop, 213
*Fuenteovejuna* (Lope): Amazons, 124–7; as answer to sovereignty questions in *Measure for Measure* (Shakespeare), 98; Catholic Kings' dilemma, 144–5; Commander's perversion, 103; death of Fernán Gómez, 133–6; debts and accounts, 143–52; *declinando,* 100–1; the enemy, 132; example or exception, 147; forgetting, 144; honor, 106–8; honor code, violability and, 122–3; honor code, Laurencia and, 114–19, 123–4; Laurencia's curse, 116–24; Laurencia's value, 116–17; love's value, 105–6; normative function, 121–2; organ transplant metaphor, 140; overview, 98–9; pastoral power, 119–20; political love, 134; politics, 129–30; power and time, 127–8; reading and writing, 112; recognition, 114–16, 140–1; repayment of violation, 122; representation of sovereignty, 104–5; representational logic, 103–4; sequencing, 99–100; sexual identity, 102–3; sovereignty's relation to body, 140–1; squadron of women, 137; subject-formation and, 102, 112–14; subjection, 102; survival, 126–7; temporality of democracy, 127–8; time, 125–6; time's movement, 101–2; tyranny, 129; violence: institutional, 118–19

Gauchet, Marcel, Christianity, 163–4
goat-stag, 168–9
God, naming of, 8–9
Goldberg, Jonathan, substitution as law, 74–6
*Golden Legend* (Voragine), 63–4
Goodrich, Peter, political love, 66
Greenberg, Mitchell, on *Fuenteovejuna* (Lope), 102–3

habeas corpus, 87–8, 92
*Hamlet or Hecuba* (Schmitt), 9–10
Haverkamp, Anselm: Benjamin's dialectical image, 15; *habeas corpus,* 87–89, 93; metaphor, 107; Schmittian paranoia, 131. *See also* Vismann, Cornelia
heretical reading, metaphorical reading, 213
history, Walter Benjamin, 15–16

*Homo Sacer: Sovereign Power and Bare Life* (Agamben), 97
honor: being and movement distinction, 108–9; Benjamin, Walter, 109; Covarrubias, 111; *Fuenteovejuna* (Lope), 106–8, 114–16, 118–19, 122–4; *New Art of Writing Plays* (Lope), 109; pastoral power, 119–20; public and private enemy and, 132; sovereignty and, 107–8
humanist subject, 54
Hutson, Lorna, two-bodies metaphor, 46–7

illusion, sovereignty, 239
image, 14–15, 164–5; abstractions, 169; blank spaces in portraiture, 165–6; chimera, 168–9; ciphers and images, 189–91; goat-stag, 168–9; monstrosity in *Life Is a Dream* (Calderón), 167; negations, 169; phantasy, 166; Suárez, 166. *See also* sign-systems
imaginary, definition, 103
imagination, 166, 169; reason and, 170–1
impossible beings, 169
institutional violence, 118–19
intellect: abstractions, 169; chimera, 169; negations, 169
international law, Suárez, Francisco, 40–1
intrinsic attribution, 42–3, 46

James I (King): 1606 Oath of Allegiance, 2–3; Christall Mirror, 34; representation *versus* metaphor, 73; similitudes, 35; *The Trew Law of Free Monarchies*, 4
Jesuit exegetes, 218–19
juridical sociology, Carl Schmitt, 12–13
jurisdiction, ecclesiastical, 3

Kahn, Victoria, two-bodies theory, 47
Kantorowicz, Ernst, 24; *The King's Two Bodies*, 34, 46–7; Richard as christomimetes (*Richard II* [Shakespeare]), 52
kings: prudence of, 188–9; service of God, 188
*The King's Two Bodies* (Kantorowicz), 34, 46–7. *See also* two-bodies theory
kingship theories, 171–2

labyrinth, *Life Is a Dream* (Calderón), 178–80
language: biblical, metaphor and, 213; Calderón, 153–4; conception and, 37; essence of the monster, 187; sovereignty and, 7–8
law: earth's relation to, 11–12; embodiment and, 78; extralegal zones, 160–1; God and, 212; *Measure for Measure* (Shakespeare), 70; metaphor and, 80–2; power and violence relationship, 159–60; readable body, 69; Schmitt, Carl, 78; speaking body, 69; Suárez, 212; substitution as, 74–6; threats from morality and interpretation, 82
law void, Carl Schmitt, 168
Legendre, Pierre: normativization, 138; political-theological dance, 138–9; psychoanalytical jurisprudence, 137–8; Roman law and sovereignty, 137; scholastic dance, 222; subject-formation, 112–14; Text, 216–19
Lezra, Jacques: Agamben, 163; incomplete secularization, 29, 47; *Measure for Measure*, 91; power, 72–3; Schmitt, 20
*Life Is a Dream* (Calderón), 153; allegory, 187; ciphers and images, what God determines, 196–7; kings in the service of God, 188; labyrinth, 178–80; modernity and, 153–4; monsters, 167; language and, 187; monsters, Clarín as, 184–6; monsters, Rosaura as, 181–4; non-legibility motif, 191–2; political-theological movement, 163–4; Protestant

allegories and, 180–1; *Richard II* (Shakespeare) and, 155–6; Segismundo's vision, 180–1; sign-system of sovereignty, 174–7; sovereignty's ideological identity, 186; sovereignty's opposite, 184; sovereignty's transformation, 195–6; throne room, 194–5; time, 157–64

Lope, 98; *El Arte Nuevo de Hacer Comedias,* 99; *New Art of Writing Plays,* 109; *El Palacio Confuso (The Confused Palace/Court),* 192–3. See also *Fuenteovejuna*

lost Mother fantasy, 223–4

Lupton, Julia Reinhard: on *Hamlet or Hecuba* (Schmitt), 10; substitution in *Measure for Measure* (Shakespeare), 88–9; on *The Winter's Tale* (Shakespeare), 229, 233

Machiavelli, Niccolò: effective truth, 39; efficacy of power, 207; *The Prince,* 39; time in relation to sovereignty, 33; truth, 206

majesty as light, 108

Marin, Louis, representation, 89–90

Mariology: Suárez, Francisco, 207–11; *The Winter's Tale* (Shakespeare), 236–7

Marion, Jean-Luc: essences, 43–4; ontological relations of sovereignty, 42–3; representation, 44–5

*Measure for Measure* (Shakespeare): Angelo as currency, 84; Angelo's sovereignty, 85; bodily exchange trope, 63–4; body of law, 66; desire, 89–90; Duke's bearing, 67–8; effects of simile and metaphor, 76–7; Elbow's inversions, 71; *habeas corpus,* 87–8; heads, 65; law, 70; metaphor's power in sovereignty, 84–5; organ transplant metaphor, 62–3, 72; organs of power, 67–8; power-effect of representation, 91; problem with the play, 93–6; representational operation, 74; setup, 64–5; the similitudes, 68; substitution, 65–6, 88–9; substitution, Barnadine and, 91–2; transfer, 61; visibility of sovereignty, 87; writing, 87

metalepsis, 18

metamorphosis, *The Winter's Tale* (Shakespeare), 236

metaphor: absolute, 21–2; Agamben, Giorgio, 79–80; Benjamin, Walter, 84; biblical language, 213; body, 23–4; conceptual function, 71–2; effects of, 76–7; epistemology of, 80; Eucharist and, 73–4; exegesis, 218–19; as figure of transport, 72; law and, 80–2; Luke's text in *Mysteries,* 219–22; metaphorical reading as heretical reading, 213; movement, 88; *Mysteries of the Life of Christ* (Suárez), 210–14; mystery and, 215–16; political-theological dance, 138–9; power of in sovereignty in *Measure for Measure* (Shakespeare), 84–5; Puttenham, George, 71–2, 76–7; representation and, 73; root metaphors in religion, 214; St. Jerome, 74; as sovereign figure of figurative speech, 85; Text and, 216–19

*Metaphysical Disputations* (Suárez), 30, 34, 41–2; categories of being, 43–4

metaphysical image, 13–14

metaphysical structures of sovereignty, 7–8

method, as digression, 14

Middle Ages, analogy, 36

modernity's narrative, 240

monsters: essence of through language, 187; *Life Is a Dream* (Calderón), 167, 181–6

mourning play, 14

*Mysteries of the Life of Christ* (Suárez), 208–10; exegesis and, 222–3; God and law, 212; historical, performative, media-theoretical

*Mysteries of the Life of Christ*
(Suárez) (cont.)
hybrid text, 222; lost Mother
fantasy, 223–4; metaphor, 210–14;
metaphor of Luke's text, 219–22
mystery: Mariology and, 208–9; media
requirements, 215–16; metaphor
and, 215

naming God, 8–9
negations, human intellect and, 169
Negri, Antonio, 45–6; constituent
power and sovereignty, 49; Neo-
Scholasticism, 46
Neo-Scholasticism, Antonio Negri, 46
*New Art of Writing Plays* (Lope), 109
new historicism, body metaphor and
sovereignty, 84–5
*The Nomos of the Earth* (Schmitt), 11–12
Norbrook, David, Kantorowicz's
two-bodies theory, 46–7
normative function, *Fuenteovejuna*
(Lope), 121–2

ontological relations of sovereignty, 7–8;
Marion, Jean-Luc, 42–3
ontology of immanence, 45
onto-theology, 36–7; Aquinas, Thomas,
37–8
organ transplant metaphor:
*Fuenteovejuna* (Lope), 140; *Measure for Measure* (Shakespeare), 62–3, 72
organs of power, *Measure for Measure*
(Shakespeare), 67–8
*The Origin of German Tragic Drama*
(Benjamin), 14–15

*El Palacio Confuso* (Lope), 192; as figure
of allegory, 193
paradigms, 24
*Paradigms for a Metaphorology*
(Blumenberg), 21
paradox of sovereignty, 8
pardon, 143–4; *Fuenteovejuna* (Lope),
145–7

pastoral power, 119–20
phantasy, 166
political enemy, 131
political love, 66; *Fuenteovejuna* (Lope),
134
political theology: bonds as media
bonds, 223; challenges, 28; God and
sovereignty, 26; problem of, 27;
psycho-political theology, 236–7;
Schmitt, Carl, 9; sovereignty and,
6, 27
*Political Theology: Four Chapters on the
Concept of Sovereignty* (Schmitt), 11
political-theological dance, 138–9; *Life Is
a Dream* (Calderón), 163–4
politics: decisionism *versus* sovereignty,
104; *Fuenteovejuna* (Lope), 129–30;
time of friendship, 126
*Politics of Friendship* (Derrida), 126–8
politics of war: Christianity and, 131;
Spanish honor code, 132
Popes, *plenitudo potestatis*, 6–7
potentiality, Giorgio Agamben, 75–6
power: definitions, 72–3; representation
and, 89–91; temporal power as
loaned power, 191–2; and time,
127–8
power and violence, 159–60
pressure, Eric Santner, 225
*The Prince* (Machiavelli), 206
proportional analogies, 41–2
Protestant allegories, *Life Is a Dream*
(Calderón) and, 181
prudence: of kings, 188–9;
representation, 189
psychoanalytical jurisprudence, 137–8
psycho-political theology, 236–7
psychotheology, 225
Puttenham, George: figure of transport,
77; metaphors, 71–2, 76–7
Pye, Christopher: *Richard II*
(Shakespeare) and modern subject,
50; aesthetics and psycho-political
anxiety in *The Winter's Tale*
(Shakespeare), 226, 228–9

reason, imagination and, 170–1
recapitulation, *The Winter's Tale* (Shakespeare) and, 223–4
recognition, 235–6; *Fuenteovejuna* (Lope), 114–16, 140–1
reflections *versus* essences, 50
religion, metaphor in, 214
religious discourse, analogy and, 35–6
representation: *Defensio fidei* (Suárez), 211; Marin, Louis, 89–90; Marion, Jean-Luc, 44–5; and metaphor, 73; power and, 89–91; prudence and, 189; representational history of sovereignty, 85–6; representational operation in *Measure for Measure* (Shakespeare), 74
representational image. *See* image
resistance theory, 3–4
rhetorical style, Calderón, 153–4
*Richard II* (Shakespeare): Calderón and, 155–6; consciousness, 55; dispersing of sovereignty, 57–8; embodied sovereignty, 47–8; relationship to time, 53–4; Richard as *christomimetes*, 52; sorrow's eyes, 48–9; tears, closing scene, 56; tears, deposition scene, 50–2; tears, Queen's, 50; transfer of sovereignty, 51–2
Ricoeur, Paul, analogy, 36
Riß, 242–5
*Roman Catholicism and Political Form* (Schmitt), 11
Roman law, sovereignty and, 137
royal propaganda, Calderón, 154
Rust, Jennifer, on *Hamlet or Hecuba* (Schmitt), 10

St. Jerome, metaphor, 74
Santner, Eric, psychotheology, 225
Schmitt, Carl, 9; duality of sovereignty theory, 20; the enemy, 130–1; extralegal zones, 160–1; *Hamlet or Hecuba*, 9–10; image, 14–15; juridical sociology, 12–13; law, 78; law void, 168; metaphysical images, 13–14; *The Nomos of the Earth*, 11–12; paranoia, 131–2; *Political Theology: Four Chapters on the Concept of Sovereignty*, 11; politics of war, Christianity and, 131; *Roman Catholicism and Political Form*, 11; sociology of concepts, 12–21; sovereign's principal operation, 77–8; violence theorization, 10–11; Weber, Max, and, 12
scholastic dance, 222
Scholasticism: Bacon, Sir Francis, 170; beings of reason, 168; goat-stag, 168; impossible beings, 168; monster, 167; sexual intercourse as mingling of blood, 226–7; Text, 216–19; thought beings, 168
Second Scholasticism, 139
secularization, sovereignty and, 6
sex, mingling of blood, 226–7
sexual identity, *Fuenteovejuna* (Lope), 103
Shakespeare: humanist subject, 54; sovereignty is nothing, 57; Suárez and, 207
shame, *The Winter's Tale* (Shakespeare), 226
Shuger, Debora, 24
sign-systems, 171; *Life Is a Dream* (Calderón), 174–7
simile, effects of, 76–7
similitudes of King James I, 35; *Measure for Measure* (Shakespeare) and, 68
sociology of concepts (Schmitt), 12–21
Sommerville, J.P., analogy, 38
sorrow's eyes, 48–9
sovereigns: conjecture *versus* divination, 189; as history's representative, 192–3; kings in the service of God, 188; prudence of, 188–9; public visibility, 171–2

sovereignty: allegory and, 195; appearance, 34–5; and constituent power and, 49; embodied, 47–8; essential circularity, 87; fire analogy, 241; historical time and, 55–6; honor and, 107–8; illusion, 239; is nothing (Shakespeare), 57; language and, 7–8; metaphysical structures, 7–8; ontological relations, 7–8; paradox of sovereignty, 8; *plenitudo potestatis*, 6–7; political theology and, 27; representational history, 85–6; Roman law and, 137; secularization and political theory, 6; seventeenth century understanding, 6; signs on the body, penal practice and torture, 86–7; sign-systems, 171; transfer of, 51–2; word's appearance, 6–7
spatiality, George Agamben, 162–3
Stafford, Barbara, analogy, 35
state of exception, 161–2
statements, essences and existences, 43–4
states, Suárez, Francisco, 41
Suárez, Francisco, 38–9; abstractions, 169; background, 29–32; biblical metaphors, 213–14; capacities of sovereignty, 40–1; categories of being, 43–4; chimera, 168–9; *De legibus* (*A Treatise on Laws and God the Lawgiver*), 40, 69; *Defensio fidei* (*A Defense of the Catholic Faith Against the Errors of the Anglican Sect*), 1–4, 206–7, 211; efficacy of power, 207; Eucharist and metaphor, 73–4; image's role in human cognition, 166; international law, 40–1; intrinsic attribution, 42–3, 46; laws, 159; *Metaphysical Disputations*, 30, 34, 41–2, 168–9; *Mysteries of the Life of Christ*, 208–10; negations, 169; Pope's effective power, 39; *potest directe*, 39; *potestas indirecta*, 39; proportional analogies, 41–2; representation, 44–5, 211; representation *versus* metaphor, James I and, 73; Shakespeare and, 207; sovereign states, 41
subject formation: *Fuenteovejuna* (Lope), 102, 114; Legendre, Pierre, 112–13
substitution: as law, 74–6; *Measure for Measure* (Shakespeare), 65–6, 88–9, 91–2
survival, *Fuenteovejuna* (Lope), 126–7

tears, 17–18; Queen's (*Richard II* [Shakespeare]), 50; *Richard II* closing, 56; *Richard II* deposition scene, 50–2
temporal power as loaned power, 191–2
temporality of democracy, 127–8
Text: exegesis, 218–19; Legendre, Pierre, 216–19; truth, 219
theater, 19–20
theory of founding, 45
Thirty Years War, burning of *Defensio fidei* and, 5
thought beings, 169
time: fold trope, 177–8; *Fuenteovejuna* (Lope), 125–6; *Life Is a Dream* (Calderón), 157–64; power and, 127–8; sovereignty and, 55–6
*Todo Sobre Mi Madre* (*All About My Mother*) (Almodóvar), 59–61
transfer of sovereignty, 51–2
transumption, 18
*Trauerspiel* (Benjamin). See *The Origin of German Tragic Drama* (Benjamin)
*A Treatise on Laws and God the Lawgiver* (Suárez). See *De legibus*
*The Trew Law of Free Monarchies* (James I), 4
tropological method of *Tears of Sovereignty*, 21–6
truth: Machiavelli, 206; Text, 219
two-bodies theory, 46–7
tyranny, *Fuenteovejuna* (Lope), 129

Vega Carpio, Lope de. *See* Lope
violability, *Fuenteovejuna* (Lope), 122–3
violence: institutional, 118–19;
    repayment of violation, 122
visibility (public) of sovereigns, 171–2
Vismann, Cornelia, *habeas corpus*, 87–9, 93. *See also* Haverkamp, Anselm
Voragine, Jacobus de, *Golden Legend*, 63–4

Weber, Max, and Carl Schmitt, Carl, 12
*The Winter's Tale* (Shakespeare), 223–4; aesthetics, 229–30; altering the body, 225; body metaphor, 205; division, 224; fidelity, 226; Leontes's affection, 227–9; Leontes's memorialization, 231–2; Leontes's recreation, 232–3; Mariology, 236–7; metamorphsis, 236; mingling of blood, 226–7; opening, 224–5; perception, 225; psychotheology, 225; recapitulation and, 223–4; recognition, 235–6; shame, 226; sovereignty and uniqueness, 231; sovereignty's return to the stage, 233–4; wrinkles, 233–7